PREFACE

REVISED EDITION

It gives us immense pleasure and satisfaction to bring out the thoroughly revised and updated edition of the book **"Disha's Alcohels, Phenols and Ethers"** The book has been designed to give a better look & feel and to make the text more lucid. The new pattern of JEE Main & Advanced has been kept in mind throughout.

The exercises at the end of each chapter have been designed in the flavour of the new pattern of JEE Main & Advanced. The questions from the previous JEE papers have been incorporated in the different exercises. A separate section having past JEE questions is also provided at the end.

1. **Exercise 1 - MCQ with One correct option :** This exercise contains a collection of question, which has been very carefully selected and it is ensured that there is no repetition. The exercise contains a collection of questions, which has been very carefully selected and it is ensured that there is no repetition. The exercise has been designed so as to cover all the concepts involved in the chapter.

2. **Exercise 2 :** This exercise contains all the four new variety of questions which have been asked in the last 3-4 JEE examinations. These variety of questions are-

    (i) **MCQ's with one or more than one correct answers :** Around 20-30 well selected problems introduced in each chapter.

    (ii) **Comprehension based questions :** More than 50 passages which tests the student's comprehension and analytical ability have been added. All these are newly framed problems.

    (iii) **Matching type question :** Match the following type of question with multiple matching have been introduced in each chapter. These are unique and newly framed problems which will definitely pose a big challenge to the student. I feel that this type of problem is the best way to check a student's concepts.

    (iv) **Assertion & Reason type questions :** Assertion and Reason type of questions have been incorporated in each and every chapter.

3. **Exercise 3 - Subjective Problems :** This exercise contains a unique collection of subjective problems which will not only give practice to the students but will also help in revising the complete chapter.

In the end, We would like to request all readers to highlight the printing errors and come forward with suggestions for further improvement of the book.

DR. O.P. AGARWAL

CONTENTS

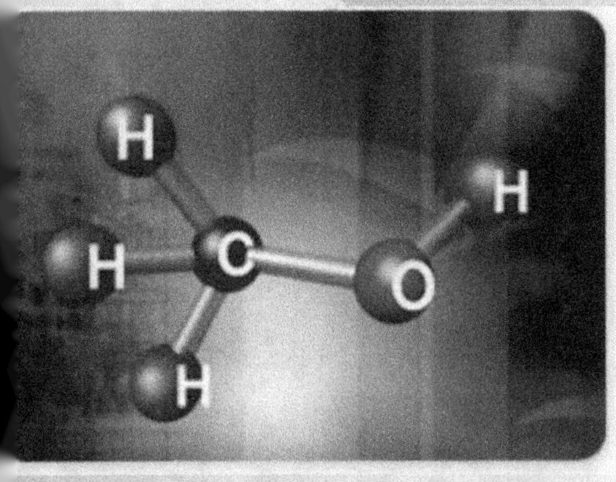

Monohydric Alcohols

11

CHAPTER HIGHLIGHTS

11.1   Nomenclature

Alcohols are compounds whose molecules have a hydroxyl group attached to a saturated carbon atom*. The saturated carbon atom may be that of an alkyl group, alkenyl or akynyl or a carbon atom attached to benzene ring.

$$CH_3CH_2OH, \quad CH_3\underset{\underset{\displaystyle OH}{|}}{C}HCH_3, \quad CH_2 = CHCH_2OH, \quad HC \equiv CCH_2OH, \quad \langle \rangle\!-\!CH_2OH$$

Alcohols may be classified as monohydric, dihydric, trihydric and polyhydric depending upon the number of —OH groups.

$$
\begin{array}{cccc}
CH_3CH_2OH &
\begin{array}{c} CH_2OH \\ | \\ CH_2OH \end{array} &
\begin{array}{c} CH_2OH \\ | \\ CHOH \\ | \\ CH_2OH \end{array} &
\begin{array}{c} CH_2OH \\ | \\ (CHOH)_4 \\ | \\ CH_2OH \end{array} \\
\\
\text{Ethyl alcohol} & \text{Glycol} & \text{Glycerol} & \text{Sorbitol} \\
\text{(Monohydric)} & \text{(Dihydric)} & \text{(Trihydric)} & \text{(Polyhydric)}
\end{array}
$$

Alternatively, an alcohol can be classified as *primary*, *secondary*, or *tertiary* according to the nature of carbon bearing —OH group.

Compounds in which a hydroxyl group is attached to an unsaturated carbon atom of a double bond (*i.e.* C = C—OH) are called **enols.**

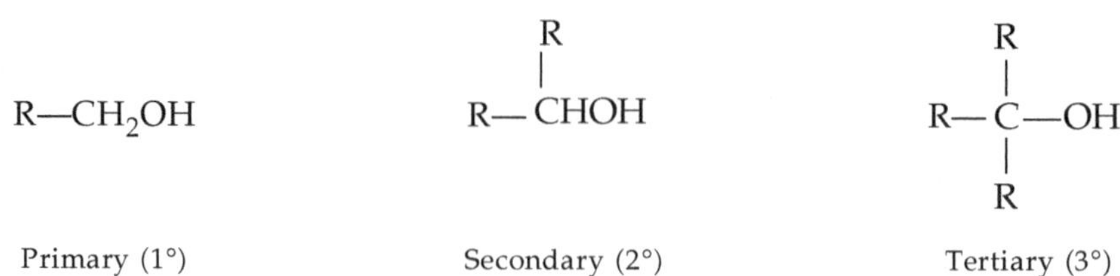

R—CH$_2$OH	R—CHOH (with R above)	R—C—OH (with R above and R below)
Primary (1°)	Secondary (2°)	Tertiary (3°)

Alcohols are named by three methods.

(i) **Carbinol method.** Alcohols are considered as derivatives of *methyl alcohol*, also known as *carbinol.*

CH$_3$CH$_2$OH	(CH$_3$)$_2$CHOH	(CH$_3$)$_3$COH
Methylcarbinol	Dimethylcarbinol	Trimethylcarbinol

(ii) **Common names** (*Radicofunctional nomenclature*). This method is most often used for the simpler alcohols. common name consists simply of the name of the alkyl group followed by the word alcohol, *e.g.*

CH$_3$CH$_2$OH	CH$_3$CHCHOH (with CH$_3$ above)	(CH$_3$)$_3$COH	(CH$_3$)$_3$CCH$_2$OH
Ethyl alcohol	Isobutyl alcohol	*tert*-Butyl alcohol	Neopentyl alcohol

(iii) **IUPAC names.** This is is the most versatile system.

CH$_3$CHCH$_2$CHCH$_2$OH (with CH$_3$, CH$_3$ above)	CH$_3$CHCH$_2$CHCH$_3$ (with OH, C$_6$H$_5$ above)	CH$_3$CHCH$_2$CH = CH$_2$ (with OH above)
2, 4-Dimethyl-1-pentanol	4-Phenyl-2-pentanol	4-Penten-2-ol

Alcohols are **functional isomers** to ethers, thus C$_4$H$_{10}$O can have following seven isomeric structures (fou alcohols and three ethers).

(i) CH$_3$CH$_2$CH$_2$CH$_2$OH	(ii) CH$_3$CHCH$_2$OH (with CH$_3$ above)	(iii) CH$_3$CH$_2$CHCH$_3$ (with OH above)
Butanol-1	2-Methylpropanol	Butanol-2

(iv) CH$_3$—C—CH$_3$ (with OH above, CH$_3$ below)	(v) CH$_3$CH$_2$OCH$_2$CH$_3$	(vi) CH$_3$OCH$_2$CH$_2$CH$_3$
2-Methylpropanol-2	Ethoxyethane	Methoxypropane

(vii) CH$_3$O.CH(CH$_3$)$_2$
Methoxy-1-methylethane

TEST YOUR UNDERSTANDING - 11.1

1. (i) Name the following alcohols by carbinol and IUPAC methods.

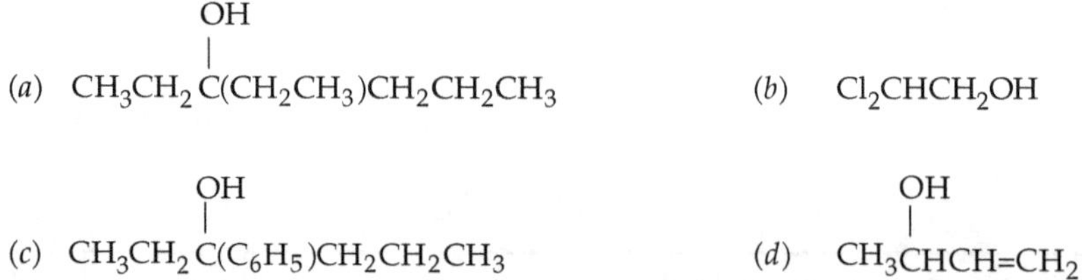

(a) CH$_3$CH$_2$ C(CH$_2$CH$_3$)CH$_2$CH$_2$CH$_3$ (with OH above)

(b) Cl$_2$CHCH$_2$OH

(c) CH$_3$CH$_2$ C(C$_6$H$_5$)CH$_2$CH$_2$CH$_3$ (with OH above)

(d) CH$_3$CHCH=CH$_2$ (with OH above)

(ii) Give IUPAC names of the following thioalcohols.

(a)

(b)

(c)

(d) $CH_3CH_2S^-Na^+$

11.2 **Preparation**

1. From alkenes.

(a) **Acid-catalyzed hydration of alkenes.** As discussed earlier in the reactions of alkenes, alkenes add water in the presence of an acid catalyst. The addition **follows Markownikov's rule.**

For example,

$$CH_2 = CH_2 + H_2O \xrightarrow{\text{dil.}H_2SO_4} CH_3CH_2OH$$

$$CH_3CH = CH_2 + H_2O \xrightarrow{H^+} CH_3CH(OH)CH_3$$

$$(CH_3)_2C = CH_2 + H_2O \xrightarrow{H^+} (CH_3)_3COH$$

(i) Hydration takes place in Markovnikov's manner.

(ii) Except for the hydration of ethene, the reaction produces 2° and 3° alcohols.

(iii) The reaction is reversible and the mechanism of hydration of an alkene is just the reverse of that for dehydration of an alcohol.

(iv) Since carbocations are formed as intermediates, rearrangement occurs whenever a less stable carbocation can rearrange by 1, 2-hydride or 1, 2-alkanide shift to the more stable carbocation. Hence this method is not used as a laboratory method for the preparation of alcohols.

2-Methylbutanol-2
(Major)

3-Methylbutanol-2
(Minor)

This is due to the fact that the intermediate 2° carbocation rearranges to the more stable 3° carbocation.

2° Carbocation

3° Carbocation

2-Methylbutanol-2

(*b*) **Oxymercuration-demercuration.** In this method alkene is treated with mercuric acetate in presence of a mixture of water and THF as solvent (*mercuration*). The mercurated product is reduced with sodium borohydride to form alcohol (*demercuration step*).

$$RCH = CH_2 \xrightarrow[\text{H}_2\text{O, 288 K}]{\text{Hg (OCOCH}_3)_2} \left[\begin{array}{c} \underset{\displaystyle \text{OH}}{R\,\underset{|}{C}H} - \underset{\displaystyle \text{HgOCOCH}_3}{\underset{|}{C}H_2} \\ \text{Not isolated} \end{array} \right] \xrightarrow[\text{OH}^-]{\text{NaBH}_4} R\,\underset{\displaystyle \underset{|}{OH}}{C}H\!-\!CH_3 + Hg + CH_3COO^-$$

(*i*) The method is fast and convenient. It takes place under mild conditions and gives excellent yield. Like acid-catalysed hydration of alkenes, this reaction is also highly *regioselective* and the elements of water (—H and —OH) add in accordance with **Markovnikov's rule**. Another striking feature of the reaction is that it does not involve any rearrangement.

$$\underset{\substack{\text{2, 3-Dimethyl-2-butanol}\\ \textbf{(Rearranged alcohol)}}}{(CH_3)_2CH\!-\!\underset{\displaystyle \underset{|}{CH_3}}{\overset{\displaystyle \overset{|}{OH}}{C}}\!-\!CH_3} \xleftarrow{\text{dil. H}_2\text{SO}_4} \underset{\text{3, 3-Dimethyl-1-butene}}{(CH_3)_3C\!-\!CH = CH_2} \xrightarrow[\text{(ii) NaBH}_4\text{, OH}^-]{\text{(i) Hg(OAc)}_2/\text{THF-H}_2\text{O}} \underset{\substack{\text{3, 3-Dimethyl-2-butanol}\\ \textbf{(Normal alcohol)}}}{(CH_3)_3C\!-\!\overset{\displaystyle \overset{|}{OH}}{C}HCH_3}$$

(*ii*) Remember here hydrogen is coming from $NaBH_4$ and hydroxyl group from water present in solvent (THF + H_2O).

(*c*) **Hydroboration-oxidation.** Alkenes react with diborane in presence of ether to form alkylboranes (*hydroboration*). Diborane is used in the form of solution in THF. Alkylboranes are then oxidised and hydrolysed by the addition of hydrogen peroxide in aqueous base.

$$\underset{\text{Propene}}{CH_3CH = CH_2} \xrightarrow{\text{THF:BH}_3} \underset{\text{Tripropylborane}}{(CH_3CH_2CH_2)_3B} \xrightarrow{\text{H}_2\text{O}_2/\text{OH}^-} \underset{\text{Propanol}}{3\,CH_3CH_2CH_2OH}$$

Here the net addition of H—OH to alkenes is *anti*-Markovnikov's and free from rearrangement.

(*i*) In hydroboration-oxidation, —H and —OH are added to the same face of the double bond, *i.e.* elements of water adds in *syn*-manner. Hence the reaction is said to be stereoselective.

$$\underset{\text{1-Methylcyclopentene}}{\text{(cyclopentene ring)}\!-\!CH_3} \xrightarrow[\text{(ii) H}_2\text{O}_2/\text{OH}^-]{\text{(i) THF : BF}_3} \underset{\substack{\text{OH}\\ \textit{trans}\text{-2-Methylcyclopentanol}}}{\text{(cyclopentane ring with CH}_3,\ H,\ H,\ OH)} + \text{ Enantiomer}$$

(*ii*) Here hydrogen that is added to carbon is derived from organoborane, and the hydroxyl group comes from hydrogen peroxide.

(*iii*) Oxymercuration-demercuration and hydroboration-oxidation methods are complement of each other, former adds water molecule in Markovnikov's manner and the latter in *anti*-Markovnikov's manner.

Comparison of the three methods for preparing alcohols from alkenes

$$\underset{}{\overset{}{>}}C = C\overset{}{<} \longrightarrow \;\; >CH\!-\!\underset{\displaystyle \underset{|}{OH}}{C}<$$

		Acid-catalysed hydration method	*Oxymercuration-demercuration method*	*Hydroboration-oxidation method*
1.	Product as per	Markovnikov's rule	Markovnikov's rule	*anti*-Markovnikov's rule
2.	Source of H	H from acid	H from $NaBH_4$	H from BH_3
3.	Source of OH	Water (solvent)	Water (solvent)	H_2O_2
4.	Rearrangement	Occurs, whenever possible	No rearranged product	No rearranged product
5.	Regioselectivity/ Stereoselectivity	Neither regioselective nor stereoselective	Regioselective, but not stereoselective	Regioselective as well as stereoselective.

TEST YOUR UNDERSTANDING - 11.2

1. Give the most stable intermediate formed during acid-catalysed hydration of each of the following alkenes.

(a) $(CH_3)_2C = CHCH_3$ (b) $(CH_3)_2CH.CH = CH_2$ (c) $(CH_3)_3C.CH = CH_2$ (d)

2. Give the final product obtained in each of the following reactions.

(a) $CH_3CH_2CH = CH_2 \xrightarrow[\text{(ii) } H_2O]{\text{(i) } D^+}$

(b) $CH_3CH_2CH = CH_2 \xrightarrow[\text{(ii) } D_2O]{\text{(i) } H^+}$

(c) $CH_3CH_2CH = CH_2 \xrightarrow[\text{(ii) } D_2O]{\text{(i) } D^+}$

(d) $\xrightarrow[\text{(ii) } D_2O]{\text{(i) } D^+}$.

3. Following alcohols can be prepared in quantitative yield by oxymercuration-demercuration of two different alkenes ; write the structures of the two alkenes in each case.

(a)   2-Methyl-2-butanol   (b)   1-Methylcyclopentanol   (c)   3-Hexanol.

4. Write the structure of the major product obtained by hydroboration-oxidation of each of the following alkenes.

(a)   *cis*-2-Butene   (b)   Cyclopentene   (c)   3-Ethyl-2-pentene   (d)   3-Ethyl-1-pentene.

5. Identify [A] to [D].

(a) $\xrightarrow[\text{(ii) } NaBH_4, OH^-]{\text{(i) } Hg(OAc)_2, THF—H_2O}$ A + B

(b) $\xrightarrow[\text{(ii) } H_2O_2, OH^-]{\text{(i) } B_2H_6, ether}$ [C]

(c) $\xrightarrow[\text{(ii) } H_2O_2, OH^-]{\text{(i) } B_2H_6, ether}$ [D]

6. Give the structure of the alcohol formed by 3-methylbutene-1 by

(a)   acid-catalysed hydration method   (b)   oxymercuration-demercuration method

(c)   hydroboration-oxidation method.

(d)   **Oxo process** (*Carbonylation or hydroformylation reaction*)

$$2RCH = CH_2 + 2CO + 2H_2 \xrightarrow[\text{heat, under P}]{[Co(CO)_4]_2 \text{ as catalyst}} RCH_2CH_2CHO + R\overset{\overset{\displaystyle CH_3}{|}}{C}HCHO$$

(Major)   (Minor)

The two aldehydes are separated by fractional distillation and then reduced catalytically to the corresponding alcohols.

(e)   **Ethanol** can be prepared by passing a mixture of ethylene and steam under pressure over Al_2O_3 or H_3PO_4 on silica at 575 K.

$$CH_2 = CH_2 + H_2O \xrightarrow[\text{575 K, Pressure}]{Al_2O_3} CH_3CH_2OH$$

2.   **From alkyl halides.**   Hydrolysis of alkyl halides with aqueous NaOH or KOH or moist Ag_2O yields alcohols (For details, consult chapter on "Alkyl halides").

$$R—X + OH^- \longrightarrow R—OH + X^-$$

(i)   Alkyl halides are converted into alcohols *via* S_N1 and/or S_N2 reactions.

(ii)   This method although quite general, it is severely limited as a method of synthesizing alcohols because alcohols are usually more available than the corresponding alkyl halides, indeed alcohols are best starting materials for alkyl halides.

(iii)   *tert*-Alkyl halides undergo a competitive elimination reaction yielding alkenes as major product.

3.   **From organometallic compounds.** As discussed in the chapter on *"Organometallic Compounds"* organolithium and organomagnesium compounds (Grignard reagents) are useful compounds for preparing the three types (1°, 2° or 3° alcohols).

(*i*)   Primary alcohols, except methyl alcohol, can be prepared by treating Grignard reagent (RMgX) with formaldehyde. Methyl alcohol can be prepared by treating the reagent with oxygen followed by hydrolysis.

(*ii*)   Primary alcohols, higher than ethanol, can be prepared by treating the reagent with epoxides (oxiranes).

Like Grignard and organolithium reagents, acetylide ions are strong bases and they add to ethylene oxide much like these reagents to form primary alcohol as the final product.

$$CH_3CH_2C \equiv C:^- + \underset{\triangle}{O} \longrightarrow CH_3CH_2C \equiv CCH_2CH_2O^- \xrightarrow{H_3O^+} CH_3CH_2C \equiv CCH_2CH_2OH$$

(*iii*)   Secondary alcohols are prepared. (*a*) from aldehydes other than formaldehyde, or (*b*) from ester of formic acid (*i.e.* HCOOR) with excess of Grignard reagent. However, in the second method the 2° alcohol will always have **identical alkyl groups**, *i.e.* R_2CHOH and not RCHOHR'.

(*iv*)   Tertiary alcohols are prepared from (*a*) ketones, or (*b*) from esters of monocarboxylic acids other than formic acid (*i.e.* R'COOR) with excess of Grignard reagent. However, in the second method those 3° alcohols can be prepared which have at least two identical alkyl groups, *i.e.* $R_2C(OH)R'$ (R and R' may be similar or different).

TEST YOUR UNDERSTANDING - 11.3

1.   Prepare the following by a Grignard reaction :

     (*a*)   1-Butanol from 1-chloropropane   (*b*)   *n*-Butanol from ethyl bromide

     (*c*)   Ethyl *p*-chlorophenylcarbinol.

2.   Identify A to E in the following reactions in each of the following reactions.

(*a*) ester + 2 (alkyl)MgBr $\xrightarrow{H_3O^+}$ [A]

(*b*) acyl chloride + [B] $\xrightarrow{H_3O^+}$ tertiary alcohol product

(*c*) cyclohexyl-MgCl + $H_2C\overset{O}{-}CHCH_3$ $\xrightarrow{H_3O^+}$ [C]

(*d*) carboxylic acid $\xrightarrow{CH_3OH, H^+}$ [D] $\xrightarrow[(ii)\ H_3O^\oplus]{(i)\ [E]}$ tertiary alcohol product

4.   **By the reduction of aldehydes and ketones.** Aldehydes and ketones are readily reduced to primary and secondary alcohols, respectively by (*a*) sodium and alcohol, (*b*) catalytic hydrogenation, (*c*) complex metal hydride like lithium aluminium hydride, $LiAlH_4$ (LAH) and sodium borohydride, $NaBH_4$ (SBH).

$$R.CHO \longrightarrow RCH_2OH \ ; \qquad \underset{R}{\overset{R}{>}}C=O \longrightarrow \underset{R}{\overset{R}{>}}CHOH$$

Benzaldehyede undergoes coupling reaction with Na/C_2H_5–OH, so it can't be reduced into alcohol by Na/C_2H_5OH

However, reduction by $LiAlH_4$ and $NaBH_4$ are more important. *Lithium aluminium hydride* reacts violently with water and alcohols, so it must be used in solvents such as anhydrous diethyl ether or tetrahydrofuran. Moreover, the reduction requires a separate hydrolysis step to liberate the alcohol product. It does not reduce the α, β-unsaturated linkage which is not conjugated with the benzene ring ; however, it reduces the double bond too when it is having a phenyl group in the β-position.

$$CH_3CH = CH.CHO \xrightarrow[\text{(ii) } H_2O]{\text{(i) } LiAlH_4, \text{ ether}} CH_3CH = CHCH_2OH$$

$$\text{Ph}{-}CH = CH.CHO \xrightarrow[\text{(ii) } H_2O]{\text{(i) } LiAlH_4} \text{Ph}{-}CH_2CH_2CH_2OH$$

Contrary to $LiAlH_4$ reductions, sodium borohydride reductions are very easy to carry out ; it needs only addition of the reagent to an aqueous or alcoholic solution of an aldehyde or ketone. It is more specific and does not reduce the carbon-carbon double bond, even when conjugated with the benzene ring. It also does not reduce —NO_2, —CN, —COOH, acid anhydrides and esters. However, it reduces —COCl to —CH_2OH.

$$CH_3CH = CHCHO \xrightarrow[\text{methanol}]{NaBH_4} CH_3CH = CHCH_2OH$$

$$\text{Ph}{-}CH = CH.CHO \xrightarrow[\text{methanol}]{NaBH_4} \text{Ph}{-}CH = CHCH_2OH$$

$$NCCH_2CH_2CHO \xrightarrow[\text{methanol}]{NaBH_4} NCCH_2CH_2CH_2OH$$

$$O_2N{-}\text{Ph}{-}CHO \xrightarrow[\text{methanol}]{NaBH_4} O_2N{-}\text{Ph}{-}CH_2OH$$

β-Benzoylpropanoic acid   →   γ-Hydroxy-γ-phenylbutanoic acid

Sodium borohydride and lithium aluminium hydride react with carbonyl compounds in much the same way that Grignard reagents do, except that they function as *hydride donors* rather than as carbanion source. Remember that one molecule of the carbonyl compound accepts one hydride ion from the reagent and thus one molecule of the reagent can reduce four molecules of the compound . Second hydrogen is coming as proton from the solvent (H—OH or H—OR) molecule.

Ketones can also be reduced to secondary alcohols by heating ketones in isopropanol with aluminium isopropoxide. The reaction is more commonly known as **Meerwein-Ponndorf-Verley (MPV) reduction.**

$$\begin{array}{c}R\\R\end{array}{>}CO + (CH_3)_2CHOH \xrightleftharpoons{Al(OCHMe_2)_3} \begin{array}{c}R\\R\end{array}{>}CHOH + (CH_3)_3CO$$

Carbonyl carbon gets hydrogen in the form of hydride from aluminium isopropoxide, while carbonyl oxygen gets hydrogen from the solvent, isopropanol.

TEST YOUR UNDERSTANDING - 11.4

1.   Complete the following :

(a) $CH_3CH=CHCOCH_3 \xrightarrow{H_2,\ CuO/Cr_2O_3}$

(b) $C_6H_5CH=CHCOCH_3 \xrightarrow[\text{methanol}]{NaBH_4}$

(c) $C_6H_5CH=CHCOCH_3 \xrightarrow[\text{(ii) } H_2O]{\text{(i) } LiAlH_4,\ \text{ether}}$

(d) $CH_3CHO \xrightarrow{NaBD_4\ \text{in } H_2O}$

(e) $CH_3COCH_3 \xrightarrow[CH_3OD]{NaBD_4\ \text{in}}$

(f) $C_6H_5CHO \xrightarrow{NaBD_4\ \text{in } CD_3OH}$

(g) $HCHO \xrightarrow[\text{(ii) } D_2O]{\text{(i) } LiAlD_4\ \text{in ether}}$

5. **By the reduction of carboxylic acids and their derivatives.**

(a) *Catalytic hydrogenation* follows the order

$$RCOCl > RCHO > R_2CO > RCOOR' > RCOOH$$

However, catalytic hydrogenation is used in industries because extremely high pressures and temperatures are required.

(b) *Bouveault-Blanc reduction* (Reduction by sodium metal in alcohol). This is applied only for esters and again used in industry.

$$RCOOC_2H_5 \xrightarrow[\text{alcohol}]{\text{Na}} RCH_2OH + C_2H_5OH$$

(c) *Reduction by lithium aluminium hydride.* Although carboxylic acids are very difficult to reduce, these can be reduced to primary alcohols by $LiAlH_4$ (not by $NaBH_4$).

$$RCOOH \xrightarrow[\text{(ii) } H_2O]{\text{(i) } LiAlH_4 \text{, diethyl ether}} RCH_2OH$$

Carboxylic acids are readily reduced to primary alcohols by borane. Actually borane, complexed with THF, reacts with the carboxyl group faster than with any other carbonyl function. It reduces selectively the –COOH group without affecting a ketonic group.

$$CH_3-\overset{O}{\overset{\|}{C}}-\!\!\!\bigcirc\!\!\!-\overset{O}{\overset{\|}{C}}-OH \xrightarrow[\text{or } B_2H_3]{BH_3 \cdot THF} CH_3-\overset{O}{\overset{\|}{C}}-\!\!\!\bigcirc\!\!\!-CH_2OH$$

Esters are more easily reduced than carboxylic acids by $LiAlH_4$. Two alcohols are formed from each ester molecule ; one is derived from the acyl part and other from the alcoholic part.

$$\bigcirc\!\!-\overset{O}{\overset{\|}{C}}-OCH_2CH_3 \xrightarrow[\text{(ii) } H_2O]{\text{(i) } LiAlH_4, \text{ diethyl ether}} \bigcirc\!\!-CH_2OH + HOCH_2CH_3$$

Ethyl benzoate   Benzyl alcohol

Although esters can also be reduced by $NaBH_4$, the reaction is too slow to be useful. Anhydrides can be reduced to alcohols by $LiAlH_4$ as well as by $NaBH_4$; however, acid chlorides can be reduced only by $LiAlH_4$.

6. **By the reduction of epoxides.** Epoxides can be converted into alcohols by reacting with Grignard reagents, organolithium compounds and lithium aluminium hydride.

$$H_2C\overset{}{-\!\!\triangle\!\!-}CH_2 + n\text{-}C_4H_9Li \xrightarrow[\text{(ii) } H_3O^+]{\text{(i) diethyl ether}} n\text{-}C_4H_9CH_2CH_2OH$$

$$H_2C\overset{}{-\!\!\triangle\!\!-}CHCH_3 \xrightarrow[\text{(ii) } H_2O]{\text{(i) } LiAlH_4} CH_3\overset{OH}{\overset{|}{C}}HCH_3$$

Like Grignard reagents, *hydride ion* (nucleophile) attacks the less substituted carbon atom.

TEST YOUR UNDERSTANDING - 11.5

1. Identify [A] to [H] in the following reactions :

(a) $CH_3CH = CH_2 \xrightarrow{C_6H_5CO_3H}$ [A] $\xrightarrow[\text{(ii) } H^+]{\text{(i) } LiAlH_4}$ [B]   (b) $\bigcirc\!\!\diagdown_O\!\!\diagup CH_3 \xrightarrow[\text{(ii) } H^+]{\text{(i) } LiAlH_4}$ [C]

(c) (benzene-1,2-dicarboxylic anhydride) $\xrightarrow[\text{(ii) H}^+]{\text{(i) LiAlH}_4}$ [D]

(d) [F] $\xleftarrow[\text{methanol}]{\text{NaBH}_4}$ (bicyclic lactone ketone) $\xrightarrow[\text{(ii) H}^+]{\text{(i) LiAlH}_4}$ [E]

(e) $\xrightarrow[\text{(ii) LiAlH}_4/\text{H}^+]{\text{(i) O}_3/\text{H}_2\text{O/Zn}}$ [G] + [H]

2. Which reducing agent, $LiAlH_4$ or $NaBH_4$, would you use to carry out the following transformations ?

(a) CH_3—⬡—COOH $\longrightarrow$ CH_3—⬡—CH_2OH

(b) CH_3—$\overset{\overset{\displaystyle O}{\|}}{C}$—⬡—COOH $\longrightarrow$ CH_3—$\overset{\overset{\displaystyle OH}{|}}{CH}$—⬡—$CH_2OH$

(c) OHC—⬡—$COOCH_3$ $\longrightarrow$ HOH_2C—⬡—$COOCH_3$

3. Give the structure of an ester that will yield a mixture containing equimolar amounts of 1-propanol and 2-propanol on reduction with lithium aluminium hydride.

4. Arrange the following in decreasing ease of reduction with LAH and SBH.

$$RCHO, \ RCOOH, \ RCOOR' \ \text{and} \ RCOR.$$

7. Other methods used for preparing alcohols are hydrolysis of esters and ethers ; and by the action of nitrous acid on primary amines.

$$RCOOR' \xrightarrow{\text{H}^+ \text{ or OH}^-} RCOOH + R'OH$$

$$R\!-\!O\!-\!R \xrightarrow[\text{pressure}]{\text{dil.H}_2\text{SO}_4} 2ROH$$

$$RCH_2NH_2 + HONO \longrightarrow RCH_2OH + N_2 + H_2O$$

11.3 Industrial Sources of Alcohols.

Natural resources constitute important ways for preparing alcohols on large scale.

(a) Petroleum is an important source of alkenes which can be converted into alcohols by (*i*) hydration and (*ii*) oxo process.

(b) Methanol is manufactured

    (*i*) as a by-product by the destructive distillation of wood, hence also known as *wood spirit or wood alcohol or naphtha*, during the manufacture of charcoal. Destructive distillation of wood gives *pyroligenous acid* (10% CH_3COOH + 2.5% CH_3OH + 0.5% acetone) from which methanol is separated by suitable treatment.

    (*ii*) Methanol is also obtained by heating a mixture of water gas (a mixture of CO and H_2 in equimolar ratio) with half of its volume of hydrogen in presence of catalyst.

$$C + H_2O \text{ (steam)} \longrightarrow \underbrace{CO + H_2}_{\text{water gas}} ; \ \underbrace{CO + H_2}_{\text{water gas}} + H_2 \xrightarrow[\text{573 K}]{\text{Cr}_2\text{O}_3,\ \text{ZnO}} CH_3OH$$

(c) Ethanol is commercially obtained by fermentation of sugars present in the form of cane-sugar (in molasses) and starch (from various grains like, maize, barley, rice etc.). Fermentation (decomposition of complex compounds into simplar by yeast) is still the most widely used method for preparing **ethanol** on large scale.

Chemical reactions involved in preparation of C_2H_5OH from molasses (a dark-brown coloured mother liquor left after the crystallization of sucrose from concentrated sugar-cane juice).

$$\underset{\substack{\text{Surose (present}\\\text{in molasses)}}}{C_{12}H_{22}O_{11}} + H_2O \xrightarrow[\text{(yeast)}]{\text{invertase}} \underset{\text{Glucose}}{C_6H_{12}O_6} + \underset{\text{Fructose}}{C_6H_{12}O_6} \xrightarrow[\text{(yeast)}]{\text{Zymase}} 2C_2H_5OH + 2CO_2\uparrow$$

Ethyl alcohol from starchy grains (hence also known as grain alcohol).

Germinated barley seeds $\xrightarrow[\begin{array}{l}(ii)\text{ Crushed with }H_2O\\(iii)\text{ Filter}\end{array}]{(i)\ 60°C\text{ to prevent further growth}}$ Filtrate (Malt extract) (It contains diastase) $\xrightarrow[\text{(starchy material + steam)}\text{ at }50°C]{\text{heat with mash}}$

Maltose $\xrightarrow[\begin{array}{l}(ii)\text{ yeast and keep}\\\text{for 2—3 days}\end{array}]{(i)\ \text{cool to }30°C}$ Wort (10% C_2H_5OH) $\xrightarrow[(ii)\text{ rectifi.}]{(i)\text{ distil.}}$ Rectified sprit

Chemical reactions involved are as follows

$$2(C_6H_{10}O_5)_n + nH_2O \xrightarrow[50—60°C]{\substack{\text{Malt extract}\\(\text{diastase})}} 2C_{12}H_{22}O_{11}$$

Mash (starch) → Maltose

$$C_{12}H_{22}O_{11} + H_2O \xrightarrow{\text{Maltase}} 2C_6H_{12}O_6 \xrightarrow{\text{Zymase}} 2C_2H_5OH + 2CO_2\uparrow.$$

Maltose → Glucose

In this process, a smaller amount of **fusel oil** is also obtained in addition to ethanol. Fusel oil is a mixture of primary alcohols mostly isopentyl alcohol with smaller amounts of n-propyl, isobutyl and 2-methyl-1-butanol (active amyl alcohol). Isopentyl and active amyl alcohols are formed by enzymatic transformation of the amino acids leucine and isoleucine derived from the hydrolysis of proteins present in starch.

$$(CH_3)_2CHCH_2\overset{*}{C}H(N^+H_3)COO^- \xrightarrow{\text{enzymes}} (CH_3)_2CHCH_2CH_2OH$$

Leucine (*chiral molecule*) → Isopentyl alcohol (*achiral*)

$$CH_3CH_2\overset{*}{C}H(CH_3)\overset{*}{C}H(NH_3^+)COO^- \xrightarrow{\text{enzymes}} CH_3CH_2\overset{*}{C}H(CH_3)CH_2OH$$

Isoleucine (*chiral*) → Active amyl alcohol (*chiral*)

Alcoholic beverages. Ethanol is the alcohol of alcoholic beverages. The particular alcoholic beverage obtained depends upon following factors.

(*a*)   Nature of fermented substance, *i.e.* where rye, corn, grapes, elderberries, barley etc.

(*b*)   Way of fermentation, *i.e.* whether CO_2 is allowed to escape or it is bottled up.

(*c*)   Treatment after fermentation, *i.e.* whether it is distilled or not remember that the special flavour of a beverage is not due to ethanol but it is either due to characteristic of the particular source or due to some flavouring substance added from outside.

Absolute alcohol (100% pure ethyl alcohol). Rectified spirit (containing 95.87% C_2H_5OH + 4.13% H_2O) cannot be converted into absolute alcohol simply by distillation because the mixture of ethanol and water in the ratio of 95.87 : 4.13 (a ratio present in rectified spirit) is a constant boiling mixture **(azeotropic mixture)** having b.p. 78.13°C. Following two special methods are used for getting absolute alcohol.

(*i*)   *Laboratory method.* Rectified spirit is kept in contact with quick lime (CaO) for 24 hours and then distilled over it. Final traces of water are removed by adding anhydrous $CuSO_4$ (white in colour) till it ceases to turn blue. It is then distilled to get absolute alcohol.

(*ii*)   *Industrial method.* By mixing rectified spirit with excess of benzene followed by distillation when first ternary mixture (74.1% benzene + 18.4% ethanol + 7.4% water) is distilled at 64.8°C, then binary mixture (67.6% benzene + 32.4% ethanol) at 68.2°C and finally absolute alcohol at 78.3°C.

In certain reactions, even a slight trace of water found in commercial absolute alcohol must be removed. This can be accomplished by treating the alcohol with metallic magnesium ; water is converted into insoluble $Mg(OH)_2$, from which dry alcohol, called absolute alcohol is collected by distillation.

$$Mg + 2H_2O \longrightarrow Mg(OH)_2\downarrow + H_2$$

Methylated spirit (Denatured alcohol). It is rectified spirit (industrial alcohol) mixed with poisonous substances like CH_3OH, pyridine, acetone, etc. to make it unfit for drinking purposes. The usual composition of denatured alcohol is 85—90% rectified spirit + 10—15% methanol.

Power alcohol. Alcohol used for the generation of power is called power alcohol. It is a mixture of petrol and alcohol in the ratio of 4 : 1 in presence of benzene or ether.

TEST YOUR UNDERSTANDING - 11.6

1.   Describe exactly what will happen when a mixture of 200 g of 95% alcohol and 74 g of benzene is distilled ?

11.4 Physical Properties

1. The lower alcohols are readily soluble in water and the solubility decreases with the increase in molecular weight. The solubility of alcohols in water can be explained due to the formation of hydrogen bond between the highly polarised —OH groups present both in alcohol and water.

$$\overset{\delta+}{H}—\overset{\delta-}{O}\cdots\cdots\overset{\delta+}{H}—\overset{\delta-}{O}\cdots\cdots\overset{\delta+}{H}—\overset{\delta-}{O}$$
$$\underset{H}{|}\qquad\underset{R}{|}\qquad\underset{H}{|}$$

Hydrogen bonding between alcohol and water molecules

However, in higher alcohols the hydrocarbon character (alkyl chain) of the molecule increases and thus alcohols tend to resemble hydrocarbon (which are insoluble in water) and hence the solubility in water decreases. When the ratio of C to OH is more than 4, alcohols have little solubility in water.

Relative solubility of isomeric alcohols in water is $1° > 2° > 3°$. Remember that ethers are also able to form hydrogen bonds with water, hence like alcohols, ethers are also soluble in water, *e.g.* diethyl ether and 1-butanol have the same solubility in water (nearly 8 g per 100 mL at room temperature).

2. Boiling points of alcohols are much higher than those of the corresponding alkanes and ethers. It is due to the formation of hydrogen bonding between the hydroxyl groups of the two molecules of an alcohol with the result several molecules are associated to form a large molecule.

$$H—O\cdots\cdots\cdots H—O\cdots\cdots\cdots H—O$$
$$\underset{R}{|}\qquad\underset{R}{|}\qquad\underset{R}{|}$$

Hydrogen bonding in alcohol molecules.

Among the isomeric alcohols, b.p. and m.p. show the following trend.

Primary > Secondary > Tertiary

This is because of the fact that in secondary and tertiary alcohols, the alkyl part (hydrocarbon character) outweighs the —OH group due to branching.

3. Lower alcohols form solid addition compounds with anhydrous metallic salts like $CaCl_2$ and $MgCl_2$, *viz.*, $CaCl_2.4C_2H_5OH$ anD $MgCl_2.6C_2H_5OH$.

By analogy to water of crystallisation, these alcohol molecules are referred to as **alcohol of crystallisation.** *For this reason, alcohols cannot be dried over anhydrous calcium chloride.*

4. Methanol is highly toxic. Ingestion of even small quantities of methanol can cause blindness; large quantities cause death. Methanol poisoning can also occur by inhalation of the vapours or by prolonged exposure to the skin. Ethanol is a **hypnotic** (*sleep producer*). Ethanol is much less toxic than methanol.

TEST YOUR UNDERSTANDING - 11.7

1. Explain why

   (*a*) Propanol, unlike propane or butane, is soluble in water.

   (*b*) *n*-Butanol is soluble in water, while *n*-hexanol is insoluble.

   (*c*) Dimethyl ether and ethyl alcohol have the same molecular weight, yet dimethyl ether boils at a very low temperature ($-24°C$) than ethanol ($78°C$).

2. Compare the solubility and boiling point of following alcohols.

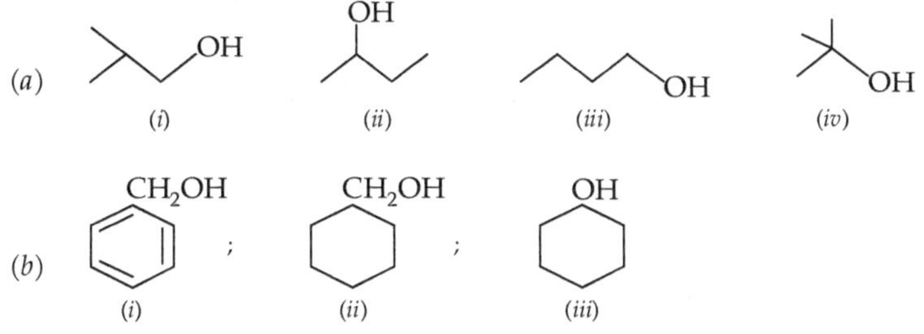

11.5   Reactions of Alcohols

Let us examine the electron distribution in the alcoholic functional group, and study its impact on the reactivity

(i)   Oxygen atom of an alcohol polarizes both the C—O bonds and the O—H bond of an alcohol. Polarization of the O—H bond makes the hydrogen partially positive and explains why *alcohols are weak acids.* In such reactions alcohols act as acids and cleavage of the O—H bond takes place. The order of reactivity of different alcohols for such reactions is

$$CH_3OH > 1° > 2° > 3° \text{ alcohols}$$

(ii)   Polarisation of the C—O bond makes the carbon atom partially positive, and hence it would have been susceptible to nucleophilic attack if OH^- were not a strong base, *i.e.* if OH^- were not a poor leaving group. However, electron pairs on the oxygen atom make alcohols both *basic* and *nucleophilic.*

$$\text{—C—OH} + \underset{\text{Strong acid}}{\text{H—A}} \rightleftharpoons \text{—C—O—H} + A^- \quad \textbf{(Basic character of alcohols)}$$

$$\underset{\text{Alcohol}}{} \qquad \qquad \underset{\text{Protonated alcohol}}{}$$

Protonation of the alcohol converts a poor leaving group (OH^-) into a good leaving one (H_2O). Protonation of the alcohol also makes the carbon atom even more positive (because $\overset{+}{—O}H_2$ is more electron withdrawing than —OH) and hence protonated alcohols become more susceptible to nucleophilic attack. In other words, protonated alcohols easily undergo nucleophilic substitution which may be S_N^2 or S_N^1 depending upon the class of alcohol. Thus these reactions involve the cleavage of the C—OH bond and replacement of —OH group by other nucleophile (substituent). The order of reactivity of different alcohols for such reactions is

$$3° > 2° > 1° > CH_3OH$$

(iii)   At a high temperature, and in the absence of a good nucleophile, protonated alcohols are capable of undergoing elimination reactions (*e.g.* dehydration).

(iv)   Alcohols act as nucleophiles while reacting with protonated alcohol (to form ethers), PBr_3 and $SOCl_2$ (to form alkyl bromides and alkyl chlorides).

(v)   Differences in the structure of the group R cause differences in reactivity and in few cases even the course of reaction is changed.

Let us apply above concepts on the various properties of alcohols.

1.   **Alcohols as acids and bases.** The polarity of the O—H bond in alcohols facilitates the departure of a proton. Further, the negative charge developed after the removal of proton can easily be accommodated by electronegative oxygen. Hence alcohols behave as acids. Acidity of alcohols is reflected by their reaction with active metals to liberate hydrogen gas.

$$\underset{\substack{\text{An alcohol} \\ \text{(a weak acid)}}}{ROH} + Na \longrightarrow \underset{\substack{\text{Sod. alkoxide} \\ \text{(a stronger base)}}}{RONa} + \frac{1}{2}H_2$$

Except methanol, all alcohols are somewhat weaker acids than water. Methanol is a slightly stronger acid than water. Among alcohols, acidity decreases with the increase in size of the alkyl group. With simpler alkyl group, water molecules are able to surround and solvate the negative oxygen of the alkoxide ion formed due to loss of a proton to a strong base. Solvation, thus stabilizes the alkoxide ion and hence increases the acidity of the alchohol.

$$R—OH + H_2O \rightleftharpoons R—O^- + H_3O^+$$

$$\underset{\substack{\text{Alkoxide ion} \\ \text{(stabilized by solvation)}}}{}$$

With the increase in the size of the alkyl group of the alcohol, solvation of the alkoxide ion (ion-dipole interaction) hindered, and the alkoxide ion is not so effectively stabilized and consequently the alcohol behaves as a weak acid. lative acidic character of some alcohols and water are given below.

$$CH_3OH \quad > \quad H_2O \quad > \quad CH_3CH_2OH \quad > \quad (CH_3)_3COH \qquad \textbf{(Relative acidic character)}$$

pK_a 15.5   15.74   15.9   18.0

All alcohols are much stronger acids than terminal alkynes, and very much stronger than hydrogen, ammonia d alkanes.

$$CH_3OH > H_2O > ROH > RC \equiv CH >> H_2 > NH_3 >> RCH = CH_2 > RH \qquad \textbf{(Relative acidity)}$$

$$CH_3O^- < OH^- < RO^- < RC \equiv C^- < H^- < NH_2^- < RCH = CH^- < R^- \qquad \textbf{(Relative basicity)}$$

The conjugate base of an alcohol is an **alkoxide ion.** Alkoxide ions of the primary or secondary alcohols are epared by the action of sodium metal, however in case of *tert*-alcohols (least reactive), more reactive metal (potassium) is rmally used. Alternatively, sodium alkoxides are sometimes prepared by the reaction of an alcohol with sodium hydride.

$$ROH + NaH \longrightarrow RONa + H_2$$

Since most alcohols are weaker acids than water, most alkoxide ions are stronger bases than the hydroxide ion d hence an alkoxide (except methoxide) is not prepared by the reaction of an alcohol with sodium hydroxide.

$$(CH_3)_3CO^- > C_2H_5O^- > OH^- > CH_3O^- \quad \textbf{(Relative basic character)}$$

Alkoxides are often used as bases in organic syntheses. Sometimes alkoxide ions are used to carry out a reaction an alcohol rather than in water (due to difference in solubility).

Like water and ammonia, alcohols are enormously stronger acids than alkanes, and hence they readily displace em from their salts, *viz.* Grignard reagents.

$$ROH \quad + \quad R'MgX \quad \longrightarrow \quad R'H \quad + \quad Mg(OR)X$$

Stronger acid   Weaker acid

In general, *a compound is shown to be a stronger acid than another by its ability to displace the second compound from salts* s illustrated below.

$$A{-}H \quad + B^- M^+ \longrightarrow \quad B{-}H \quad + A^- M^+$$

Stronger acid   Weaker acid

Due to presence of unshared electron pairs on oxygen, alcohols also act as Lewis bases.

$$ROH \quad + H_2SO_4 \rightleftharpoons \quad ROH_2^+ \quad + \quad HSO_4^-$$

Stronger base   Protonated alcohol   Weaker base

TEST YOUR UNDERSTANDING - 11.8

1.   Which of the member of following pairs is a stronger acid ?

(*a*)   (*i*) 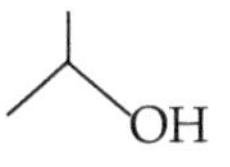   and   (*ii*) 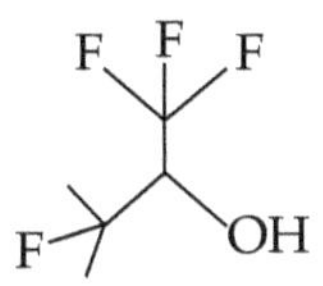   (*b*)   (*i*)    and   (*ii*)

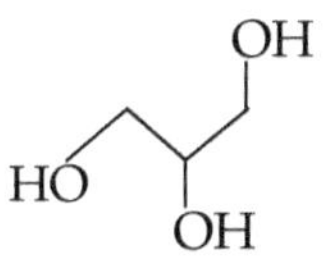

(*c*)   Which of the above member of each pairs is a stronger nucleophile ?

2.   Action of acids (Esterification).

(*a*)   **Esters of carboxylic acids.** Carboxylic acids react with alcohols in presence of a little amount of conc. H_2SO_4 or dry hydrogen chloride to form esters, and the reaction is known as **Fischer esterification.**

$$R'COOH \ + \ H{-}OR \ \underset{}{\overset{H^+}{\rightleftharpoons}} \ R'COOR \ + \ H_2O$$

(*i*)   Fischer esterification is an acid catalyzed reaction. It proceeds very slowly in the absence of strong acid.

(*ii*) It is a reversible reaction and the position of equilibrium can be made more favourable towards esters by using either the alcohol or the carboxylic acid in excess. The yield of ester can also be increased by removing water from the reaction mixture as soon as it is formed. This can be accomplished by adding benzene as co-solvent and distilling the azeotropic mixture of benzene and water. (Benzene-water azeotrope contains 9% water and boils at 69°C).

On the other hand, if we want to hydrolyze an ester, we must use a large excess of water, *i.e.* ester is refluxed with dilute aqueous HCl or dil aqueous H_2SO_4.

(*iii*) The presence of bulky groups near the site of reaction, whether in the alcohol or in the acid slows down esterification (as well as its reverse, hydrolysis).

Reactivity in $CH_3OH > 1° > 2° > 3°$

esterification $HCOOH > CH_3COOH > RCH_2COOH > R_2CHCOOH > R_3CCOOH$

Thus *tert*-alcohols react so slowly in acid-catalyzed esterifications that they usually undergo elimination reaction to form alkenes ; or they form *tert*-alkyl chlorides. Hence for the preparation of esters of *tert*-alcohols or esters of acids like 2, 4, 6-trimethyl benzoic acid, the steric hindrance is so marked that special methods are used for their preparation.

(*iv*) With the help of labelled experiment (by taking O^{18} in alcohols), it has been proved that esterification involves cleavage of the O—H bond of alcohols and not the C—OH bond, *i.e.* H atom is removed from alcohol and OH group from acid.

$$C_6H_5-\overset{O}{\overset{\|}{C}}-OH + CH_3-\overset{18}{O}-H \underset{\longleftarrow}{\overset{H^+}{\longrightarrow}} C_6H_5-\overset{O}{\overset{\|}{C}}-\overset{18}{O}CH_3 + H_2O$$

acyl group

(*v*)   Esters are also formed by the reaction of alcohols with acyl chlorides or acid anhydrides.

$$CH_3-\overset{O}{\overset{\|}{C}}-Cl + H-OC_2H_5 \xrightarrow{\text{pyridine}} CH_3-\overset{O}{\overset{\|}{C}}-OC_2H_5 + HCl$$

Pyridine is often added to react with the HCl formed.

$$CH_3-\overset{O}{\overset{\|}{C}}-O-\overset{O}{\overset{\|}{C}}-CH_3 + H-OR \longrightarrow CH_3-\overset{O}{\overset{\|}{C}}-O-R + CH_3-\overset{O}{\overset{\|}{C}}-OH$$

Unlike the reaction with carboxylic acids, these reactions are irreversible, hence yields of esters *via* this route are always high.

(*vi*) The fact that the acyl group of the carboxylic acid, acyl chloride or acid anhydride is transferred to the oxygen of the alcohol is most clearly evident in the esterification of chiral alcohols.

$$C_6H_5-\overset{C_2H_5}{\underset{CH_3}{\overset{*}{C}}}-O-H + ClC\overset{O}{\overset{\|}{}}-\langle\!\langle\,\rangle\!\rangle-NO_2 \longrightarrow C_6H_5-\overset{C_2H_5}{\underset{CH_3}{\overset{*}{C}}}-O-\overset{O}{\overset{\|}{C}}-\langle\!\langle\,\rangle\!\rangle-NO_2$$

R-(+)-2-Phenyl-2-butanol   (R)-(–)-1-Methyl-1-phenylpropyl- *p*-nitrobenzoate

Retention in configuration indicates that none of the bonds to the stereogenic center is broken in the process.

Mechanism of esterification will be discussed in detail in the chapter on "carboxylic acids". Further note that since acid-catalysed esterification is a reversible reaction, the mechanism of acidic hydrolysis of esters will be the exact reverse of esterification.

TEST YOUR UNDERSTANDING - 11.9

1. Arrange the following alcohols in the decreasing tendency of ester formation with acetic acid in presence of conc. H_2SO_4.

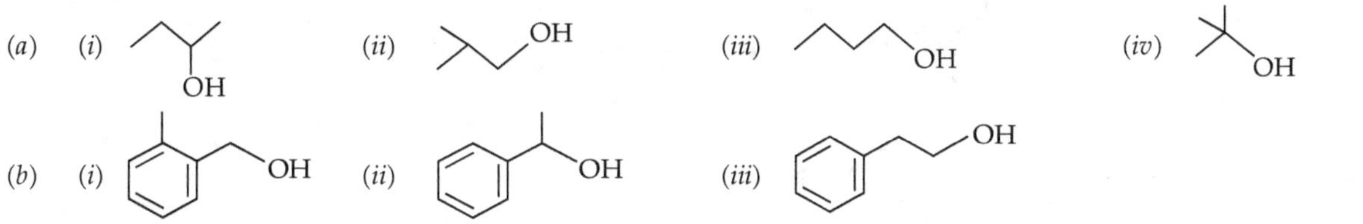

    (a) (i) (ii) (iii) (iv)

    (b) (i) (ii) (iii)

2. Complete the following reactions.

    (a) $\xrightarrow[\text{H}^+]{\text{CH}_3\text{COCl}}$

    (b) $+$ $\xrightarrow{\text{heat}}$

(b) **Esters of sulphonic acids.** Alcohols react with sulphonyl chlorides (remember that like carboxylic acids, sulphonic acids are less reactive than the corresponding chlorides and anhydrides) to form **sulphonates.**

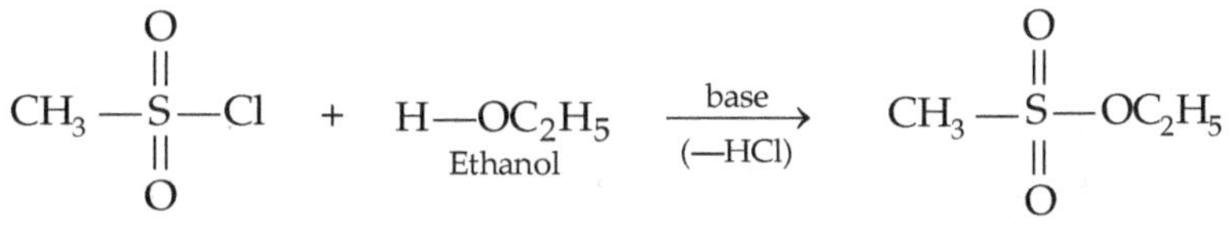

$$CH_3-\underset{\underset{O}{\|}}{\overset{\overset{O}{\|}}{S}}-Cl \ + \ H-OC_2H_5 \xrightarrow[(-HCl)]{\text{base}} CH_3-\underset{\underset{O}{\|}}{\overset{\overset{O}{\|}}{S}}-OC_2H_5$$

Methanesulphonyl chloride   Ethanol   Ethyl methanesulphonate (Ethyl mesylate)

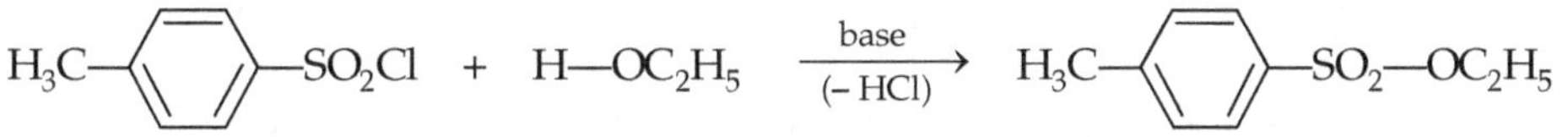

$$H_3C-\!\!\left\langle\ \right\rangle\!\!-SO_2Cl \ + \ H-OC_2H_5 \xrightarrow[(-HCl)]{\text{base}} H_3C-\!\!\left\langle\ \right\rangle\!\!-SO_2-OC_2H_5$$

p-Toluenesulphonyl chloride   Ethyl *p*-toluenesulphonate (Ethyl tosylate)

Name of methanesulphonyl, trifluoromethanesulphonyl and *p*-toluenesulphonyl groups are shortened to mesyl (Ms), trifyl (Tf) and tosyl (Ts) respectively.

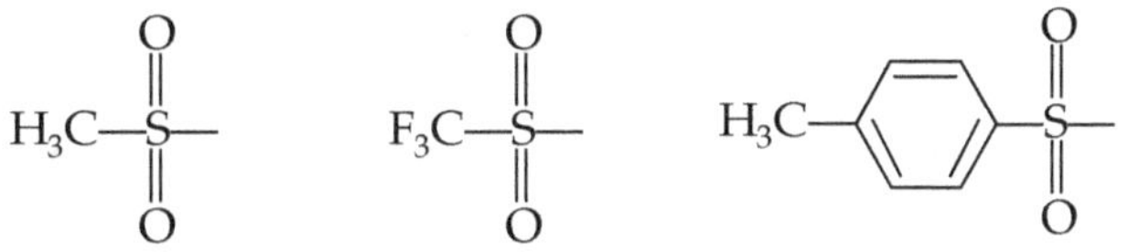

Mesyl or Ms   Trifyl or Tf   Tosyl or Ts

Since sulphonate ions are excellent leaving groups*, alkyl sulphonates are frequently used as substrates for nucleophilic substitution or elimination reactions.

$$\text{Nu}\!:^- \ + \ RCH_2-O-SO_2R' \ \longrightarrow \ Nu-CH_2R \ + \ {}^-OSO_2R'$$

Alkyl sulphonate, tosylate or mesylate   Sulphonate ion (a very weak base, hence a good leaving group)

(where $\text{Nu}:^- = {}^-OH, {}^-C\equiv N, Br^-, {}^-OR, :NH_3, LiAlH_4$)

Trifluoromethanesulphonate ($CF_3SO_2O^-$) is one of the best known leaving groups.

Actually, the triflate ion is such a good leaving group that even vinylic triflates undergo S_N^1 reactions.

$$H_2C=CH-OSO_2CF_3 \xrightarrow[\text{Vinylic cation}]{\text{solvolysis}} H_2C=\overset{+}{C}H \ + \ {}^-OSO_2CF_3$$

Triflate ion

---

* Although protonation of alcohols also generates a good leaving group ($-\overset{+}{O}H_2$), it limits our choice of reagents to those compatible with an acidic medium. Alkyl sulphonates, on the other hand, can be used with any nucleophile or base.

TEST YOUR UNDERSTANDING - 11.10

1.   Write down the structure of products A and B in the following reaction.

$$\underset{\substack{R' \\ }}{\overset{R}{\diagdown}}\!\!C\text{—OH} \ + \ ClTs \ \longrightarrow \ [A] \ \xrightarrow[(S_N 2)]{OH^-} \ [B]$$

(where Ts is *p*-toluenesulphonyl, H_3C—⟨ ⟩—SO_2—).

(c)   **Esters of inorganic acids.** Alcohols react with inorganic acids, *viz.* nitric acid, sulphuric acid, H_3PO_3 and H_3PO_4 to form esters of inorganic acids. For example,

$$\underset{\text{Alcohol}}{ROH} \ + \ \underset{\text{Nitric acid}}{HONO_2} \ \xrightarrow{H^+} \ \underset{\text{Alkyl nitrate}}{RONO_2} \ + \ H_2O$$

$$CH_3OH + HO\!-\!\overset{O}{\underset{O}{\overset{\|}{\underset{\|}{S}}}}\!-\!OH \ \longrightarrow \ \underset{\text{Methyl hydrogen sulphate}}{CH_3O\!-\!\overset{O}{\underset{O}{\overset{\|}{\underset{\|}{S}}}}\!-\!OH} \ \xrightarrow{CH_3OH} \ \underset{\text{Dimethyl sulphate}}{CH_3O\!-\!\overset{O}{\underset{O}{\overset{\|}{\underset{\|}{S}}}}\!-\!OCH_3}$$

$$\underset{\substack{\text{Trimethyl phosphite} \\ \text{(Ester to phosphorous} \\ \text{acid, } H_3PO_3)}}{CH_3O\!-\!\overset{\cdot\cdot}{\underset{OCH_3}{P}}\!-\!OCH_3} \qquad \underset{\substack{\text{Dimethyl hydrogen phosphate}}}{CH_3O\!-\!\overset{O}{\underset{OCH_3}{\overset{\|}{P}}}\!-\!OH} \qquad \underset{\text{Trimethyl phosphate}}{CH_3O\!-\!\overset{O}{\underset{OCH_3}{\overset{\|}{P}}}\!-\!OCH_3}$$

$$\text{(Esters of phosphoric acid, } H_3PO_4)$$

Dimethyl sulphate is used as methylating agent in synthetic organic chemistry ; *e.g.*

$$C_2H_5OH + (CH_3)_2SO_4 \longrightarrow \underset{\text{Ethylmethyl ether}}{C_2H_5\text{—O—}CH_3} + CH_3HSO_4$$

Methylation is used for determining the number of – OH group in alcohols.

$$\text{No. of – OH gps.} \ = \frac{\text{Mol. mass of methylated product – Mol. mass of alcohol}}{14}$$

Action of conc. sulphuric acid on alcohols is very interesting as it gives different products under different conditions.

(i)   Alcohols dissolve in cold conc. H_2SO_4 (*i.e.* at 0°C) forming oxonium salts, $R\overset{+}{O}H_2HSO_4^-$.

(ii)   At room temperature, esterification takes place forming alkyl hydrogen sulphate.

$$\underset{\text{Ethyl hydrogen sulphate}}{CH_3CH_2HSO_4} \xleftarrow{\text{room temp.}} CH_3CH_2OH + H_2SO_4 \xrightarrow{0°\,C} CH_3CH_2\overset{+}{O}H_2HSO_4^-$$

Ethyl hydrogen sulphate is an important intermediate and can be converted into different products under different conditions.

(a)   When heated alone, it forms diethyl sulphate

$$2C_2H_5HSO_4 \xrightarrow{\text{heat}} (C_2H_5)_2SO_4 + H_2SO_4$$

(b)   When heated with excess of H_2SO_4 at 160°C, it forms ethylene.

$$CH_3CH_2HSO_4 \xrightarrow{H^+,\,160°\,C} CH_2 = CH_2 + H_2SO_4$$

(c)   When heated with excess of ethanol, it forms diethyl ether

$$C_2H_5HSO_4 + HOC_2H_5 \xrightarrow{140°C} C_2H_5\text{—O—}C_2H_5 + H_2SO_4$$

3. Conversion of alcohols into alkyl halides

(a) Reaction with hydrogen halides.

$$R—OH + HX \longrightarrow R—X + H_2O$$

The order of reactivity of the hydrogen halides is **HI > HBr > HCl** (HF is generally unreactive), and the order of reactivity of alcohols is **3° > 2° > 1° < CH$_3$.**

(i) The reaction is *acid-catalysed**. Alcohols react with strongly acidic hydrogen halides, but not with non acidic NaCl, NaBr or NaI. Primary and secondary alcohols can be converted to alkyl chlorides and bromides by allowing them to react with a mixture of sodium halide and sulphuric acid.

$$R—OH + NaX \xrightarrow{H_2SO_4} R—X + NaHSO_4 + H_2O \ (X = Cl \ or \ Br)$$

(ii) The least reactive hydrogen halide, *i.e.* HCl **generally requires the presence of ZnCl$_2$*** (a Lewis acid) for reaction with 1° and 2° alcohols ; however, the highly reactive 3° alcohols do not require ZnCl$_2$.

$$CH_3CH_2CH_2CH_2OH \xrightarrow[\text{heat}]{\text{dry HBr or NaBr} + H_2SO_4} CH_3CH_2CH_2CH_2Br$$

$$CH_3CH_2CH_2OH \xrightarrow{HCl + ZnCl_2,\ heat} CH_3CH_2CH_2Cl$$

$$\underset{\textit{tert-}\text{Butyl alcohol}}{(CH_3)_3COH} \xrightarrow{\text{conc. HCl, room temperature}} \underset{\textit{tert-}\text{Butyl alcohol}}{(CH_3)_3COH}$$

This relative reactivity of alcohols towards HCl forms the basis of **Lucas test.**

(iii) Except with *most primary alcohols*, rearrangement of the alkyl group occurs, *i.e.* rearranged halides are formed.

3, 3-Dimethyl-2-butanol
(a 2° alcohol)

2-Chloro-2, 3-dimethylbutane

Neopentyl alcohol
(a 1° alcohol)

tert-Pentyl chloride

(iv) One of the important aspects of this reaction is that by converting an ROH into RX , we have replaced a very poor leaving group (—OH) into a very good leaving group (—X) instantaneously ; *i.e.* highly reactive compounds are formed from lesser reactive compounds.

Mechanism. Secondary, tertiary, allylic, and benzylic alcohols appear to react by S$_N$1 mechanism.

Step 1. $(CH_3)_3C—OH + H—Cl \rightleftharpoons (CH_3)_3C—\overset{+}{O}H_2 + Cl^-$

Step 2. $(CH_3)_3C—\overset{+}{O}H_2 \rightleftharpoons (CH_3)_3C^+ + H_2O$

Step 3. $(CH_3)_3 C^+ + Cl^- \longrightarrow (CH_3)_3C—Cl$
$$\textit{tert-}\text{Butyl chloride}$$

Most of the primary alcohols and methyl alcohol react by S$_N$2 mechanism.

$$R—\overset{+}{O}H_2 + X^- \longrightarrow \left[\overset{\delta-}{X}\cdots\cdots R\cdots\cdots\overset{\delta+}{O}H_2 \right] \longrightarrow X—R + H_2O$$

Why CH$_3$OH reacts faster than other primary alcohols ? Actually, methyl substrate is least capable of heterolysis and thus reacts by a full-fledged S$_N$2 reaction. Although most of the primary substrates also react by S$_N$2 mechanism, but because of greater steric hindrance they react less rapidly than the methyl.

---

* Although the aqueous HX are themselves strong acids, presence of H$_2$SO$_4$ speeds up the reaction.
** Recall that Cl$^-$ is a weaker nucleophile than Br$^-$ or I$^-$.

Function of ZnCl₂ in Lucas reagent. Since chloride ion is a weaker nucleophile than bromide or iodide ions, H does not react with less reactive 1° and 2° alcohols unless some good Lewis acid like $ZnCl_2$ is added to the reaction mixture. Primary alcohols, being least reactive, requires some heat in addition to $ZnCl_2$. Zinc chloride a good Lewis acid, forms a complex with the alcohol. This complex provides a better leaving group for the reaction than H_2O.

$$R\!-\!\overset{\cdot\cdot}{\underset{H}{O}}\!:\ +\ ZnCl_2\ \rightleftharpoons\ R\!-\!\overset{\cdot\cdot}{\underset{H}{\overset{+}{O}}}\!-\!\overset{-}{Z}nCl_2$$

(Actual substrate)

$$:\overset{\cdot\cdot}{\underset{\cdot\cdot}{Cl}}\ +\ R\!-\!\overset{+}{\underset{H}{O}}\!-\!\overset{-}{Z}nCl_2\ \longrightarrow\ Cl\!-\!R\ +\ [Zn(OH)Cl_2]^-\ \overset{\overset{+}{H}}{\rightleftharpoons}\ ZnCl_2 + H_2O$$

Now we can explain why the reactions of alcohols with hydrogen halides are acid catalyzed.

(*i*) In case of 3° and 2° alcohols, the function of acid is to help in the formation of carbocations.

(*ii*) In case of methyl and 1° alcohols, the function of acid is to produce a substrate in which the leaving group a weakly basic species (H_2O or $Zn(OH)Cl_2^-$) rather than a strongly basic hydroxide ion.

(*b*) **Reaction with phosphorus trihalides or thionyl chloride.**

$$3R\!-\!OH\ +\ PX_3\ \longrightarrow\ 3R\!-\!X\ +\ H_3PO_3$$
  (1° or 2°) (X = Br or I) Phosphorous acid

Phosphorus is a water-soluble and may be removed by washing the alkyl halide with water or with dilute aqueous base.

Cyclopentyl bromide $\xleftarrow{PBr_3}$ Cyclopentanol $\xrightarrow{P\ and\ I_2}$ Cyclopentyl iodide

$$R\!-\!OH\ +\ SOCl_2\ \longrightarrow\ R\!-\!Cl\ +\ SO_2\uparrow\ +\ HCl\uparrow$$
(1° or 2°)

Since SO_2 and HCl, both are gases at room temperature, these are easily removed. Reactions with thionyl chloride are normally carried out in the presence of potassium carbonate or the weak organic base pyridine.

(*i*) Since *tert*-alcohol are readily converted into halides, phosphorous trihalides and thionyl chloride are mainly used for preparing primary and secondary halides.

(*ii*) Since carbocations are not formed as intermediates, the reaction with both the reagents occurs *without rearrangement*.

TEST YOUR UNDERSTANDING - 11.11

1. Identify [A] to [D] in the following reactions.

(*a*) $\xrightarrow{HCl}$ [A]   (*b*) $\xrightarrow{HBr}$ [B]

(*c*) $\xrightarrow{HBr}$ [C]   (*d*) $\xrightarrow{HBr}$ [D] Major

2. Explain the following :

(*a*) Neopentyl alcohol reacts with hydrogen halides slowly.

(*b*) 1-Chloro-2-propanol is although a secondary alcohol, it reacts with hydrogen halides slowly than the parent compound 2-propanol.

3. Neopentyl chloride can't be prepared from neopentyl alcohol, can you suggest a method for the preparation of neopentyl chloride in quantitative yield ?

4. Identify the compounds [A] to [F] in the following reactions.

(a) [cyclopentylmethanol] $\xrightarrow{\text{HCl/ZnCl}_2}$ [A]

(b) [cyclopentylmethanol] $\xrightarrow{\text{SOCl}_2}$ [B]

(c) [2,4-dimethylpentan-2-ol structure] $\xrightarrow{\text{HCl/ZnCl}_2}$ [C]

(d) [2,4-dimethylpentan-2-ol structure] $\xrightarrow{\text{SOCl}_2}$ [D]

(e) [cyclohexanol] $\xrightarrow[\text{(ii) Mg/ether}]{\text{(i) PBr}_3}$ [E] $\xrightarrow[\text{H}_3\text{O}^+]{\text{epoxide}}$ [F]

---

4. Dehydration to alkenes. (Intramolecular dehydration)

Heating of most of alcohols with a strong acid causes loss of a water molecule to form alkenes (for mechanism, consult chapter on "Alkenes").

$$\overset{\underset{\displaystyle H}{|}}{\underset{}{C}}-\overset{\underset{\displaystyle OH}{|}}{\underset{}{C}} \xrightarrow{\;H^+\;} \quad {>}C = C{<} \;+\; H_2O$$

(i) The reaction is an elimination and is favoured at high temperatures. Most commonly used acids in the laboratory are H_2SO_4 and H_3PO_4, while alumina is often used in industries.

(ii) The order of dehydration among three types of alcohols is $3° > 2° > 1°$. Thus dehydrating conditions become milder as we proceed from $1°$ to $3°$ alcohols.

$$CH_3CH_2OH \xrightarrow{\;\text{conc.}\,H_2SO_4,\,180°C\;} CH_2 = CH_2 + H_2O$$

[cyclohexanol] $\xrightarrow{\;85\%\,H_3PO_4,\,165\text{--}170°C\;}$ [cyclohexene] $+ H_2O$

$$(CH_3)_3COH \xrightarrow{\;20\%\,H_2SO_4,\,85°C\;} (CH_3)_2C = CH_2 + H_2O$$

This behaviour is related to the relative stabilities of carbocations $(3° > 2° > 1°)$.

(iii) Since carbocations are formed as intermediate, rearranged olefins, where possible, are formed (consult Ch. on alkenes).

(iv) Whenever dehydration can produce two different alkenes, major product is formed according to **Saytzeff rule** *"poor becomes poorer"* *i.e.* more substituted alkene (alkene having lesser number of hydrogen atoms on the two doubly bonded carbon atoms) is the major product.

[2-Methylcyclohexanol] $\xrightarrow[\text{heat}]{\text{H}_3\text{PO}_4}$ [1-Methylcyclohexene] + [3-Methylcyclohexene]

2-Methylcyclohexanol   1-Methylcyclohexene **(Major)**   3-Methylcyclohexene (Minor)

Such reactions which can produce two or more structural isomers but one of them in greater amounts than the other are called **regioselective** *; in case a reaction is 100% regioselective, it is termed as* **regiospecific.**

(v) In addition to being regioselective, alcohol dehydrations are **stereoselective** *(a reaction in which a single starting material can yield two or more stereoisomeric products, but gives one of them in greater amount than any other).*

$$CH_3CH_2\overset{\underset{\displaystyle OH}{|}}{\underset{}{C}}HCH_2CH_3 \xrightarrow[\text{heat}]{\text{H}_2\text{SO}_4}$$

3-Pentanol

[*cis*-2-Pentene structure] + [*trans*-2-Pentene structure]

cis-2-Pentene (Minor)   *trans*-2-Pentene (Major)

TEST YOUR UNDERSTANDING - 11.12

1. Write down the structure of the compound(s) by the acid-catalyzed dehydration of the following alcohols. Mention the major product, if any, in each case.

(a)   (b)   (c)

(d)   (e)   (f)

---

5. **Dehydration to ethers (Intermolecular dehydration).** Primary alcohols when heated in presence of an acid catalyst (usually H_2SO_4) undergo intermolecular dehydration to form ethers.

$$R—OH + HO—R \xrightarrow{H^+,\,heat} R—O—R$$

(i) Dehydration of an alcohol to an ether usually takes place at a lower temperature than dehydration to alkene.

$$CH_2 = CH_2 \xleftarrow[180°C]{excess\ of\ H_2SO_4} CH_3CH_2OH \xrightarrow[H_2SO_4,\,140°C]{excess\ of\ ethanol} CH_3CH_2OCH_2CH_3$$

(ii) As mentioned above, the reaction is effective only with primary alcohols ; secondary and tertiary alcohols on such treatment mainly give alkenes. However, diols having primary alcoholic groups can undergo dehydration (intramolecular) to form a 5-membered or 6-membered ring.

$$\xrightarrow[heat]{H_2SO_4}\quad + \quad H_2O$$

1, 5-Pentanediol   Oxane

(iii) This method is not useful for the preparation of unsymmetrical ethers because the reaction leads to a mixture of products.

$$R—OH + HO—R' \xrightarrow{H^+} R—O—R' + R—O—R + R'—O—R'$$

The most common method for preparing unsymmetrical ethers is **Williamson synthesis** (discussed in ethers).

Mechanism. Reaction is a nucleophilic substitution in which substrate is a protonated alcohol and nucleophile is the second alcohol molecule.

$$CH_3CH_2OH \xrightarrow{H^+} CH_3CH_2\overset{+}{O}H_2 \ + \ CH_3CH_2OH \longrightarrow \left[CH_3CH_2\overset{\delta+}{—O}\cdots CH_2\cdots\overset{\delta+}{OH_2} \right]$$

1st molecule of alcohol   Protonated alcohol (substrate)   2nd molecule of alcohol (nucleophile)   Transition state

$$\xrightarrow[(-H_2O)]{} CH_3CH_2\overset{+}{—O}—CH_2CH_3 \xrightarrow{HSO_4^-} CH_3CH_2—O—CH_2CH_3 \ + \ H_2SO_4$$

Ether

Mechanism for the conversion of 1, 5-pentanediol to oxane.

$$+ \ H—\overset{..}{\underset{..}{O}}SO_2OH \xrightarrow{-:\overset{..}{\underset{..}{O}}SO_2OH} \xrightarrow[(-H_2O)]{} \xrightarrow{HSO_4^-} + \ H_2SO_4$$

1, 5-Pentanediol   Substrate is $-\overset{..}{O}H_2$ Oxane

nucleophile is $-\overset{..}{\underset{..}{O}}H$

pinacol–pinacolone rearrangement.

Pinacols, ditertiary 1, 2-diols, on heating with acids lose a molecule of water along with the rearrangement to form ketones, commonly known as pinacolones.

$$CH_3-\underset{\underset{CH_3}{|}}{\overset{\overset{OH}{|}}{C}}-\underset{\underset{CH_3}{|}}{\overset{\overset{OH}{|}}{C}}-CH_3 \xrightarrow[heat]{H^+} CH_3-\underset{\underset{CH_3}{|}}{\overset{\overset{O}{\|}}{C}}-\underset{\underset{CH_3}{|}}{C}-CH_3$$

Pinacol   Pinacolone

6. **Oxidation of alcohols.** Oxidation of an alcohol involves the loss of one or more hydrogens (α-hydrogens) from the carbon bearing the —OH group. Hence the nature of product obtained depends upon the number of α-hydrogen atoms present in the alcohol. Thus,

A carboxylic acid $\xleftarrow{\text{loss of } 2\alpha\text{-H}}$ A 1° alcohol (2α-H atoms) $\xrightarrow{\text{loss of } 1\alpha\text{-H}}$ An aldehyde

A 2° alcohol (1α-H atom) → A ketone ; A 3° alcohol (no α-H atom) → Oxidation not possible

Thus, in short a primary alcohol may be oxidised to an aldehyde or a carboxylic acid, a secondary alcohol to a ketone, and a tertiary alcohol is not oxidisable easily. However, a tertiary alcohol can be dehydrated by an acidic oxidising agent to an alkene which can then be oxidised.

(*a*) **Oxidation of primary alcohols to carboxylic acids.** Primary alcohols can be oxidised to carboxylic acids by acidic or basic aqueous solution of potassium permanganate. As the oxidation takes place Mn (VII) is reduced to Mn (IV) in the form of brown precipitate of MnO_2.

$$RCH_2OH + KMnO_4 \xrightarrow{OH^-, H_2O, \text{heat}} RCOOK + MnO_2\downarrow + KOH$$

1° Alcohol   Purple   Solution in H_2O Brown

$$\xrightarrow{H^+} RCOOH$$

Insoluble in water

Primary alcohols can be oxidised to carboxylic acids also by $Cr_2O_7^{2-} + H_2SO_4 + H_2O$ and chromic acid, H_2CrO_4, prepared by dissolving CrO_3 or $K_2Cr_2O_7$ in aqueous sulphuric acid.

(b)   **Oxidation of primary alcohols to aldehydes.** The oxidation of aldehydes to carboxylic acids **in aqueous solution** usually takes place with less powerful oxidizing agents than those required to oxidize 1° alcohols to aldehydes, thus **it is difficult to stop oxidation at the aldehydic stage in aqueous solution.** Hence special oxidizing agents must be used for oxidizing 1° alcohols to the aldehydic stage. One of the best and most convenient reagents for this purpose is **pyridinium chlorochromate (PCC),** obtained by dissolving chromium oxide (CrO_3) in hydrochloric acid in presence of pyridine.

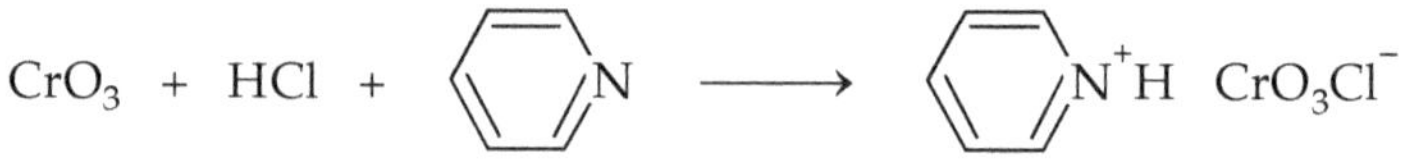

$$CrO_3 \ + \ HCl \ + \ \text{(pyridine)} \longrightarrow \text{(pyridinium)} N^+H \ \ CrO_3Cl^-$$

Pyridinium chlorochromate (PCC)

Other such reagent is **pyridinium dichromate (PDC),** $(C_5H_5NH)_2^+ \ Cr_2O_7^{2-}$. Both of these reagents are used in presence of dichloromethane, CH_2Cl_2 in which these reagents are soluble.

$$CH_2 = CH-CH_2OH \ \xrightarrow{PCC/CH_2Cl_2} \ CH_2 = CHCHO$$

Remember that aldehyde hydrates, $RCH(OH)_2$ are more easily oxidisable than aldehydes, hence aqueous medium is avoided whenever aldehyde is to be obtained as final product.

(c)   **Oxidation of secondary alcohols to ketones.** Secondary alcohols are oxidised to ketones, at which stage reaction usually stops because further oxidation requires breaking of C—C bond. Secondary alcohols can be oxidised to ketone either by (i) chromic acid (H_2CrO_4), prepared by adding CrO_3 or $Na_2Cr_2O_7$ to aqueous sulphuric acid, or by a complex of chromium trioxide and pyridine (**Collins reagent**) or by (iii) CrO_3 in aqueous acetone (**Jones reagent**) ; or by (iv) PDC/PCC in CH_2Cl_2. Although Jones reagent rarely affects double bond, the last reagent is especially useful for oxidising unsaturated alcohols to unsaturated carbonyl compounds.

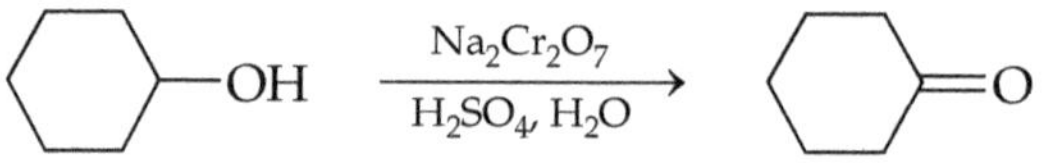

$$\text{Cyclohexanol} \xrightarrow[H_2SO_4,\ H_2O]{Na_2Cr_2O_7} \text{Cyclohexanone}$$

Cyclohexanol   Cyclohexanone

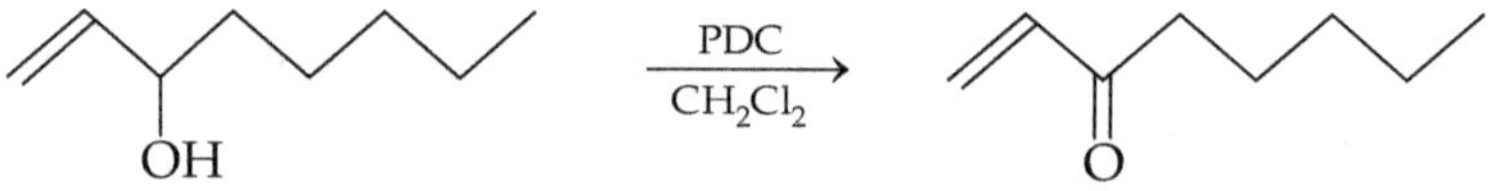

$$\text{1-Octen-3-ol} \xrightarrow[CH_2Cl_2]{PDC} \text{1-Octen-3-one}$$

1-Octen-3-ol   1-Octen-3-one

(d)   **Oxidation by manganese dioxide.** Manganese dioxide selectively oxidises the alcoholic groups of allylic and benzylic 1° and 2° alcohols to give aldehydes and ketones respectively.

(i) $HOCH_2CH_2CH = CHCH_2OH \ \xrightarrow{MnO_2} \ HOCH_2CH_2CH = CHCHO$

(ii) $\text{(Ph)}-CH_2OH \ \xrightarrow{MnO_2} \ \text{(Ph)}-CHO$ (iii) $\text{(cyclopentenol)} \xrightarrow{MnO_2} \text{(cyclopentenone)}$

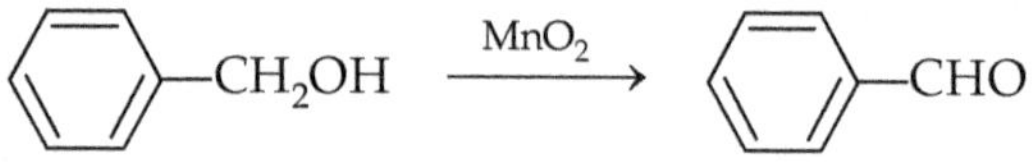

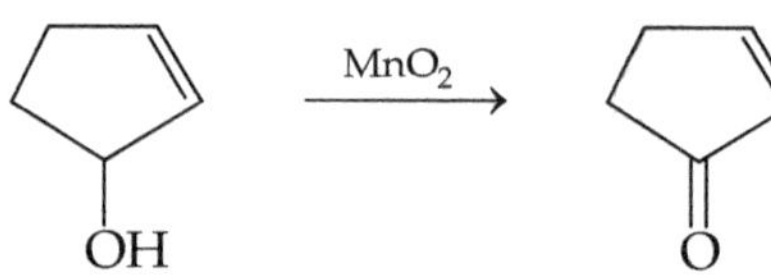

(iv) $\text{(Ph)}-CHOHCH_2CH_2OH \ \xrightarrow{MnO_2} \ \text{(Ph)}-COCH_2CH_2OH$

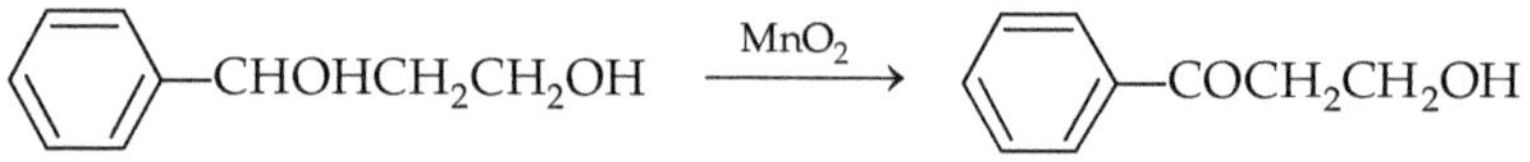

(e)   **Swern oxidation** of 1° and 2° alcohols gives aldehydes and ketones respectively. It uses dimethylsulfoxide (DMSO) as as the oxidizing agent; DMSO and oxalyl chloride are added to the alcohol at low temperature, followed by a hindered base such as triethylamine. The by-products of this reaction are all volatile, and are easily separated from the organic products. Thus it provides a useful alternative to PCC that uses chromium reagents.

$$\underset{(R'=H\ or\ alkyl)}{R-\overset{R'}{\underset{|}{C}}HOH} + \underset{DMSO}{H_3C-\overset{O}{\overset{||}{S}}-CH_3} + Cl-\overset{O}{\overset{||}{C}}-\overset{O}{\overset{||}{C}}-Cl \xrightarrow[CH_2Cl_2]{(CH_3CH_2)_3N} R-\overset{R'}{\underset{|}{C}}=O + H_3C-S-CH_3 + CO_2 + CO + 2HCl$$

(f)   **Chemical test for 1° and 2° alcohols.** Primary and secondary alcohols can be easily distinguished from tertiary alcohols on the basis of the fact that the former are readily oxidised by a solution of CrO_3 in aqueous sulphuric acid which is accompanied by change of clear orange solution containing Cr (VI) ions to greenish opaque solution containing Cr(III) ions.

$$\underset{\text{Clear orange solution}}{\underline{RCH_2OH \ or \ R_2CHOH + CrO_3 / aq. \ H_2SO_4}} \longrightarrow \underset{\text{Greenish opaque solution}}{\underline{\text{Oxidation products} + Cr^{3+}}}$$

This colour change, associated with the reduction of $Cr_2O_7^{2-}$ to Cr^{3+} forms the basis for **Breathalyzer tubes** used to detect intoxicated auto drivers. In the Breathalyzer, the dichromate salt is coated on granules to silica gel.

(g) **Distinction between 1°, 2° and 3° alcohols.** We have learnt that

(i) Oxidation of 1° alcohols gives first aldehydes and then acids, both having same number of carbon atoms as the parent alcohol.

$$CH_3CH_2OH \longrightarrow CH_3CHO \longrightarrow CH_3COOH$$
$$\text{2C} \qquad\qquad \text{2C} \qquad\qquad \text{2C}$$

(ii) Oxidation of 2° alcohols gives ketones which are difficult to oxidise, however on vigourous oxidation ketones give carboxylic acids having lesser number of carbon atoms than the parent alcohol.

$$(CH_3)_2CHOH \longrightarrow (CH_3)_2CO \longrightarrow CH_3COOH + HCOOH$$
$$\text{3C} \qquad\qquad \text{3C} \qquad\qquad \text{2C} \qquad \text{1C}$$

(iii) Tertiary alcohols are not oxidised easily, however on treatment with acidic reagents, they first undergo **dehydration** to form alkenes. Alkenes are then oxidized first to ketones and then to acids, both having lesser number of carbon atoms than the parent alcohol.

$$CH_3 - \underset{\underset{\text{4C}}{\overset{\displaystyle CH_3}{|}}}{\overset{\overset{\displaystyle OH}{|}}{C}} - CH_3 \xrightarrow[\text{oxidizing agent}]{\text{acidic}} \left[\underset{\text{Alkene}}{CH_3 - \underset{\underset{\displaystyle CH_3}{|}}{C} = CH_2} \right] \xrightarrow{[O]} \underset{\text{3C}}{(CH_3)_2CO} \xrightarrow{[O]} \underset{\text{2C}}{CH_3COOH} + \underset{\text{1C}}{HCOOH}$$

7. **Dehydrogenation (oxidation) of alcohols by copper at 573 K.** This reaction is also considered as oxidation. In this reaction primary alcohols give aldehydes and secondary give ketones ; while tertiary alcohols undergo dehydration to form alkenes.

$$\underset{\text{1° Alcohol}}{CH_3CH_2OH} \longrightarrow \underset{\text{Aldehyde}}{CH_3CHO} \ ; \ \underset{\text{2° Alcohol}}{(CH_3)_2CHOH} \longrightarrow \underset{\text{Ketone}}{(CH_3)_2CO} \ ; \ \underset{\text{3° Alcohol}}{(CH_3)_3COH} \longrightarrow \underset{\text{An alkene}}{(CH_3)_2C = CH_2}$$

8. **Oxidation of alcohols by hypohalites.** Ethyl alcohol and secondary alcohols having at least one of the alkyl groups as —CH_3 undergo haloform reaction on treatment with alkaline halogen, $(X_2 + NaOH)$ or hypohalites. For details, consult iodoform in the chapter on "**Alkyl Halides**".

Remember that the reaction takes place in presence of alkaline solution, so CH_3CH_2Cl and CH_3CHClR will also respond haloform test because these halides are converted by aqueous alkali into corresponding alcohols which then undergo haloform reaction.

TEST YOUR UNDERSTANDING - 11.13

1. Predict the product obtained by the oxidation of benzyl alcohol with *(a)* $KMnO_4/OH^-$, *(b)* $CrO_3/aq.\ H_2SO_4$, *(c)* CrO_3/pyridine HCl.

2. Show how each of the following transformations could be accomplished ?

(a)   *(b)*

(c)   *(d)*

3. Which of the following compounds give a positive haloform test ? Also give the structure of the carboxylic acid formed.

(a) $C_6H_5CH_2OH$ *(b)* $C_6H_5CHOHCH_3$

(c)   Cyclopentylmethyl carbinol   *(d)*   1-Methylcyclohexanol.

11.6　Distinction Between Primary, Secondary and Tertiary Alcohols

1. **Lucas test.** Lucas reagent (a mixture of conc HCl and zinc chloride) reacts with alcohols to form corresponding alkyl chlorides which are insoluble. Formation of a chloride from an alcohol is indicated by the cloudiness that appars when the chloride separates from the solution. Hence the time required for cloudiness to appear is a measure of reactivity of the alcohol.

   A tertiary alcohol reacts immediately, a secondary alcohol reacts within five minutes, and a primary alcohol does not react appreciably at room temperature. However, remember that allyl alcohol, $CH_2 = CHCH_2OH$ reacts as rapidly as tertiary alcohols with the Lucas reagent to form *soluble* allyl chloride.

2. **Victor Meyer test.** This test is based upon the fact that the three types (1°, 2° or 3°) of nitroalkanes (formed by alcohols) react differently with nitrous acid followed by sodium hydroxide. The three types of alcohols are first converted to corresponding nitro compounds.

$$\overset{}{>}C\text{—OH} \xrightarrow{P/I_2} \overset{}{>}C\text{—I} \xrightarrow{AgNO_2} \underset{\text{Nitroalkane}}{\overset{}{>}C\text{—NO}_2}$$

Nitroalkane, so obtained, is treated first with nitrous acid and then with sodium hydroxide to get different colours at the end.

$$CH_3CH_2NO_2 \xrightarrow{HONO} \underset{\overset{\|}{NOH}}{CH_3\,CNO_2} \xrightarrow{NaOH} \underset{\overset{\|}{NOHa}}{CH_3\,CNO_2}$$

1° Nitroalkane　　　　　　　Nitrolic acid (blue)　　　　　　Sod. nitrolate **(red)**
(from 1° alcohol)

$$(CH_3)_2CHNO_2 \xrightarrow{HONO} \underset{\overset{|}{NO}}{(CH_3)_2\,CNO_2} \xrightarrow{NaOH} \text{No reaction}$$

2° Nitroalkane　　　　　　　Pseudonitrol **(blue)**
(from 2° alcohol)

$$(CH_3)_3CNO_2 \xrightarrow{HONO} \text{No reaction } \textbf{(no colour)}$$

3° Nitroalkane

3. **Oxidation method :** With this method, we can distinguish 1° and 2° alcohols from 3° alcohols; primary and secondary alcohols are easily oxidised by chromic anhydride (CrO_3) in aqueous sulphuric acid, indicated by change in colour from clear orange solution to blue-green opaque.

$$\underset{\text{1° or 2° alcohol}}{RCH_2OH/R_2CHOH} + \underset{\underset{\text{solution}}{\text{Clear orange}}}{H_2CrO_4} \longrightarrow R COOH/R_2CO + \underset{\underset{\text{opaque}}{\text{greenish}}}{Cr^{3+}}$$

tert-Alcohols are not oxidised, hence do not respond this test.

TEST YOUR UNDERSTANDING - 11.14

1. There are five isomeric compounds of the molecular formula $C_5H_{12}O$, only one of which (A) gives white turbidity immediately with conc. HCl/$ZnCl_2$, while the other four do not respond the reagent at room temperature. Identify the five compounds.

2. Identify the alcohol(s) from the given reaction.

   (*a*)　An alcohol of the formula C_3H_8O decolorises acidic $KMnO_4$ solution.

   (*b*)　An aromatic compound of the formula C_7H_8O turns orange solution of dichromate to green.

   (*c*)　A cyclic alcohol of the formula $C_7H_{14}O$ reacts immediately with Lucas reagent.

1.7 Illustrative Examples

Here some problems in the form of reactions or descriptive language are given. Each problem has one or more ncept in it.

Example 1 :

Identify A and B in the following reactions.

$$B \xleftarrow[\text{(ii) } H_2O_2/OH^-]{\text{(i) } BH_3.THF} CH_3C \equiv CH \xrightarrow{H_2SO_4/Hg^{2+}} A.$$

Solution :

Recall that hydration of alkenes/alkynes by H_2SO_4 takes place in Markovnikov's way, while hydration by hydroboration-oxidation occurs in *anti*-Markovnikov's manner.

$$\underset{(A)}{CH_3COCH_3} \qquad \underset{(B)}{CH_3CH_2CHO}$$

Example 2 :

Write steps in the acidic degradative oxidation of $(CH_3)_3COH$ to CH_3COOH and CO_2.

Solution :

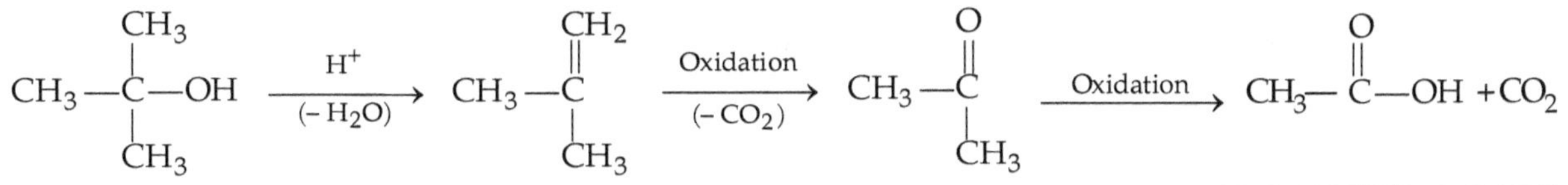

Example 3 :

Supply the missing compounds in the following series of reactions.

$$[A] \xrightarrow{C_6H_5CO_3H} [B] \xrightarrow{CH_3CH_2MgCl} CH_3CH_2CH_2CH_2OH \xrightarrow[CH_2Cl_2]{PCC} [C]$$

Solution :

Note that the product has two carbon atoms more than the Grignard reagent used, hence the compound B should be ethylene oxide, and hence A as ethylene.

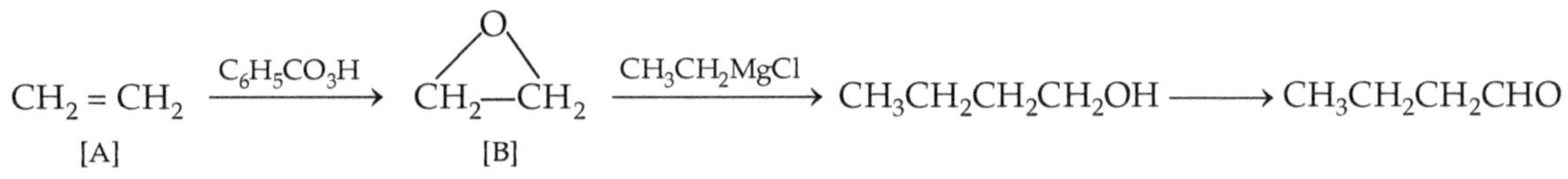

Example 4 :

Identify A to [C] in the following reactions.

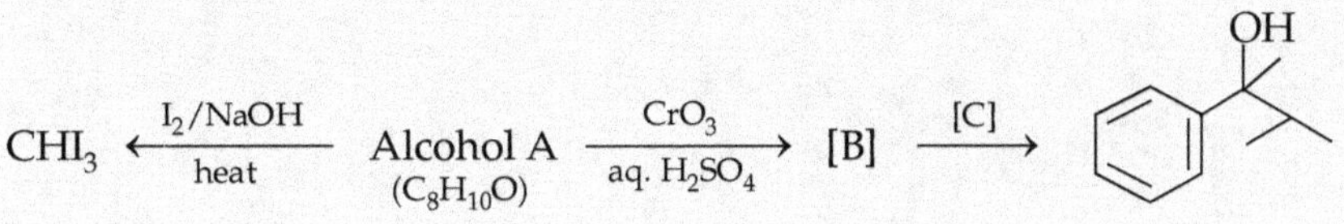

Solution :

Above reactions indicate that alcohol A has benzene nucleus and —$CHOHCH_3$ part, hence it is $C_6H_5CHOH\ CH_3$. Thus

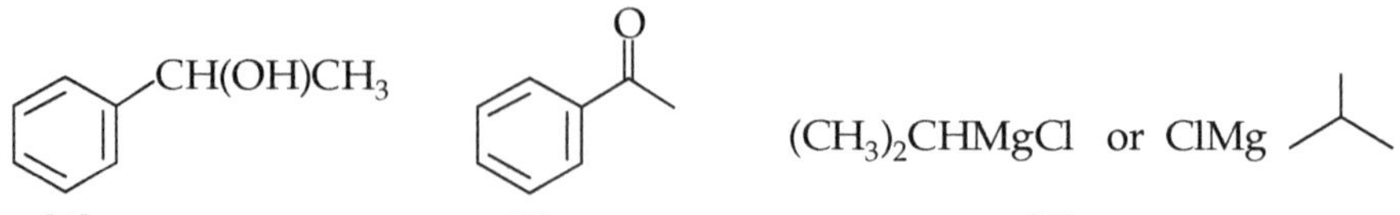
CH(OH)CH3
O
(CH3)2CHMgCl or ClMg

[A] [B] [C]

Example 5 :

Identify A and B ; what is relation of B with the starting compound ?

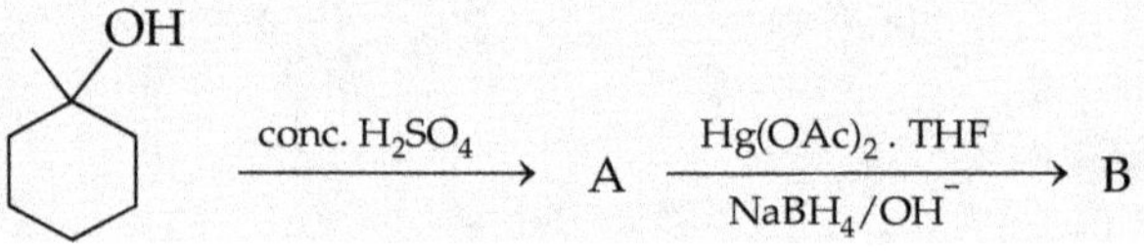
OH
conc. H2SO4
A
Hg(OAc)2 . THF
NaBH4/OH⁻
B

Solution :

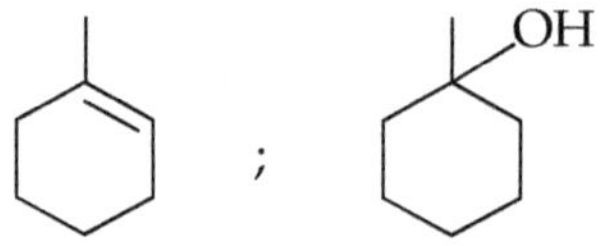
OH

A ; B ; B and starting compounds are same.

Example 6 :

Give the structures of A, B and C

A cyclic alcohol A ($C_6H_{12}O$) $\xrightarrow{\text{conc. } H_2SO_4}$ **B** $\xrightarrow[\text{heat}]{\text{conc. } HNO_3}$ **$C_6H_{10}O_4$ (C)**

Solution :

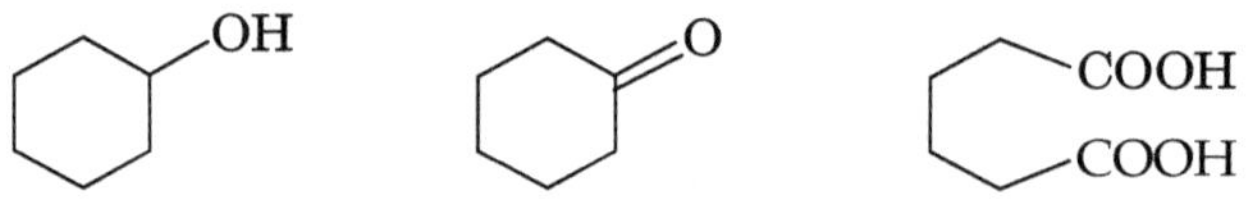
OH
O
COOH
COOH

(A) (B) (C) Adipic acid

Example 7 :

Starting from cyclohexanol, prepare cyclohexene, and 1, 3-cyclohexadiene.

Solution :

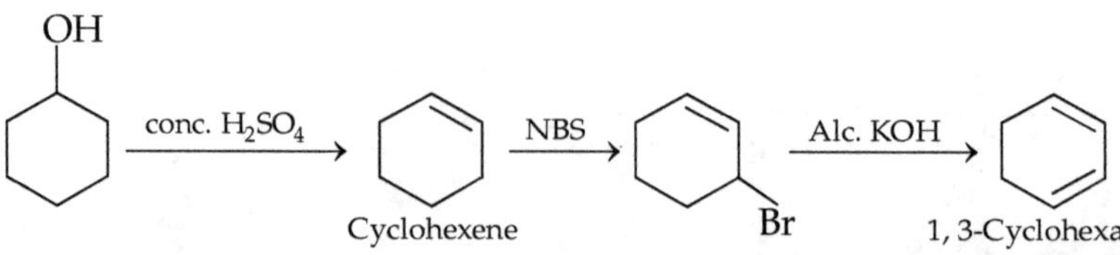
OH
conc. H2SO4
NBS
Alc. KOH
Br

Cyclohexene 1, 3-Cyclohexadiene

Example 8 :

Complete the following reactions.

(i) (cyclopentanol) $\xrightarrow[\text{pyridine}]{\text{TsCl}}$ **[A]** $\xrightarrow{\text{LiAlH}_4}$ **[B]**; $\xrightarrow{\text{NaBr}}$ **[C]**

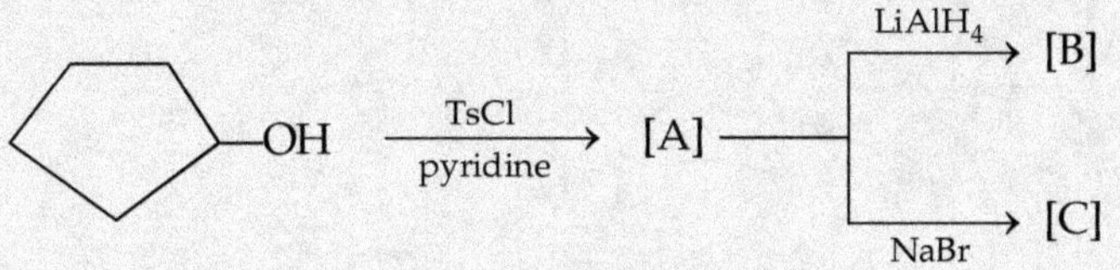

(ii) **[F]** $\xleftarrow{\text{PBr}_3}$ (cyclopentane diol with H, H, OH, CH$_3$) $\xrightarrow[\text{pyridine}]{\text{TsCl}}$ **[D]** $\xrightarrow{\text{NaBr}}$ **[E]**

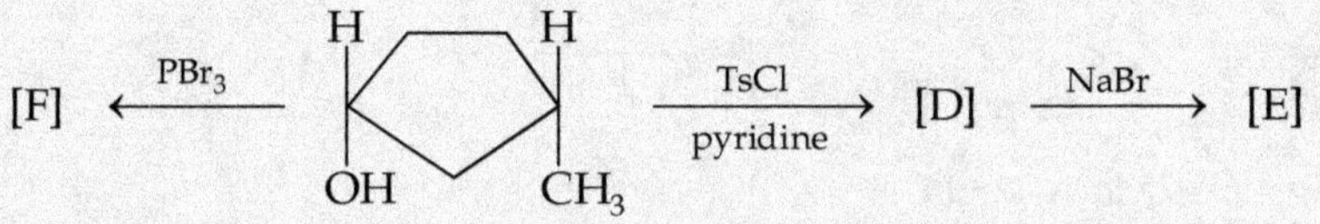

(iii) (cyclohexanol) $\xrightarrow{\text{conc. H}_2\text{SO}_4}$ **[G]** $\xrightarrow[\text{H}_2\text{O}]{\text{C}_6\text{H}_5\text{CO}_3\text{H}}$ **[H]**

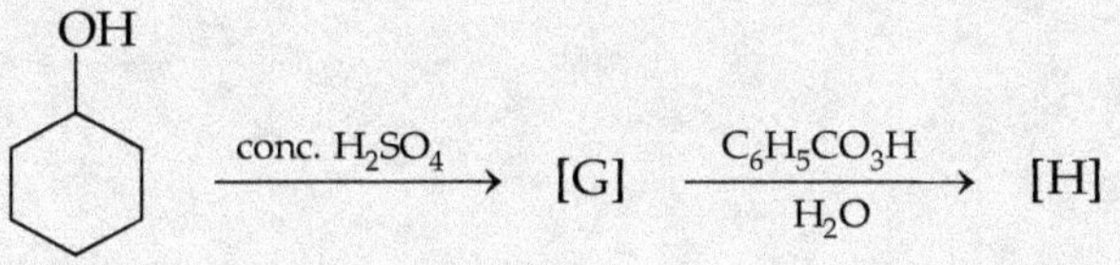

(iv) (1-methylcyclohexanol) $\xrightarrow{\text{conc. H}_2\text{SO}_4}$ **[I]** $\xrightarrow[\text{(ii) H}_2\text{O}_2/\text{OH}^-]{\text{(i) BH}_3 . \text{THF}}$ **[J]**

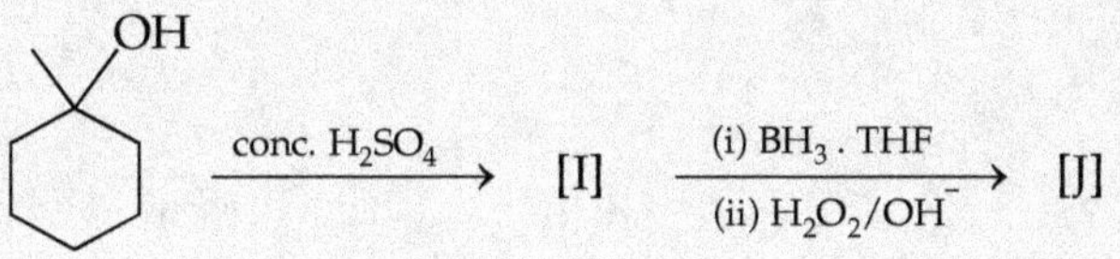

Solution :

Carry out the reactions keeping in mind the stereochemical implication, if any.

(i)

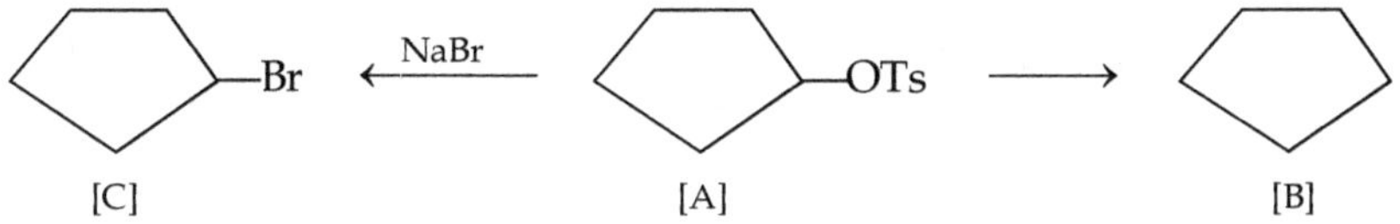

(cyclopentyl-Br) **[C]** $\xleftarrow{\text{NaBr}}$ (cyclopentyl-OTs) **[A]** $\longrightarrow$ (cyclopentane) **[B]**

(ii)

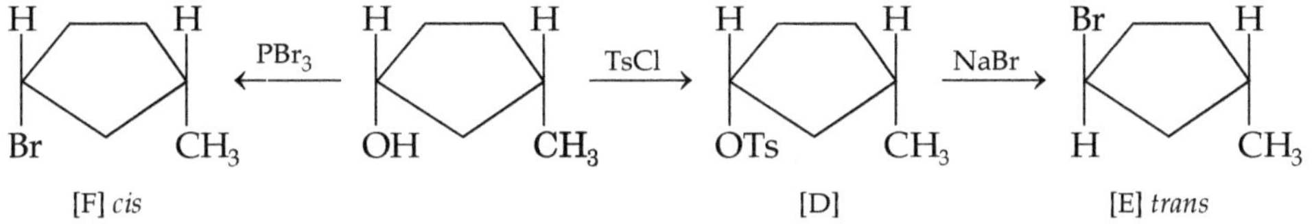

(cyclopentane with H, Br, H, CH$_3$) **[F]** *cis* $\xleftarrow{\text{PBr}_3}$ (cyclopentane with H, OH, H, CH$_3$) $\xrightarrow{\text{TsCl}}$ (cyclopentane with H, OTs, H, CH$_3$) **[D]** $\xrightarrow{\text{NaBr}}$ (cyclopentane with Br, H, H, CH$_3$) **[E]** *trans*

(iii)

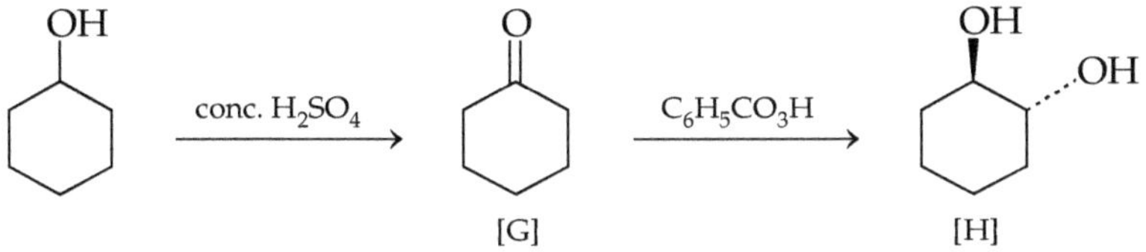

(cyclohexanol) $\xrightarrow{\text{conc. H}_2\text{SO}_4}$ (cyclohexanone) **[G]** $\xrightarrow{\text{C}_6\text{H}_5\text{CO}_3\text{H}}$ (cyclohexane with OH and OH) **[H]**

(iv)

(1-methylcyclohexanol) $\xrightarrow{\text{conc. H}_2\text{SO}_4}$ (methylcyclohexene) **[I]** $\xrightarrow[\text{(ii) H}_2\text{O}_2/\text{OH}^-]{\text{(i) BH}_3 . \text{THF}}$ (cyclohexane with CH$_3$ and OH) **[J]**

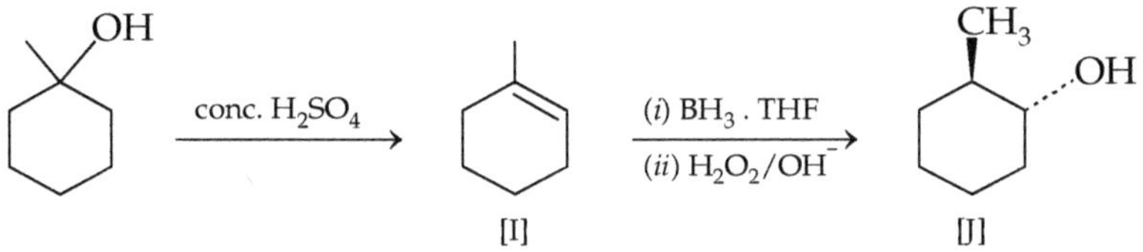

Example 9 :

Identify the products A and B in the following reaction.

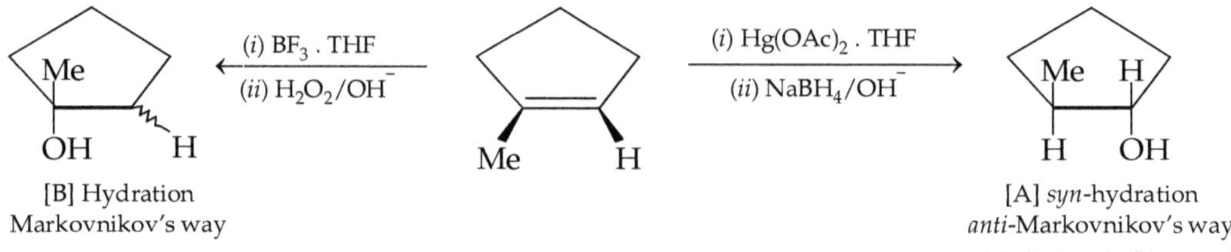

Solution :

[B] Hydration
Markovnikov's way

[A] *syn*-hydration
anti-Markovnikov's way

Example 10 :

Supply proper structures to the compounds A to C

$$\text{C}_6\text{H}_6 + \text{ClCH}_2\text{CH}=\text{CH}_2 \xrightarrow{\text{AlCl}_3} [A] \xrightarrow[\text{(ii) } \text{H}_2\text{O}_2/\text{OH}^-]{\text{(i) BH}_3.\text{THF}} [B] \xrightarrow[\text{heat}]{\text{HF}} \text{C}(\text{C}_9\text{H}_{10})$$

Solution :

First step seems to be Friedel-Craft reaction, second *anti*-Markovnikov's hydration and the last step is again an example of Friedel-Craft reaction causing cyclization.

[A] [B] [C] C_9H_{10}

Example 11 :

Write the intermediate steps involved in the following reactions.

(i) $\text{C}_6\text{H}_5\text{CH(OH)} \, \text{C} \equiv \text{CH} \xrightarrow{\text{H}_3\text{O}^+} \text{C}_6\text{H}_5\text{CH} = \text{CHCHO}$ **(ii)**

Solution :

(i) $\text{C}_6\text{H}_5\text{CH(OH)} \, \text{C} \equiv \text{CH} \xrightarrow[\text{(ii) } - \text{H}_2\text{O}]{\text{(i) H}^+} \text{C}_6\text{H}_5\overset{+}{\text{C}}\text{H}-\text{C} \equiv \text{CH} \longleftrightarrow \text{C}_6\text{H}_5\text{CH}=\text{C}=\overset{+}{\text{C}}\text{H} \xrightarrow{\text{H}_2\text{O}}$

$$\text{C}_6\text{H}_5\text{CH}=\text{C}=\text{CH} \quad (\overset{\oplus}{\text{O}}\text{H}_2) \xrightarrow{-\text{H}^+} \text{C}_6\text{H}_5\text{CH}=\text{C}=\text{CHOH} \underset{\text{tautomerization}}{\rightleftharpoons} \text{C}_6\text{H}_5\text{CH}=\text{CH}-\text{CHO}$$

(ii)

Example 12 :
Prepare *n*-butanol and isobutanol from ethyne.

Solution :

$$HC \equiv CH \xrightarrow{\text{1 mol NaNH}_2} HC \equiv CNa \xrightarrow{CH_3CH_2Br} HC \equiv CCH_2CH_3$$
$$\text{Butyne-1}$$

$$\underset{\text{Isobutanol}}{CH_3\overset{\overset{\displaystyle OH}{|}}{C}HCH_2CH_3} \xleftarrow[\text{(ii) Hg(OAc)}_2/\text{NaBH}_4]{\text{(i) Li/NH}_3} \underset{\text{Butyne-1}}{HC \equiv CCH_2CH_3} \xrightarrow[\substack{\text{(ii) BH}_3.\text{THF} \\ \text{(iii) H}_2O_2/OH^-}]{\text{(i) Li/NH}_3} \underset{\text{n-Butanol}}{HOH_2CCH_2CH_2CH_3}$$

Example 13 :
Give chemical reactions involved in the conversion of ethyl chloride to 2-methylbut-3-yn-2-ol.

Solution :

First write down the structure of the required compound, observe the functional group(s) and recall that how these can be introduced. In the present case, the required compound has a 3° alcohol and an acetylenic linkage ; so first introduce acetylenic linkage, convert it to Grignard reagent and then treat it with ketone (acetone) to get 3° alcohol.

$$CH_3CH_2Cl \xrightarrow{\text{alc. KOH}} CH_2 = CH_2 \xrightarrow{Br_2} BrCH_2\!-\!CH_2Br \xrightarrow{\text{2NaNH}_2} CH \equiv CH$$

$$\xrightarrow{CH_3MgBr} CH \equiv CMgBr \xrightarrow{CH_3COCH_3} CH_3\!-\!\overset{\overset{\displaystyle OH}{|}}{\underset{\underset{\displaystyle CH_3}{|}}{C}}\!-\!C \equiv CH$$

Example 14 :
You are given acetophenone and methyl iodide as the main organic compounds, how will you convert these into 2-phenyl-2-methylethanol.

Solution :

$$CH_3I \xrightarrow[\text{(ii) C}_6\text{H}_5\text{COCH}_3]{\text{(i) Mg}} C_6H_5\overset{\overset{\displaystyle OH}{|}}{C}(CH_3)_2 \xrightarrow{H_2SO_4} C_6H_5\overset{\overset{\displaystyle CH_3}{|}}{C} = CH_2 \xrightarrow[\text{(ii) H}_2O_2/OH^-]{\text{(i) BH}_3/\text{THF}} C_6H_5\overset{\overset{\displaystyle CH_3}{|}}{C}H.CH_2OH$$

Example 15 :
Propane can be converted into 1-propanol, 2-propanol and propen-2-ol without using any other organic compound? Illustrate it.

Solution :

$$CH_3CH_2CH_3 \xrightarrow{Cl_2,\,h\nu} CH_3CHClCH_3 \xrightarrow{aq,\,KOH} \underset{\text{2–Propanol}}{CH_3CHOHCH_3}$$

$$CH_3CHClCH_3 \xrightarrow[\text{KOH}]{\text{alc.}} CH_3CH = CH_2 \xrightarrow[\text{(ii) H}_2O_2/OH^-]{\text{(i) BH}_3.\text{THF}} \underset{\text{1–Propanol}}{CH_3CH_2CH_2OH}$$

$$\downarrow \text{NBS}$$

$$BrCH_2CH = CH_2 \xrightarrow[\text{KOH}]{\text{aq.}} \underset{\text{Propen-2-ol}}{HOCH_2CH = CH_2}$$

Example 16 :

How will you prepare 2, 3-dimethyl-2-butanol from isopropanol as the only available organic compound ?

Solution :

Let us draw structure of the required compound,
$$CH_3\!-\!\underset{\underset{OH}{|}}{\overset{\overset{CH_3}{|}}{C}}\!-\!\overset{\overset{CH_3}{|}}{CH}\!-\!CH_3$$

Since it is has six carbon atoms and it is a tertiary alcohol, it can be easily prepared through Grignard reagent route.

$$(CH_3)_2CHOH$$
$$\downarrow MnO_4^-/H^+$$

$$(CH_3)_2CHOH \xrightarrow[\text{(ii) Mg}]{\text{(i) PBr}_3} (CH_3)_2CHMgBr \xrightarrow{(CH_3)_2CO} (CH_3)_2\,\underset{\underset{OH}{|}}{C}\!-\!\underset{\underset{CH_3}{|}}{CH}CH_3$$

Example 17 :

You are given methanol and allyl chloride as the main compounds, how these two can be converted into butanol-1 by using inorganic reagents ?

Solution :

$$CH_3OH \xrightarrow{\text{P and I}_2} CH_3I \xrightarrow[\text{(ii) 2CuI}]{\text{(i) Li}} (CH_3)_2CuLi \xrightarrow{ClCH_2CH=CH_2} CH_3CH_2CH=CH_2$$

$$\xrightarrow[\text{(ii) H}_2O_2/OH^-]{\text{(i) BH}_3.\text{THF}} CH_3CH_2CH_2CH_2OH$$

Example 18 :

Is it possible to carry out the following transformation in quantitative yield ?

$$CH_3CH_2\overset{\overset{CH_3}{|}}{C}HCH_2OH \longrightarrow CH_3CH_2\overset{\overset{CH_3}{|}}{C}=CH_2$$

Solution :

Note that the above dehydration can't be achieved by treating the alcohol with conc. H_2SO_4 since it will lead to the more stable (more substituted) alkene as major product.

$$CH_3CH_2\overset{\overset{CH_3}{|}}{C}HCH_2OH \xrightarrow{H^+} CH_3CH_2\overset{\overset{CH_3}{|}}{\overset{+}{C}}HCH_2 \xrightarrow{\text{1, 2-hydride shift}} CH_3CH_2\underset{\oplus}{\overset{\overset{CH_3}{|}}{C}}CH_3$$

$$\xrightarrow{-H^+} CH_3CH=\overset{\overset{CH_3}{|}}{C}\!-\!CH_3 + CH_3CH_2\overset{\overset{CH_3}{|}}{C}=CH_2$$

2-Methyl-2-butene   2-Methyl-1-butene
(Major)   (Minor)

Hence the required alkene is prepared by dehydrohalogenation route.

$$CH_3CH_2\overset{\overset{CH_3}{|}}{C}HCH_2OH \xrightarrow{PBr_3} CH_3CH_2\overset{\overset{CH_3}{|}}{C}HCH_2Br \xrightarrow{\text{alc. KOH}} CH_3CH_2\overset{\overset{CH_3}{|}}{C}=CH_2$$

2-Methyl-1-butene

Example 19 :

Give the product and write a mechanism for the acid dehydration of cyclobutylcarbinol.

Solution :

[Reaction mechanism scheme: Cyclobutylcarbinol (CH_2OH) $\xrightarrow{H^+}$ ($CH_2OH_2^+$) $\xrightarrow{-H_2O}$ (cyclopentyl cation) $\xrightarrow{-H^+}$ Cyclopentene]

Cyclobutylcarbinol → Cyclopentene

Expansion of four to a five-membered ring relieves ring strain.

Example 20 :

Give the step involved in the hydration of cyclobutylethene in dilute sulphuric acid to 2-methyl cyclopentanol.

Solution :

[Reaction scheme: Cyclobutylethene $\xrightarrow{H^+}$ → (cation) $\xrightarrow[-H^+]{H_2O}$ cis- and trans-2-Methylcyclopentanol]

Cyclobutylethene → *cis*- and *trans*-2-Methylcyclopentanol

Example 21 :

An organic compound A ($C_9H_{12}O$) gives a positive iodoform test. On vigorous oxidation, it gives benzoic acid. Identify the compound and give its various isomers which on oxidation gives benzoic acid.

Solution :

Since the compound and its isomers on oxidation gives benzoic acid, these must be monosubstituted benzene. Further, the compound (A) undergoes haloform reaction, it must have —$CHOHCH_3$ or —$COCH_3$ grouping. Thus compound A is $C_6H_5CH_2CHOHCH_3$; $C_6H_5CH_2COCH_3$ is not possible because its molecular formula is $C_9H_{10}O$. Other possible isomers are II, III and IV.

$$C_6H_5CH_2CHOHCH_3 \qquad C_6H_5CHOHCH_2CH_3 \qquad C_6H_5CH_2CH_2CH_2OH \qquad C_6H_5\overset{\overset{\displaystyle CH_3}{|}}{CH}.CH_2OH$$

$$\text{A} \qquad\qquad\qquad \text{II} \qquad\qquad\qquad \text{III} \qquad\qquad\qquad \text{IV}$$

Example 22 :

An aromatic alcohol of the formula $C_{10}H_{14}O_2$ when heated with sodium hypoiodite forms two moles of iodoform per mole of the alcohol, and a dibasic salt which on acidification gives a molecule of terphthalic acid. Identify the compound A.

Solution :

Since the aromatic alcohol undergoes haloform reaction to form two moles of iodoform, it must contain two —$CHOHCH_3$ groupings. Further formation of terphthalic acid indicates that these two groups are present in *p*-position to each other. Hence the alcohol should be p-$C_6H_4(CHOHCH_3)_2$.

$$\text{p-(CHOHCH}_3)_2\text{C}_6\text{H}_4 \xrightarrow{\text{NaIO}} 2\text{CHI}_3 + \text{p-(COO}^-\text{Na}^+)_2\text{C}_6\text{H}_4 \xrightarrow{\text{H}^+} \text{p-(COOH)}_2\text{C}_6\text{H}_4$$

Example 23 :

An alkene A of the formula C_7H_{14} reacts with BH_3.THF followed by H_2O_2/OH^- to give a chiral compound B. Reductive ozonolysis of A gives compound C, which is also obtained by oxidation of 2-methyl-3-pentanol with $KMnO_4$. Identify the alkene A and explain all reactions.

Solution :

Going backward, we can easily solve the problem.

$$
\underset{\textbf{A}}{\overset{\displaystyle \overset{CH_2}{\|}}{C_2H_5CCH(CH_3)_2}} \xrightarrow[\text{(ii) Zn}]{\text{(i) O}_3} \underset{\textbf{C}}{\overset{\displaystyle \overset{O}{\|}}{C_2H_5CCH(CH_3)_2}} \xleftarrow{\text{Oxi.}} \underset{\text{2- Methyl- 3- pentanol}}{\overset{\displaystyle \overset{OH}{|}}{C_2H_5CHCH(CH_3)_2}}
$$

$$\downarrow \begin{array}{l}\text{(i) BH}_3.\text{THF} \\ \text{(ii) H}_2\text{O}_2 , \text{OH}^-\end{array}$$

$$
\underset{\textbf{B}}{\overset{\displaystyle CH_2OH}{C_2H_5 - \overset{|}{\underset{|}{C}} - CH(CH_3)_2}} \quad \overset{|}{H}
$$

Example 24 :

Give the stereochemical formulas for each of the bracketed compound ,

(a) [cyclobutane with CH_3] $\xrightarrow[\text{(ii) H}_2\text{O}_2,\ \text{OH}^-]{\text{(i) THF.BH}_3}$ [A] $\xrightarrow[\text{OH}^-]{\text{TsCl}}$ [B] $\xrightarrow{\text{OH}^-}$ [C]

What is the stereoisomeric relationship between A and C?

(b) $CH_3CH_2 - C \overset{CH_3}{\underset{OH}{\langle}} H$ (R)-2-Butanol $\xrightarrow{\text{NaH}}$ [D] $\xrightarrow{\text{CH}_3\text{I}}$ [E]

$\xrightarrow{\text{MsCl}}$ [F] $\xrightarrow{\text{CH}_3\text{ONa}}$ [G]

What is the stereoisomeric relationship between [E] and [G] ?

Solution :

(a) $A =$ [structure: cyclobutane with CH_3 (wedge up) and OH] $+$ enantiomer $B =$ [structure: cyclobutane with CH_3 and OTs] $+$ enantiomer $C =$ [structure: cyclobutane with CH_3 and OH] $+$ enantiomer

A and **C** are diastereomers

(b) $D = CH_3CH_2 - C$ (with CH_3, H, ONa) $E = CH_3CH_2 - C$ (with CH_3, H, OCH_3)

  $F = CH_3CH_2 - C$ (with CH_3, H, OMs) $G = CH_3CH_2 - C$ (with CH_3, OCH_3, H)

E and **G** are enantiomers.

Example 25 :

Give the product when the two isomeric 3-bromo-2-butanols A and B are treated with HBr. Explain the formation of products by proper mechanism.

(a) [structure A: $H\cdots C - C$ with Br, H_3C, CH_3, H, OH] $\xrightarrow{\text{HBr}}$ (b) [structure B: $H\cdots C - C$ with Br, H_3C, H, CH_3, OH] $\xrightarrow{\text{HBr}}$

Solution :

The reactions proceed through the formation of bromonium ions identical to those formed in the bromination of *trans*- and *cis*-2-butenes.

(a) [structure A] $\xrightarrow{\text{HBr}}$ [protonated $\overset{+}{O}H_2$ intermediate $+ Br^-$] $\xrightarrow{-H_2O}$ [bromonium ion with Br^+ and Br^-] $\longrightarrow$ [*meso*-2,3-Dibromobutane]

(Attack at the other carbon atom of the brominium ion gives the same product).

(b) [structure B] $\xrightarrow{\text{HBr}}$ [protonated $\overset{+}{O}H_2$ intermediate] $\xrightarrow{-H_2O}$ [bromonium ion intermediate with attack by Br^- at (a) and (b) positions giving]

(a) → [structure: H_3C, H, Br, CH_3, Br, H]

(b) → [structure: Br, H, H, CH_3, H_3C, Br]

(±)-2,3-Dibromobutane

Example 26 :

Propose a mechanism to explain the formation of two products in the following reaction.

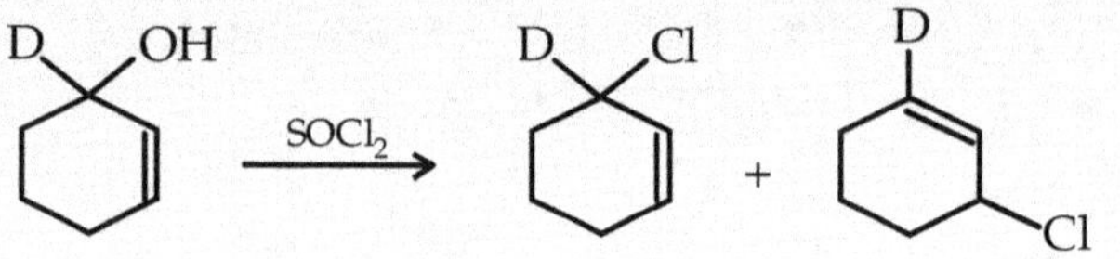

Solution :

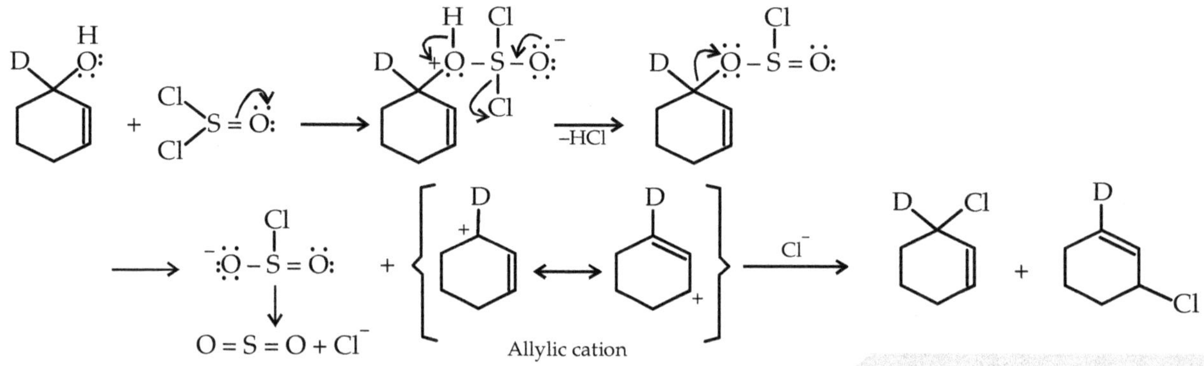

Allylic cation

Example 27 :

Vinyl alcohols are generally unstable, and quickly isomerize to carbonyl compounds. Propose mechanism for the following isomerizations.

(a)

(b)

Solution :

(a)

$+ H - B$

(b)

$+ OH^-$

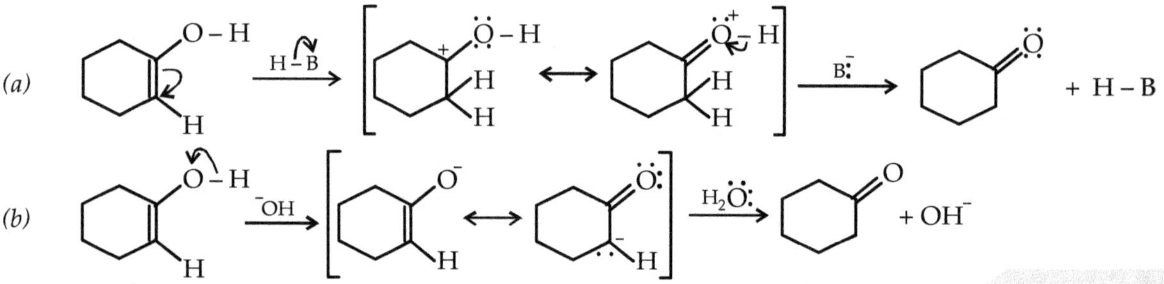

Example 28 :

Propose a mechanism to explain the following unexpected transformation.

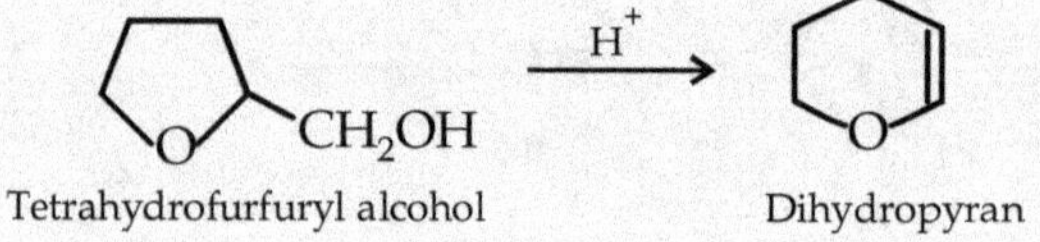

CH_2OH

Tetrahydrofurfuryl alcohol

Dihydropyran

Solution :

CH_2OH $\xrightarrow[(-H_2O)]{H^+}$ CH_2 $\xrightarrow[\text{ring expansion}]{\text{alkyl shift}}$

$2°$ carbocation is resonance-stabilized

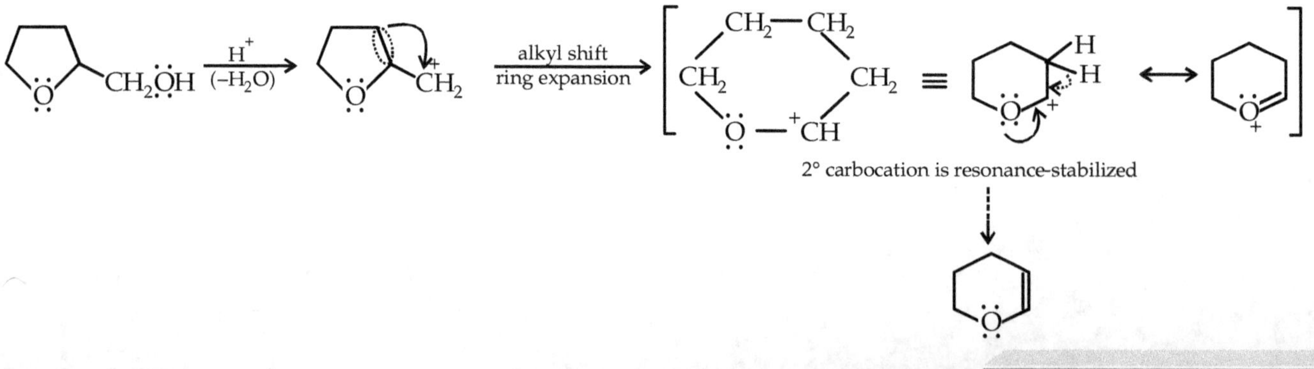

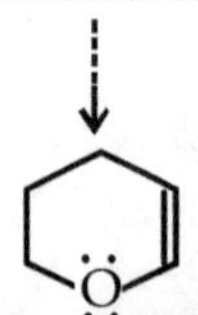

Example 29 :

An organic compound A ($C_9H_{12}O$) exhibits following characteristics.

(a)   It reacts with metallic sodium to give a colourless odorless gas

(b)   It is oxidised by $KMnO_4$ to benzoic acid.

Write all the possible structures for the compound. In addition to the above reactions, the compound A shows following properties.

(c)   It can be resolved.

(d)   It does not give precipitate with iodine in presence of NaOH.

(e)   It changes the colour of $Cr_2O_7^{2-}$ from orange to blue, and gives a chiral compound.

Assign structure to compound A.

Solution :

(i)   Oxidation to benzoic acid indicates that it is a monosubstituted benzene derivative.

(ii)   Its reaction with Na indicates the presence of an alcoholic group. The possible structures for the compound. A can be

$$\underset{I}{C_6H_5\overset{OH}{\underset{|}{C}}HCH_2CH_3} \quad \underset{II}{C_6H_5\overset{OH}{\underset{|}{\underset{CH_3}{\underset{|}{C}}}}CH_3} \quad \underset{III}{C_6H_5CH_2\overset{OH}{\underset{|}{C}}HCH_3} \quad \underset{IV}{C_6H_5\overset{OH}{\underset{|}{\underset{CH_3}{\underset{|}{C}}}}HCH_2OH} \quad \underset{V}{C_6H_5CH_2CH_2CH_2OH}$$

(iii)   Since the compound can be resolved, it can't be V.

(iv)   The compound does not respond haloform reaction (*d*), it can't be III.

(v)   Its oxidation with $Cr_2O_7^{2-}$ indicates that it is either a 1° or a 2° alcohol, hence possibility for the structure II is discarded.

(vi)   Its oxidation product with $Cr_2O_7^{2-}$ is found to be a chiral compound, so structure I is discarded and hence the compound **A** has structure IV.

$$\underset{\substack{IV \\ Chiral}}{C_6H_5\overset{CH_3}{\underset{|}{C}}HCH_2OH} \xrightarrow{Cr_2O_7^{2-}} \underset{Chiral}{C_6H_5\overset{CH_3}{\underset{|}{C}}HCHO}$$

Example 30 :

An optically active 2° alcohol A undergoes two different reactions to form compounds B and C.

$$C \xleftarrow[\text{(ii) Mg, ether}]{\text{(i) PBr}_3} A \xrightarrow[\text{acid}]{\text{chromic}} B \ (\text{Ketone})$$

Compound B is added to the solution of compound C and the resulting solution on acidic hydrolysis gives a compound, identified as **3,4-dimethyl-3-hexanol**. Identify compounds A, B and C.

Solution :

Proceed backward, by first writing the structure of the final product.

3,4-Dimethyl-3-hexanol

(B)

(C)

(A)

EXERCISE 11.1　(MCQ - ONE option correct)

1. According to carbinol system, $C_6H_5CH_2CH_2CH_2OH$ is
   (a) benzyl carbinol
   (b) β-phenylethylcarbinol
   (c) benzylmethylcarbinol
   (d) γ-phenylpropylcarbinol.

2. Common name for $CH \equiv C.CH_2OH$ is
   (a) allylcarbinol
   (b) allyl alcohol
   (c) propargyl alcohol
   (d) none of the three.

3. Which of the following alcohol is known as rubbing alcohol ?
   (a) CH_3OH
   (b) C_2H_5OH
   (c) $CH_3CH_2CH_2OH$
   (d) $(CH_3)_2CHOH$.

4. When 20 ml of ethanol is mixed with 10 ml of water, the total volume of the solution will be
   (a) 30 ml
   (b) > 30 ml
   (c) < 30 ml
   (d) not definite.

5. The correct order of boiling points of the following alcohols is 1-pentanol (A), 2-methyl-2-butanol (B), 3-methyl-2-butanol(C)
   (a) A > B > C
   (b) A > C > B
   (c) C > B > A
   (d) B > C > A.

6. Predict the nature of P in the following hydration reaction of alkenes

   (a) 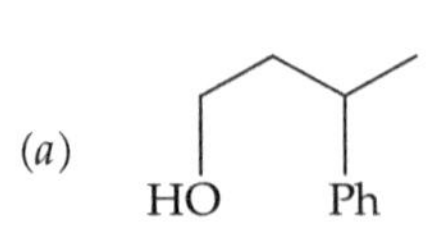
   (b) 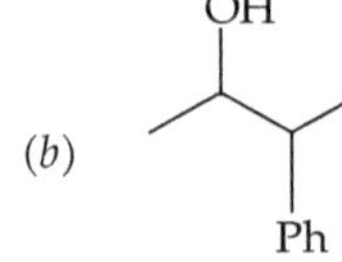
   (c) 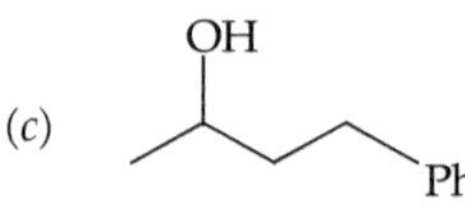
   (d) 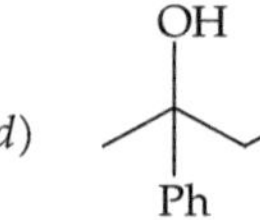

7. Predict the nature of reducing agent in the following reaction.

   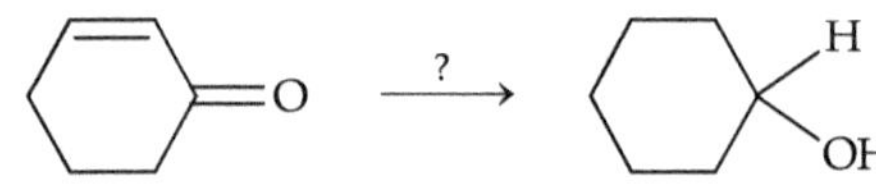

   (a) $LiAlH_4$
   (b) $NaBH_4$
   (c) H_2/Pt
   (d) Both (a) and (c)

8. In the following reaction, alkene A is

   A $\xrightarrow{\text{cold conc. }H_2SO_4}$ Intermediate $\xrightarrow{H^+/H_2O}$ rac
   $$CH_3CHOHCH_2CH_3$$
   (a) cis-2-Butene
   (b) trans-2-Butene
   (c) Butene-1
   (d) All the three.

9. Which of the following is the best leaving group toward nucleophilic substitution ?
   (a) Iodide
   (b) Mesyl
   (c) Tosyl
   (d) Trifyl.

10. Lucas test is useful only for
    (a) alcohols having at the maximum four carbon atoms
    (b) alcohols having six or less carbon atoms
    (c) alcohols having twenty or less carbon atoms
    (d) all alcohols.

11. Identify the main product P in the following reaction

    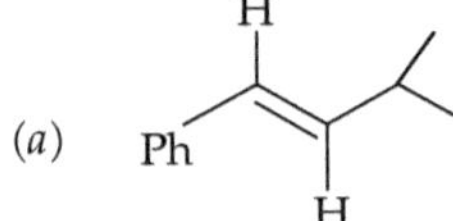

    (a) 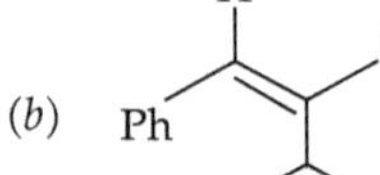
    (b) 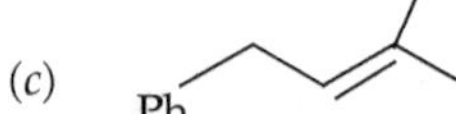
    (c)
    (d) All are formed in equal amounts.

12. Dehydration of 3, 3-dimethylbutanol-2 gives
    (a) 3, 3-dimethylbutene-1
    (b) 2, 3-dimethylbutene -1
    (c) 2, 3-dimethylbutene-2
    (d) Being 3° alcohol, dehydration is not possible.

13. $CH_3CH = CHCHOHCH_3 \xrightarrow[\text{aq. acetone}]{H_2CrO_4 \text{ in}} X$; here X is
    (a) $CH_3COOH + COOH.CO.CH_3$
    (b) $CH_3CHOH.CHOH.CHOH.CH_3$
    (c) $CH_3CH = CH.COCH_3$
    (d) $CH_3CHOH.CHOH.CO.CH_3$.

14. Identify the reagent in the following reaction
    $$(CH_3)_3CCH_2OH \xrightarrow{\text{reagent}} (CH_3)_3CCH_2Cl$$
    (a) conc. HCl
    (b) HCl in presence of $ZnCl_2$
    (c) $SOCl_2$
    (d) Either of the three.

15. Dehydration of 1-phenyl-2-propanol in acidic medium gives 1-phenyl-1-propene rather than 1-phenyl-2-propene because
    (a) 1-Phenyl-1-propene is more substituted alkene than 1-phenyl-2-propene
    (b) In 1-phenyl-1-propene, the double bond is conjugated with the ring
    (c) Both the above statements are true
    (d) None of the above statement is true and both alkenes are formed nearly in equal amounts.

16. Identify C in the following series of reactions.
    $$CH_3CH = CHCHO \xrightarrow{NaBH_4} [A] \xrightarrow{HCl/ZnCl_2} [B]$$
    $$\xrightarrow{HCN, H^+} [C]$$
    (a) $CH_3CH_2CH_2CH_2CN$
    (b) $CH_3CH_2CH_2CH_2COOH$
    (c) $CH_3CH = CHCH_2CN$
    (d) $CH_3CH = CHCH_2COOH$.

17. Identify [A] and [E] in the following series of reactions.
    $$[A] \xrightarrow{PBr_5} CH_3CH_2CH_2Br \xrightarrow{\text{alc. KOH}} [B] \xrightarrow{Br_2} [C]$$
    $$\xrightarrow[\text{(ii) NaNH}_2]{\text{(i) alc. KOH}} [D] \xrightarrow{Hg^{2+}, H_2SO_4} [E]$$
    (a) $CH_3CH_2CH_2OH, CH_3CH_2CHO$
    (b) $CH_3CH_2CH_2OH, CH_3CH_2CH_2CHO$
    (c) $CH_3CH_2CH_2OH, CH_3COCH_3$
    (d) $CH_3CH_2CH_2OH, CH_2COCH_2CH_3$.

18. The correct structure for the compound B will be

    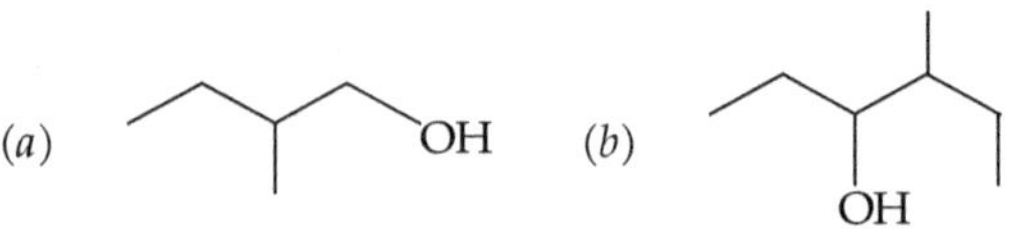

    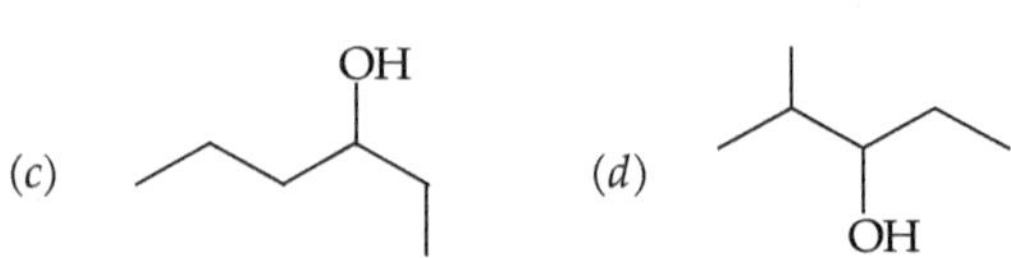

    (a) 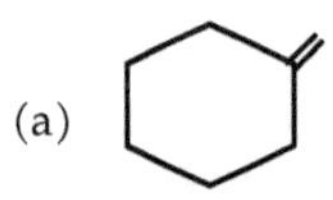
    (b) 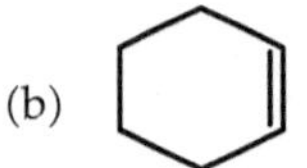
    (c) 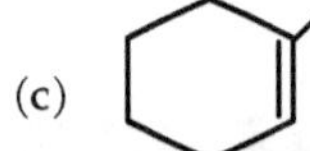
    (d) 

19. Acid catalysed hydration, hydroboration-oxidation, and oxymercuration-demercuration will give different products in
    (a)
    (b)
    (c)
    (d)

During dehydration of t-butanol, which of the following carbocation is more likely to be formed as an intermediate?

(a) $CH_3CH_2CH_2 \overset{+}{C}H_2$ (b) $CH_3CH_2 \overset{+}{C}HCH_3$

(c) Both   (d) None

Primary, secondary and tertiary alcohols can be distinguished by the action of
(a) Reduced Cu
(b) Acidic $KMnO_4$
(c) HCl in presence of anhydrous $ZnCl_2$
(d) PCl_5

Ethyl alcohol when treated with conc. H_2SO_4 may give
(a) Only diethyl sulphate
(b) Only diethyl ether
(c) Only ethylene
(d) All the three

1–Propanol and 2–propanol can be distinguished by
(a) oxidation with alkaline $KMnO_4$ followed by reaction with Fehling solution
(b) oxidation with acidic dichromate followed by reaction with Fehling solution
(c) oxidation by heating with copper followed by reaction with Fehling solution
(d) oxidation with concentrated H_2SO_4 followed by reaction with Fehling solution

4.

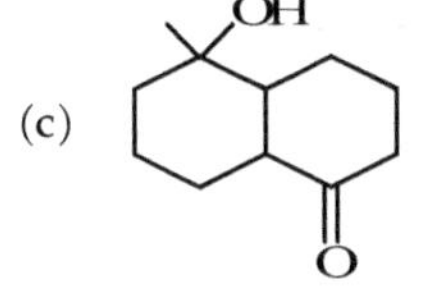

$$\xrightarrow[\Delta]{H^\oplus / KMnO_4} \text{ Product is}$$

(a) (b)

(c) (d)

5. What will be the product of following reaction ?

$$\xrightarrow{Br_2} \text{ 'X', X will be}$$

(a) (b)

(c) (d) (a) and (b) both

26. $CH_2 = CH - CH - CH = CH - CH_3 \xrightarrow{CH_3OH/H^\oplus}$
with OH substituent

major products is

(a) $CH_3O - CH_2 - CH = CH - CH = CH - CH_3$

(b) $CH_2 = CH - CH - CH = CH - CH_3$ with OCH_3

(c) $CH_2 = CH - CH = CH - CH - CH_3$ with OCH_3

(d) $CH_2 = CH - CH_2 - CH - CH = CH_2$ with OCH_3

27. $HC \equiv CH \xrightarrow[\text{Fe Tube}]{\text{Red Hot}} P \xrightarrow[(1.eq.)]{Br_2/Fe} Q \xrightarrow{Mg/Ether} S$;

$$T \xleftarrow[\text{Distill}]{Ca(OH)_2/\Delta} R \xleftarrow{KMnO_4} CH_3CH_2OH$$

S and T are mixed and product is hydrolysed and heated in presence of conc. H_2SO_4 and product is ozonolysed then following is obtained.

(a) Acetophenone   (b) Benzophenone
(c) Benzaldehyde   (d) Acetone

28. $CH_2O \xrightarrow[H_3O^\oplus]{CHD_2MgI} X \xrightarrow[\Delta]{Conc. H_2SO_4} Y$

In the above reaction compound X and Y respectively will be

(a) $\overset{OH}{C}HD - CH_2 - OH, \ CHO - CHO$

(b) $CHD_2 - CH_2 - OH, CHO - CHO$

(c) $CHD_2 - CH_2 - OH, CD_2 = CH_2$

(d) $\overset{OH}{C}HD - CH_2 - OD, \ CD_2 = CH_2$

29. The correct order of reactivity of following alcohols towards conc. $HCl/ZnCl_2$ is :

I. II.

III. IV.

(a) I > II > III > IV   (b) I > III > II > IV
(c) IV > III > II > I   (d) IV > III > I > II

30. Which one of the following will most readily be dehydrated in acidic condition ?

(a) (b)

(c) (d)

31. The product B in the reaction is

$$(CH_3)_3COH \xrightarrow{Cu}_{573K} A \xrightarrow[OH^-/D_2O]{B_2H_6} B$$

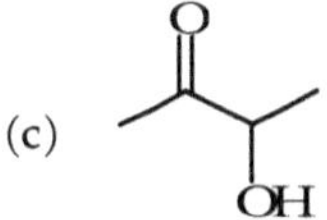

(a) (b)

(c) (d)

32. The following alcohol is treated with conc. H_2SO_4, the major product obtained is

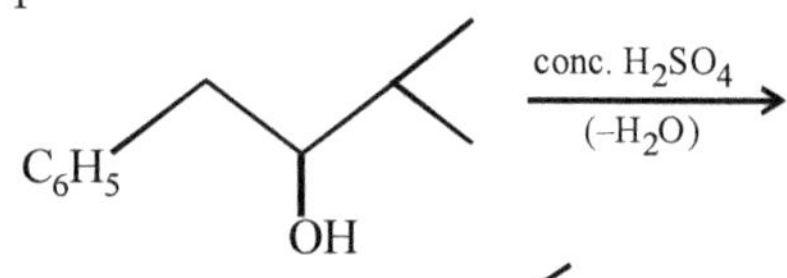

(a) 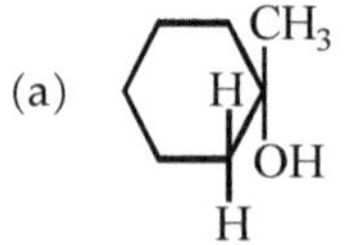

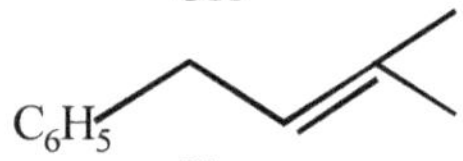

(b)

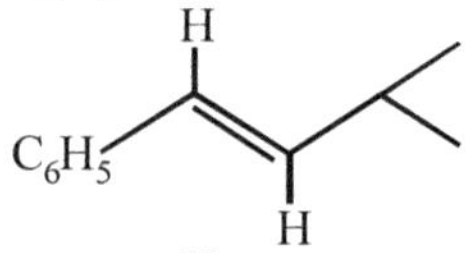

(c)

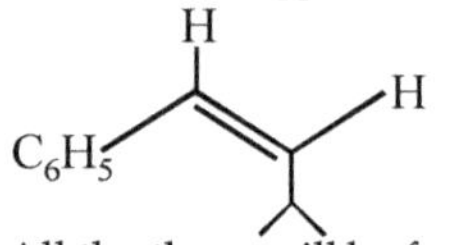

(d) All the three will be formed in equal amounts

33. 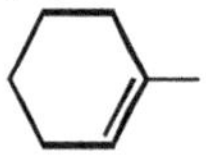 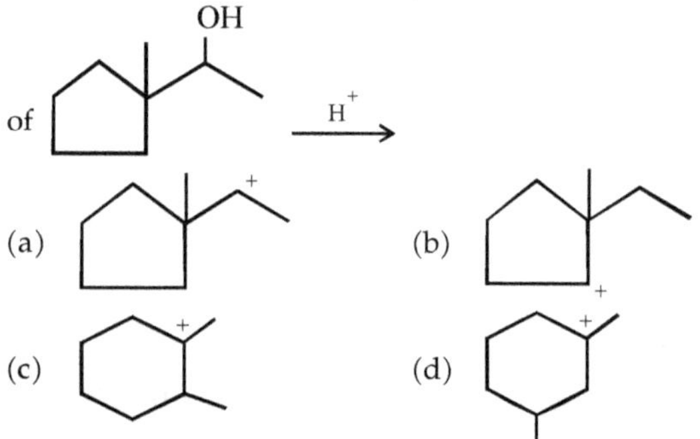 $\xrightarrow[\text{(ii) } H_2O_2, \, OH^-]{\text{(i) } B_2H_6}$ X. The compound X is

(a) (b)

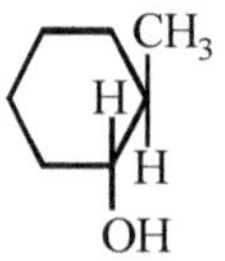

(c) 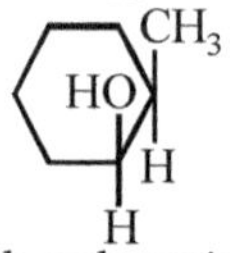 (d) Both (b) and (c)

34. Which carbocation is more likely to be formed in the dehydration of

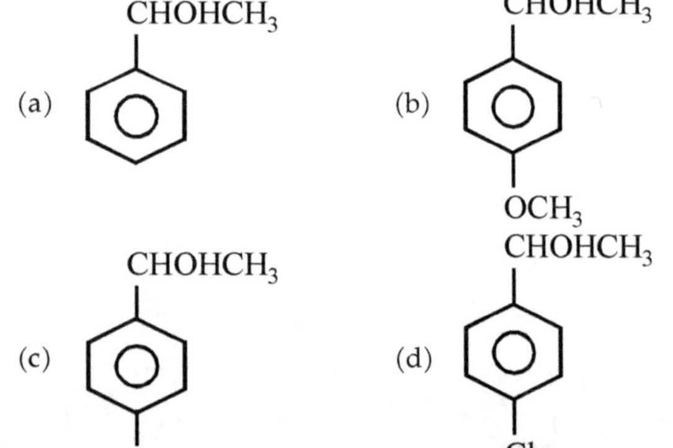

(a) (b)

(c) (d)

35. Energy of activation is lowest for which reaction ?
(a) $R\overset{+}{C}H_2\overset{+}{O}H_2 \rightarrow R\overset{+}{C}H_2$ (b) $R_2\overset{+}{C}HOH_2 \rightarrow R_2\overset{+}{C}H$
(c) $R_3\overset{+}{C}OH_2 \rightarrow R_3C^+$ (d) All have same E_{act}.

36. Dehydration of an alcohol in presence of sulphuric acid gives alkene

$$CH_3CH_2OH \xrightarrow{H_2SO_4} CH_2 = CH_2 + H_2O$$

Here sulphuric acid acts as
(a) an acid   (b) a base
(c) a catalyst   (d) all the three

37. Which of the following alcohols is dehydrated most readily with conc. H_2SO_4 ?

(a) (b)

(c) (d)

38. $CH_3CH_2OH + HCl \xrightarrow{ZnCl_2} CH_3CH_2Cl + H_2O$
In the above reaction, the leaving group is
(a) OH^- (b) H_2O
(c) $HOZn^-Cl_2$ (d) H_3O^+

39. Dehydration of alcohols by conc. H_2SO_4 takes place according following steps :

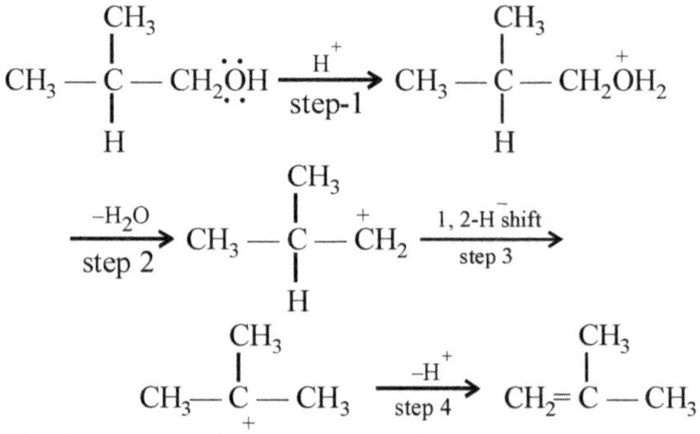

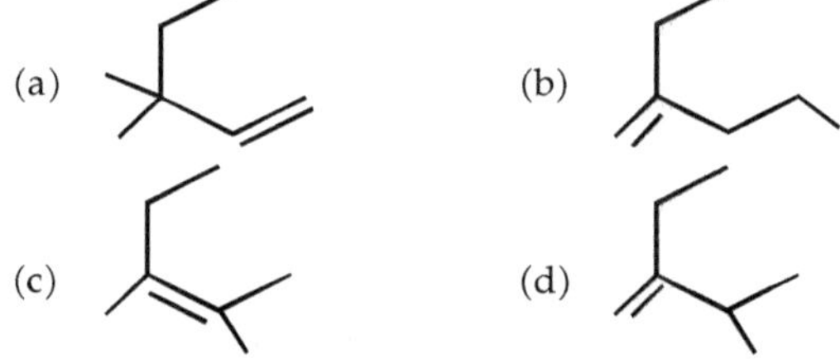

The slowest and fastest steps in the above reaction are
(a) step 1 is slowest, while 3 is fastest
(b) step 2 is slowest, while 3 is fastest
(c) step 2 is slowest, while 4 is fastest
(d) all steps proceed at equal rate

40. 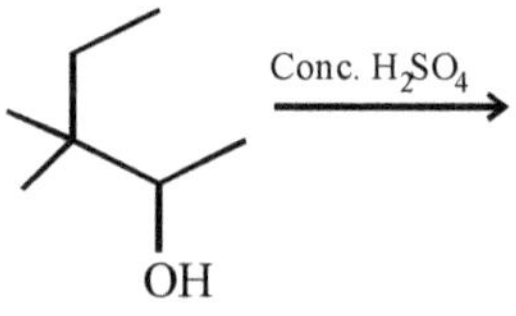 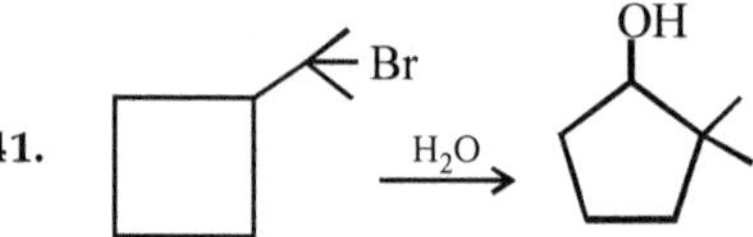 $\xrightarrow{\text{Conc. } H_2SO_4}$ Major product is

(a) (b)

(c) (d)

41. 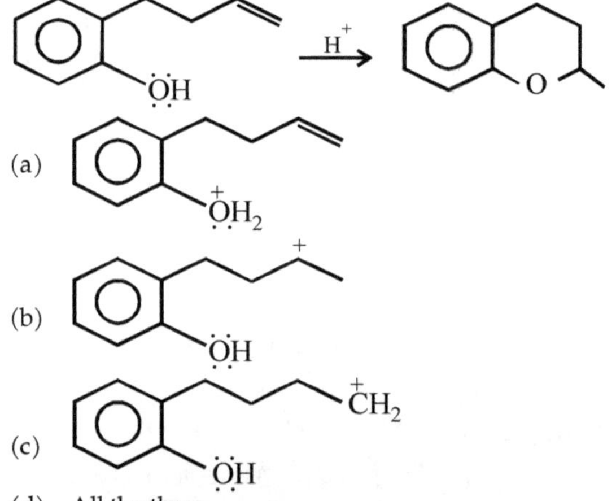 $\xrightarrow{H_2O}$
The driving force in the above reaction is
(a) conversion of 1° carbocation to 2° carbocation
(b) conversion of 1° carbocation to 3° carbocation
(c) releif in steric strain due to expansion of ring
(d) both (a) and (c)

42. Which of the following ion is formed in the following reaction?

$\xrightarrow{H^+}$

(a)

(b)

(c)

(d) All the three

43. Which reacts rapidly with Lucas reagent?
(a) $CH_2=CHCH_2OH$ (b) $(CH_3)_3COH$
(c) Both (a) and (b)   (d) CH_3CH_2OH

EXERCISE 11.2 (MCQ 1 or >1 option correct, Passage based, Matching, A/R)

DIRECTIONS for Q. 1 to Q. 23 : Multiple choice questions with one or more than one correct option(s).

1. Which of the following statements is false?
(a) No aldehyde can be prepared by the oxidation of primary alcohol with acidic $KMnO_4$.
(b) Aldehyde having a boiling point less than 100°C can be prepared by the oxidation of primary alcohol with acidic dichromate.
(c) Secondary alcohols on oxidation with PCC in dichloromethane give carboxylic acids having lesser number of carbon atoms
(d) None of the statement is correct.

2. $A \xrightarrow{\text{dil. } H_2SO_4/Hg^{2+}}$ 1-Methylcyclohexanol. Here A is

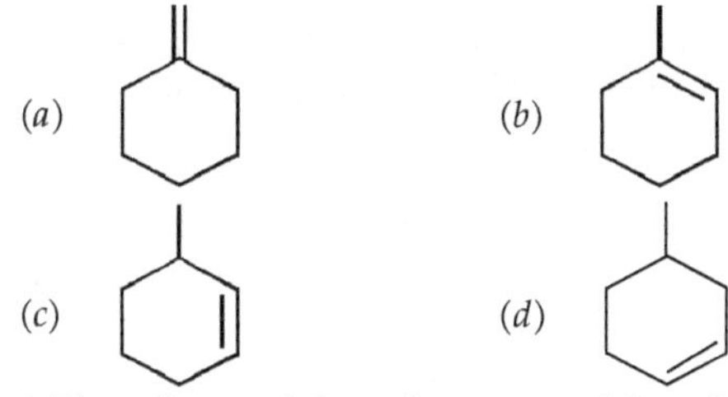

3. 2-Phenylbutanol-2 can be prepared by which of the following combinations ?
(a) $C_6H_5COCH_3 + C_2H_5MgBr$
(b) $C_2H_5COCH_3 + C_6H_5MgBr$
(c) $C_6H_5COC_2H_5 + CH_3MgBr$
(d) $C_6H_5COC_6H_5 + C_2H_5MgBr$

4. Which of the alcohol gives a positive iodoform test ?
(a) Benzylmethylcarbinol
(b) Phenylethylcarbinol
(c) Cyclopentylmethylcarbinol
(d) Isopropanol.

5. $C_6H_5COCH_2CH_2Br + LiAlD_4 \xrightarrow{H_2O} X$, here X does not have
(a) $C_6H_5CD(OD)CH_2CH_2Br$
(b) $C_6H_5CD(OH)CH_2CH_2D$
(c) $C_6H_5CD(OH)CH_2CH_2Br$
(d) $C_6H_5CH(OH)CH_2CH_2D$.

6. Which of the following alcohol will mainly give the rearranged chloride, when treated with HCl?

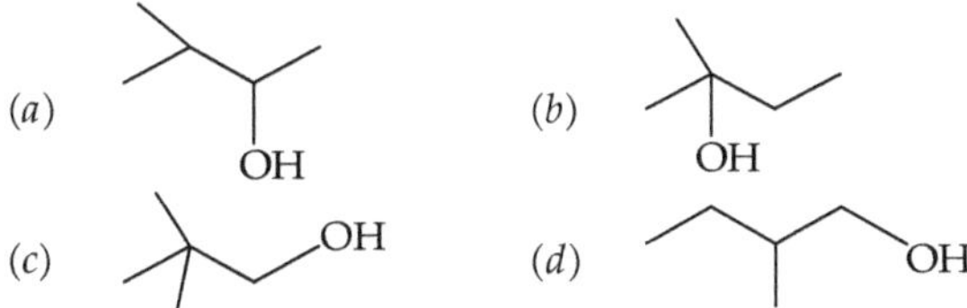

7. On treatment with a concentrated solution of zinc chloride in concentrated HCl at room temperature, an alcohol immediately gives, an oily product. The alcohol can be
(a) $C_6H_5CH_2OH$
(b) $CH_3CHOHCH_3$
(c) $CH_3 - \underset{\underset{CH_3}{|}}{\overset{\overset{CH_3}{|}}{C}} - OH$
(d) $CH_3CH_2 \underset{\underset{CH_3}{|}}{\overset{\overset{CH_3}{|}}{C}} - OH$

8. Which of the following are correct?
(a) ordinary ethyl alcohol is known as rectified spirit
(b) the alcohol sold in the market for polishing, etc., is known as methylated spirit
(c) absolute alcohol is 100% ethanol
(d) power alcohol is 100% ethanol

9. $CH_3 - \underset{\underset{CH_3}{|}}{CH} - CH = CH_2 \xrightarrow{\text{reagent R}}$ alcohol

Which is/are true about alcohol and R?
(a) alcohol is $CH_3 - \underset{\underset{CH_3}{|}}{CH} - CH_2 - CH_2OH$ when reagent R is $BH_3 / THF - H_2O_2 / OH^-$
(b) alcohol is $CH_3 - \underset{\underset{CH_3}{|}}{CH} - \underset{\underset{OH}{|}}{CH} - CH_3$ when reagent R is $Hg(OAc)_2/NaBH_4 - H_2O$
(c) alcohol is $CH_3 - \underset{\underset{CH_3}{|}}{\overset{\overset{OH}{|}}{C}} - CH_2 - CH_3$ when reagent is H_3O^+
(d) none is correct

10. Chromic anhydride in H_2SO_4 is turned blue by :
(a) 1° alcohol
(b) 2° alcohol
(c) 3° alcohol
(d) ![cyclohexanol]

11. Which gives turbidity with HBr?

12. Which are correct statements?
(a) Rectified spirit is a binary azeotrope
(b) Denatured spirit contains CH_3OH ($\approx$ 5%)
(c) Ternary azeotrope is obtained when benzene is added to rectified spirit
(d) Pyrolegenous acid contains CH_3OH, CH_3COCH_3 and CH_3COOH

13. Which is/are correct statements?
(a) Oxidation product of 1, 2-ethanediol with HIO_4 is formaldehyde
(b) 1° alcohol turns $K_2Cr_2O_7/H^+$ solution green
(c) t-butyl alcohol is converted to isobutene on heating with Cu
(d) CH_3OH is also called wood spirit

14. Which of the following combination of reactants can be used to prepare the following compound ?

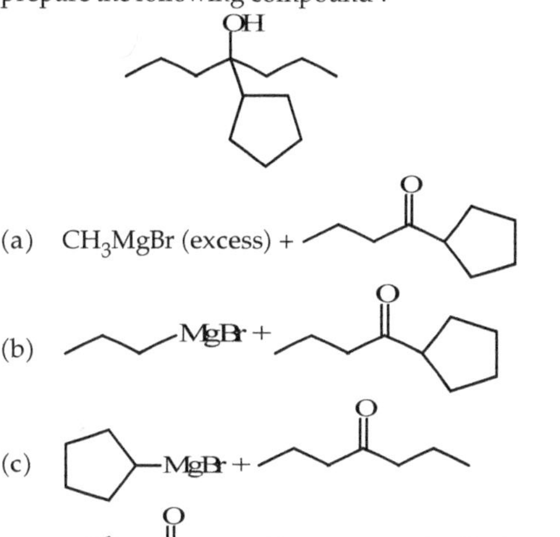

15. The following compounds are reacted with Mg/Ether followed by O_2 and then acidified. Lucas test is not positive with the final product of :

(a) 

(b) $CH_3—\underset{\underset{CH_3}{|}}{\overset{\overset{CH_3}{|}}{C}}—Br$

(c)

(d) $CH_2 = CH – Br$

16. 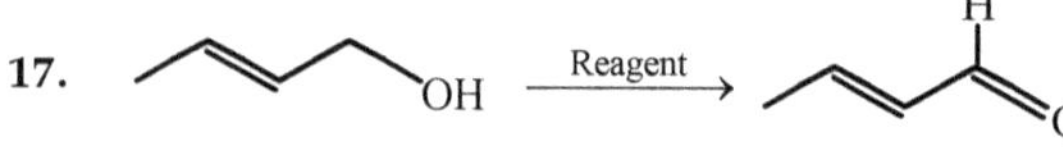

The above reaction involves
(a) Conversion of 2° to 3° carbocation
(b) Conversion of 3° to 2° carbocation
(c) Expansion of ring
(d) Conversion of 3° to the more stable benzylic carbocation

17. 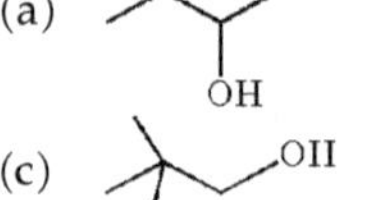

Reagent in the above reaction may be
(a) Collines reagent   (b) Tollen's reagent
(c) PCC   (d) PDC

18. Which of the following alcohol will mainly give the rearranged chloride, when treated with HCl?

(a) 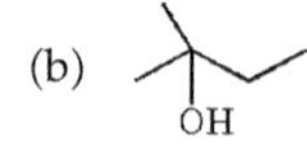

(b)

(c)

(d)

19. Pick up the correct statements in the following reaction

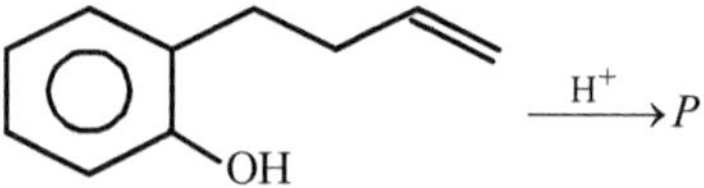

(a) protonation occurs at –OH
(b) protonation occurs at C = C linkage
(c) P is
(d) P is

20. 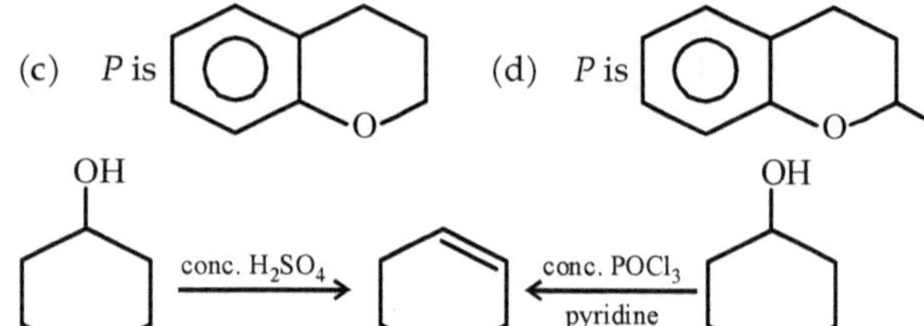

Which of the following statement is true regarding above reaction?
(a) Dehydration by conc. H_2SO_4 is slower than with $POCl_3$
(b) Both involve carbocation as intermediate
(c) Dehydration by $POCl_3$ involves elimination of –$OPOCl_2$ which is a better leaving group.
(d) Elimination of – $OPOCl_2$ and abstraction of proton by pyridine take place simultaneously.

21. 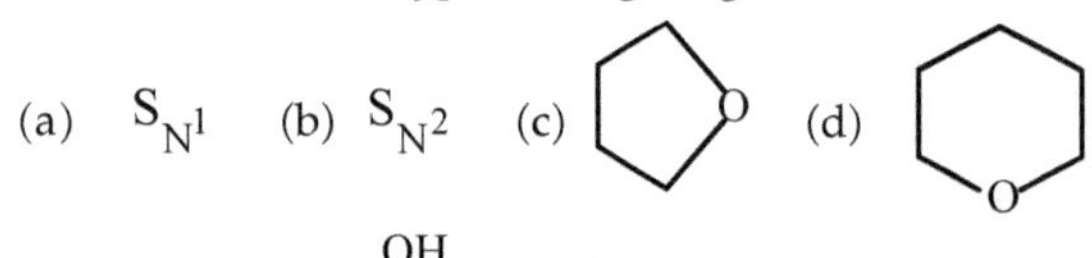 undergoes intramolecular nucleophilic substitution of the type.......... giving...........

(a) S_N1 (b) S_N2 (c)   (d)

22.

The above transformation involves
(a) protonation at the C = C linkage
(b) protonation at –OH group
(c) formation of 2° carbocation
(d) formation of 3° carbocation

23. In the reaction 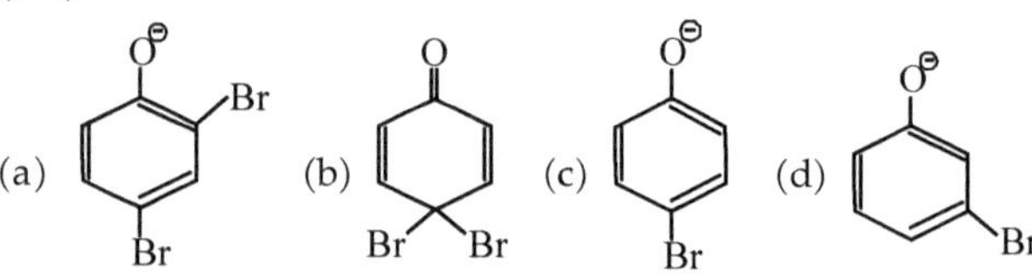 the intermediate (s) is (are)

(a)   (b)   (c)   (d)

DIRECTIONS for Q. 24 to Q. 35 : Read the following passages and answer the questions that follows :

PASSAGE 1

An organic compound **A** $(C_9H_{12}O)$ exhibits following characteristics.
(a) It reacts with metallic sodium to give a colourless odorless gas
(b) It is oxidised by $KMnO_4$ to benzoic acid.
(c) It can be resolved.
(d) It does not give precipitate with iodine in presence of NaOH.
(e) It changes the colour of $Cr_2O_7^{2-}$ from orange to blue, and gives a chiral compound.

On the basis of the above reaction & the following 5 structures, answer the following questions :

$$C_6H_5\ \underset{\underset{}{|}}{\overset{\overset{OH}{|}}{C}}HCH_2\ CH_3 \qquad C_6H_5\ \underset{\underset{CH_3}{|}}{\overset{\overset{OH}{|}}{C}}CH_3 \qquad C_6H_5CH_2\ \overset{\overset{OH}{|}}{C}HCH_3$$

$$I \qquad\qquad II \qquad\qquad III$$

$$C_6H_5\ \underset{\underset{CH_3}{|}}{C}HCH_2OH \qquad C_6H_5CH_2CH_2CH_2OH$$

$$IV \qquad\qquad V$$

24. Which of the following given characteristics discard the possibility of compound V
(i) (b)   (ii) (c)   (iii) (d)   (iv) (e)
(a) (i) and (ii)   (b) (ii) and (iv)
(c) (i), (ii) and (iii)   (d) all the four

25. The above characteristics establish the structure of A as
(a) I   (b) II   (c) III   (d) IV

26. The total number of isomeric alcohols to IV would be
(a) 4   (b) 6   (c) 8   (d) 9

PASSAGE 2

Study the following road map and answer questions 16-18 :

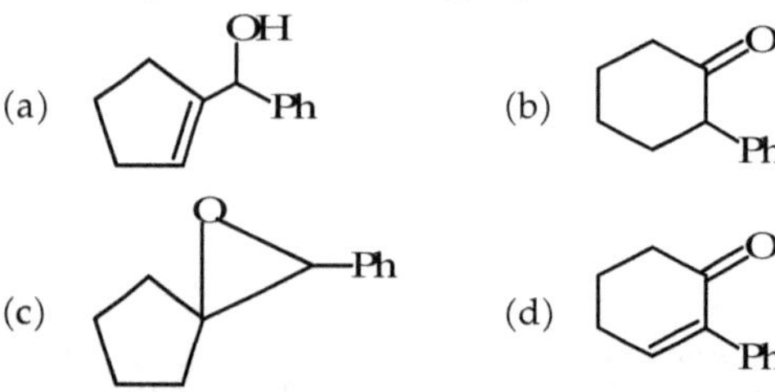

27. The compound (X), (the major product) is

(a)   (b)   (c)   (d)

28. The reagent Y can be
(a) Baeyer's reagent
(b) Lucas reagent
(c) I_2/NaOH
(d) 2, 4-Dinitrophenylhydrazine

The product Z is :

(a) 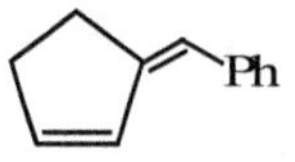 [structure]

(b) 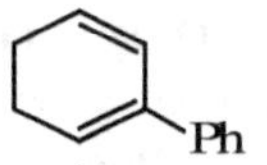 [structure]

(c) 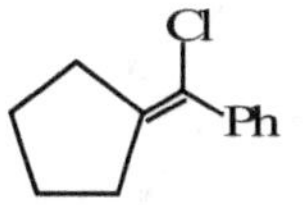 [structure]

(d) 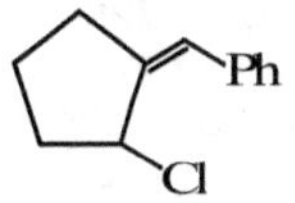 [structure]

PASSAGE 3

Hydration, hydroboration-oxidation and oxymercuration-demercuration are three important methods for the synthesis of alcohols from alkenes. The overall process in each case corresponds to the addition of elements of water (H^+, OH^-) to the alkenes. Whereas both hydration and oxymercuration-demercuration produce alcohols corresponding to Markovnikov's addition of water, hydroboration-oxidation produces alcohols corresponding to anti-Markovnikov's addition of water to the alkene with the only difference that hydration occurs through carbocation intermediate and thus often produces unexpected alcohols having rearranged carbon skeleton. In contrast, hydroboration-oxidation does not involve carbocation intermediate and produces only expected alcohols.

30. Hydration of 3-phenylbut--1-ene with dil. H_2SO_4 mainly gives
(a) 3-Phenylbutan-1-ol   (b) 3-Phenylbutan-2-ol
(c) 2-Phenylbutan-1-ol   (d) 2-Phenylbutan-2-ol

31. 2-Methylpropene upon hydroboration-oxidation gives
(a) 2-Methyl-1-propanol   (b) 2-Methyl-2-propanol
(c) 2-propanol   (d) 1-propanol

32. The product of the following reaction,

$$CH_3 - \underset{\underset{CH_3}{|}}{\overset{\overset{CH_3}{|}}{C}} - CH = CH_2 \xrightarrow[\text{(ii) NaBH}_4]{\text{(i) Hg(OAc)}_2, H_2O} \text{ is}$$

(a) $CH_3 - \underset{\underset{CH_3}{|}}{\overset{\overset{CH_3}{|}}{C}} - CH - CH_3$ (b) $CH_3 - \underset{\underset{CH_3}{|}}{\overset{\overset{CH_3}{|}}{C}} - CH_2 - CH_2OH$

(c) $CH_3 - \underset{\underset{CH_3}{|}}{\overset{\overset{OH}{|}}{C}} - CH - CH_3$ (d) $HOCH_2 - \underset{\underset{CH_3}{|}}{\overset{\overset{OH}{|}}{C}} - CH_2CH_3$

PASSAGE 4

Secondary and tertiary alcohols always give E1 reactions in dehydraton. Primary alcohols whose β-carbon is 3° or 4° also give E1 reactions. However, the primary alcohols whose β-carbon is 1° or 2° give E2 reactions. Dehydrating agents like conc. H_2SO_4, Al_2O_3, anhydrous $ZnCl_2$ are used.

The reactivity of alcohols for elimination reaction lies in following sequence :

    Tertiary alcohol > secondary alcohol > primary alcohol

Electron attracting groups present in alcohols increase the reactivity for dehydration. Greater is the –I effect of the group present in alcohol, more will be its reactivity. Both E1 and E2 mechanism give the product according to Saytzeff's rule, i.e., major product is the most substituted alkene.

$$CH_3 - CH - \underset{\underset{CH_3}{|}}{CH} - CH_3 \xrightarrow[\text{above 413 K}]{\text{Conc. H}_2SO_4}$$

with OH on the second carbon

1-Methylbutan-2-ol

$$CH_3 - \underset{\underset{CH_3}{|}}{C} = CH - CH_3 + CH_3 - \underset{\underset{CH_3}{|}}{CH} - CH = CH_2$$

2-Methylbut-2-ene (Major product)   3-Methylbut-1-ene (Minor product)

---

33. Arrange the reactivity of given four alcohols in decreasing order for dehydration.

A. 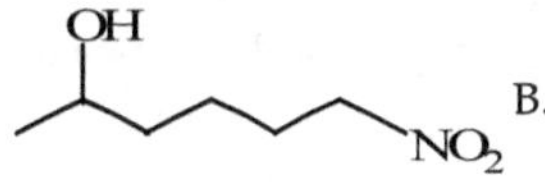 [structure with OH and NO_2]
B. 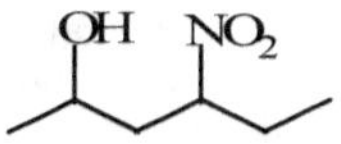 [structure with OH and NO_2]
C. 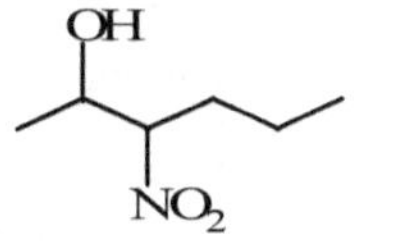 [structure with OH and NO_2]
D. 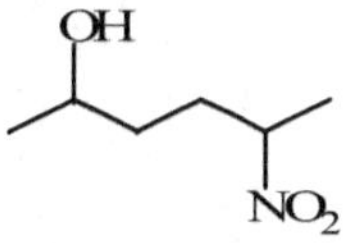 [structure with OH and NO_2]

(a) A > B > C > D   (b) D > C > B > A
(c) C > B > D > A   (d) B > C > A > D

34. Which among the following sequences of reactivity for dehydration is incorrect ?

(a) 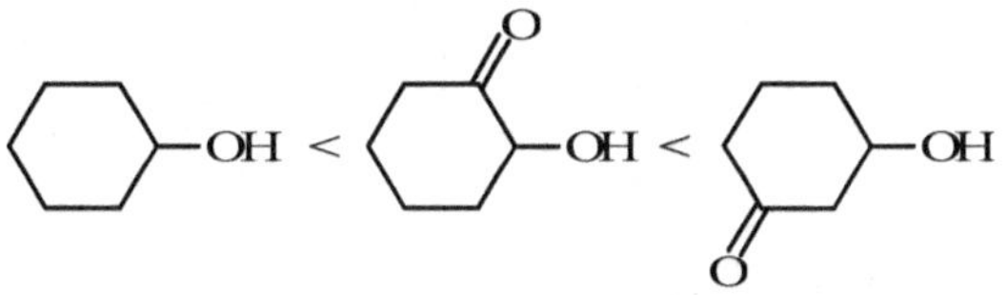 [cyclohexyl-OH] < [2-oxocyclohexyl-OH] < [3-oxocyclohexyl-OH]

(b) $CH_3CH_2CH_2CH_2OH < CH_3 - \underset{\underset{OH}{|}}{CH} - CH_2 - CH_3 < CH_3 - \underset{\underset{CH_3}{|}}{\overset{\overset{CH_3}{|}}{C}} - OH$

(c) 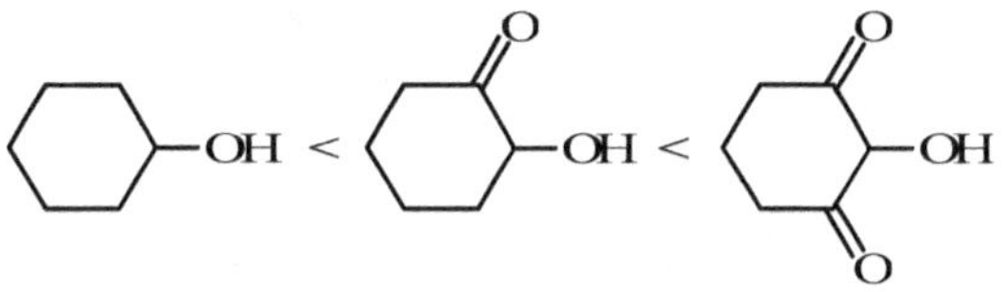 [cyclohexyl-OH] < [2-oxocyclohexyl-OH] < [2,6-dioxocyclohexyl-OH]

(d) 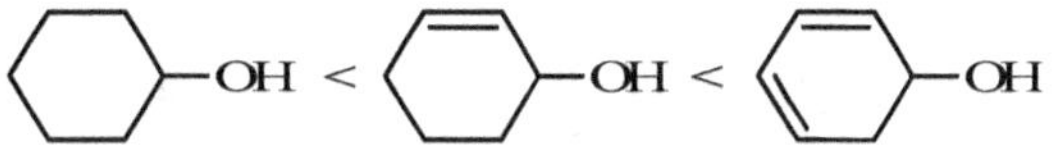 [cyclohexyl-OH] < [cyclohexyl-OH] < [cyclohexenyl-OH]

35. Which of the following dehydration products is incorrect ?

(a) 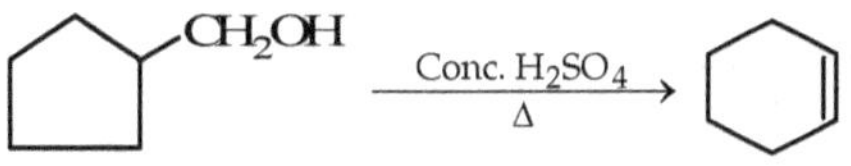 [cyclopentyl-CH_2OH] $\xrightarrow[\Delta]{\text{Conc. H}_2SO_4}$ [cyclohexene]

(b) $CH_3 - \underset{\underset{CH_3}{|}}{\overset{\overset{CH_3}{|}}{C}} - \underset{\underset{OH}{|}}{CH} - CH_3 \xrightarrow[\Delta]{\text{Conc.H}_2SO_4} CH_3 - \underset{\underset{CH_3}{|}}{\overset{\overset{CH_3}{|}}{C}} - CH = CH_2$

(c) $CH_3CH_2CH_2CH_2OH \xrightarrow[\Delta]{\text{Conc. H}_2SO_4}$

        $CH_3 - CH = CH - CH_3$

(d) 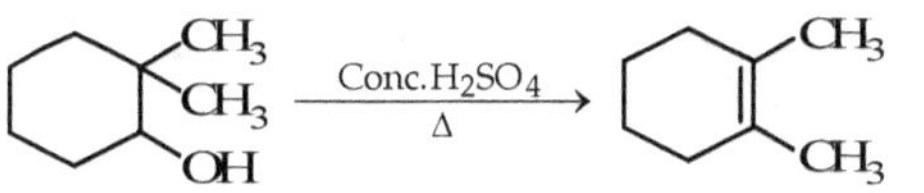 [cyclohexane with CH_3, CH_3, OH] $\xrightarrow[\Delta]{\text{Conc.H}_2SO_4}$ [cyclohexene with CH_3, CH_3]

DIRECTIONS for Q. 36 to Q. 40 : The following questions are matching type questions. Match Column I with Column II

36. *Column I*   *Column II*
(A) Fuel   (a) Alkenes
(B) Lewis acid   (b) Ammonical silver nitrate
(C) Tollen's reagent   (c) Anhydrous $AlCl_3$
(D) Yeast   (d) Ethanol

37.

Column I		Column II	
(A)	Acid-catalysed hydration of alkenes	(a)	Markovnikov hydration
(B)	Oxymercuration-demercuration of alkenes	(b)	*anti*-Markovnikov hydration
(C)	Hydroboration-oxidation of alkenes	(c)	Stereoselective
(D)	Dehydration of alcohols to alkenes	(d)	Regioselective

38. Match the column :

Column-I (Compounds)   **Column-II (Can be differentiated by)**

A. $CH_3 - \underset{\underset{OH}{|}}{CH} - CH_3$ and   (p) Lucas reagent

   $CH_3 - CH_2 - CH_2 - OH$

B. $CH_2 = CH - CH_2 - OH$ (q) Victor Meyer test

   and $CH_3 - \underset{\underset{OH}{|}}{\overset{\overset{CH_3}{|}}{C}} - CH_3$

C.   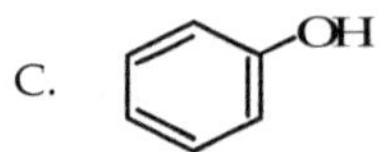 and 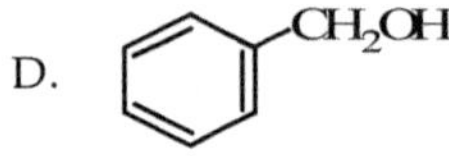   (r) Iodoform test

   (s) Aqueous $AgNO_3$

39. Match the following column :

Column-I   **Column-II**

A. $CH_3 - CH_2 - OH$ (p) No response to Victor Meyer's reagent

B. $H_3C - \underset{\underset{CH_3}{|}}{\overset{\overset{CH_3}{|}}{C}} - OH$ (q) Turbidity immediately when treated with Lucas reagent

C.   (phenol, OH on ring)   (r) No response to Lucas reagent

D.   (benzyl alcohol, CH_2OH on ring)   (s) Red colour in Victor Meyer's test

   (t) Gives test with dil. $AgNO_3$

40.

	Column-I		Column-II
A.	Allyl alcohol	(p)	Gives ppt with Lucas reagent immediately
B.	Benzyl alcohol	(q)	Reaction with sodium vigorously
C.	Ter-butyl alcohol	(r)	Reacts with sodium slowly
D.	Ethyl alcohol	(s)	Does not give precipitate with Lucas reagent at room temperature

Instructions for Q. 41 to 44 : Following questions are Assertion an Reasoning Type Questions :

Note : Each question contains STATEMENT-1 (Assertion) an STATEMENT-2 (Reason). Each question has 5 choices (a), (b), ((d) and (e) out of which ONLY ONE is correct.

(a) Statement-1 is True, Statement-2 is True; Statement-2 is correct explanation for Statement-1.

(b) Statement-1 is True, Statement-2 is True; Statement-2 is NO a correct explanation for Statement-1.

(c) Statement -1 is True, Statement-2 is False.

(d) Statement -1 is False, Statement-2 is True.

(e) Statement -1 is False, Statement-2 is False.

41. **Statement 1 :** Alcoholic fermentation involves conversion sugar into ethyl alcohol by yeast.

Statement 2 : Fermentation involves the slow decompositio of complex organic molecules.

42. **Statement 1 :** Acid catalysed dehydration of *t*-butanol is slow than *n*-butanol.

Statement 2 : Dehydration involves formation of the protonate alcohol, ROH_2^+.

43. **Statement 1 :** The ease of dehydration of alcohols follows th order : Primary > Secondary > Tertiary.

Statement 2 : Dehydration proceeds through the formation oxonium ions.

44. **Statement-1 :** Solubility of *n*-alcohols in water decreases wit increase in its relative molar mass.

Statement-2 : The relative proportion of the hydrocarbon pa in alcohols increases with increasing molar mass, which premit enhanced hydrogen bonding with water.

Instructions for Q. 45 to 46 : Following questions are Integer Typ Questions :

45.

$$\underset{Et}{\overset{Me}{\underset{Ph}{|}{C}}} - OH \xrightarrow{HI}$$

How many iodides are produced in more than 5% yield ?

46.

$$\xrightarrow[(-H_2O)]{H^+} [F] \xrightarrow{Br_2, CCl_4} C_4H_8Br_2 \text{ (5 isomers)}$$

How many structures are possible for F ?

EXERCISE 11.3   (Subjective Problems)

1. Give IUPAC name of the following compounds.

(a)

(b)

(c) C_6H_4-Cl-*m*

(d)

. Write the structures and names of all isomeric cyclic alcohols of **the formula** C_4H_7OH. Indicate which one of the isomer is (are) chiral.

. Arrange the following compounds in order of decreasing boiling point.
3-Hexanol, *n*-hexane, 2-methyl-2-pentanol, *n*-octyl alcohol and *n*-hexyl alcohol.

. Predict the structure of the alcohol formed in each of the following cases.

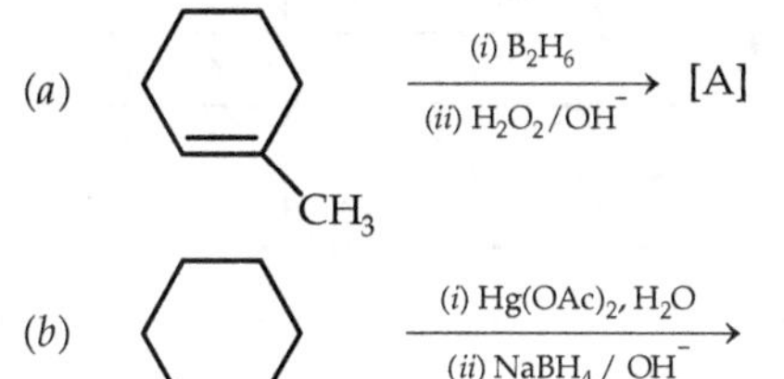

(*a*) $\xrightarrow[\text{(ii) H}_2\text{O}_2/\text{OH}^-]{\text{(i) B}_2\text{H}_6}$ [A]

(*b*) $\xrightarrow[\text{(ii) NaBH}_4 / \text{OH}^-]{\text{(i) Hg(OAc)}_2, \text{H}_2\text{O}}$ [B]

(*c*) $\xrightarrow{\text{dil. H}_2\text{SO}_4}$ [C]

(*d*) $\xrightarrow[\text{(ii) NaBH}_4/\text{OH}^-]{\text{(i) Hg(OAc)}_2, \text{H}_2\text{O}}$ [D]

5. Explain the following :
(*a*) Reaction of *tert*-butyl chloride with OH⁻ gives no *tert*-butyl alcohol, while reaction with H_2O in dioxane gives appreciable amount of *tert*-butanol.
(*b*) Methanol and ethanol are reasonably good solvents for many ionic substances.
(*c*) Cyclohexanol is more soluble in water than 1-hexanol.
(*d*) Acid catalysed dehydration of *tert*-butanol is faster than that of *n*-butanol.

6. Give the synthesis of each of the following alcohols from an alkene with the same number of carbon atoms.
(*a*) 2-Butanol   (*b*) Isobutanol
(*c*) Cyclopentylcarbinol   (*d*) 2-methyl-2-butanol.

7. Give the possible pairs of Grignard reagent and other component that can be used for preparing following alcohols.

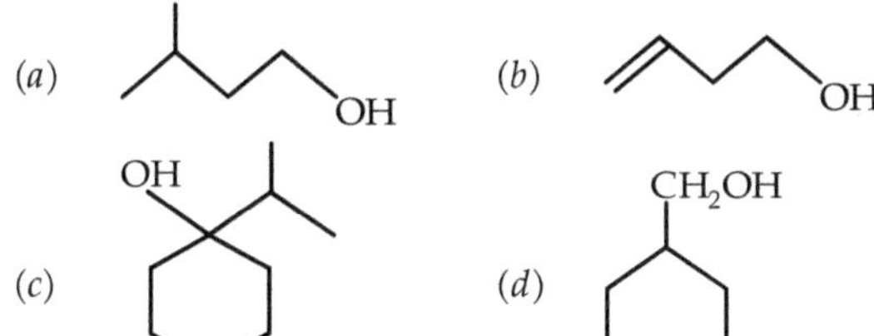

8. Give the expected product obtained by reducing following compounds with $LiAlH_4$.
(*a*) $CHO.CH_2COOCH_3$ (*b*) $CH_3COCH_2CH_2Br$

(*c*) [cyclohexenone structure] =O (*d*) OHC—[benzene ring]—NO_2.

9. Give the products for the reaction of isopropanol with conc. H_2SO_4 at
(*a*) 0°C,   (*b*) room temperature, (*c*) 130°C, and   (*d*) 180°C.

10. How does the Lewis theory of acids and bases explain the functions of
(*a*) $ZnCl_2$ in the Lucas reagent, and
(*b*) ether as solvent in the Grignard reagent.

11. Arrange the following alcohols in order of their decreasing reactivity with HBr.

(*a*)

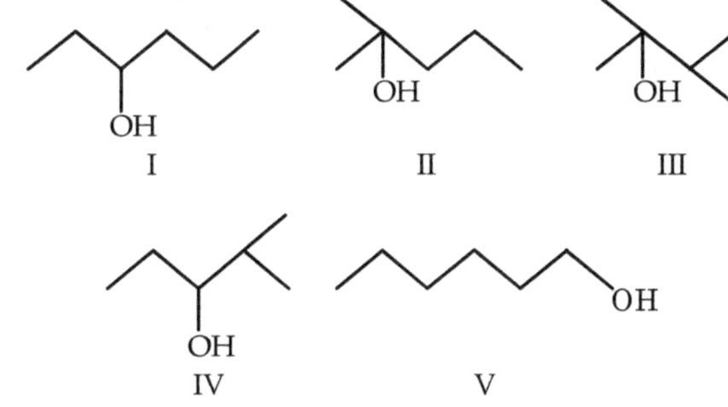

(*i*)   (*ii*)

(*iii*)   (*iv*)

(*b*)

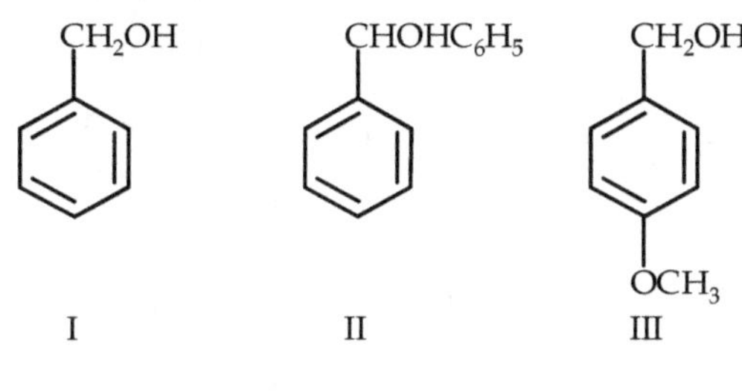

(*i*)   (*ii*)   (*iii*)

(*c*)

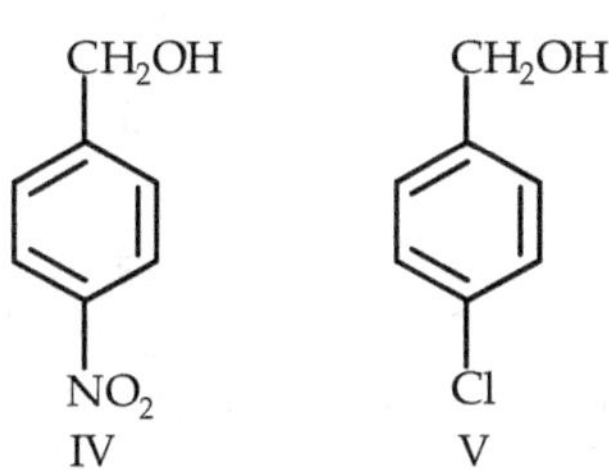

(*i*)   (*ii*)

(*iii*)   (*iv*)

12. Arrange the following benzyl alcohols in order of their decreasing reactivity with HBr.

CH_2OH $CHOHC_6H_5$ CH_2OH

I   II OCH_3 III

CH_2OH CH_2OH

NO_2 IV Cl V

13. Arrange the following alcohols in decreasing order of dehydration with sulphuric acid.

OH I   OH II   OH III

OH IV   V OH

14. Give structures and names of the main product expected from the reaction (if any) of isopropyl alcohol with
(*a*) C_2H_5MgBr (*b*) *aq.* NaOH
(*c*) cold. dil. $KMnO_4$
(*d*) CrO_3, H_2SO_4 (*e*) tosyl chloride, OH⁻.

15. Give necessary steps involved in the conversions of
(*a*) 1- butanol to *n*-butane-1-deuterium
(*b*) 1-Butanol to *n*-butyraldehyde
(*c*) 1-Butanol to *n*-octane
(*d*) 2-Methyl-2-propanol to isobutane.

16. 3, 3-Dimethylbutan-2-ol loses a molecule of water in the presence of a concentrated sulphuric acid to give tetramethylethylene as a major product. Suggest a suitable mechanism.

SOLUTIONS

EXERCISE 11.1

6	(d)	11	(a)	16	(d)	21	(d)	26	(a)	31	(c)	36	(d)	41	(c)
7	(c)	12	(c)	17	(c)	22	(d)	27	(a)	32	(b)	37	(b)	42	(b)
8	(d)	13	(c)	18	(b)	23	(c)	28	(c)	33	(b)	38	(c)	43	(c)
9	(d)	14	(c)	19	(d)	24	(c)	29	(c)	34	(c)	39	(c)		
10	(b)	15	(c)	20	(b)	25	(c)	30	(a)	35	(c)	40	(c)		

1. (*a*) Carbinol is CH_3OH, hence for $C_6H_5\overset{\beta}{C}H_2\overset{\alpha}{C}H_2CH_2OH$ option (*b*) is correct.

2. $CH \equiv C—CH_2—$ is propargyl group.

3. Isopropanol is used for rubdowns and its evaporation reduces fevers ; it is cheaper than ethanol hence replaced ethanol for this purpose.

4. Hydrogen bonding between ethanol and water permits the two unlike molecules to move close together in the solution than can ethanol to ethanol and water to water molecules.

5. n-$C_4H_9CH_2OH$ **(A)** ; $CH_3—\underset{\underset{OH}{|}}{\overset{\overset{CH_3}{|}}{C}}—CH_2CH_3$ **(B)** ; $CH_3—\underset{\underset{OH}{|}}{CH}—\underset{\underset{CH_3}{|}}{C}—CH_3$ **(C)**

With the increase in branching, the shape of the molecule becomes more compact and spherical ; hence less surface contact is available for van der Waals forces.

6.

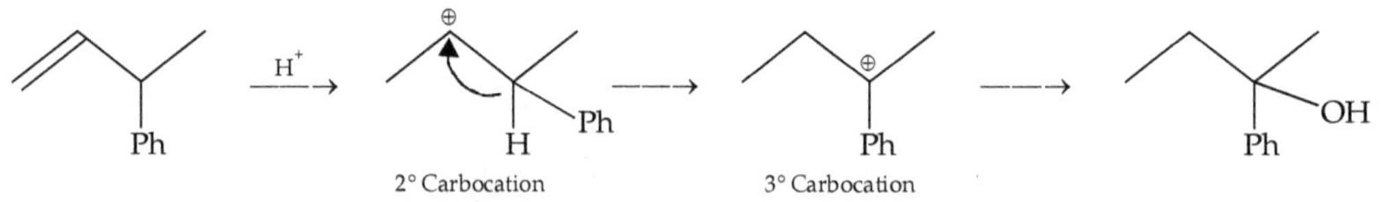

7. Catalytic hydrogenation reduces double bond as well as carbonyl group.

8. $CH_3CH = CHCH_3$ or $CH_3CH_2CH = CH_2 \xrightarrow{Cold, Conc\ H_2SO_4} CH_3CH_2\underset{\underset{\underset{rac-}{OSO_3H}}{|}}{C}HCH_3 \longrightarrow CH_3CH_2\underset{\underset{\underset{rac-}{OH}}{|}}{C}HCH_3$

cis-or trans-Butene-2   Butene-1

9. Weaker a base better is the leaving group. Triflate (trifluoromethanesulphonate, $F_3CSO_2O^-$) anion is an extremely weak base because it has three powerful electron-withdrawing fluorine atoms which help to stabilize the triflate anion $F_3CSO_2O^-$ and thus make the parent acid F_3CSO_2OH (triflic acid) one of the strongest known Lowry-Bronsted acids, much stronger than H_2SO_4 or $HClO_4$.

10. For Lucas test, initially the alcohol must be soluble in the reagent. Alcohols having seven or more carbon atoms are not soluble, hence they form two layers at the start.

11. Remember that conjugated isomer is more stable than the non-conjugated ; neglecting the option (*c*) which is Saytzeff product. Out of *cis*- and *trans*-isomers, *trans*- is more stable and hence option (*a*) is main product.

12.

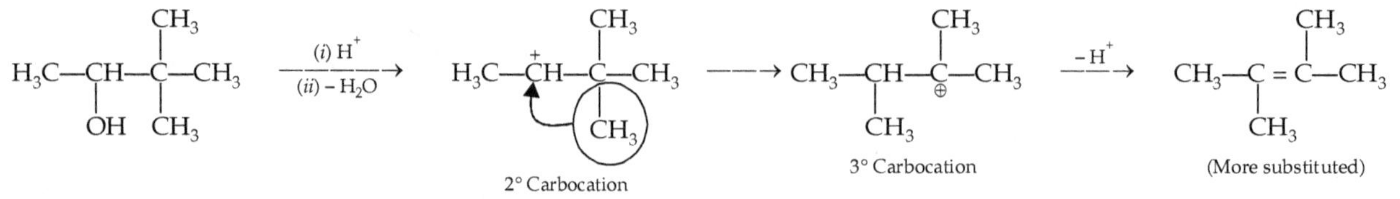

13. Jones reagent (chromic acid in aq. acetone solution) is a mild oxidizing agent and oxidizes alcohols without oxidising double bond.

14. Reaction of an alcohol with $SOCl_2$ does not cause rearrangement, while with HCl and HCl + $ZnCl_2$, rearranged product, $(CH_3)_2CClCH_2CH_3$ will be formed.

15. $C_6H_5CH_2\overset{\overset{OH}{|}}{C}HCH_3 \xrightarrow{H^+} C_6H_5CH = CHCH_3 + C_6H_5CH_2CH = CH_2$

1–Phenyl–2–propanol   1-Phenyl-1-propene (Major)   1-Phenyl-2-propene

16. $NaBH_4$ does not reduce double bound, but only CHO to CH_2OH.

17. $\underset{[A]}{CH_3CH_2CH_2OH}$, $\underset{[B]}{CH_3CH = CH_2}$, $\underset{[C]}{CH_3CHBr.CH_2Br}$, $\underset{[D]}{CH_3C \equiv CH}$, $\underset{[E]}{CH_3.CO.CH_3}$

(d) acid-catalysed product
(rearranged Markownikov)   hydro-oxidation product
(*anti*-Markownikov)

oxymerc-demerc product
(Mark., no rearranged)

4. (c)
$$\xrightarrow[\Delta]{H^{\oplus}/KMnO_4}$$
$$\xrightarrow{\Delta}$$

5. (c)
$$\xrightarrow[(-HBr)]{\text{Cylization}} (C)$$

6. (a) $CH_2 = CH - \overset{+}{C}H - CH = CH - CH_3 \xrightarrow[(ii)-H^+]{(i)CH_3OH}$

7. (a) $C_6H_5MgBr + CH_3COCH_3 \underset{S}{\quad} \underset{T}{\quad} C_6H_5 - \overset{CH_3}{\underset{CH_3}{\overset{|}{\underset{|}{C}}}} - OH \xrightarrow[H_2SO_4]{\text{conc.}} C_6H_5 - \overset{CH_2}{\underset{CH_3}{\overset{||}{C}}} \xrightarrow{O_3} C_6H_5 - \overset{O}{\overset{||}{C}} - CH_3$

8. (c)
$$\overset{H}{\underset{H}{C}} \overset{}{=} O + \overset{\delta\ominus}{CD_2} - Mg - I \longrightarrow \overset{CD_2-H}{\underset{OMg-I}{C-H}} \xrightarrow{H_2O} \overset{CD_2-H}{\underset{OH}{C-H}}$$
(X)

$$\xrightarrow[\Delta]{\text{Conc. } H_2SO_4} D_2C = CH_2$$
(Y)

9. (c) According to carbocation stability IV > III > II > I

10. (a) Option (a) will lead to conjugated ketone with highly substituted C = C.

11. (c) Hydroboration – oxidation of alkenes leads to *anti*-Markownikoff's hydration.

12. (b)
$$C_6H_5 \overset{OH}{\underset{}{\diagdown}} \xrightarrow{\overset{+}{H}} C_6H_5 \overset{\oplus}{\diagdown} \xrightarrow{\text{rearranges}} C_6H_5 \overset{\oplus}{\diagdown}$$
Benzyl carbocation is more stable

$$\xrightarrow{-\overset{+}{H}} C_6H_5 \overset{H}{\diagdown} + C_6H_5 \overset{H}{\diagdown} H$$

trans–(more stable due to steric relief)   *cis*– (less stable due to bulky gps. lying on same side)

13. (b) Hydroboration – oxidation reaction of alkenes leads to anti-Markovnikov's hydration. Further addition of water adds in *syn*-manner, i.e., H and OH are added to the same face of the double bond leading *trans*-product. In short, hydroboration-oxidation of alkenes is regioselective as well as stereoselective.

14. (c)
$$\xrightarrow{\overset{+}{H}} \xrightarrow{} \equiv \xrightarrow{-\overset{+}{H}}$$
2° cabocation

35.   **(c)**   Higher is the stability of a species, more likely it is formed, hence lower will be the E_{act} for its precursor.

36.   **(d)** $CH_3CH_2OH \xrightarrow[\text{(from } H_2SO_4)]{H^+} CH_3CH_2\overset{+}{O}H_2 \rightarrow CH_3\overset{+}{C}H_2 \xrightarrow[\text{(from } H_2SO_4)]{HSO_4^-} CH_2 = CH_2 + H_2SO_4$

Thus note that H_2SO_4 is acting as an acid in step (i), as a base in step (iii). Since it is regenerated back as such it also acts as a cataly

37.   **(b)**   The reaction involves the formation of carbocation as intermediate. Hence more the stability of the carbocation, more will be the ra of reaction. Let us draw the structure of the corresponding carbocation and observe the relative stability of the four benzyl carbocation

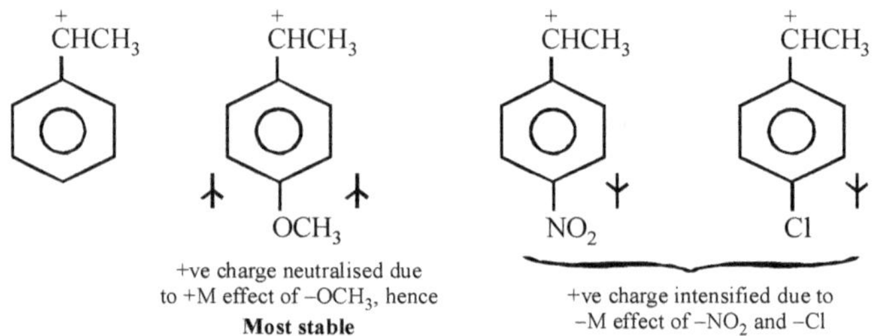

The relative stability of the four carbocations is

38.   **(c)**   Zinc chloride is a Lewis acid and coordinates with the alcoholic group.

$$R-\overset{..}{\underset{..}{O}}H + ZnCl_2 \longrightarrow R-\overset{+}{\underset{H}{O}}-\overset{\ominus}{Z}nCl_2 \longrightarrow R^+ + HO-\overset{\ominus}{Z}nCl_2$$
Leaving group

$$R^+ + Cl^- \text{(from HCl)} \rightarrow RCl + H^+$$

$$H^+ + HO^- - ZnCl_2 \rightarrow H_2O + ZnCl_2$$

39.   **(c)**   Step 2 involves the formation of carbonium ion by the loss of weakly basic H_2O molecule, hence it is slowest step. Step 4 involves th conversion of an unstable (or intermediate) species into a quite stable product, hence it is fastest step.

40.   **(c)**   It is an example of dehydration of alcohol. The 2° carbocation formed at first stage rearranges to the more stable 3°.

41.   **(c)**

42.   **(b)**

43.   **(c)** $\overset{+}{C}H_2 = CH\overset{+}{C}H_2$ and $(CH_3)_3\overset{+}{C}$ are quite stable.

EXERCISE 11.2

	1	(a,c)	9	(a, b, c)	17	(a, c, d)
	2	(a,b)	10	(a, b, d)	18	(a, c, d)
	3	(a,b,c)	11	(a, b, c)	19	(b, d)
>1 CORRECT	4	(a,c,d)	12	(a, b, c, d)	20	(a, c, d)
OPTION	5	(a,c,d)	13	(a, b, c, d)	21	(a, c)
	6	(a,c,d)	14	(b, c, d)	22	(b, c, d)
	7	(c, d)	15	(c, d)	23	(a, c)
	8	(a, b, c)	16	(b, c)		
PASSAGE 1	24	(b)	25	(d)	26	(c)
PASSAGE 2	27	(b)	28	(d)	29	(c)
PASSAGE 3	30	(d)	31	(a)	32	(a)
PASSAGE 4	33	(c)	34	(c)	35	(b)
MATCH THE FOLLOWING	36	(A) – a, d; (B) – c; (C) – b; (D) – d				
	37	(A) - a, (B) - a, d, (C) - b, c, d, (D) - c, d				
	38	(A) - a,b,c (B) - b, (C) - b, c, d				
	39	(A) - c, d (B) - a, b, (C) - a, c; (D) - b, d				
	40	(A) - b,d (B) - a, b, (C) - a, c, (D) - b, d				
A/R	41	(a)	42	(d)	43	(d)
	44	(c)				
INTEGER	45	2	46	3		

1. If the aldehyde has a boiling point less than 100°C, it can be prepared by the oxidation of 1° alcohols with regular oxidising agents like acidic permanganate or dichromate. Since the aldehyde has a lower boiling point than the alcohol, it is distilled off as soon as it is formed ; so further oxidation to a carboxylic acid is minimized.

2.

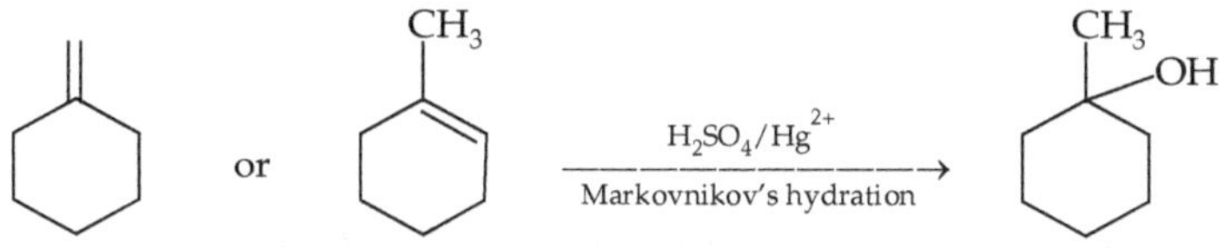

3. 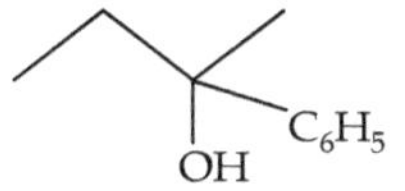 is a 3° alcohol ; the first three combinations can be applied for its preparation.

4. Phenylethylcarbinol, $PhCH(OH)CH_2CH_3$ does not have —CHOHCH$_3$ group, so does not respond haloform test.

5. $LiAlH_4$ reduces —CO as well as Br group. Hydride ions from $LiAlH_4$ are transferred to carbonyl carbon and carbon bearing Br atom.

6. Option (b) will form the most stable (3°) carbocations, hence it does not rearrange.

14. (b, c, d)

(b)

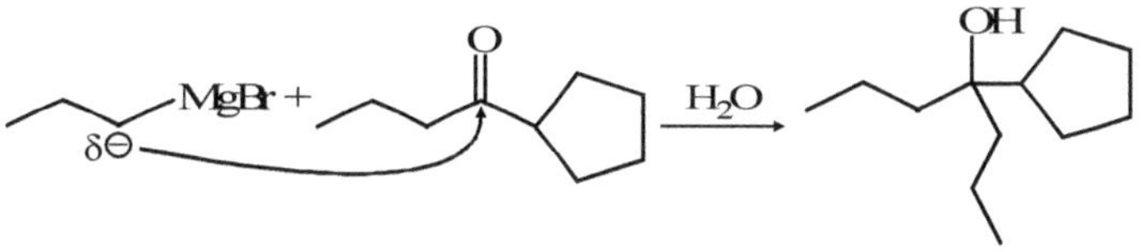

(c)

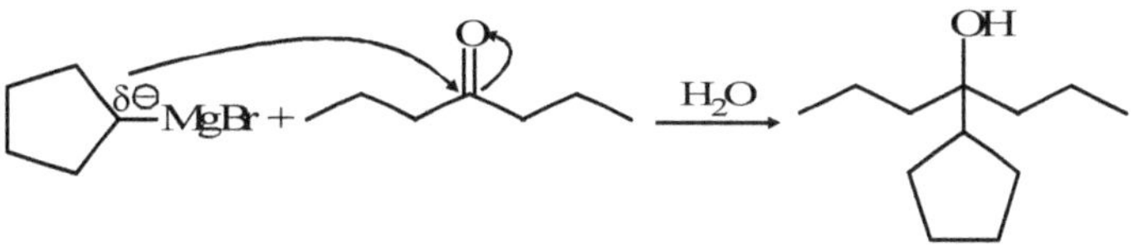

(d)

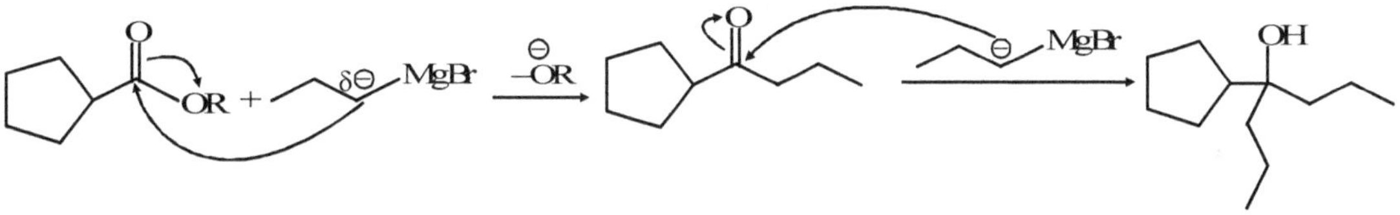

15.   (c, d) (c) and (d) do not form RMgX, hence no alcohol; while (a) and (b) form alcohol which responds Lucas test.

16.   (b, c)

3° carbocation $\xrightarrow[\text{steric strain}]{\text{relief in}}$ 2° carbocation (more stable, 6 membered)

18.   (a, c, d)   Option (b) will form the most stable (3°) carbocation, hence it does not rearrange.

19.   (b, d)

$\xrightarrow{H^+}$

P

22.   (b,c,d)

$\xrightarrow[\text{(ii) }-H_2O]{\text{(i) }H^+}$

2° carbocation

3° carbocation

23.   (a, c)

OH $\xrightarrow[-H_2O]{NaOH}$ $\xrightarrow[-Br]{Br_2}$ (I) $\xrightarrow[-Br]{Br_2}$ (II) (III)

$\xrightarrow[-Br]{Br_2}$ (IV)

Product of reaction of phenol with $NaOH/Br_2$ is sodium salt of 2,4,6-tribromophenol. Hence, species (I), (II), (III) are formed as intermediate.

30.   (d) $CH_2 = CH - \underset{\underset{Ph}{|}}{CH} - CH_3 \xrightarrow{H^+} CH_3 - \overset{+}{CH} - \underset{\underset{Ph}{|}}{CH} - CH_3$

$\longrightarrow CH_3 - CH_2 - \underset{\underset{Ph}{|}}{\overset{+}{C}} - CH_3 \xrightarrow{OH^-} CH_3CH_2 - \underset{\underset{OH}{|}}{\overset{Ph}{|}} C - CH_3$

35.   (b) $CH_3 - \underset{\underset{CH_3}{|}}{\overset{CH_3}{|}}C = \overset{CH_3}{\underset{|}{C}} - CH_3$

38.   A - (p, q, r); B - (q); C - (q, r, s)

(A) $CH_3 - \underset{\underset{OH}{|}}{CH} - CH_3$ & $CH_3 - CH_2 - CH_2 - OH$
      2° alcohol (can give iodoform)   1° alcohol

Lucas & Victor Meyer rest can also be used.

(B) $CH_2 = CH - CH_2 - OH$ & $CH_3 - \underset{\underset{OH}{|}}{\overset{\overset{CH_3}{|}}{C}} - CH_3$
    1° alcohol   3° alcohol

Lucas test can not be used since both give immediate turbidity. Victor Meyer test can be used.

(C)

Lucas test can not be used. **Victor Meyer, iodoform & AgNO₃** tests can be used.

39.   A - (r, s); B - (p, q); C - (p, r); D - (q, s)

40.   A - (q, s); B - (p, q); C - (p, r); D - (q, s)
Though allyl alcohol reacts with Lucas reagent, the ppt reacts with HCl and dissolves in it.

44.   (c)   As hydrocarbon part increases, capacity to make hydrogen bonding decreases. So if molar mass increases, solubility decreases.

45.   **Two**

46.   **3**

Sol. (27-29) :

$\xrightarrow{H^{\oplus}}$ $\longrightarrow$

$\xrightarrow{-H^{\oplus}}$ (X) $\xrightarrow[(Y)]{2,4\text{-DNP}}$ [Yellow orange ppt.]

Cl_2 (excess) $\longrightarrow$ $\xrightarrow[\Delta]{\text{alc. KOH}}$ Ph + HCl (Z)

$\xrightarrow[(-H_2O)]{H^+}$ cis-Butene-2 + trans-Butene-2 + Butene-1

$\downarrow Br_2$ $\downarrow Br_2$ $\downarrow Br_2$

d- and l-forms   meso-   d- and l

EXERCISE 11.3

(*a*) 2-Methyl-4-octanol

(*c*) 5-Chloro-6-methyl-6-(3-chlorophenyl)-2-hepten-1-ol

(*b*) 3-Buten-2-ol

(*d*) 4, 4-Dimethyl-2-cyclohexen-1-ol.

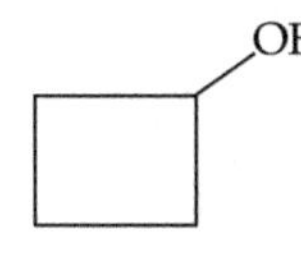

Cyclobutanol

Cyclopropylmethanol

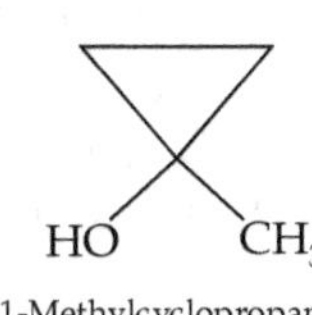

1-Methylcyclopropanol

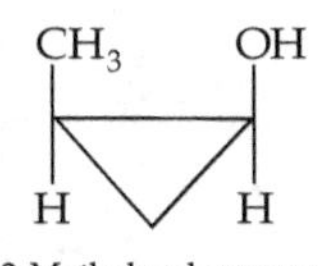

cis-2-Methylcyclopropanol
(**Chiral**)

trans-2-Methylcyclopropanol
(**Chiral**)

n-Octyl alcohol > *n*-Hexyl alcohol > 3-Hexanol > 2-Methyl-2-pentanol > *n*-Hexane.

In hydroboration-oxidation of alkenes, H_2O is added in *cis*– anti-Markovnikov's way. In oxymercuration-demercuration of alkenes, H_2O is added in Markovnikov's way without rearrangement. In acid-catalyzed hydration of alkenes, H_2O is added with rearrangement, if possible.

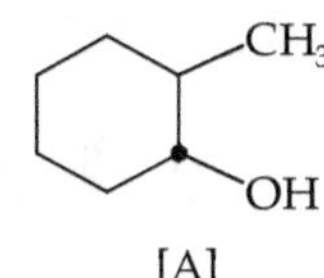

[A]

trans-2-Methylcyclohexanol
(*cis*-Anti-Markovnikov's hydration)

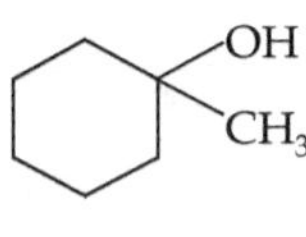

[B]

1-Methylcyclohexanol
(Markovnikov's hydration)

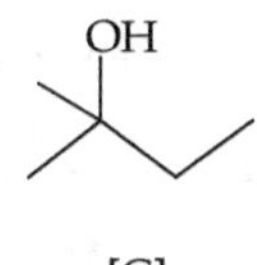

[C]

2-Methyl-2-butanol
(Markovnikov's hydration
with rearrangement)

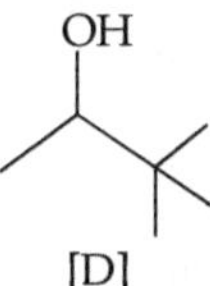

[D]

3, 3-Dimethyl-2-butanol
(Markovnikov's hydration
without rearrangement)

(*a*) 3° Halides react with bases to eliminate HCl forming alkenes ; they do not undergo S_N^2 displacement to give alcohols. However, when heated with water in dioxane, 3° halides undergo S_N^1 reaction forming 3° alcohols in good yield.

(*b*) Like water, methanol and ethanol form H-bond and have relatively high dielectric constant for organic compounds. They are able to insulate charges by solvation, minimizing attractions between unlike ions.

(*c*) The R in cyclohexanol is more compact than in 1-hexanol. Its OH group is more exposed and available for H-bonding with water. In addition, its small compact shape results in fewer water-water H-bonds being broken.

(*d*) Due to formation of more stable *tert*-butyl carbocation.

In such cases, first write down the structure of the required compound and then go backward for knowing the structure of the parent alkene. However, keep in mind that Markovnikov hydration can be achieved by dil. H_2SO_4 or by oxymercuration-demercuration; while *anti*-Markovnikov's hydration is done by BH_3—THF followed by oxidation with H_2O_2 in *aq.* OH⁻.

(*a*) $\underset{\text{2-Butanol}}{CH_3\overset{\overset{\displaystyle OH}{|}}{C}HCH_2CH_3} \xleftarrow[\text{hydration}]{\text{Markovnikov's}} CH_3CH=CHCH_3 \quad \text{or} \quad CH_3CH_2CH=CH_2$

(*b*) $\underset{\text{Isobutyl alcohol}}{(CH_3)_2CHCH_2OH} \xleftarrow[\text{hydration}]{\textit{anti}\text{-Markovnikov's}} (CH_3)_2C=CH_2$

(*c*) $\text{—CH}_2\text{OH} \xleftarrow[\text{hydration}]{\textit{anti}\text{-Markovnikov's}} \text{=CH}_2$

(*d*) $CH_3\overset{\overset{\displaystyle CH_3}{|}}{\underset{\underset{\displaystyle OH}{|}}{C}}CH_2CH_3 \xrightarrow[\text{hydration}]{\text{Markovnikov's}} (CH_3)_2C=CHCH_3 \quad or \quad H_2C=\overset{\overset{\displaystyle CH_3}{|}}{C}CH_2CH_3$

Observe the nature of alcohol (1°, 2° or 3°) and recall how these are prepared from Grignard reagents.

(*a*) $HCHO +$ [alkyl]MgX or   [epoxide] $+$ [isopropyl]MgX

(*b*) $HCHO + CH_2=CHCH_2MgX$ or $\overset{O}{\overset{\diagup\diagdown}{CH_2-CH_2}} + CH_2=CHX$

(*c*) [cyclohexanone] $+ (CH_3)_2CHMgX$

(*d*) [cyclopentyl]$MgX + CH_2O$

8. In addition to carbonyl group, LiAlH$_4$ also reduces groups like —NO$_2$, —X, —NO$_2$, —COOH, —COOR, etc. NaHB$_4$ does not redu~~ either of these groups except carbonyl. Also remember that unsaturation present in α, β-position with respect to carbonyl group~ neither reduced by LiAlH$_4$ nor by NaBH$_4$.

(a) CH$_2$OH.CH$_2$CH$_2$OH

(b) CH$_3$CHOHCH$_2$CH$_3$

(c) [cyclohexene ring]—OH

(d) HOH$_2$C—[benzene ring]—NH$_2$

9. (a) (CH$_3$)$_2$CHOH$_2^+$.HSO$_4^-$
Isopropyloxoniumhydrogen sulphate

(b) (CH$_3$)$_2$CHOSO$_3$H
Isopropylhydrogen sulphate

(c) (CH$_3$)$_2$CH.O.CH(CH$_3$)$_2$
Diisopropyl ether

(d) CH$_3$CH = CH$_2$.
Propene

10. (a) $\underset{\text{Lewis acid}}{ZnCl_2} + 2HCl \longrightarrow \underset{\text{(A stronger acid than HCl)}}{H_2ZnCl_4} \xrightarrow{ROH} ROH_2^+ \xrightarrow{Cl^-} RCl + H_2O$

(b) Magnesium of RMgX can coordinate with two molecules of ether *via* the electron pairs of their oxygen atoms to form an eth~ soluble addition compound.

11. In general, the order of reactivity is 3° > 2° > 1° < CH$_3$OH. Electronic factors are important except for 1° alcohols, for which steric facto~ are controlling.

(a) All are primary alcohols, greater the steric hindrance near the carbon of the alcoholic group, lesser will be its reactivity towards HB~ Thus

(i) > (ii) > (iv) > (iii)

(b) (iii) > (i) > (ii)
   3°   2°   1°

(c) (i) > (iv) > (ii) > (iii)

All are 2°, rate decreases with the nearness and number of electron-withdrawing fluorines.

12. This is an S$_N^1$ reaction and involves formation of carbocation as intermediate. Hence greater the stability of a carbocation, higher wi~ be reactivity of its parent alcohol. Recall that

(a) electron withdrawing groups like NO$_2$ and Cl in the *para* position will destabilize the carbocation by intensifying the positiv~ charge. Further NO$_2$ is more effective since it destabilizes by both resonance and induction, while Cl destabilizes only by inductio~

(b) Electron releasing group like OCH$_3$ will stabilize the carbocation.

(c) More the number of phenyl groups on the benzylic carbon, more stable will be the carbocation.

III > II > I > V > IV.

13. Ease of dehydration of alcohols is 3° > 2° > 1°. Further among same type of alcohol (*viz.* 3°) the alcohol which gives a more substitute~ alkene will be dehydrated more easily than the other. Thus

III > II > IV > I > V

14. (a) C$_2$H$_6$
Ethane

(b) and (c) No reaction

(d) (CH$_3$)$_2$CO
Acetone

(e) (CH$_3$)$_2$CHOTs (Isopropyl tosylate)

15. (a) n-C$_3$H$_7$CH$_2$OH $\longrightarrow$ n-C$_3$H$_7$CH$_2$Br $\xrightarrow{Mg}$ n-C$_3$H$_7$CH$_2$MgBr $\xrightarrow{D_2O}$ n-C$_3$H$_7$CH$_2$D

(b) n-C$_3$H$_7$CH$_2$OH $\xrightarrow{PCC, CH_2Cl_2}$ n-C$_3$H$_7$CHO

(c) n-C$_3$H$_7$CH$_2$OH $\longrightarrow$ n-C$_3$H$_7$CH$_2$Br $\xrightarrow{Li}$ n-C$_3$H$_7$CH$_2$Li $\xrightarrow{CuI}$ (n-C$_3$H$_7$CH$_2$–)$_2$–CuLi

$\xrightarrow{n\text{-}C_3H_7CH_2Br}$ n-C$_3$H$_7$CH$_2$CH$_2$C$_3$H$_7$-n

(d) (CH$_3$)$_3$COH $\xrightarrow{HBr}$ (CH$_3$)$_3$CBr $\xrightarrow[(ii)\,H_2O]{(i)\,Mg}$ (CH$_3$)$_3$CH

16. [reaction scheme] $\xrightarrow{H^+}$ [structure] $\xrightarrow{-H_2O}$ [2° Carbocation] $\longrightarrow$ [3° Carbocation] $\xrightarrow{-H^+}$ [alkene]

OH $_+$OH$_2$ 2° Carbocation   3° Carbocation

Ethers, Epoxides and Polyhydric Alcohols

12

CHAPTER HIGHLIGHTS

ETHERS

 Nomenclature

Ethers are compounds containing a C—O—C unit, hence their general formula is R—O—R (R may be alkyl or aryl). Ethers are named in radicofunctional way or IUPAC (substitutive) way.

	$CH_3CH_2OCH_2CH_3$	$CH_3CH_2OCH_3$	$CH_3OCH_2CH_2Cl$
Radicofunctional name :	Diethyl ether	Ethyl methyl ether	2-Chloroethyl methyl ether
IUPAC name :	Ethoxyethane	Methoxyethane	1-Chloro-2-methoxyethane

If the two groups bonded to oxygen are identical, the ether is said to be **symmetrical or simple** (*e.g.* diethyl ether, diisopropyl ether) ; if these groups are different, then the ether is named as **unsymmetrical or mixed** (*e.g.* ethyl methyl ether, *tert*-butyl ethyl ether).

In cyclic ethers, oxygen is present inside the ring, they may be considered as heterocyclic compounds.

Oxirane
(Ethylene oxide)

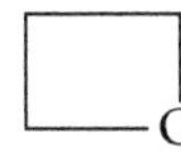

Oxetane

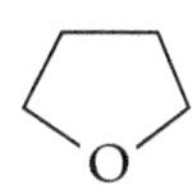

Oxalone
(Tetrahydrofuran)

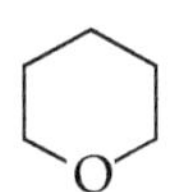

Oxane
(Tetrahydropyran)

Ethers are functional isomers of alcohols.

(*i*) CH_3OCH_3 and CH_3CH_2OH

(*ii*) $CH_3OCH_2CH_3$, $CH_3CH_2CH_2OH$ and $(CH_3)_2CHOH$

Examples of diethers and triethers (compounds containing two and three ether linkages) are

$$CH_3-O-CH_2CH_2-O-CH_3 \qquad CH_3-O-CH_2CH_2-O-CH_2CH_2-O-CH_3$$

1, 2-Dimethoxyethane   1, 4-Dioxane   Diethylene glycol dimethyl ether (Diglyme)

TEST YOUR UNDERSTANDING - 12.1

1.   Give derived and IUPAC name for the following ethers.

(*a*) $C_6H_5OCH_2CH_3$ (*b*) $(CH_3)_2CHOCH(CH_3)CH_2CH_3$ (*c*) p-$NO_2.C_6H_4OCH_3$.

2.   Write the structure of each of these ethers.

(*a*)   Chloromethyl methyl ether   (*b*)   2-(Chloromethyl) Oxirane   (*c*)   3, 4-Epoxy-1-butene.

12.2   Preparation of Ethers

The first two methods given below are used for preparing simple ethers, while the rest for mixed ethers.

1.   **By intermolecular dehydration of alcohols *or* acid catalysed condensation of alcohols.**   (For details, consult properties of alcohols). This method is limited for the preparation of those *symmetrical ethers* in which both alkyl groups are primary because in 2° and 3° alcohols, alkenes will be formed in significant amount. This is industrial method for the preparation of symmetrical ethers.

2.   **By treating alkyl halide with dry silver oxide.**

$$2(CH_3)_2CHCl + Ag_2O \longrightarrow (CH_3)_2CHOCH(CH_3)_2 + 2AgCl$$

3.   **By the acid-catalyzed addition of alcohols to alkenes.**

$$(CH_3)_2C = CH_2 + CH_3OH \xrightarrow{\text{H}^+} (CH_3)_3C.O.CH_3$$
$$\text{2-Methylpropene} \qquad\qquad\qquad \textit{tert}-\text{Butyl methyl ether*}$$

Reaction involves the protonation of alkene to form carbocation followed by attack by alcohol (nucleophile) on the more stable carbocation to form ether as final product.

***tert*-Butyl ethers as protecting group.** Reaction between isobutene and alcohol is of special significance, in the sense that the reactive alcoholic group is converted into non-reactive ether linkage, *i.e.* the alcoholic group is protected by *tert*-butyl group which can be easily removed by treating the ether with dil. aqueous acid, after carrying out the required reaction at other functional group. Consider the preparation of 4-pentyn-1-ol from 3-bromo-1-propanol and sodium acetylide. Direct reaction between them will not give the required product because the strongly basic acetylide will react first with the hydroxyl group and not with the bromine.

$$HC \equiv CH + NaOCH_2CH_2CH_2Br \xleftarrow{\text{NaC} \equiv \text{CH}} HOCH_2CH_2CH_2Br \xrightarrow{\text{NaC} \equiv \text{CH}} HOCH_2CH_2CH_2C \equiv CH$$
$$\textit{(Not formed)}$$

However, the reaction at the carbon bearing Br can be achieved by protecting the —OH group in the form of —$OCMe_3$ and then carrying the reaction as usual.

---

*   *tert*-Butyl methyl ether is added to gasoline to increase octane number.

$$HOCH_2CH_2CH_2Br \xrightarrow[\text{(ii) } CH_2=C(CH_3)_2]{\text{(i) } H_2SO_4} (CH_3)_3COCH_2CH_2CH_2Br \xrightarrow{NaC\equiv CH} (CH_3)_3COCH_2CH_2CH_2C\equiv CH$$

$$\xrightarrow{H_3O^+/H_2O} HOCH_2CH_2CH_2C\equiv CH + (CH_3)_3COH$$

4-Pentyn-1-ol

4. **By the use of diazomethane.**

This method is used for preparing only methyl ethers..

$$n\text{-}C_4H_9OH + CH_2N_2 \xrightarrow{BF_3 \text{ (Lewis acid)}} n\text{-}C_4H_9OCH_3 + N_2$$

n-Butyl methyl ether

$$C_6H_5OH + CH_2N_2 \xrightarrow{BF_3} C_6H_5OCH_3$$

Anisole

5. **By solvomercuration-demercuration of alkenes.**

We have studied oxymercuration-demercuration as a method of preparing alcohols from alkenes.

$$RCH=CH_2 \xrightarrow[\text{(ii) } NaBH_4/OH^-]{\text{(i) } Hg(OAc)_2-THF-H_2O} RCH-CH_2-H$$

OH **From water present in solvent (THF.H_2O)**

H from $NaBH_4$

Markovnikov orientation

The above reaction can be modified for preparing ethers by taking an alcohol as solvent instead of aqueous tetrahydrofuran.

$$\underset{\text{2-Phenylpropene}}{C_6H_5-\underset{CH_3}{\overset{}{C}}=CH_2} \xrightarrow[\text{(ii) } NaBH_4/OH^-]{\text{(i) } Hg(OAc)_2, CH_3OH} \underset{\text{2-Methoxy-2-phenylpropane}}{C_6H_5-\underset{CH_3}{\overset{OCH_3}{C}}-CH_3}$$

TEST YOUR UNDERSTANDING - 12.2

1. Reaction between allyl alcohol and isopropanol gives a good yield of a mixed ether. Write down its structure and explain its formation in quantitative yield.

2. Complete the reactions, giving the position of labelled oxygen in the product.

$$(CH_3)_3C^{18}OH + CH_3OH \xrightarrow{conc.H_2SO_4} \text{Ether} + \text{Water.}$$

3. Give mechanism involved in the following reaction.

$$\text{(cyclohexane with } CH=CH_2) + CH_3OH \xrightarrow{H_2SO_4} \text{A mixture of ethers}$$

4. Complete the following reaction.

$$\text{(alkene)} \xrightarrow[H_2SO_4]{C_2H_5OH} \text{Major product.}$$

5. Show how each of the following ethers can be prepared by solvomercuration-demercuration process.

(a) $\underset{CH_3}{\overset{}{C_6H_5CHOCH_2CH_2CH_3}}$

(b) $\underset{OCH_2CH_3}{\overset{}{CH_3CHCH_2CH_2CH_2CH_3}}$

(c) $\underset{OCH_3}{\overset{}{(CH_3)_3C.CHCH_3}}$

(d) $\underset{OC_2H_5}{\overset{}{\text{(cyclopropyl)}CHCH_2CH_3}}$

6. Write the structure of the ether obtained by solvomercuration-demercuration process ?

(a) $\text{(cyclohexene)} \xrightarrow[\text{(ii) } NaBH_4/OH^-]{\text{(i) } Hg(OAc)_2, \text{ } iso\text{-}C_3H_7OH}$

(b) $\text{(alkene)} \xrightarrow[\text{(ii) } NaBH_4/OH^-]{\text{(i) } Hg(OAc), \text{ } C_6H_5OH}$

6.   **Williamson synthesis.** Williamson synthesis involves the reaction of a sodium alkoxide with an alkyl halide, alkyl sulphonate, or dialkyl sulphate.

$$R—ONa + X—R' \longrightarrow R—O—R' + Na—X$$

where   X = Cl, Br, I, OSO_2R'',   or OSO_2OR''

$$(CH_3)_2CHOH \xrightarrow{\text{Na or NaH}} (CH_3)_2CHO^-Na^+ \xrightarrow{CH_3CH_2I} (CH_3)_2CHOCH_2CH_3$$
Ethyl isopropyl ether

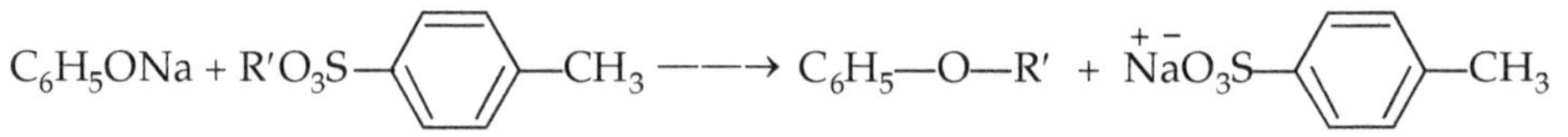

Williamson synthesis can be applied for the synthesis of symmetrical as well as unsymmetrical ethers. It follows S_N2 path, hence it is most successful when the alkyl halide, sulphonate, or sulphate is primary (or methyl). If the alkyl halide (substrate) is tertiary or secondary they react with alkoxide base by E2 elimination rather than by S_N2 substitution. Thus if we want to prepare *tert*-butyl ether, we must take *tert*-butyl group in the form of alkoxide rather than halide,

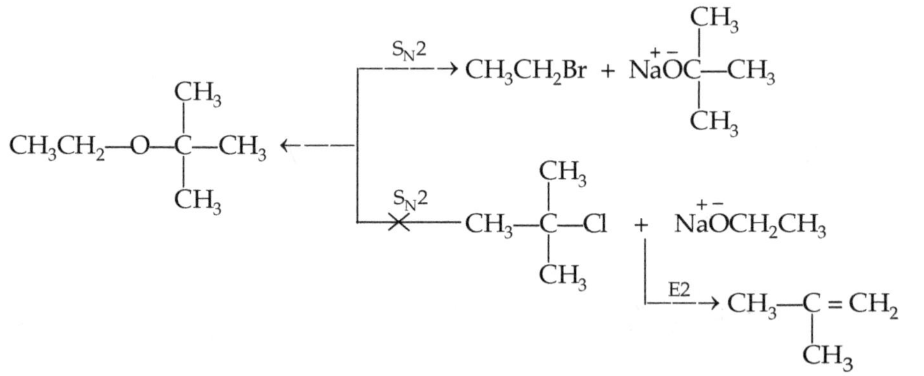

Isobutene

Note that the alkoxides as well as alkyl halides are prepared from alcohols, we can say that the Williamson synthesis ultimately involves the synthesis of an ether from two alcohols.

TEST YOUR UNDERSTANDING - 12.3

1.   Choose the correct combination of alkyl halide and alkoxide for the preparation of each of the following ethers by the Williamson synthesis.

    (*i*) $CH_2 = CHCH_2OCH(CH_3)_2$ (*ii*)   (cyclopentyl)$-OCH_2CH_3$ (*iii*)   (cyclohexyl)$-OCH_2CH_3$

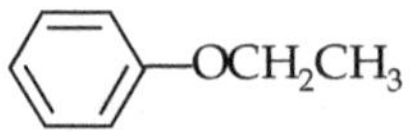

2.   (*a*)   Rank the following alkyl halides in decreasing order of reactivity in the Williamson synthesis.

        Me_3CCH_2Br (A), $ClCH_2CH = CH_2$ (B), $ClCH_2CH_2CH_3$ (C), $BrCH_2CH_2CH_3$ (D).

    (*b*)   Among the three methods for preparing ethers, *viz.* intermolecular dehydration, alkoxymercuration-demercuration and Williamson synthesis, which can best be used for preparing following ethers.

        (*i*) Cyclohexyl ether   (*ii*) $CH_3(CH_2)_2OCH_2CH_3$ (*iii*) $CH_3CH_2\overset{\overset{\displaystyle CH_3}{|}}{C}HOC_3H_7\text{-}n$

12.3 Structure and Physical Properties

1. Like water, the central oxygen atom of ethers is sp^3 hybridised. Hence bonding in ethers can best be understood by comparing ethers (R—O—R) with water (H—O—H) and alcohols (R—O—H). In ether, van der Waals strain involving alkyl groups causes the bond angle at oxygen to be larger than in alcohols, which in turn is larger than in water. An extreme example is di-*tert*-butyl ether, where steric hindrance between the bulky *tert*-butyl groups increases the C—O—C bond angle to a larger extent.

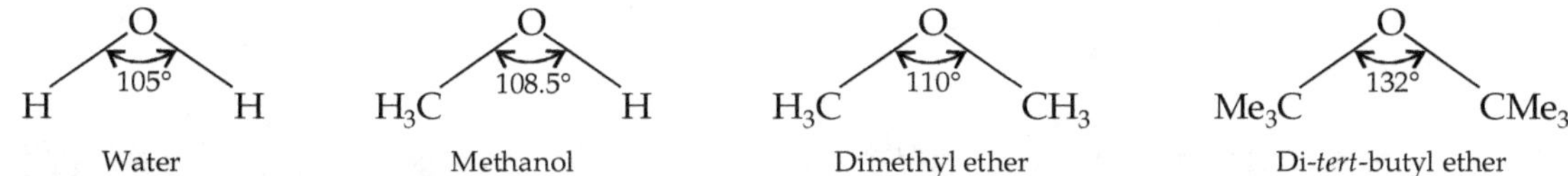

Water   Methanol   Dimethyl ether   Di-*tert*-butyl ether

2. Since the C—O—C bond angle is not 180°, the dipole moments of the two C—O bonds do not cancel each other, hence ethers possess a small net dipole moment, *e.g.* 1.18 D for diethyl ether.

3. Boiling points of ethers are comparable with those hydrocarbons of the same molecular weight. However, boiling points of ethers are much lower than those of comparable alcohols, because alcohol molecules can associate with each other through H-bonding, while ether molecules cannot.

4. Although ethers are not able to form H-bond with themselves, they are able to form hydrogen bonds with water, hence ethers are nearly as much soluble, in water, as alcohols of comparable molecular weight.

12.4 Chemical Properties

Ethers are one of the least reactive functional groups. Dialkyl ethers react with very few reagents other than acids. Ethers resist attack by nucleophiles and by bases. This lack of reactivity, coupled with the ability of ethers to solvate cations, by donating an electron pair from their oxygen atom, makes ethers especially useful as solvents for many reactions. Diethyl ether, used as solvent in the preparation of Grignard reagent, must be free of traces of water and alcohol. This so-called **absolute ether** can be prepared by distilling ordinary ether over conc. H_2SO_4, which removes water, alcohol and peroxides, followed by storing over metallic sodium. The only reactive sites in a molecule of dialkyl ether are the C—H bonds of the alkyl groups and the $-\ddot{O}-$ group of the ether linkage.

1. Due to the presence of unshared electron pairs on oxygen, ethers are basic and hence react with proton donors (*e.g.* HCl, HBr, H_2SO_4) to form oxonium salts.

$$CH_3CH_2\overset{..}{\underset{..}{O}}CH_2CH_3 \; + \; HBr \; \underset{\longleftarrow}{\overset{\text{Low temp.}}{\rightleftharpoons}} \; CH_3CH_2-\overset{..+}{\underset{\underset{H}{|}}{O}}-CH_2CH_3Br^-$$

Diethyl ether   Diethyl ether oxonium bromide

The oxonium salts are stable only at low temperature and in a strongly acidic medium. On dilution, they decompose to give back the original ether and acid.

2. **Formation of peroxides -** On standing in contact with air, ethers are converted into unstable peroxides *which are highly explosive* even in low concentrations. Hence *ether is always purified before distillation.* Purification (removal of peroxide) can be done by washing ether with a solution of ferrous salt (which reduces peroxide to alcohols, ROOH $\longrightarrow$ ROH) or by distillation with conc. H_2SO_4 (which oxidises peroxides).

The presence of peroxides in ether is indicated by formation of red colour when ether is shaken with an aqueous solution of ferrors ammonium sulphate and potassium thiocyanate. The peroxide oxidises Fe^{2+} to Fe^{3+} which reacts with thiocyanate ion to give red colour of ferric thiocyanate.

$$\text{Peroxide} + Fe^{2+} \longrightarrow Fe^{3+} \xrightarrow{\;CNS^-\;} \underset{\text{Red}}{Fe(CNS)_3}$$

However, the formation of peroxide is prevented by adding a little Cu_2O to it.

$$CH_3CH_2OCH_2CH_3 + O_2 \longrightarrow CH_3\underset{\underset{\textstyle OOH}{|}}{C}HOCH_2CH_3$$

1-Ethoxyethyl hydroperoxide

The reaction is free-radical, and oxidation occurs at the α-carbon atom.

Combustion of ethers gives CO_2 and H_2O.

$$CH_3CH_2OCH_2CH_3 + 6O_2 \longrightarrow 4CO_2 + 5H_2O$$

TEST YOUR UNDERSTANDING - 12.4

1. Does peroxide formation occur more rapidly with $(RCH_2)O$ or $(R_2CH)_2O$?

2. Why do free-radical substitution reactions of ethers occur preferentially on the α-carbon ?

3. **Acid-catalyzed cleavage of ethers.** As in alcohols, the carbon-oxygen bond of ethers is cleaved by reaction with hydrogen halides.

$$R—O—R' + HX \longrightarrow R—OH + R'—X$$

Reactivity of HX : HI > HBr >> HCl.

$$CH_3OCH_2CH_3 + HI \longrightarrow CH_3I + HOCH_2CH_3$$

However, when excess of HX is used, the alcohol formed as one of the products is subsequently converted into an alkyl halide, and thus the reaction typically leads to two alkyl halide molecules. Cleavage of ethers takes place only under vigorous conditions, *viz.* use of concentrated acids (HI or HBr) and at high temperature.

$$CH_3.CH.CH_2CH_3 \xrightarrow[\text{heat}]{HBr} CH_3 CHCH_2CH_3 + CH_3Br$$

$|$ $|$ Bromomethane

OCH_3 Br

sec-Butyl methyl ether   2-Bromobutane

$$\xrightarrow[150°C]{HI} ICH_2CH_2CH_2CH_2I$$

Tetrahydrofuran   1, 4-Diiodobutane

Reaction of ethers with HI forms the basis of **Zeisel method** for the detection and estimation of alkoxy group in a compound.

$$R'-O-CH_3 + HI \longrightarrow CH_3I \xrightarrow{AgNO_3} AgI + CH_3NO_3$$

Thus, moles of $-OCH_3$ = moles of AgI

$$\% \text{ of } -OCH_3 \text{ group} = \frac{31 \times \text{Wt. of AgI} \times 100}{\text{Mol. mass of AgI} \times \text{Wt. of ether}}$$

Mechanism. It is similar to reaction of alcohols with hydrogen halide in presence of acid to form alkyl halides ($ROH + HX \longrightarrow RX$), *i.e.* S_N1 or S_N2 depending upon the nature of the alkyl group.

$$R\text{—}O\text{—}R' + HI \xrightarrow[(-I^-)]{} R\overset{\oplus}{\underset{H}{\text{—}O\text{—}}}R' \xrightarrow[(-R'OH)]{} R^{\oplus} \xrightarrow{I^-} R\text{—}I \quad (S_N^1 \text{ when R is } 3°)$$

$$\downarrow I^-$$

$$I^-\ldots\ldots R\ldots\ldots\underset{H}{\overset{}{O\text{—}}}R' \longrightarrow I\text{—}R + HO\text{—}R' \qquad (S_N^2 \text{ when R is } 1°)$$

On heating with sulphuric acid, ethers give alkyl hydrogen sulphate.

$$C_2H_5OC_2H_5 + H_2SO_4 \xrightarrow{heat} C_2H_5OH + C_2H_5HSO_4$$

4. **Hydrolysis of ethers**. Ethers, when treated with dil. aqueous acid, give alcohols.

$$R\text{—}O\text{—}R \xrightarrow{H_3O^+/H_2O} 2ROH$$

$$CH_3CH_2OC(CH_3)_3 \xrightarrow{H_3O^+/H_2O} CH_3CH_2OH + HOC(CH_3)_3$$

5. **Halogenation** (action of chlorine or bromine). In dark, substitution occurs at α-carbon atoms, while in presence of light all hydrogen atoms are substituted to form perhalo (fully halogenated) ether.

$$CH_3CH_2OCH_2CH_3 \xrightarrow{\underset{dark}{Cl_2}} CH_3\overset{\overset{\displaystyle Cl}{|}}{C}HO\overset{\overset{\displaystyle Cl}{|}}{C}HCH_3 \xrightarrow{\underset{light}{Cl_2}} CCl_3.CCl_2\text{—}O\text{—}CCl_2.CCl_3$$

$$\text{Perchlorodiethyl ether}$$

6. **Action of phosphorus pentachloride.**

$$R\text{—}O\text{—}R' + PCl_5 \longrightarrow RCl + R'Cl + POCl_3$$

TEST YOUR UNDERSTANDING - 12.5

1. (*i*)   Why HI is considered as a better reagent that HBr for the reaction ?

$$R\text{—}O\text{—}R + HX \longrightarrow R\text{—}OH + RX$$

(*ii*)   Di-*tert* butyl ether is rapidly cleaved by HCl and that too at room temperature.

2. Identify A in the following reaction.

(*a*) $B \xleftarrow[\text{HI, ether}]{\text{anhydrous}} CH_3OC(CH_3)_3 \xrightarrow{\text{aq. HI}} A$ (*b*) $C_6H_5\text{—}O\text{—}CH_3 + HI \longrightarrow C + D$

(*c*) $CH_3\overset{\overset{\displaystyle OCH_3}{|}}{C}HCH_2CH_3 \xrightarrow{\text{conc. HI}}$

3. Assign the structure to the three ethers, which when treated with excess of hydrogen bromide gave following results.

(*a*)   One gave only benzyl bromide

(*b*)   Other gave a mixture of bromocyclopentane and 1-bromobutne

(*c*)   The third gave one mole of 1, 5-dibromopentane per mole of ether.

4. An ether A of the formula $C_6H_{14}O$ when treated with PCl_5 gives two chlorides which on treatment with aqueous NaOH give corresponding alcohols B and C. Both alcohols respond haloform test. B, when treated with sodium hypoiodite followed by acidic hydrolysis gives ethanoic acid. Give structures of the ether A and alcohols B and C.

EPOXIDES (OXIRANES)

12.5   Nomenclature

Epoxides are cyclic ethers with three-membered rings. At one time, these were named as oxides of alkenes. IUPAC nomenclature. these are called **oxiranes,** while according to substitutive IUPAC nomenclature, these are named *epoxy derivatives of alkanes.*

Common name	:	Ethylene oxide	Propylene oxide
IUPAC name	:	Oxirane	2-Methyloxirane
Substitutive IUPAC name	:	Epoxyethane	1, 2-Epoxypropane

However, substitutive IUPAC names are the widely used names.

1, 2-Epoxycyclohexane   2-Methyl-2, 3-epoxybutane

12.6   Preparation

1.   Epoxides are commonly prepared by the **oxidation of alkenes by peroxy acids** (also called per acid), *e.g.* peroxybenzoic acid ($C_6H_5CO_3H$), peroxyacetic acid (CH_3CO_3H), etc. This process is known as **epoxidation.**

$$\text{C} = \text{C} \;+\; \text{R}-\overset{\text{O}}{\underset{}{\text{C}}}-\text{O}-\text{O}-\text{H} \longrightarrow \text{C}-\text{C}\;(\text{O}) \;+\; \text{R}-\overset{\text{O}}{\underset{}{\text{C}}}-\text{OH}$$

$$CH_2 = CH(CH_2)_9CH_3 \;+\; CH_3COOOH \longrightarrow CH_2-CH(CH_2)_9CH_3 \;+\; CH_3COOH$$

1-Dodecene   1, 2-Epoxydecane

Cyclopentene   + C_6H_5COOOH $\longrightarrow$ 1,2-Epoxycyclopentane   + C_6H_5COOH

(*i*)   Epoxidation of alkenes with peroxy acids involves *syn* addition to the double bond.

cis-2-Butene   + RCOOOH $\longrightarrow$ *cis*-2, 3-Dimethyloxirane (a *meso* compound)

trans-2-Butene   + RCOOOH $\longrightarrow$ *trans*-2, 3-Dimethyloxiranes (racemic)

(ii) Presence of electron-releasing alkyl groups on the double bond increases the rate of epoxidation, suggesting that the peroxy acid acts as an electrophile towards he alkene.

$$(CH_3)_2C = CHCH_3 > (CH_3)_2C = CH_2 > CH_3CH = CH_2 > CH_2 = CH_2 \quad \textbf{(Rate of epoxidation)}$$

2.　Base catalysed cyclization of vicinal chlorohydrins

$$R_2C = CR_2 \xrightarrow{Cl_2, H_2O} \underset{\overset{|}{HO}\ \overset{|}{Cl}}{R_2C-CR_2} \xrightarrow{OH^-} R_2C\underset{O}{\diagdown\diagup}CR_2$$

This method can be used for preparing 5- and 6-membered oxygen containing heterocyclic compounds.

$$\underset{\underset{Cl\ \ \ OH}{\overset{|}{CH_2}\ \ \overset{|}{CH_2}}}{\overset{CH_2-CH_2}{\diagup\ \ \ \ \diagdown}} \xrightarrow{NaOH} \underset{\underset{Cl\ \ \diagdown O}{\overset{|}{CH_2}\ \ \overset{|}{CH_2}}}{\overset{CH_2-CH_2}{\diagup\ \ \ \ \diagdown}} \longrightarrow \underset{\underset{O}{\overset{|}{CH_2}\ \ \ \overset{|}{CH_2}}}{\overset{CH_2-CH_2}{\diagup\ \ \ \ \ \diagdown}} + Cl^-$$

Tetrahydrofuran

TEST YOUR UNDERSTANDING - 12.6

1.　*(a)*　Give IUPAC name of the following expoxide,

H　O　H

(b)　also draw the structure of the alkene from which this important sex attractant (disparlure) can be prepared.

2.　Give two methods for converting propylene to 1, 2-epoxypropane.

12.7　Properties

Epoxides react rapidly with nucleophiles under conditions in which ordinary ethers are inert. This enhanced reactivity is due to highly strained three membered ring which is opened up during reaction and thus strain is relieved.

1.　Acid-catalyzed cleavage of ethers.

These reactions either involve an acid as a reactant or occur under conditions of acid catalysis.

$$\underset{O}{\overset{|\ \ \ |}{-C-C-}} + H^+ \rightleftharpoons \underset{\underset{H}{\overset{\oplus}{O}}}{\overset{|\ \ \ |}{-C-C-}} \xrightarrow{Z:} \underset{\underset{OH}{}}{\overset{|\ \ \overset{Z}{|}}{-C-C-}}$$

Protonated epoxide

Where : Z is a nucleophile, *e.g.* Br⁻ or solvent like H_2O, CH_3OH, etc.

$$\underset{O}{\overset{CH_2-CH_2}{\diagdown\diagup}} + HBr \longrightarrow \underset{\underset{Br\ \ \ \ OH}{\overset{|}{CH_2}-\overset{|}{CH_2}}}{}$$

2-Bromoethanol

$$\underset{O}{\overset{CH_2-CH_2}{\diagdown\diagup}} + C_2H_5OH \xrightarrow{H^+} \underset{\underset{OH\ \ \ \ OC_2H_5}{\overset{|}{CH_2}-\overset{|}{CH_2}}}{}$$

2-Ethoxyethanol

$$\underset{O}{\overset{CH_2-CH_2}{\diagdown\diagup}} + H_2O \xrightarrow{H^+} \underset{\underset{OH\ \ \ \ OH}{\overset{|}{CH_2}-\overset{|}{CH_2}}}{}$$

1, 2-Ethanediol

In the acid-catalyzed ring opening of an unsymmetrical epoxide, the nucleophile attacks primarily at the more substituted carbon atom. For example,

$$CH_3OH \; + \; (CH_3)_2C\!-\!\!CH_2 \quad \xrightarrow{\; HA \;} \quad (CH_3)_2C\!-\!CH_2OH$$

with the epoxide O bridge shown between the two carbons and OCH_3 below the left carbon.

Attack of nucleophile on the more highly substituted carbon atom is because of the fact that such atom of the protonated epoxide acquires a considerable positive charge and thus resembles like a more stable 3° or 2° carbocation and hence the reaction is S_N^1 like.

$$CH_3\!-\!\overset{\overset{\displaystyle CH_3}{|}}{\underset{\underset{\displaystyle CH_3\ddot{O}H}{+}}{C}}\!-\!CH_2 \longrightarrow CH_3\!-\!\overset{\overset{\displaystyle CH_3}{|}}{\underset{\underset{\displaystyle {}_+^{}OCH_3}{|}}{C}}\!-\!CH_2OH \xrightarrow[(-H^+)]{} CH_3\!-\!\overset{\overset{\displaystyle CH_3}{|}}{\underset{\underset{\displaystyle OCH_3}{|}}{C}}\!-\!CH_2OH$$

Thus alkenes can be easily converted to 1, 2,-diols by epoxidation followed by hydrolysis. This is a stereoselective reaction and the 1, 2-diols formed correspond to *anti*-addition to the carbon-carbon double bond (Similarity with the hydroxylation of alkenes by peroxyformic acid, but different with the hydroxylation of alkenes by permanganate or by osmium tetroxide which involves *syn*-addition).

2.   **Base-catalyzed cleavage of ethers.** Unlike ordinary ethers, epoxides can also undergo base-catalyzed ring opening, provided the attacking nucleophile is a strong base like alkoxide, phenoxide, ammonia, etc. Here the nucleophile attacks on the less substituted carbon atom which is least hindered to form alkoxide ion which is then protonated.

$$R\!-\!\ddot{O}\!:^- \; + \; H_2C\!-\!\!CHCH_3 \longrightarrow ROCH_2\overset{}{\underset{\underset{\displaystyle O_-}{|}}{C}}HCH_3 \xrightarrow{\; ROH \;} ROCH_2\overset{}{\underset{\underset{\displaystyle OH}{|}}{C}}HCH_3 \; + \; RO^-$$

A strong nucleophile is able to open the strained epoxide ring in a direct S_N2 reaction.

$$C_2H_5ONa \; + \; CH_2\!-\!\!CHCH_3 \longrightarrow C_2H_5OCH_2\overset{}{\underset{\underset{\displaystyle OH}{|}}{C}}HCH_3$$

1-Ethoxy-2-propanol

$$NH_3 \; + \; CH_2\!-\!\!CH_2 \longrightarrow H_2NCH_2CH_2OH$$

2-Aminoethanol

$$CH_3CH_2CH_2SK \; + \; CH_2\!-\!\!CH_2 \longrightarrow CH_3CH_2CH_2SCH_2CH_2OH$$

2-(Propylthio) ethanol

3.   **Cleavage of ethers by Grignard reagents and lithium aluminium hydride.** In case of Grignard reagent, the nucleophilic end *i.e.* R part attacks on the carbon atom of the epoxide. This cleavage is also regioselective because here the nucleophile attacks at the less substituted ring carbon.

$$C_6H_5MgBr \; + \; H_2C\!-\!\!CHCH_3 \xrightarrow[\text{(ii) } H_3O^+]{\text{(i) diethyl ether}} C_6H_5CH_2\overset{}{\underset{\underset{\displaystyle OH}{|}}{C}}HCH_3$$

1-Phenyl-2-propanol

Thus this reaction is used for the preparation of alcohols having at least two carbon atoms more than the Grignard reagent.

Epoxides are reduced to alcohols on treatment with lithium aluminium hydride ; hydride ion is transferred to the less crowded carbon.

$$H_2C\!-\!\!CH(CH_2)_7CH_3 \xrightarrow[\text{(ii) } H_2O]{\text{(i) } LiAlH_4} CH_3\overset{}{\underset{\underset{\displaystyle OH}{|}}{C}}H(CH_2)_7CH_3$$

1, 2-Epoxydecane   2-Decanol

TEST YOUR UNDERSTANDING - 12.7

1. Which alkene, *cis-* or *trans-*2-butene, would give *meso-*2, 3-butanediol

   (*a*) by epoxidation followed by acid-catalysed hydrolysis, and (*b*) by osmium tetroxide hydroxylation ?

2. Write down the product formed by treating each of the following epoxide with HI.

   (*a*) 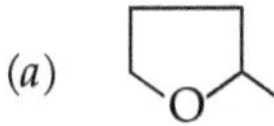   (*b*) 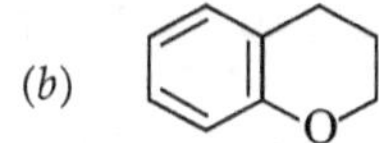   (*c*) 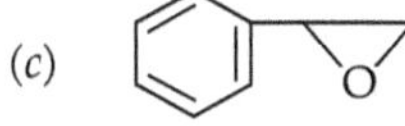

3. What is the principal product formed in the reaction of ethylene oxide with each of the following ?

   (*a*)   NaOH in water   (*b*)   NaCN in water   (*c*) NaN_3 (sodium azide) in water

   (*d*)   Phenyllithium in ether, followed by addition of dil. H_2SO_4 (*e*)   1-Butynylsodium in liq. NH_3.

4. Predict the chief product of each of the following reactions.

   (*a*)   Propylene oxide + NH_3 (*b*)   Trimethylene oxide + HCl   (*c*)   Ethylene oxide in presence of acid.

5. Provide structure to the final product.

$$CH_3CH = CH_2 \xrightarrow{CF_3CO_3H} [A] \xrightarrow{DCl} [B] \xrightarrow{H_2O} [C].$$

6. Give the second reactant for the following conversions.

   (*a*)   3-Methyl-1-butanol from ethylene oxide   (*b*)   1-Phenylcyclohexanol from 1-phenylcyclohexene oxide.

7. Write down the structures of the alcohols obtained in the following reactions.

Example 1 :

3-Methylbutene is converted to ethers via following three different routes. Identify the ether in each case.

(a) $\xrightarrow[\text{(ii) }CH_2N_2/HBF_4^-]{\text{(i) }H_3O^+}$ [A]   **(b)** $\xrightarrow[\text{(ii) }H_2O_2/OH^-]{\text{(i) }BH_3 \cdot THF}$ [ ] $\xrightarrow[\text{HBF}_4^-]{CH_2N_2}$ [B]

(c) $\xrightarrow[\text{(ii) }NaBH_4/OH^-]{\text{(I) }Hg(OAc)_2/CH_3OH}$ [C].

Solution :

(*a*)   Here alcohol is formed by simple hydration which leads to Markovnikov's product with rearranged carbocation; alcohol is then converted to methyl ether by diazomethane.

(*b*)   Here alcohol is formed by hydroboration-oxidation method which leads to *anti-*Markovnikov addition without rearrangement, the alcohol so formed is then converted to methyl ether by diazomethane.

(*c*)   Here ether is formed by solvomercuration-demercuration process according to Markovnikov addition without rearrangement.

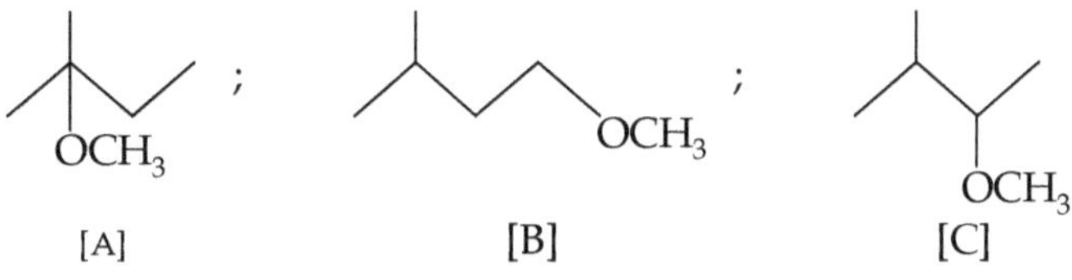

Example 2 :

Give steps involved in the following reaction.

$$OHCH_2CH_2CH_2CH_2Cl \xrightarrow{OH^-} \text{(tetrahydrofuran)}$$

Solution :

(A)

Note that the intermediate (A) acts both as an alkoxide group as well as a halide, hence intramolecular cyclization (Williamson synthesis) takes place forming cyclic compound.

Example 3 :

Give necessary steps involved in the following conversions.

(a) $CH_2 = CHC(CH_3)_2OH \longrightarrow BrCH_2CH_2C(CH_3)_2OH$ (b) $HOCH_2C \equiv CH \longrightarrow HOCH_2C \equiv CCH_3$

(c) $HOCH_2C(CH_3)_2CH_2Br \longrightarrow HOCH_2C(CH_3)_2CH_2D.$

Solution :

(a)   Although the reaction involves simply addition of HBr in presence of peroxide, the direct reaction will also involve conversion of allylic —OH group to Br, so OH must first be protected.

(b)   Here also CH_3 group can't be directly introduced in place of acetylenic hydrogen atom, because this will lead to conversion of OH to reactive alkoxide ion. Hence OH group must first be protected, here benzyl group can't be used as protecting group because this will lead to reduction of the $C \equiv C$ bond during catalytic hydrogenation required for removing the protecting benzyl group (as in above example). Hence trimethylsilyl group is used for protecting the OH group.

$$HOCH_2C \equiv CH + \underset{\text{Chlorotrimethylsilane}}{M_3SiCl} \xrightarrow{\text{amine base}} Me_3Si—OCH_2C \equiv CH$$

$$\xrightarrow[\text{(ii) CH}_3\text{I}]{\text{(i) BuLi}} Me_3Si—OCH_2C \equiv CCH_3 \xrightarrow{\text{mild H}^+} Me_3Si—OH + HOCH_2C \equiv CCH_3$$

(c)   Here also OH group must first be protected to avoid its reaction with Grignard reagent formed during main reaction.

Example 4 :

Identify A to D in the following reactions.

(a) [structure] $\xrightarrow[\text{NaBH}_4/\text{OH}^-]{\text{Hg(OAc)}_2 \,.\, \text{(CH}_3\text{)}_2\text{CHOH}}$ **[A]**

(b) [structure] $\xrightarrow[\text{NaBH}_4/\text{OH}^-]{\text{Hg(OAc)}_2/\text{Phenol}}$ **[B]**

(c) [structure] $\xrightarrow[\text{H}_2\text{O}_2/\text{OH}^-]{\text{BH}_3 \,.\, \text{THF}}$ **[C]** $\xrightarrow[\text{heat}]{\text{NaOH}}$ **[D]**

Solution :

[A]   [B]   [C]   [D]

Example 5 :

An ether of the molecular formula $C_5H_{12}O$ when treated with phosphorus pentachloride gives two compounds B and C. B when refluxed with metallic sodium in presence of ether gives *n*-butane, while C on similar treatment gives, 1, 1, 2, 2-tetramethylethane. Deduce the structure of A and, explain the formation of hydrocarbons from compounds B and C.

Solution :

In such cases, students are advised to sketch a map of the complete problem as below.

$$C_5H_{12}O \xrightarrow{\text{PCl}_5} \quad B \quad + \quad C$$

Na/ether ↓   Na/ether ↓

Structures of the hydrocarbons formed indicates that one alkyl group of ether is normal (unbranched) and the other is branched. Since products have 4 + 6 = 10 carbon atoms, it indicates that the chlorides B (having 2 carbon atoms) and C (having 3 carbon atoms) have undergone Wurtz reaction to form higher hydrocarbons. Hence the ether should be $CH_3CH_2OHC(CH_3)_2$.

[structure] $(C_5H_{12}O, \text{ether})$ $\xrightarrow{\text{PCl}_5}$ [B] + [C]

↓   ↓

n-Butane   1, 1, 2, 2-Tetramethylethane

Example 6 :

Complete the following giving importance to configuration of the compounds A, B and C.

$$[C] \xleftarrow[\text{(ii) } C_2H_5Br]{\text{(i) Na}} \quad \underset{\text{(R)-2-Octanol}}{\overset{C_6H_{13}}{\underset{CH_3}{H-\overset{|}{\underset{|}{C}}-OH}}} \quad \xrightarrow[\substack{\text{Solvent of low} \\ \text{dielectric constant}}]{HBr} [A] \xrightarrow{C_2H_5ONa} [B].$$

Solution :

In the reaction of alcohol with metallic sodium, since no bond to the chiral carbon is cleaved the product (C) will have R configuration. However, reaction of alcohol with HBr in solvent of low dielectric constant follows S_N^2 mechanism, the chiral carbon is inverted, *i.e.* product will have S configuration. Further attack by $C_2H_5O^-$ is also an S_N^2 reaction, again inverted product [B] will be obtained. Thus the net result of two inversions is retention of configuration.

$$\underset{\substack{[C] \\ (R)}}{\overset{C_6H_{13}}{\underset{CH_3}{H-\overset{|}{\underset{|}{C}}-OC_2H_5}}} \xleftarrow[\text{(ii) } C_2H_5Br]{\text{(i) Na}} \underset{\substack{\text{(R)-2-Octanol} \\ (R)}}{\overset{C_6H_{13}}{\underset{CH_3}{H-\overset{|}{\underset{|}{C}}-OH}}} \xrightarrow{HBr} \underset{\substack{[A] \\ (S)}}{\overset{C_6H_{13}}{\underset{CH_3}{Br-\overset{|}{\underset{|}{C}}-H}}} \xrightarrow{C_2H_5ONa} \underset{\substack{[B] \\ (R)}}{\overset{C_6H_{13}}{\underset{CH_3}{H-\overset{|}{\underset{|}{C}}-OC_2H_5}}}$$

Example 7 :

Supply structures for compounds (A) to (C)

$$(CH_3)_3CBr + \text{alc. KOH} \longrightarrow [A] \xrightarrow{HOCl} [B] \xrightarrow{NaCl} [C]$$

Solution :

$$\underset{(A)}{(CH_3)_2C = CH_2} \qquad \underset{(B)}{\underset{\quad OH\;\;Cl}{(CH_3)_2C{-}CH_2}} \qquad \underset{(C)}{(CH_3)_2C\underset{O}{\overset{}{\diagdown\diagup}}CH_2}$$

Example 8 :

Complete the following reactions and identify the end product in each case ?

(a)   (epoxide) $\xrightarrow{C_2H_5OH,\ H^+}$ [A] $\xrightarrow{\text{(epoxide)},\ H^+}$ [B]

(b) $H_2O \xrightarrow{\text{(epoxide)},\ H^+}$ [C] $\xrightarrow{\text{(epoxide)},\ H^+}$ [D] $\xrightarrow{\text{(epoxide)},\ H^+}$ [E]

Solution :

All steps of these reactions involve acid-catalyzed cleavage of ethers.

(a)   (epoxide) $\xrightarrow[H^+]{C_2H_5OH}$ $\underset{[A]}{C_2H_5OCH_2CH_2OH}$ $\xrightarrow{\text{(epoxide)},\ H^+}$ $\underset{[B]}{C_2H_5OCH_2CH_2OCH_2CH_2OH}$

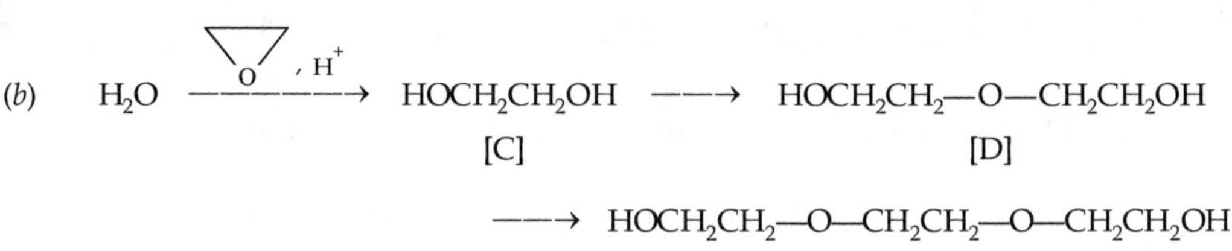

(b) $H_2O \xrightarrow[\triangle O, H^+]{} HOCH_2CH_2OH \longrightarrow HOCH_2CH_2—O—CH_2CH_2OH$

$\qquad\qquad\qquad\qquad\qquad$ [C] $\qquad\qquad\qquad\qquad\qquad\qquad$ [D]

$\longrightarrow HOCH_2CH_2—O—CH_2CH_2—O—CH_2CH_2OH$

Triethylene glycol [E]

Example 9 :

Supply the missing reagent or organic compound in the following series of reactions.

$$CH_3CH\overset{O}{\underset{\triangle}{-}}CH_2 \xrightarrow{[A]} [B] \xrightarrow{CH_3I} CH_3\underset{OCH_3}{CH}CH_2C \equiv CCH_3 \xrightarrow{H_2/Pd/BaSO_4} [C].$$

Solution :

Proceed backward from the given structure

$$CH_3\underset{OCH_3}{CH}CH_2C \equiv CCH_3 \xleftarrow{CH_3I} CH_3\underset{O^-}{CH}CH_2C \equiv CCH_3 \xleftarrow[{[A]}]{^-C \equiv CCH_3} CH_3CH\overset{O}{-}CH_2$$

$$\qquad\qquad\qquad\qquad\qquad\qquad\qquad [B]$$

$$\Big\downarrow H_2/Pd$$

$$cis\text{-}CH_3\underset{OCH_3}{CH}CH_2CH = CHCH_3$$

$$[C]$$

Example 10 :

Propose mechanism for the following reaction.

$$ClCH_2 - \overset{O}{\underset{}{CH - \overset{14}{CH_2}}} \xrightarrow{C_2H_5ONa} H_2C - \overset{O}{\underset{}{CH - \overset{14}{CH_2}}} -OC_2H_5$$

Solution :

Ethoxide ion attacks the epoxide ring at the primary carbon because it is less hindered.

$$ClCH_2 - \overset{O}{\underset{}{CH - \overset{14}{CH_2}}} \xrightarrow{^-OC_2H_5} Cl - CH_2 - \underset{-O}{CH} - \overset{14}{C}H_2OC_2H_5 \longrightarrow \overset{O}{\underset{}{CH_2 - CH - \overset{14}{CH_2}}} - OC_2H_5 + Cl^-$$

Example 11 :

Give necessary steps involved in the conversion of benzene to 1, 2-diphenylethanol through styrene.

Solution :

First, we will have to convert benzene to styrene, $C_6H_5CH = CH_2$

$$C_6H_6 + CH_3CH_2Cl \xrightarrow{AlCl_3} C_6H_5CH_2CH_3 \xrightarrow{NBS} C_6H_5CHBrCH_3 \xrightarrow{alc.\ KOH} C_6H_5CH = CH_2$$

$$\qquad\qquad\qquad\qquad\qquad\qquad\qquad\qquad\qquad\qquad\qquad\qquad\qquad Styrene$$

$$\xrightarrow{C_6H_5CO_3H} C_6H_5CH\overset{O}{-}CH_2 \xrightarrow[(ii)\ H_3O^+]{(i)\ C_6H_5MgBr} C_6H_5CH_2\underset{OH}{CH}C_6H_5$$

$$\qquad\qquad\qquad\qquad\qquad\qquad\qquad\qquad\qquad 1,\ 2\text{-Diphenylethanol}$$

GLYCOLS OR DIOLS

Alcohols containing two hydroxyl groups are commonly called **glycols.** In IUPAC substitutive system, they are named as **diols.**

$$
\begin{array}{ccc}
CH_2 - CH_2 & CH_3\,CH - CH_2 & CH_2\,CH_2\,CH_2 \\
|\quad\quad | & |\quad\quad | & |\quad\quad\quad | \\
OH\quad\ OH & OH\quad OH & OH\quad\quad OH
\end{array}
$$

Common Name :   Ethylene glycol   Propylene glycol   Trimethylene glycol
IUPAC Name   :   1, 2-Ethanediol   1, 2-Propanediol   1, 3-Propanediol

12.9   Preparation

1.   **Oxidation of alkenes.** Of the numerous oxidizing agent that bring about hydroxylation, two of the most commonly used are (*a*) cold alkaline potassium permanganate (also known as *Baeyer's reagent*) and (*b*) peroxy acids, such as performic acid.

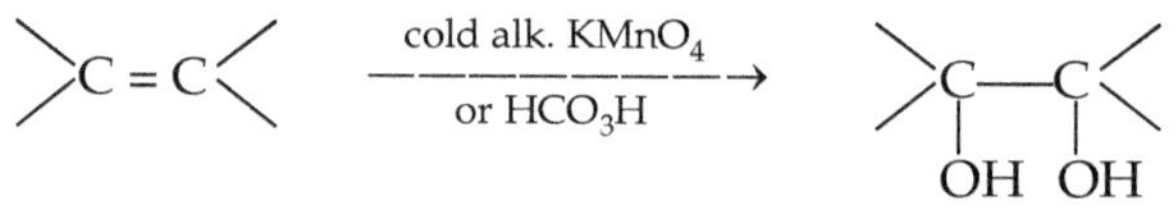

$$
>\!C = C\!< \quad \xrightarrow[\text{or } HCO_3H]{\text{cold alk. } KMnO_4} \quad >\!\!\underset{\underset{OH\ \ OH}{|\quad\ |}}{C-C}\!\!<
$$

A 1, 2-diol

Hydroxylation with permanganate is carried out by stirring together the alkene and the aqueous permanganate solution, either neutral or better slightly alkaline at room temperature. Mild conditions are the key factors, and thus heat and addition of acid are avoided since these will promote further oxidation of the diol. Permanganate oxidation gives *syn*-hydroxylation. Thus

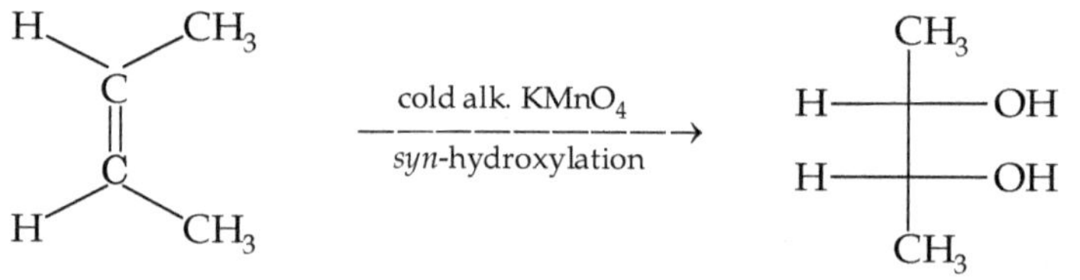

meso-2, 3-Butanediol (M.P. 34°C)

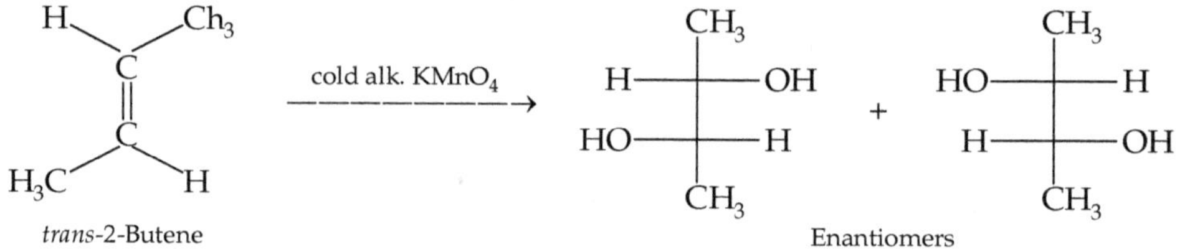

trans-2-Butene   Enantiomers   *rac*-2, 3-Butanediol (M.P. 19°C)

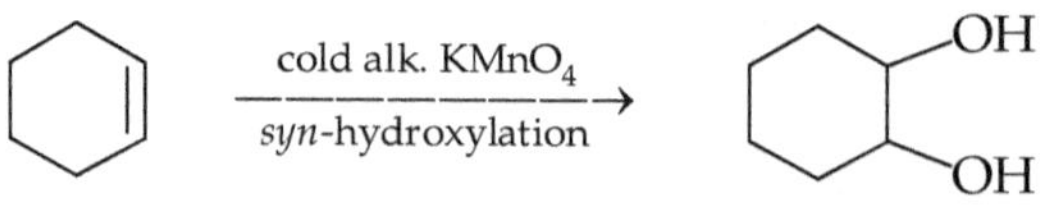

cis-1, 2-Cyclohexanediol

Hydroxylation of alkenes by **means of osmium tetroxide** in presence of hydrogen peroxide also takes place in *cis*-manner.

Hydroxylation with peroxy formic acids is carried out by allowing the alkene to stand with a mixture of hydrogen peroxide and formic acid, for a few hours, and then heating the product with water. Peroxy acids give *anti*-hydroxylation, and thus

$$
cis\text{-2-Butene} \xrightarrow[\text{(ii) } H_2O]{\text{(i) } HCO_3H} rac\text{-2, 3-Butanediol}
$$

$$
trans\text{-2-Butene} \xrightarrow[\text{(ii) } H_2O]{\text{(i) } HCO_3H} meso\text{-2, 3-Butanediol}
$$

$$\text{Cyclohexene} \xrightarrow[\text{\textit{anti}-hydroxylation}]{(i)\ HCO_3H\ (ii)\ H_2O} \text{trans-1, 2-Cyclohexanediol}$$

2. By the hydrolysis of alkylene dihalides, halohydrins and epoxides

$$\begin{array}{c} RCH\text{---}CHR \\ |\quad\ | \\ X\quad X \end{array} \text{ or } \begin{array}{c} RCH\text{---}CHR \\ |\quad\ | \\ OH\ \ X \end{array} \xrightarrow{OH^-} \begin{array}{c} RCH\text{---}CHR \\ |\quad\ | \\ OH\ \ OH \end{array} \xleftarrow[H^+]{H_2O} \begin{array}{c} RCH\text{---}CHR \\ \diagdown\ \ \diagup \\ O \end{array}$$

Recall that hydrolysis of epoxides produces *anti*-hydroxylation.

3. By the reduction of carbonyl compounds.

Symmetrical 1, 2-glycols, known as **pinacols,** are prepared by **bimolecular reduction** of aldehyddes or ketones.

$$R_2C = O \xrightarrow[\text{ether}]{\text{Mg in}} \begin{array}{c} R_2C\text{---}CR_2 \\ |\qquad| \\ {}^-O\ Mg^{2+}\ O^- \end{array} \xrightarrow{H_2O} \begin{array}{c} R_2C\text{---}CR_2 \\ |\qquad| \\ OH\ \ OH \end{array} + Mg(OH)_2$$

A pinacol

Dicarbonyl compounds may be reduced easily to diols by catalytic hydrogenation, by reduction with $NaBH_4$ or $LiAlH_4$.

$$CHO.CHO \longrightarrow CH_2OH.CH_2OH$$

$$\begin{array}{c} CHOCH_2CH.CH_2CHO \\ | \\ CH_3 \end{array} \longrightarrow \begin{array}{c} HOCH_2CH_2CHCH_2CH_2OH \\ | \\ CH_3 \end{array}$$

3-Methyl-1, 5-pentanediol

TEST YOUR UNDERSTANDING - 12.8

1. (*a*) Prepare ethylene glycol from ethanol.

(*b*) Name the reagent used for preparing *cis*- and *trans*-cyclopentene glycol from cyclopentene.

(*c*) Give the structure of the glycol, called a pinacol, obtained by the reductive coupling of each of the following ketone using Mg in ether.

(*i*) CH_3COCH_3,   (*ii*) $C_6H_5COCH_3$,   (*iii*) $C_6H_5COC_6H_5$.

2. Identify the product obtained in each case.

(*a*) $\xrightarrow[H_2O_2]{OsO_4}$ (*b*) $\xrightarrow[H_2O_2]{OsO_4}$

12.10 Properties

Presence of two hydroxyl groups in glycols provides more sites for *intermolecular hydrogen bonding* than monohydric alcohols. Hence diols are more soluble in water and have much higher boiling and melting points as compared to monohydric alcohols of comparable molecular weights. Due to its very high boiling point and water solubility, ethylene glycol is used in automobiles as an antifreeze.

Chemical properties : Diols, *e.g.* ethylene glycol, are expected to exhibit chemical reactions similar to compounds containing two hydroxyl groups. However, when one hydroxyl group has undergone the chemical reaction, it modifies the reactivity of the other group.

1. Acidic nature. The two hydroxyl groups do not react simultaneously, but react one after the other, first —OH is very much reactive than the second. The electron-withdrawing inductive effect of one hydroxyl group makes the other more acidic than the —OH group of a monohydric alcohol ; hence diols react with the sodium metal more quickly. However, the alkoxide ion so formed makes the second —OH group less acidic because of its electron releasing effect, hence it requires higher temperature.

$$\begin{array}{c} R\,CHOH \\ | \\ RCHOH \end{array} \xrightarrow[50°C]{Na} \begin{array}{c} RCHO^-Na^+ \\ | \\ RCHOH \end{array} \xrightarrow[160°]{Na} \begin{array}{c} RCHO^-Na^+ \\ | \\ RCHO^-Na^+ \end{array}$$

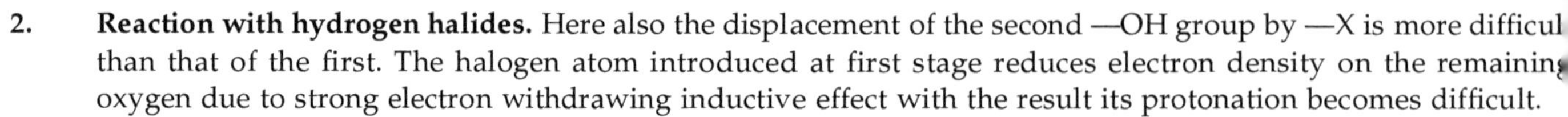

2. **Reaction with hydrogen halides.** Here also the displacement of the second —OH group by —X is more difficult than that of the first. The halogen atom introduced at first stage reduces electron density on the remaining oxygen due to strong electron withdrawing inductive effect with the result its protonation becomes difficult.

$$CH_2OH \atop CH_2OH \xrightarrow[150°C]{H^+} CH_2\overset{+}{O}H_2 \atop CH_2OH \xrightarrow[(S_N1\ or\ S_N2)]{HCl} CH_2Cl \atop CH_2OH \xrightarrow[200°C]{H^+} CH_2Cl \atop CH_2Cl$$

Protonation difficult
due to –I effect of Cl

3. **Other substitution reactions.**

$$CH_2 \atop CH_2 \xleftarrow{-I_2} \left[CH_2I \atop CH_2I \right] \xleftarrow{P+I_2} CH_2OH \atop CH_2OH \xrightarrow{PBr_3} CH_2Br \atop CH_2Br$$

Ethylene   Two heavy atoms   Glycol
                  on adjacent carbons

4. **Esterification.**

$$CH_2OH \atop CH_2OH \xrightarrow[or\ CH_3COCl\ or\ (CH_3CO)_2O]{(i)\ 2CH_3COOH,\ H_2SO_4} CH_2OCOCH_3 \atop CH_2OCOCH_3$$

Glycol   Glycol diacetate

Esterification with terphthalic acid (p-HOOC.C_6H_4.COOH) produces a polyester synthetic fibre known as **terylene** or **dacron**, while with phthalic acid (o-HOOC.C_6H_4.COOH), polymer known as **glyptal** is produced.

5. **Dehydration**

(i)
$$CH_2OH \atop CH_2OH \xrightarrow[500°]{heat} \overset{CH_2}{\underset{CH_2}{\big\langle}} O$$

(ii)
$$\begin{matrix} H \\ | \\ H-C-OH \\ | \\ HO-C-H \\ | \\ H \end{matrix} \xrightarrow[or\ P_2O_5]{ZnCl_2} \begin{matrix} CHOH \\ \| \\ CH_2 \end{matrix} \rightleftharpoons \begin{matrix} CHO \\ | \\ CH_3 \end{matrix}$$
Glycol   Acetaldehyde

(iii)
$$\begin{matrix} HO \quad\quad OH \\ + \\ HO \quad\quad OH \end{matrix} \xrightarrow[or\ H_3PO_4]{conc.\ H_2SO_4} \text{(Dioxane)} + 2H_2O$$

Dioxane
(a useful solvent)

(iv) Diols easily undergo intramolecular dehydration to form cyclic ethers when a five-membered or six-membered ring is formed.

$$\xrightarrow[heat]{H_2SO_4} \text{(Oxane)} + H_2O$$

1, 5-Pentanediol   Oxane

6. **Oxidation involving carbon-carbon bond fission.** 1, 2-Diols, when treated with an aqueous solution of **periodic acid** (H_5IO_6 or $HIO_4.2H_2O$), give aldehydes or ketones.

$$\begin{matrix} R-CHOH \\ | \\ R'-CHOH \end{matrix} + HIO_4 \longrightarrow RCHO + R'CHO + HIO_3 + H_2O$$
                                                              Iodic acid

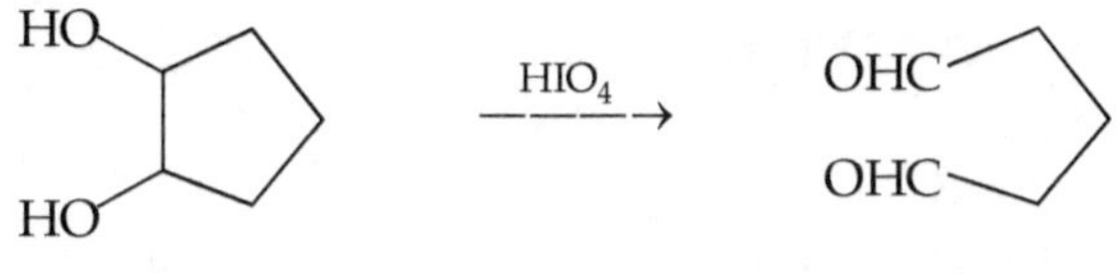

$$\text{1, 2-Cyclopentanediol} \xrightarrow{HIO_4} \text{1, 5-Pentanedial}$$

(*i*)   A 1° alcohol gives CH_2O, a 2° alcohol gives RCHO, a 3° alcohol gives a ketone.

(*ii*)   In case of polyhydric alcohols, one mole of HIO_4 is consumed between every two adjacent hydroxy groups.

(*iii*) An alcholic group, attacked on both sides by HIO_4, is converted into carboxylic acid.

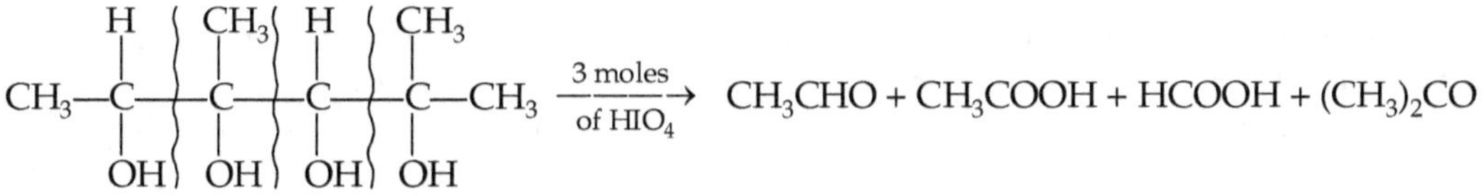

$$CH_3\!-\!\underset{OH}{\overset{H}{C}}\!-\!\underset{OH}{\overset{CH_3}{C}}\!-\!\underset{OH}{\overset{H}{C}}\!-\!\underset{OH}{\overset{CH_3}{C}}\!-\!CH_3 \xrightarrow[\text{of } HIO_4]{\text{3 moles}} CH_3CHO + CH_3COOH + HCOOH + (CH_3)_2CO$$

Thus periodic oxidation has been used for determining the structure of compounds by knowing the number of moles of HIO_4 consumed and nature of the product formed. The technique has found its widest application in carbohydrate chemistry.

Lead tetraacetate also oxidises 1, 2-diols to aldehydes and ketones.

$$RCHOH\!-\!R'CHOH \xrightarrow{Pb(OCOCH_3)_4} RCHO + R'CHO$$

7.   **Oxidation in which carbon-carbon bond remains intact.** Following products have been obtained depending upon the nature of the oxidising agent.

$\underset{CHO}{\overset{CH_2OH}{|}}$	$\underset{COOH}{\overset{CH_2OH}{|}}$	$\underset{CHO}{\overset{CHO}{|}}$	$\underset{COOH}{\overset{CHO}{|}}$	$\underset{COOH}{\overset{COOH}{|}}$
Glycollic aldehyde	Glycollic acid	Glyoxal	Glyoxalic acid	Oxalic acid

8.   **Formation of cyclic acetals (from aldehydes) and ketals** (from ketones)

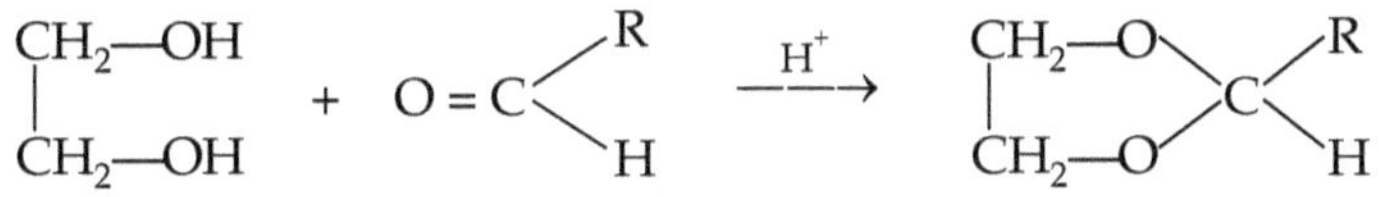

$$\underset{CH_2-OH}{\overset{CH_2-OH}{|}} + O=C\!\!\begin{smallmatrix}R\\H\end{smallmatrix} \xrightarrow{H^+} \underset{CH_2-O}{\overset{CH_2-O}{|}}\!\!C\!\!\begin{smallmatrix}R\\H\end{smallmatrix}$$

An acetal

$$\underset{CH_2-OH}{\overset{CH_2-OH}{|}} + O=C\!\!\begin{smallmatrix}R\\R\end{smallmatrix} \xrightarrow{H^+} \underset{CH_2-O}{\overset{CH_2-O}{|}}\!\!C\!\!\begin{smallmatrix}R\\R\end{smallmatrix}$$

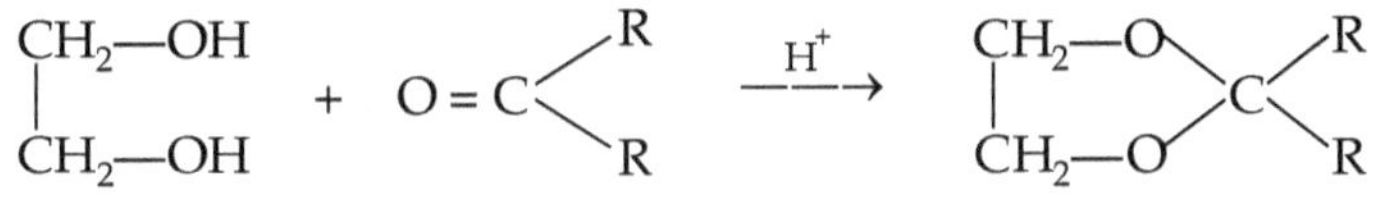

A ketal

These reactions are used in organic synthesis for protecting the carbonyl group. The acetals and ketals are stable in alkaline media whereas the "rest" of the molecule can be subjected to desired conversions under these conditions. The carbonyl group is regenerated in the final stage either by the addition of periodic acid to aqueous solution or by acidic hydrolysis.

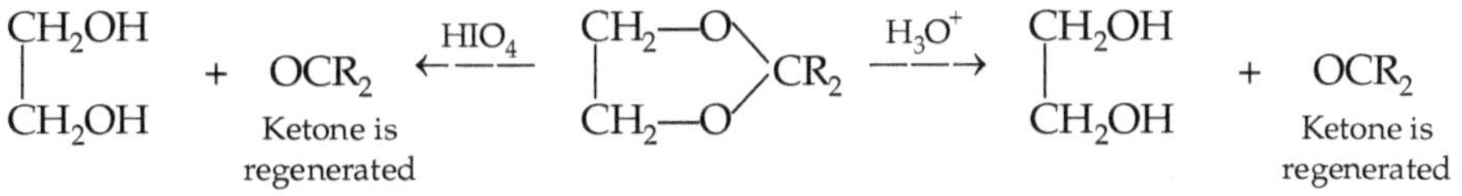

$$\underset{CH_2OH}{\overset{CH_2OH}{|}} + \underset{\substack{\text{Ketone is}\\\text{regenerated}}}{OCR_2} \xleftarrow{HIO_4} \underset{CH_2-O}{\overset{CH_2-O}{|}}\!\!CR_2 \xrightarrow{H_3O^+} \underset{CH_2OH}{\overset{CH_2OH}{|}} + \underset{\substack{\text{Ketone is}\\\text{regenerated}}}{OCR_2}$$

9.   **Acid-catalyzed rearrangement of glycols.** 1, 2-Diols on treatment with acids rearrange to form carbonyl compounds, the classic example being the acid catalyzed rearrangement of 2, 3-dimethyl -2, 3-butanediol **(pinacol)** into methyl *tert*-butyl ketone **(pinacolone)**. Thus the reaction is commonly known as **pinacol-pinacolone rearrangement.**

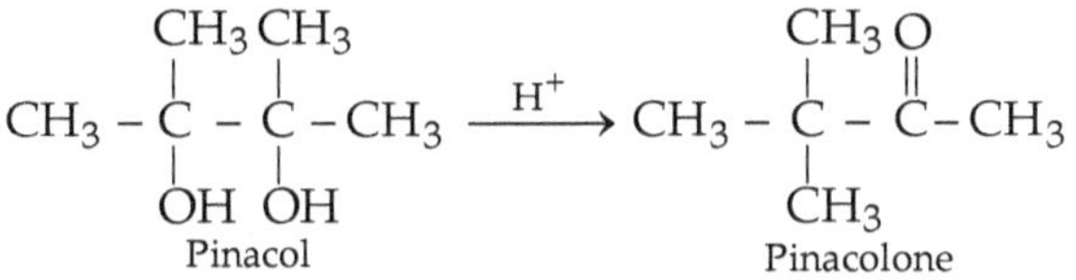

$$CH_3 - \underset{OH}{\overset{CH_3}{\underset{|}{\overset{|}{C}}}} - \underset{OH}{\overset{CH_3}{\underset{|}{\overset{|}{C}}}} - CH_3 \xrightarrow{H^+} CH_3 - \underset{CH_3}{\overset{CH_3}{\underset{|}{\overset{|}{C}}}} - \overset{O}{\overset{||}{C}} - CH_3$$

Pinacol   Pinacolone

TEST YOUR UNDERSTANDING - 12.9

1. Write down the chemical reactions between following compounds.

    (*a*)   1, 3-Butanediol is heated with alumina at 350°C   (*b*)   1, 2,-Dimethyl-1, 2-ethanediol is treated with $KMnO_4$

    (*c*)   2, 3-Butanediol is treated with acetophenone   (*d*)   Ethane-1, 2-diol and ethylene oxide are treated in presence of ac

    (*e*)   2-Methyl-3-phenylpropanediol is treated with periodic acid.

2. Write down the structures of cyclic acetals derived from

    (*a*)   1, 2-Ethanediol and cyclopentanone   (*b*)   Ethylene glycol and isobutyl methyl ketone

    (*c*)   Benzaldehyde and 1, 3-propanediol   (*d*)   2, 2-Dimethyl-1, 3-propanediol and isobutyl methyl ketone.

3. Give the products formed and the number of HIO_4 consumed in the reactions of each of the following glycols.

    (*a*) $CH_3CHOHCH_2OH$ (*b*) $(CH_3)_2COHCHOHCH_3$

    (*c*) $HOCH_2CH_2CH_2OH$ (*d*) $CH_3CHOHC(CH_3)OH.CHOH.COH(CH_3)_2$

    (*e*)

4. Deduce the structure of the following glycol which on oxidation gives following results.

    (*a*)   A $\xrightarrow{\text{1 mole } HIO_4}$ ... $+ CH_2O$ (*b*)   B $\xrightarrow{\text{2 moles } HIO_4}$ $C_6H_5CHO + HCOOH + CH_3CHO.$

12.11   Illustrative Examples

Example 12 :

Identify the products [A] to [D], and explain your answer.

(a)   ... $\xrightarrow{H_3PO_4}$ [A] + [B]

(b)   ... $\xrightarrow{\text{alk. } KMnO_4}$ [C] $\xrightarrow{CrO_3/\text{glacial } CH_3COOH}$ [D]

Solution :

(*a*)   Note that the two OH groups are different, C_2—OH is 3° (more basic) and hence behaves as a base while C_5—OF is 2° (less basic than 3° alcoholic OH) and hence behaves as an acid. Thus during intramolecular dehydration F from C_5—OH and OH from C_2—OH will be eliminated as water. Consequently O^{18} will appear in the cycli ether, and not in water.

(*b*)

In compound [C], only 2° alcohol group is oxidised, the second OH group being 3° is resistant to oxidation.

Example 13 :

Give steps involved in the following reaction.

(a) $\underset{\displaystyle OH}{CH_2CH_2CH_2CH_2CH_2}\ \underset{\displaystyle OH}{\Big|}\ \xrightarrow[\text{heat}]{H_2SO_4}$ [cyclic ether]

(b) [epoxide] $\xrightarrow{H^+}$ [diol with OH groups]

Solution :

(a) [mechanism scheme: diol $\xrightarrow{H^+}$ protonated intermediate $\xrightarrow{(-H_2O)}$ oxocarbenium $\xrightarrow{HSO_4^-}$ tetrahydropyran + H_2SO_4]

(b) [mechanism scheme: epoxide $\xrightarrow{H^+}$ protonated epoxide $\xrightarrow{:\ddot{O}H_2}$ intermediate $\xrightarrow{-H^+}$ diol]

Example 14 :

How will you carry out following transformations ?

(a) $CH_3COCH_2CH_2C \equiv CH \longrightarrow CH_3COCH_2CH_2C \equiv CCH_3$

(b) $\underset{\displaystyle O}{CH_3-\overset{\displaystyle \|}{C}}-\!\!\!\bigcirc\!\!\!-COOH \ \dashrightarrow\ \underset{\displaystyle O}{CH_3-\overset{\displaystyle \|}{C}}-\!\!\!\bigcirc\!\!\!-CH_2OH$

Solution :

(a) Here it is not possible to directly convert $-C \equiv CH$ to $-C \equiv CCH_3$ by means of $NaNH_2$ followed by CH_3I because of following reasons.

   (*i*) The carbonyl group in the given acetylenic compound will not tolerate the strongly basic reagent ($NaNH_2$).

   (*ii*) The carbonyl group will react with the carbanion, formed at first step.

   Hence it becomes necessary to protect the carbonyl group by acetal formation which can easily be removed at the desired stage by acidic hydrolysis.

$CH_3COCH_2CH_2C \equiv CH \xrightarrow[H^+]{HOCH_2CH_2OH}$ [cyclic acetal: H_3C and $CH_2CH_2C \equiv CH$]

$\xrightarrow[(ii)\ CH_3I]{(i)\ NaNH_2,\ NH_3}$ [cyclic acetal: H_3C and $CH_2CH_2C \equiv CCH_3$] $\xrightarrow{H_2O,\ HCl} CH_3COCH_2CH_2C \equiv CCH_3$

   5-Heptyn-2-one

(b) Direct reduction of $-COOH$ will also reduce $-COCH_3$ group, hence latter should first be protected by reaction with ethylene glycol.

$\underset{\displaystyle CH_3}{O=\overset{\displaystyle}{C}}-\!\!\!\bigcirc\!\!\!-COOH \xrightarrow[H^+,\ heat]{CH_2OHCH_2OH}$ [protected acetal] $-COOH \xrightarrow[(ii)\ H_2O]{(i)\ LiAlH_4}$

[acetal] $-CH_2OH \xrightarrow{H_2O,\ H^+} \underset{\displaystyle CH_3}{O=\overset{\displaystyle}{C}}-\!\!\!\bigcirc\!\!\!-CH_2OH + CH_2OHCH_2OH$

TRIHYDRIC ALCOHOLS OR TRIOLS

12.12   Glycerol

12.12.1 Preparation of Glycerol

The simplest and most important trihydric alcohol is **propane-1, 2, 3-triol,** commonly known as **glycerol.**

It is present in all oils and fats which are esters of glycerol (alcohol) with higher fatty acids, *e.g.* palmitic, stearic and oleic acids. Oils and fats are industrially used for the manufacture of **soaps** and **candles,** glycerol is obtained as a by product in each case. (*a*) In soap manufacture, oils are hydrolysed in presence of alkali (NaOH), (*b*) while in candle industry, oils are hydrolysed with steam.

$$
(a) \quad
\begin{array}{l}
CH_2O-COR \\
| \\
CHO-COR \\
| \\
CH_2O-COR
\end{array}
\;+\; 3\,NaOH \;\xrightarrow{\text{Saponification}}\;
\begin{array}{l}
CH_2OH \\
| \\
CHOH \\
| \\
CH_2OH
\end{array}
\;+\;
\begin{array}{l}
3RCOONa \\
\text{Sod. salts of fatty acids} \\
\text{(Soap)}
\end{array}
$$

Oil or Fat   Glycerol

(where R = $C_{15}H_{31}$, $C_{17}H_{33}$ or $C_{17}H_{35}$; R may be similar or different)

Filtrate after removing soap contains mainly glycerol and known as **spent lye** (app. 5% glycerol)

$$(b) \quad Oil \xrightarrow{\text{steam}} \text{Fatty acids} + \text{Glycerol}$$

Fatty acids are removed and mixed with paraffin wax to get candles. Product obtained after removing fatty acids mainly contains glycerol, and known as **sweet water.**

Glycerol from fermentation of sugars. Glycerol is also obtained as a by-product during alcoholic fermentation ; the yield of glycerol can be considerably improved by adding sodium sulphite.

Synthetic glycerol. Now-a-days, glycerol is mainly obtained from propene which is either synthesized from elements (carbon and hydrogen) or obtained as one of the products of cracking of petroleum.

$$
2C + H_2 \xrightarrow[\text{arc}]{\text{electric}} CH \equiv CH \xrightarrow[Hg^{2+}]{H_3O^+} CH_3CHO \xrightarrow[\text{(ii) Ca(OH)}_2]{\text{(i) oxi}} (CH_3COO)_2Ca \xrightarrow{\text{dry distillation}} \begin{array}{c} CH_3 \\ | \\ CO \\ | \\ CH_3 \end{array} \xrightarrow[Na/C_2H_5OH]{\text{Reduction}}
$$

Acetone

$$
\begin{array}{l}
CH_3 \\
| \\
CHOH \\
| \\
CH_3
\end{array}
\xrightarrow{H^+,\,\text{heat}}
\begin{array}{l}
CH_3 \\
| \\
CH \\
\| \\
CH_2
\end{array}
\xrightarrow[500°C]{Cl_2}
\begin{array}{l}
CH_2Cl \\
| \\
CH \\
\| \\
CH_2
\end{array}
\xrightarrow{\text{aq. Na}_2CO_3}
\begin{array}{l}
CH_2OH \\
| \\
CH \\
\| \\
CH_2
\end{array}
\xrightarrow[\substack{anti\text{-Marko.}\\ \text{addition}}]{HOCl}
\begin{array}{l}
CH_2OH \\
| \\
CHCl \\
| \\
CH_2OH
\end{array}
\xrightarrow{OH^-}
\begin{array}{l}
CH_2OH \\
| \\
CHOH \\
| \\
CH_2OH
\end{array}
$$

Propene   Allyl chloride   Glycerol

12.12.2 Properties of Glycerol

It is a colourless, viscous liquid boiling at 290° with decomposition. It is miscible, in all proportions, with water due to availability of three hydroxyl groups for H-bonding with water. Glycerol gives chemical reactions, typical to that of a primary and secondary alcohol.

1.   **Reaction with metals.** At low temperature it forms monosodium salt, and at higher temperature it forms disodium salt (both 1° alcohols have reacted). Trisodium salt is generally not formed.

2.   **Reaction with hydrogen halides.**

$$\underset{\substack{\text{CH}_2\text{OH} \\ | \\ \text{CHOH} \\ | \\ \text{CH}_2\text{OH}}}{}\xrightarrow[110°C]{\text{HCl}}\underset{\substack{\text{CH}_2\text{Cl} \\ | \\ \text{CHOH} \\ | \\ \text{CH}_2\text{OH} \\ \text{(Major)}}}{}+\underset{\substack{\text{CH}_2\text{OH} \\ | \\ \text{CH}_2\text{Cl} \\ | \\ \text{CH}_2\text{OH} \\ \text{(Minor)}}}{}\xrightarrow{\text{HCl}}\underset{\substack{\text{CH}_2\text{Cl} \\ | \\ \text{CHOH} \\ | \\ \text{CH}_2\text{Cl} \\ \text{(Major)}}}{}+\underset{\substack{\text{CH}_2\text{Cl} \\ | \\ \text{CHCl} \\ | \\ \text{CH}_2\text{OH} \\ \text{(Minor)}}}{}$$

Low reactivity of the 2° alcoholic group is due to —I effect of the two 1° alcoholic group or chlorine and OH group which decrease the electron density on oxygen at 2-position, required for protonation. Either of the dichloro derivative or even glycerol, when treated with PCl_5 gives 1, 2, 3-trichloropropane.

$$\underset{\substack{\text{CH}_2\text{Cl} \\ | \\ \text{CHOH} \\ | \\ \text{CH}_2\text{Cl}}}{}\ \text{or}\ \underset{\substack{\text{CH}_2\text{Cl} \\ | \\ \text{CHCl} \\ | \\ \text{CH}_2\text{OH}}}{}\ \text{or}\ \underset{\substack{\text{CH}_2\text{OH} \\ | \\ \text{CHOH} \\ | \\ \text{CH}_2\text{OH}}}{}\xrightarrow{\text{PCl}_5}\underset{\substack{\text{CH}_2\text{Cl} \\ | \\ \text{CHCl} \\ | \\ \text{CH}_2\text{Cl} \\ \text{1, 2, 3-Trichloropropane}}}{}$$

3.   **Reaction with hydroiodic acid** (a very strong acid).

$$\underset{\substack{\text{CH}_2\text{OH} \\ | \\ \text{CHOH} \\ | \\ \text{CH}_2\text{OH}}}{}\xrightarrow[\text{or PI}_3]{\text{3HI}}\underset{\substack{\text{CH}_2\text{I} \\ | \\ \text{CHI} \\ | \\ \text{CH}_2\text{I}}}{\left[\;\;\right]}\xrightarrow{-\text{I}_2}\underset{\substack{\text{CH}_2 \\ \| \\ \text{CH} \\ | \\ \text{CH}_2\text{I} \\ \text{Allyl iodide}}}{}\xrightarrow{\text{HI}}\underset{\substack{\text{CH}_3 \\ | \\ \text{CHI} \\ | \\ \text{CH}_2\text{I}}}{\left[\;\;\right]}\xrightarrow{-\text{I}_2}\underset{\substack{\text{CH}_3 \\ | \\ \text{CH} \\ \| \\ \text{CH}_2 \\ \text{Propene}}}{}\xrightarrow{\text{HI}}\underset{\substack{\text{CH}_3 \\ | \\ \text{CHI} \\ | \\ \text{CH}_3 \\ \text{Isopropyl iodide}}}{}$$

Two bulky atoms present on adjacent C's

4.   **Reaction with conc. HNO_3 in presence of conc. H_2SO_4**

$$\underset{\substack{\text{CH}_2\text{OH} \\ | \\ \text{CHOH} \\ | \\ \text{CH}_2\text{OH}}}{}+\ 3\text{HONO}_2\xrightarrow[10°C]{\text{conc. H}_2\text{SO}_2}\underset{\substack{\text{CH}_2\text{ONO}_2 \\ | \\ \text{CHONO}_2 \\ | \\ \text{CH}_2\text{ONO}_2 \\ \text{Glyceryl trinitrate}}}{}$$

Remember that **glyceryl trinitrate is an ester,** and not a nitro compound, although commonly but wrongly named as trinitroglycerine, TNG. Glyceryl trinitrate is a highly poisonous oil and explodes violently when detonated. Due to its high sensitivity, its transportation is very hazardous task. However, Alfred Nobel discovered that this oil can be transported easily when adsorbed on keiselguhr ; glyceryl trinitrate adsorbed on keiselguhr was called **dynamite**, a patent registered by Alfred Nobel. **Cordite** (smokeless powder) is a mixture of glyceryl trinitrate, gun cotton (cellulose nitrate) and vaseline. **Blasting gelatine** is a mixture of glyceryl trinitrate with gum cotton.

Glycerol reacts with acetic anyhdride or acetyl chloride to form **glyceryl triacetate (triacetin).**

5.   **Reaction with oxalic acid**

(*a*)   *At low temperature (120°)*

$$\underset{\substack{\text{CH}_2\text{OH} \\ | \\ \text{CHOH} \\ | \\ \text{CH}_2\text{OH}}}{}+\underset{\substack{\text{HOOC} \\ | \\ \text{HOOC}}}{}\xrightarrow{120°C}\underset{\substack{\text{CH}_2\text{O—CO} \\ | \quad\ \ | \\ \text{CHOH}\ \ \text{COOH} \\ | \\ \text{CH}_2\text{OH} \\ \text{Glyceryl monoxalate}}}{}\xrightarrow{(-\text{CO}_2)}\underset{\substack{\text{CH}_2\text{O—CHO} \\ | \\ \text{CHOH} \\ | \\ \text{CH}_2\text{OH} \\ \text{Glyceryl monoformate}}}{}\xrightarrow{\text{H}_2\text{O}}\underset{\substack{\text{CH}_2\text{OH} \\ | \\ \text{CHOH} \\ | \\ \text{CH}_2\text{OH}}}{}+\ \textbf{HCOOH}$$

The overall reaction of glycerol with oxalic acid at low temperature (120°C) appears to be **conversion of oxalic acid to formic acid** with glycerol as a catalyst.

(b)   *At high temperature (260°C). Allyl alcohol is the main product.*

$$\underset{\substack{| \\ CH_2OH}}{\overset{\substack{CH_2OH \\ |}}{\underset{}{CHOH}}} + \underset{HOOC}{\overset{HOOC}{|}} \xrightarrow{260°C} \underset{\substack{| \\ CH_2OH}}{\overset{CH_2-O-CO}{\underset{|}{CH-O-CO}}} \longrightarrow \underset{\substack{| \\ CH_2OH}}{\overset{CH_2}{\underset{}{CH}}} + 2CO_2$$

Glyceryl dioxalate   Allyl alcohol

6.   Dehydration

$$\underset{\substack{| \\ CH_2OH}}{\overset{\substack{CH_2OH \\ |}}{CHOH}} \xrightarrow[\text{heat}]{KHSO_4} \underset{\substack{| \\ CHO}}{\overset{CH_2}{CH}} + 2H_2O$$

Acrolein

7.   Oxidation

Various oxidation products of glycerol are

$\underset{\substack{| \\ CHO}}{\overset{\substack{CH_2OH \\ |}}{CHOH}}$	$\underset{\substack{| \\ COOH}}{\overset{\substack{CH_2OH \\ |}}{CHOH}}$	$\underset{\substack{| \\ COOH}}{\overset{\substack{COOH \\ |}}{CHOH}}$	$\underset{\substack{| \\ COOH}}{\overset{\substack{COOH \\ |}}{CO}}$	$\underset{\substack{| \\ CH_2OH}}{\overset{\substack{CH_2OH \\ |}}{CO}}$
Glyceraldehyde	Glyceric acid	Tartronic acid	Mesoxalic acid	Dihydroxyacetone

Equimolar mixture of glyceraldehyde and dihydroxyacetone, called **glycerose,** is obtained by the oxidation of glycerol with bromine water or Fenton's reagent.

Periodic oxidation of glycerol forms two moles of formaldehyde and one mole of formic acid by consuming two mole of periodic acid.

$$H-\underset{\substack{| \\ OH}}{\overset{\substack{H \\ |}}{C}}\underset{\substack{| \\ OH}}{\overset{\substack{H \\ |}}{C}}\underset{\substack{| \\ OH}}{\overset{\substack{H \\ |}}{C}}-H \xrightarrow{2HIO_4} HCHO + HCOOH + HCHO$$

8.   Reduction

Glycerol when heated strongly with phosphorus and HI gives propane, $CH_3CH_2CH_3$.

EXERCISE 12.1 (MCQ - ONE option correct)

1. IUPAC name of the compound (cyclohexenyl—OCH(CH$_3$)$_2$)

(a) 3-Cyclohexenyl isopropyl ether
(b) 2-Cyclohexenyl isopropyl ether
(c) Isopropoxycyclohexene-2
(d) Isopropoxycyclohexene.

2. (aromatic ring with OCH$_2$CH=^{14}CH$_2$, two D substituents) $\xrightarrow{\text{heat}}$ X ; X is

(a) (ring with OH, two D, CH$_2$CH=^{14}CH$_2$)

(b) (ring with OD, two D, CH$_2$CH=^{14}CH$_2$)

(c) (ring with OD, D, ^{14}CH$_2$CH=CH$_2$)

(d) (ring with OH, D, ^{14}CH$_2$CH=CH$_2$)

3. Identify the compound Y in the following reactions.

$$CH_3CH_2CH_2CH_2OH \xrightarrow{\text{conc. H}_2\text{SO}_4} [X] \xrightarrow[\text{H}_2\text{SO}_4]{CH_3OH} Y$$

(a) $CH_3CHOHCH_2CH_3$ (b) $HOCH_2CH_2CH_2CH_3$
(c) $CH_3OCH_2CH_2CH_2CH_3$ (d) $CH_3CH(OCH_3)CH_2CH_3$.

4. Which of the following can be prepared by the typical Williamson reaction ?
(a) R_3COCR_3 (b) $ArOAr$
(c) $RCH=CHOCH=CHR'$ (d) none of the three.

5. Di-*tert*-butyl ether can be obtained by
(a) Williamson synthesis
(b) by dehydration of Me_3COH
(c) both (a) and (b)
(d) None of the two.

6. Benzyl ethyl ether can be prepared by which combination of components ?
(a) $C_6H_5CH_2Br + C_2H_5ONa$ (b) $C_6H_5CH_2ONa + C_2H_5Br$
(c) both (a) and (b)   (d) $C_6H_5CH_2OH + C_2H_5OH$.

7. Following reaction can be carried out in three different ways

(isobutylene) $\xrightarrow{?}$ (tert-butyl methyl ether, OCH$_3$)

Use of which of the following reagents will give best result ?
(a) (i) H_3O^+, (ii) Na, (iii) CH_3Br

(b) $Hg(OAc)_2.THF.H_2O$, (ii) $NaBH_4/OH^-$, (iii) Na, (iv) CH_3Br
(c) (i) $BH_3.THF/H_2O_2$, OH^- (ii) Na (iii) CH_3Br
(d) None of the above.

8. Which of the following ether will form hydroperoxide easily ?
(a) *n*-propyl ether   (b) *iso*-propyl ether (c)
Both (d)   None.

9. Identify A in the following reactions

(methylcyclohexene) $\xrightarrow[\text{NaBH}_4/\text{OH}^-]{Hg(OAc)_2.CH_3OH}$ [A]

(a) (1-methyl-1-methoxycyclohexane, OCH$_3$)
(b) (1-methyl-2-methoxycyclohexane, OCH$_3$) (c)
(c) (1-methyl-3-methoxycyclohexane, OCH$_3$)

Both (a) and (b)   (d)

10. Identify the nature of (B)

$$CH_3CH=CH_2 \xrightarrow{Cl_2, H_2O} [A] \xrightarrow{aq.\ NaOH} B$$

(a) $CH_3CHOH.CH_2OH$ (b) $CH_2Cl.CHOH CH_2OH$
(c) $CH_2OH CHOHCH_2OH$ (d) $CH_3CH\!-\!\!-\!CH_2$ (epoxide, O)

11. Which of the following is an example of acid cleavage of ethylene oxide ?
(a) Reaction of ethylene oxide with methanol in presence of a little sulphuric acid
(b) Reaction of ethylene oxide with methanol in presence of a little amount of sodium methoxide.
(c) Reaction of ethylene oxide with methylamine
(d) None of the three.

12. Following two compounds are isomers

(I) $CH_2\!-\!\!-\!CHCH_2CH_3$ (epoxide, O)   (II) (oxolane/tetrahydrofuran, O)

(I)   (II)

What is true about their enthalpies of combustion ?
(a) Both have equal enthalpies of combustion
(b) Enthalpy of combustion of I > II
(c) Enthalpy of combustion of II > I
(d) It can't be predicted.

13. Identify the nature of the compound (A)

(2,2-dimethyloxirane) $\xrightarrow{HCl/H_2O^{18}}$ A

(a) $(CH_3)_2C(OH).CH_2O^{18}H$
(b) $(CH_3)_2C(O^{18}H)CH_2OH$
(c) $(CH_3)_2C(O^{18}H)CH_2O^{18}H$
(d) $(CH_3)_2C(OH)CH_2OH$.

14. Identify the end product in the following reaction.

(cyclohexyl—OH) $\xrightarrow[\text{heat}]{\text{conc. H}_2\text{SO}_4} [X] \xrightarrow{CH_3CO_3H} [Y] \xrightarrow[\text{H}_3\text{O}^+]{C_6H_{11}MgBr} [Z]$

(a) (cyclohexyl—CHOHC$_6$H$_{11}$)   (b) (cyclohexyl—OC$_6$H$_{11}$)   (c)

(d) (cyclohexyl with OH and C$_6$H$_{11}$)   (cyclohexyl—C$_6$H$_{11}$CH$_2$OH)

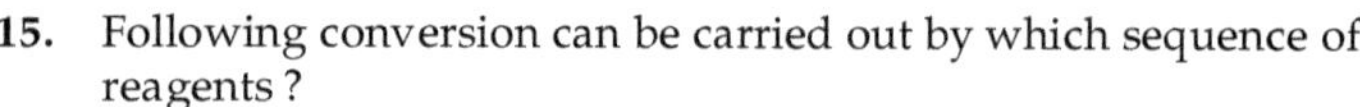

15. Following conversion can be carried out by which sequence of reagents ?

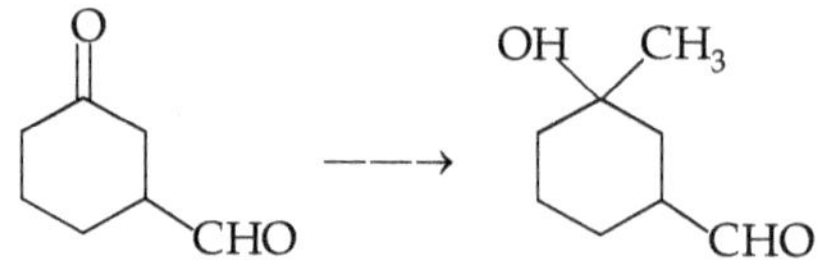

(a)   1CH$_3$MgI, H$_3$O$^+$
(b)   2CH$_3$MgI, H$_3$O$^+$
(c)   (CH$_2$OH)$_2$, CH$_3$MgI, H$_3$O$^+$, H$^+$
(d)   Not possible.

16. Arrange the following glycols in order of decreasing rate of oxidation with periodic acid.

$$\begin{array}{ccc} CH_2OH & CH_3CHOH & (CH_3)_2COH \\ CH_2OH, & CH_3CHOH, & CH_2OH \\ I & II & III \end{array}$$

(a)   I > II > III
(b)   II > III > I
(c)   III > II > I
(d)   All will be oxidised at the same rate.

17. Identify the end product in the following reaction.

$$2(CH_3)_2CO \xrightarrow[\text{(ii) } H_3O^+]{\text{(i) Mg}} [A] \xrightarrow{HIO_4} [B]$$

(a)   (CH$_3$)$_3$COH
(b)   (CH$_3$)$_2$C = CH$_2$ (c) 2(CH$_3$)$_2$CO
(d)   Reaction not feasible.

18. The compound which is not isomeric with diethyl ether is
(a)   n-propylmethyl ether
(b)   butanol-1
(c)   2-methylpropanol
(d)   Butanone

19.

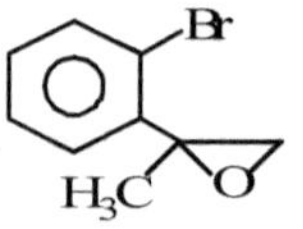

$$\xrightarrow{NH_3/CH_3OH} A, \; A \text{ is}$$

(a) 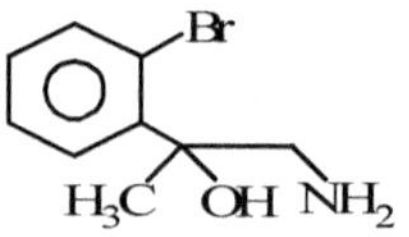   (b)

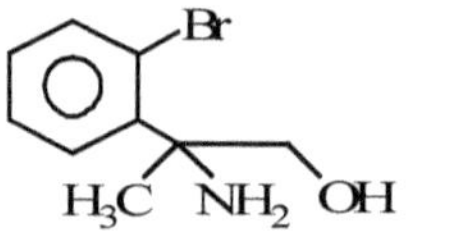

(c) 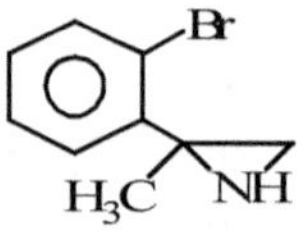   (d)   None of these

20. Hydrolysis product of given compound is

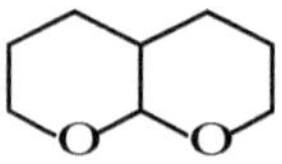

(a) 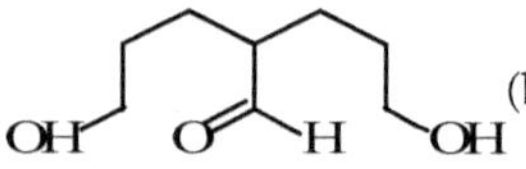   (b)

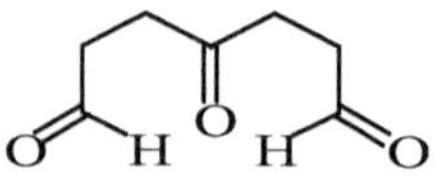

(c) 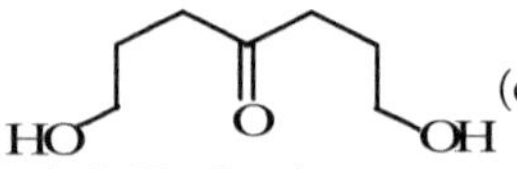   (d)   No hydrolysis

21. A chiral C$_5$H$_{10}$O ether reacts with hot HI to give a C$_5$H$_{10}$I$_2$ product. Treatment of this with hot KOH in ethanol produces 1, 3-pentadiene. What is the structure of the original ether ?

(a) 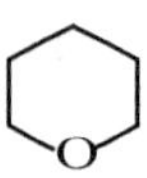   (b)

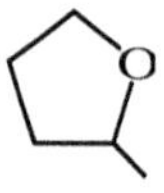

(c) 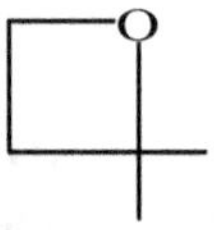   (d)

22. Which of the following would work best for the synthesis of the ether shown below ?

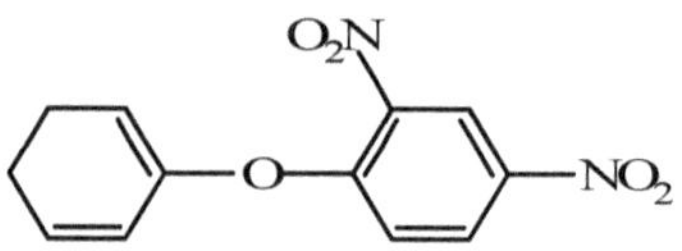

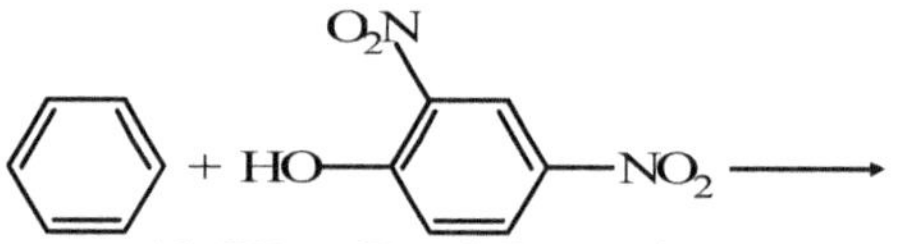

23. HBr reacts with CH$_2$ = CH – OCH$_3$ under anhydrous conditions at room temperature to give
(a)   BrCH$_2$ – CH$_2$ – OCH$_3$
(b)   H$_3$C – CHBr – OCH$_3$
(c)   CH$_3$CHO and CH$_3$Br
(d)   BrCH$_2$CHO and CH$_3$OH

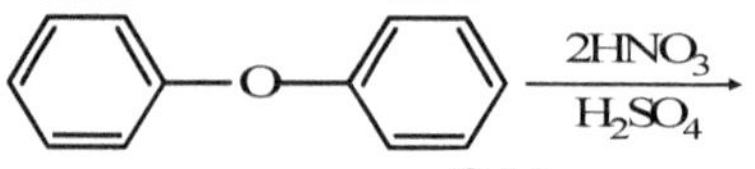

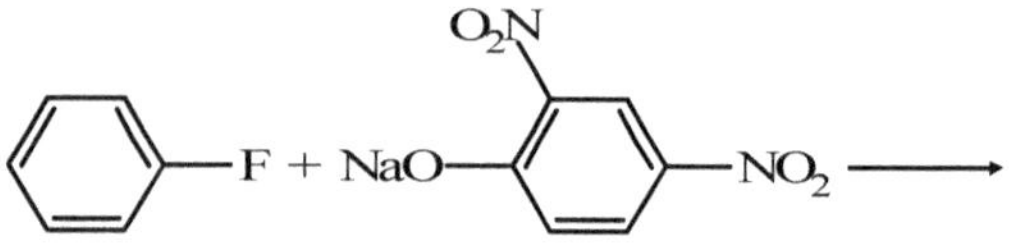

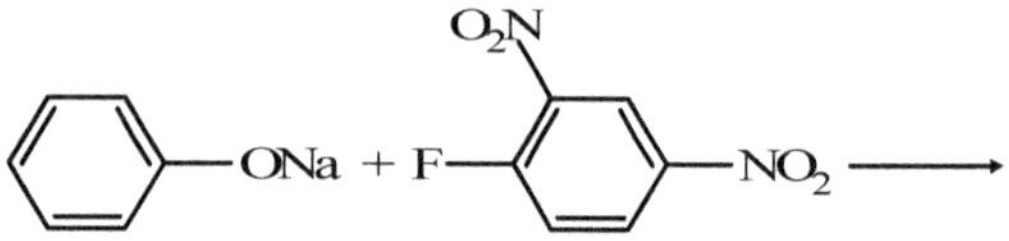

24. Anisole is treated with HI under two different conditions.

$$C + D \xleftarrow{HI(g)} C_6H_5OCH_3 \xrightarrow{\text{conc. HI}} A + B$$

The nature of A to D will be
(a)   A and B are CH$_3$I and C$_6$H$_5$OH, while C and D are CH$_3$OH and C$_6$H$_5$I
(b)   A and B are CH$_3$OH and C$_6$H$_5$I, while C and D are CH$_3$I and C$_6$H$_5$OH
(c)   Both A and B as well as both C and D are CH$_3$I and C$_6$H$_5$OH
(d)   A and B are CH$_3$I and C$_6$H$_5$OH, while there is no reaction in the second case.

25.

$$\text{Products}(P_2) \xleftarrow{\text{anhy. HI}} (CH_3)_3C-O-CH_3 \xrightarrow{\text{conc. HI}} \text{Products } (P_1)$$

The products P$_1$ and P$_2$ respectively are
(a)   (CH$_3$)$_3$COH + CH$_3$I and (CH$_3$)$_3$CI + CH$_3$OH
(b)   (CH$_3$)$_3$CI + CH$_3$OH and (CH$_3$)$_3$COH + CH$_3$I
(c)   (CH$_3$)$_3$CCI + CH$_3$OH in both cases
(d)   CH$_3$I and (CH$_3$)$_3$COH in both cases

26. *tert*-Butyl ethyl ether can't be prepared by which reaction?

(a)   *tert* – Butanol + ethanol $\xrightarrow{H^+}$
(b)   *tert*-Butyl bromide + sodium ethoxide →
(c)   Sodium *tert*-butoxide + ethyl bromide →
(d)   Isobutene + ethanol $\xrightarrow{H^+}$

27.

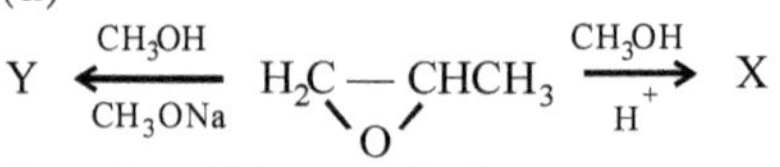

$$Y \xleftarrow{CH_3OH}_{CH_3ONa} H_2C-CHCH_3 \xrightarrow[H^+]{CH_3OH} X$$

Here X and Y respectively are
(a)   CH$_2$ – CHCH$_3$ and HOCH$_2$ – CHCH$_3$ with OCH$_3$, OH / OCH$_3$
(b)   HOCH$_2$ – CHCH$_3$ and CH$_2$ – CHCH$_3$
(c)   CH$_2$ – CHCH$_3$ in both cases (OCH$_3$, OH)
(d)   HOCH$_2$ – CHCH$_3$ in both cases (OCH$_3$)

Predict the product in the following reaction

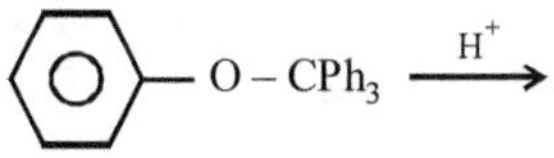

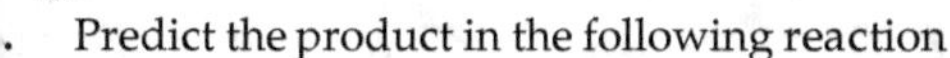

Product is

(a) 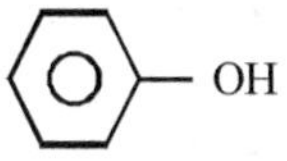 (b) Ph_3COH

(c) 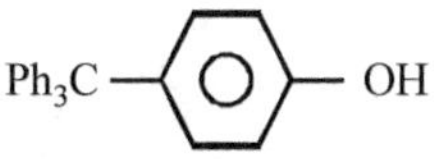 (d) All the three

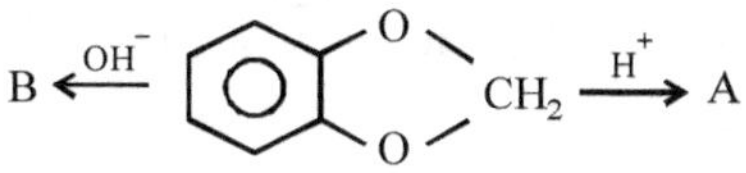

A and B are

	A	B
(a)	Catechol + Methanal	Catechol + Methanal
(b)	Catechol + Methanal	Sodium salt of catechol + Methanal
(c)	No reaction	Catechol + Methanal
(d)	Catechol + Methanal	No reaction

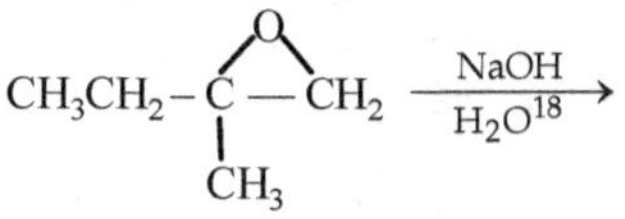

Major product is

(a) $CH_3CH_2-C(^{18}OH)(CH_3)-CH_2(OH)$ (b) $CH_3CH_2-C(OH)(CH_3)-CH_2(^{18}OH)$

(c) $CH_3CH_2-C(OH)(CH_3)-CH_2(OH)$ (d) $CH_3CH_2-C(^{18}OH)(CH_3)-CH_2(^{18}OH)$

31. 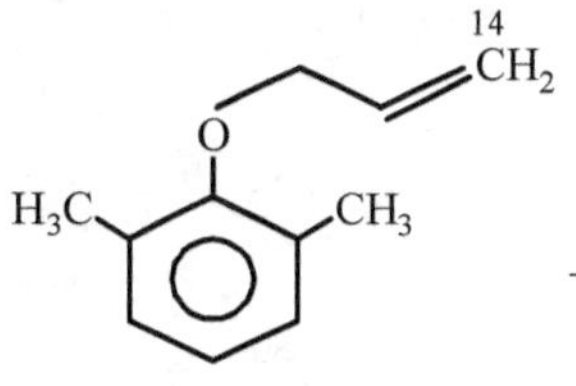 $\xrightarrow{heat}$ P. P is

(a) 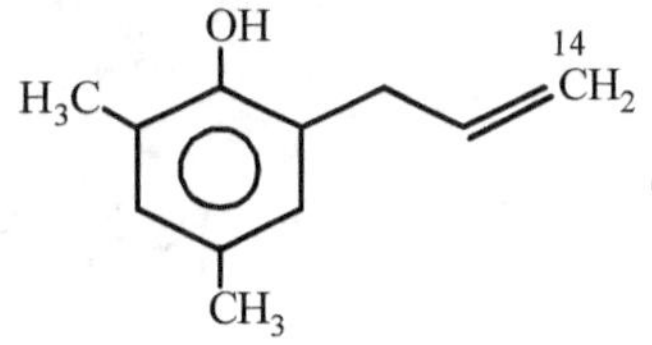 (b) 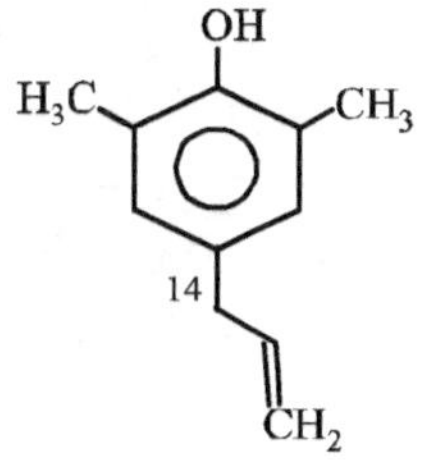

(c) 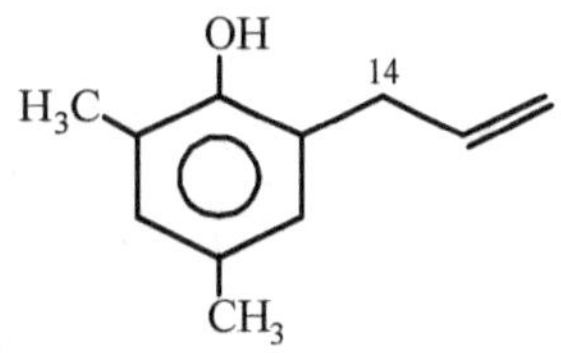 (d) 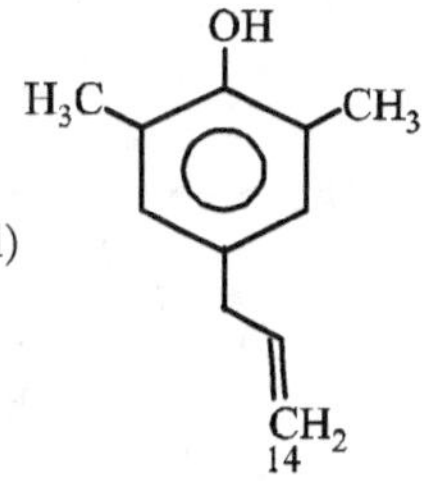

32. The major product of the following reaction is

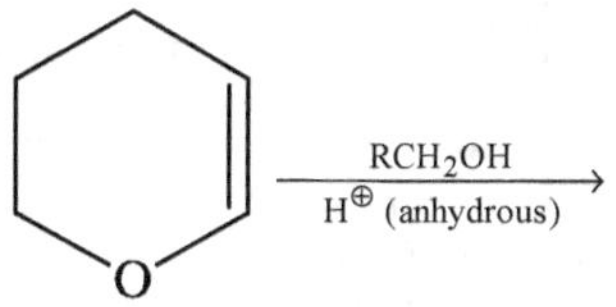

(a) a hemiacetal (b) an acetal
(c) an ether (d) an ester

EXERCISE 12.2 (MCQ 1 or >1 option correct, Passage based, Matching, A/R)

DIRECTIONS for Q. 1 to Q.15 : Multiple choice questions with one or more than one correct option(s).

Which of the following statement is true ?
(a) Ethers are soluble in water
(b) Ethers are soluble in alcohols
(c) Alcohols are soluble in ethers
(d) All alcohols are soluble in water

Which of the following reaction is not possible ?
(a) $C_6H_5OH + HBr \longrightarrow C_6H_5Br + H_2O$
(b) $(CH_3)_3CCl + NaOCH_3 \longrightarrow (CH_3)_3COCH_3 + NaCl$
(c) 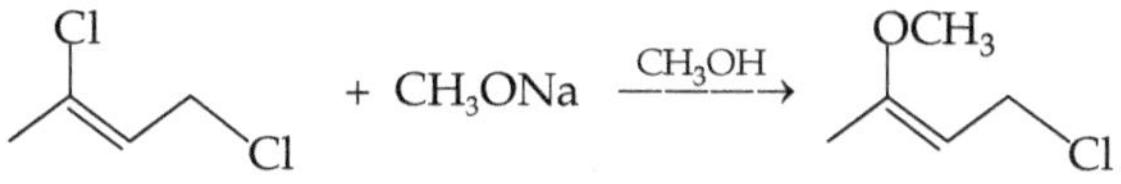
(d) 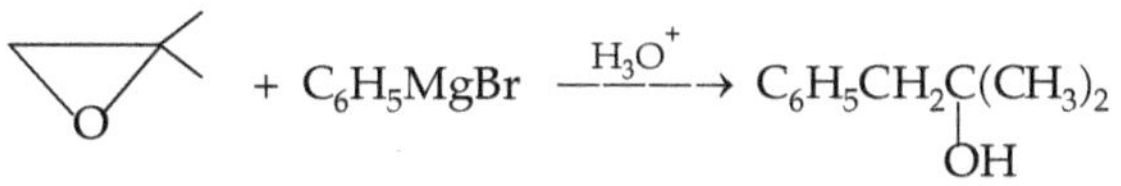

Which of the following statements about ethers are correct?
(a) Peroxide is obtained in the presence of air
(b) Ethers are weakly acidic
(c) Ethers form oxonium salts
(d) Ethers form stable complexes with Lewis acids

4. Diethyl ether reacts with
(a) sulphuric acid (b) hydrochloric acid
(c) acetic acid (d) hydroiodic acid

5. The ether 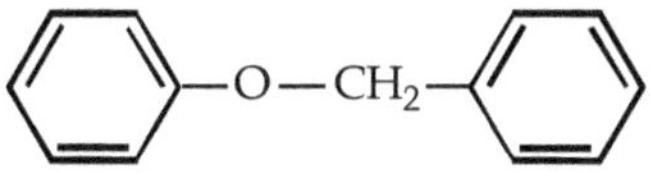 when treated with HI produces

(a) 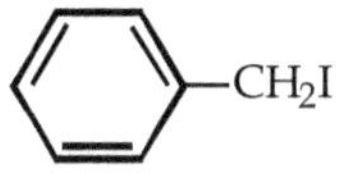 (b) 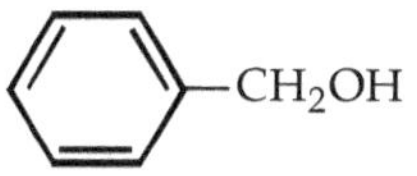

(c) 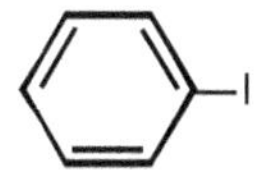 (d) 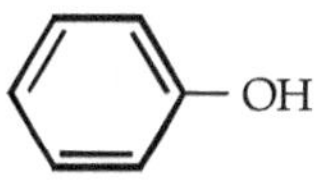

6. C_3H_6O(A) does not reduce Tollen's reagent, does not give iodoform test, but reacts with HI. A can be :
(a) CH_3COCH_3 (b) CH_3CH_2CHO
(c) $CH_2 = CH - O - CH_3$ (d) 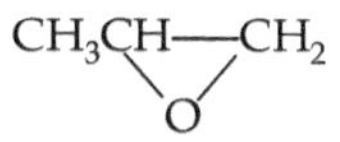

7. Which of the following reaction are feasible?

(a) $CH_3CH_2 - \underset{\underset{CH_2CH_3}{|}}{\overset{\overset{CH_2CH_3}{|}}{C}} - Br + OH^- \xrightarrow[CH_3OH]{25°C} CH_3CH_2 - \underset{\underset{CH_2CH_3}{|}}{\overset{\overset{CH_2CH_3}{|}}{C}} - OH$

(b) $C_6H_5{-}Cl + NaOCH_3 \longrightarrow C_6H_5{-}OCH_3$

(c) $C_6H_5{-}ONa + CH_3Br \longrightarrow C_6H_5{-}OCH_3$

(d) $CH_3 - \underset{\underset{CH_3}{|}}{\overset{\overset{CH_3}{|}}{C}} - ONa + CH_3Br \longrightarrow CH_3 - \underset{\underset{CH_3}{|}}{\overset{\overset{CH_3}{|}}{C}} - O - CH_3$

8. The reaction products of $C_6H_5OCH_3 + HI \xrightarrow{\Delta}$ is :
(a) C_6H_5OH (b) CH_3I
(c) C_6H_5I (d) CH_3OH

9. Select the correct statement(s) :
(a) Methoxyethane gives iodoethane with one equivalent of anhydrous HI
(b) Order of basicity in aqueous medium is $MeNH_2 < Me_2NH < Me_3N$
(c) Optically active alkanol will show total retention of configuration during its reaction with $SOCl_2$
(d) S-2-Bromobutane gives R-2-methylbutane nitrile with AgCN as major product

10. Compound (x) C_3H_6O decolorises bromine water, with dil. H_2SO_4 it undergoes hydrolysis to give (y) and (z). The correct statements are :
(a) (x) is an ether
(b) (x) is an alkene
(c) (x) is cyclic compound
(d) Both (y) and (z) are crbonyl compounds

11. Choose the correct statement(s) regarding to the product formed in the reaction given below ($-Bu^t$ stands for tertiary butyl group)

$$\underset{Me}{\overset{Me}{>}}C=C=C\overset{H}{\underset{Bu^t}{<}} \xrightarrow[\text{of } CH_3CO_3H]{2 \text{ equivalent}} \text{(epoxide product)}$$

Epoxidation at double bond takes place one by one
(a) the final product formed does not contain plane of symmetry
(b) the initial attack takes place on more substituted double bond from the least hindered side
(c) the mono-epoxide obtained in (b) undergoes further epoxidation more rapidly than the first epoxidation.
(d) the final product contains two fold axis of symmetry

12. The reaction of $CH_3CH=CH{-}C_6H_4{-}OH$ with HBr gives

(a) $CH_3CHBrCH_2{-}C_6H_4{-}OH$

(b) $CH_3CH_2CHBr{-}C_6H_4{-}OH$

(c) $CH_3CHBrCH_2{-}C_6H_4{-}Br$

(d) $CH_3CH_2CHBr{-}C_6H_4{-}Br$

13. The ether $C_6H_5{-}O{-}CH_2{-}C_6H_5$ when treated with HI produces

(a) $C_6H_5{-}CH_2I$ (b) $C_6H_5{-}CH_2OH$

(c) $C_6H_5{-}I$ (d) $C_6H_5{-}OH$

14. Which of the following combination can't be used for preparing an ether ?
(a) $C_6H_5OH + (CH_3)_2 SO_4$
(b) $C_6H_5Br + CH_3CH_2OH$
(c) $p\text{-}NO_2C_6H_4Br + CH_3CH_2OH$
(d) $C_6H_5OH + (CH_3)_3CBr$

15. $C_6H_5{-}O{-}\overset{14}{C}H_2{-}CH=CH_2 \xrightarrow{200°} P.$ Product (P) may be

(a) 2-($\overset{14}{C}H_2CH=CH_2$)phenol

(b) 2-($CH_2CH=\overset{14}{C}H_2$)phenol

(c) 4-($\overset{14}{C}H_2CH=CH_2$)phenol

(d) 4-($CH_2CH=\overset{14}{C}H_2$)phenol

DIRECTIONS for Q. 16 to Q. 30 : Read the following passages and answer the questions that follows :

PASSAGE 1

Cyclic acetal may be formed by the reaction of CH_3CHO (a) with the 1- and 2- OH groups, and (b) with 1- and 3- OH groups.

$$\underset{CH_2OH}{\overset{\overset{CH_2{-}OH}{|}}{\underset{|}{CH{-}OH}}} + O=C\overset{H}{\underset{CH_3}{<}} \longrightarrow \text{(cis and trans cyclic acetals)}$$

$$\underset{CH_2{-}OH}{\overset{\overset{CH_2{-}OH}{|}}{\underset{|}{CHOH}}} + O=C\overset{H}{\underset{CH_3}{<}} \longrightarrow \text{(cis and trans cyclic acetals)}$$

6. Total number of compounds formed in the first reaction is
(a) 1   (b) 2   (c) 3   (d) 4

7. The total number of compounds formed in the second reaction is
(a) 1   (b) 2   (c) 3   (d) 4

8. The mixture of both of the reactions can be separated to give .... compounds.
(a) 3   (b) 4   (c) 5   (d) 6

PASSAGE 2

3-Methylbutene is converted to ethers via following three different routes.

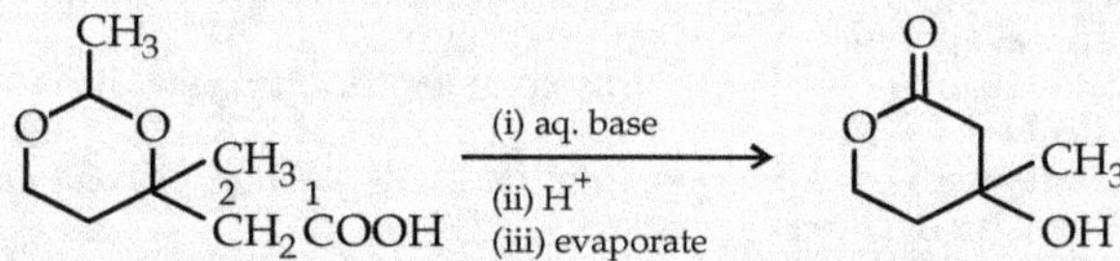

19. The set of reactions in (a) involve
(a) Markownikoff addition
(b) Rearrangement of carbocation
(c) Both
(d) Oxidation

20. The set of reactions in (b) involve
(a) Anti-Markownikoff addition
(b) Hydroboration-oxidation
(c) No rearrangement
(d) All the three

21. The set of reactions in (c) involve
(a) Markownikoff addition   (b) no rearrangement
(c) Both   (d) None

PASSAGE 3

Acetals are resistant to base, while these are hydrolysed to acids to aldehydes and diols.

22. The functional groups present in the reactant and product are

	Reactant	Product
(a)	ether, carboxylic acid	cyclic ketone, ether
(b)	hemiacetal, carboxylic acid	lactone, 3° alcohol
(c)	acetal, carboxylic acid	cyclic ester, 3° alcohol
(d)	diether, carboxylic acid	ether, ketone, 3° alcohol

23. Conversion of reactant to product involves
(a) hydrolysis and cyclisation
(b) hydrolysis and esterification
(c) Both (a) and (b)
(d) Hydrolysis and dehydration

24. What is the fate of C_1 of the reactant, when it converts into product?
(a) It will appear in the form of $-C-OH$
(b) It will appear in the form of $C = O$
(c) It will be removed as CO_2
(d) It will be appearing in the α-position to $C = O$ group

PASSAGE 4

Observe the following reaction

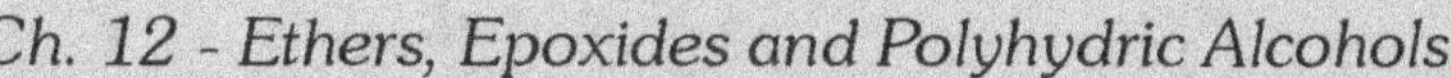

$$\xrightarrow{H^{\oplus}/H_2O} (P) + (Q) + (R)$$

the product P shows positive test towards neutral $FeCl_3$, Q towards $I_2/\overset{\ominus}{O}H$ and R towards Fehling solution.

25. 'P' on reaction with bromine water followed by Zn dust gives a substituted benzene which was [X], number of halogens in X is
(a) 2   (b) 3
(c) 4   (d) 5

26. Q and R respectively are

(a) $CH_3 - \underset{OH}{CH} - CH_3$, CH_3COCH_3

(b) $CH_3 - \underset{O}{\overset{\|}{C}} - CH_3$, CH_3CH_2CHO

(c) $CH_3 - \underset{O}{\overset{\|}{C}} - C_2H_5$, CH_3CHO

(d) $CH_3 - \underset{O}{\overset{\|}{C}} - H$, $CH_3\overset{\overset{O}{\|}}{C}CH_3$

27. $M \xrightarrow{DBr\ (Anhydrous)\ 1\ eq.}$ Product is

PASSAGE 5

Read and observe the following sketch of organic transformation carefully and then answer the questions given below :

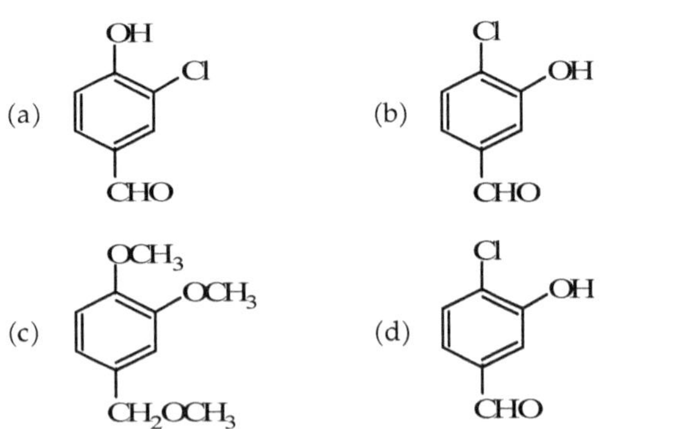

$$+ HCHO \xrightarrow{\text{NaOH}} \text{"S"} \xrightarrow[\text{Acetone}]{2CH_3I} \text{"T"}$$

28. The structure of 'T' is :

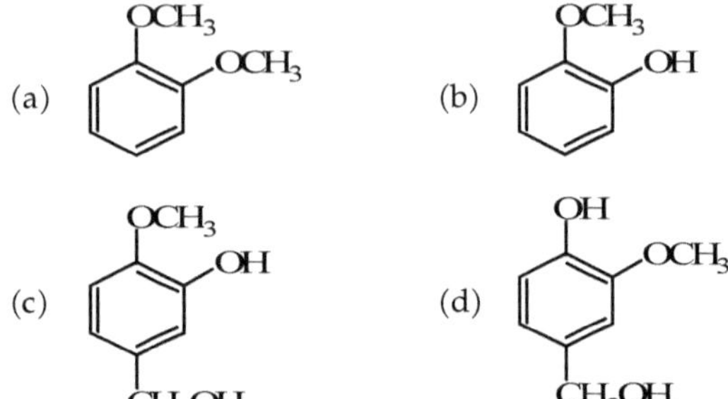

(a)   (b)   (c)   (d)

29. The structure of 'S' is

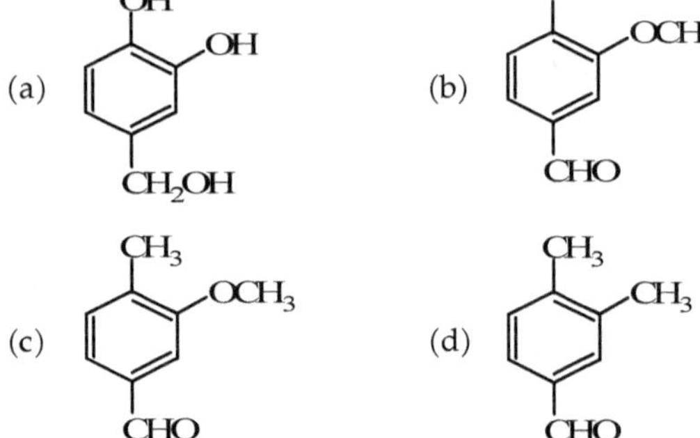

(a)   (b)   (c)   (d)

30. If 'T' is treated with H_3O^+ the compound formed is

(a)   (b)   (c)   (d)

DIRECTIONS for Q. 31 & Q. 33 : The following questions are matching type questions. Match Column I with Column II

31.

Column I (Reactant)		Column II (Product)	
(A)	Glycerol	(a)	Glycerol
(B)	Acetone	(b)	Acetone
(C)	Dimethylcadmium	(c)	Chloroform
(D)	Propene	(d)	Methanoic acid

32.

Column I		Column II	
(Conversion of glycerol to)		(Reagent required)	
(A)	Methanal	(a)	Oxalic acid
(B)	Formic acid	(b)	P + HI
(C)	Propene	(c)	Periodic acid
(D)	Propane	(d)	HI

33. Match the column :

Column-I		Column-II	
A.	$C_6H_5OCH_3 \xrightarrow{\text{HI, 100°C}}$	(a)	CH_3CH_2I
B.	$C_6H_5CH_2OCH_3 \xrightarrow[\text{100°C}]{\text{HI (1 mole)}}$	(b)	C_6H_5OH
C.	$CH_3CH_2OCH_3 \xrightarrow[\text{100°C}]{\text{HI (1 mole)}}$	(c)	$C_6H_5CH_2I$
D.	$CH_3CH_2OCH_2CH_3 \xrightarrow{\text{HI, 100°C}}$	(d)	CH_3I

Instructions for Q. 34 to 41 : Following questions are Assertion and Reasoning Type Questions :

Note : Each question contains STATEMENT-1 (Assertion) and STATEMENT-2 (Reason). Each question has 5 choices (a), (b), (c), (d) and (e) out of which ONLY ONE is correct.

(a)   Statement-1 is True, Statement-2 is True; Statement-2 is a correct explanation for Statement-1.
(b)   Statement-1 is True, Statement-2 is True; Statement-2 is NOT a correct explanation for Statement-1.
(c)   Statement -1 is True, Statement-2 is False.
(d)   Statement -1 is False, Statement-2 is True.
(e)   Statement -1 is False, Statement-2 is False.

34. **Statement 1 :** Ethers behaves as bases in the presence of mineral acids.
Statement 2 : It is due to the presence of lone pair of electrons on the oxygen.

35. **Statement 1 :** The major products formed by heating $C_6H_5CH_2OCH_3$ with HI are $C_6H_5CH_2I$ and CH_3OH.
Statement 2 : Benzyl cation is more stable than methyl cation.

36. **Statement 1 :** t-butyl methyl ether is not prepared by the reaction of t-butyl bromide with sodium methoxide.
Statement 2 : Sodium methoxide is a strong nucleophile.

37. **Statement 1 :** Preparation of ethers by acid dehydration of secondary or tertiary alcohols is not a suitable method.
Statement 2 : Ethers cannot be prepared by the dehydration of secondary or tertiary alcohols.

38. **Statement-1 :** Ethers behave as bases in the presence of mineral acids.
Statement-2 : Due to the presence of lone pairs of electrons on oxygen.

39. **Statement-1 :** High boiling point of glycerol is due to hydrogen bonding.
Statement-2 : Glycerol decomposes much below its boiling point and evaporation is carried in vacuum.

40. **Statement-1 :** With HI, anisole gives iodobenzene and methyl alcohol.
Statement-2 : Iodide ion combines with smaller group to avoid steric hindrance.

41. **Statement-1 :** With HI at 373 K, *ter*-butyl methyl ether gives *ter*-butyl iodide and methanol.
Statement-2 : The reaction occurs by S_N2 mechanism.

Instructions for Q. 42 to 43 : Following questions are Integer Type Questions :

42. Sum of molecular mass of iodides produced in following reaction is

(a) $\xrightarrow{\text{conc. HI}}$

(b) $\xrightarrow[\text{HI}]{\text{anhydrous}}$

(c) $Ph - O - Me \xrightarrow[\text{excess}]{\text{HI}}$

If answer of part (a) is x, part (b) is y and part (c) is z then present sum of x + y + z in the OMR sheet. For example : if answer (a) is 12, (b) is 13 and (c) is 3 you will fill 0028 in OMR sheet.

43. How many ethers will be formed when a mixture of C_2H_5OH and methyl alcohol are treated with conc. H_2SO_4 ?

EXERCISE 12.3 (Subjective Problems)

Give IUPAC name to each of the following compound :

(a) $ClCH_2CH_2OCH_3$

(b) $p\text{-}NO_2.C_6H_4OC_2H_5$

(c) ⬡—$OCH_2CH_2CH_3$

(d) $CH_2 = CHOCH_2C_6H_5$

(e) $CH_3CHOHCH_2CH_2CH_2OCH_3$.

Upon treatment with sulphuric acid, a mixture of ethyl alcohol and *n*-propyl alcohol gives a mixture of three ethers, while a mixture of *tert*-butyl alcohol and ethyl alcohol gives a single ether in quantitative yield. Explain.

How will you carry out following conversions ?

(a) Phenol to *p*-nitrophenyl ethyl ether
(b) Benzene to diphenyl ether
(c) Cyclohexanol to cyclohexyl methyl ether
(d) Toluene to dibenzyl ether
(e) Ethylene to divinyl ether.

Give the mechanism for the formation of hydroperoxide from ethers and oxygen.

Cleavage of optically active *sec*-butyl methyl ether by anhydrous HBr yields mainly methyl bromide and *sec*-butyl alcohol having same configuration and optical purity as the starting material. Can you suggest the mechanism (*i.e.* S_N^2, or S_N^1) involving in this reaction ?

Write the structures of the products when following ethers are exposed to oxygen.

(a) $CH_2 = CHCH_2OCH_2CH_2CH_3$
(b) $CH_3CH_2CH_2OCH_2C_6H_5$.

7. (a) Give a simple chemical test to distinguish an ether from a hydrocarbon of comparable molecular weight.
(b) Give chemical tests for distinguishing alcohols from ethers.

8. Explain the following :
(a) Ethers are soluble in conc. H_2SO_4 but separate out on addition of water.
(b) Ethers are used as solvents for BF_3 and Grignard reagent.

9. Give main products of (a) mononitration of *p*-methylanisole, and (b) monobromination of *p*-ethoxyphenol.

10. Give the products of the reactions of styrene oxide with
(a) *aq.* NaCN
(b) *aq.* NaN_3
(c) dry HCl
(d) excess NH_3
(e) $LiAlD_4$, then H_2O
(f) CH_3CH_2SH followed by bases.

11. Give the products obtained by treating 1, 2-epoxypropane (propylene oxide) with the following reagents.
(a) Methanol in presence of HCl
(b) Methanol
(c) Methanol in presence of sod. methoxide.

12. Give the various possible products that can be obtained from the following reaction.

$$\text{cyclohexene-}CH_2Br + C_2H_5OH \xrightarrow{\text{heat}}$$

13. What reagent will yield (a) *cis*- and (b) *trans*-cyclopentene glycol from cyclopentene ?

14. Predict the products in presence of periodic acid (or lead tetra acetate)oxidation of
(a) CH_2OHCH_2OH
(b) $CH_3CHOHCH_2OCH_3$
(c) 1, 2-Cyclopentanediol.

15. One mole of compound $C_6H_{14}O_5$ reacts with 4 moles of HIO_4. The moles of products formed are : $1CH_2O$, $1CH_3CHO$, and $3HCOOH$. Suggest a possible structure for $C_6H_{14}O_5$.

16. Suggest the structure of the compound whose one mole on oxidation with one mole of periodic acid gives
(a) one mole each of CH_3COCH_3 and HCHO
(b) one mole of $CHO.(CH_2)_4.CHO$.

17. An alkene is treated with OsO_4 followed by aqueous sodium bisulphite to form compound X. The compound X is treated with periodic acid, it forms an unsubstituted cyclic ketone with molecular formula $C_6H_{10}O$. What is the structure of the alkene?

SOLUTIONS

EXERCISE 12.1

1	(c)	6	(c)	11	(a)	16	(a)	21	(b)	26	(b)	31	(d)
2	(c)	7	(b)	12	(b)	17	(c).	22	(c).	27	(b).	32	(b)
3	(d)	8	(b)	13	(b)	18	(d)	23	(b)	28	(d)		
4	(d)	9	(a)	14	(c)	19	(a).	24	(c).	29	(d).		
5	(d)	10	(d)	15	(c)	20	(a)	25	(b)	30	(b)		

1.   Double bond is the principal functional group.

2.   (c)   Remember that in migration to ortho position, allyl group rearranges only once, hence position of C^{14} is changed.

3.   [X] is $CH_3CH = CHCH_3$, formed via 2° carbocation ; Y is $CH_3.\overset{\overset{\displaystyle OCH_3}{|}}{C}HCH_2CH_3$

4.   *tert-* and *sec-*carbocations are liable to undergo elimination reaction in presence of strong alkoxide bases. Aryl and vinyl halides do not undergo nucleophilic substitution.

5.   Williamson synthesis and dehydration of Me_3COH will lead to alkene (isobutene) as the main product because the *tert*-butyl cation will undergo dehydration readily than the attack of a bulkier nucleophile Me_3COH. However, di-*tert*-butyl ether can be prepared in low yield by following reaction.

$$2Me_3C—Cl \xrightarrow{Ag_2CO_3} Me_3C—O—CMe_3$$

6. $C_6H_5CH_2Br + NaOC_2H_5$ or $C_6H_5CH_2ONa + C_2H_5Br \longrightarrow C_6H_5CH_2OC_2H_5$

7.   (*a*)   Acidic hydration leads to hydration according to Markovnikov addition, but with rearranged carbon skeleton.

      (*b*)   Oxymercuration-demercuration leads to hydration according to Markovnikov rule and without any rearrangement. This process will produce required ether.

      (*c*)   Hydroboration-oxidation leads to hydration in *anti*-Markovnikov's way without rearrangement.

      Three respective main products are :

      (A) ;   (B) ;   (C)

8.   In isopropyl ether more stable (2°) intermediate is formed than in *n*-propyl ether which forms 1° intermediate.

9.   It is an example of solvomercuration and demercuration.

10. $CH_3CH = CH_2 \xrightarrow{Cl_2, H_2O} \underset{\underset{\displaystyle OH \quad Cl}{|\quad\quad|}}{CH_3CH—CH_2} \xrightarrow{aq. NaOH} CH_3CH{\underset{O}{\diagdown\diagup}}CH_2$

11. Only option (*a*) involves the use of an acid.

12. Epoxide has higher value of enthalpy of combustion because the three-membered ring is more strained.

13. In presence of acid, nucleophile H_2O^{18} attacks the more substituted carbon of the epoxide.

14. [X] ;   [Y] ;   [Z]   *trans-*

15. Here reaction is to be carried out only on —CO, so —CHO should be protected by ethylene glycol, otherwise Grignard reagent will react with both functional groups, *i.e.* —CO as well as CHO.

16. Greater the steric hindrance, slower is the oxidation.

17. Reaction is bimolecular reduction followed by oxidation

$$2CH_3—\overset{\overset{\displaystyle CH_3}{|}}{C}=O \xrightarrow[\text{(ii) }H_3O^+]{\text{(i) Mg}} CH_3—\underset{\underset{\displaystyle OH}{|}}{\overset{\overset{\displaystyle CH_3}{|}}{C}}—\underset{\underset{\displaystyle OH}{|}}{\overset{\overset{\displaystyle CH_3}{|}}{C}}—CH_3 \xrightarrow{HIO_4} 2CH_3—\overset{\overset{\displaystyle CH_3}{|}}{C}=O$$

21. (b)

$C_5H_{10}O$ $C_5H_{10}I_2$ 1, 3-pentadiene

22. (c) In (b) aryl fluoride does not undergo S_N reaction.

23. (b) Methyl vinyl ether under anhydrous condition at room temperature undergoes addition reaction.

$$CH_2 = CH - OCH_3 \xrightarrow{HBr} CH_3 - \underset{\underset{Br}{|}}{CH} - O - CH_3$$

24. (c) Although in both cases products are CH_3I and C_6H_5OH; the two reactions follow different mechanism.

$$C_6H_5 - O - CH_3 \xrightarrow[S_N2]{HI(g)} CH_3I + C_6H_5OH$$

$$C_6H_5 - O - CH_3 \xrightarrow[S_N1]{conc.HI} CH_3I + C_6H_5OH$$

Remember that during S_N1 reaction, CH_3^+ is formed because it is more stable than $C_6H_5^+$.

25. (b) When one of the alkyl groups is 3° and another is 1°, nature of reagent determines the type of mechanism (S_N^1 or S_N^2). A polar solvent or reagent capable of forming ions (viz. conc. HI) will cause S_N^1 reaction, while a non-polar solvent or a reagent not capable of forming ions (anhydrous HI) will cause S_N^2 reaction.

26. (b) $(CH_3)_3CBr + NaOC_2H_5$ can't be applied for synthesising the ether because sod. ethoxide, being a strong base, will preferentially cause elimination reaction.

$$(CH_3)_3CBr \xrightarrow{^-OC_2H_5} (CH_3)_2C = CH_2 + HBr$$

In isobutene + ethanol, isobutene will form *tert*-butyl cation which reacts with ethanol, a nucleophile to form ether.

$$(CH_3)_2C = CH_2 \xrightarrow{H^+} (CH_3)_2\overset{+}{C}CH_3$$

$$\xrightarrow[\text{(ii) } -H^+]{\text{(i) } CH_3CH_2OH} (CH_3)_3COCH_2CH_3$$

27. (b) In the acid-catalysed ring opening of an unsymmetrical epoxide, the nucleophile attacks primarily at the more substituted carbon atom because such carbon of the protonated epoxide acquires a considerable positive charge.

This resembles like a more stable 2° or 3° carbocation and hence the reaction is S_N1 like.

In case of CH_3ONa, $^-OCH_3$, being a strong nucleophile, opens the strained epoxide ring in a direct S_N2 reaction, i.e. by attacking at the least hindered carbon atom.

28. (d)

29. (d) The compound is a cyclic acetal; hence it is stable to alkalies and hydrolysed by acids.

30. (b) Base catalysed epoxide opening is a typical S_N2 reaction in which attack of the nucleophile takes place at the less hindered epoxide.

31. (d) It is an example of Claisen rearrangement.

32. (b)

EXERCISE 12.2

MCQ >1	1	(a,b,c)	2	(a,b,c)	3	(a, c, d)
CORRECT	4	(a, b, d)	5	(a, d)	6	(c, d)
OPTION	7	(c, d)	8	(a, b)	9	(a, b, d)
	10	(a, b)	11	(a, b, c)	12	(b)
	13	(a, d)	14	(b, b)	15	(a, d)
PASSAGE 1	16	(d)	17	(b)	18	(b)
PASSAGE 2	19	(c)	20	(d)	21	(c)
PASSAGE 3	22	(c)	23	(c)	24	(b)
PASSAGE 4	25	(c)	26	(b)	27	(b)
PASSAGE 5	28	(c)	29	(d)	30	(a)
Match the Following	31	(A)-d ; (B)-c ; (C)-b ; (D)-a				
	32	(A) - c, (B) - a, c, (C) - d, (D) - b				
	33	(A) - b, d; (B) - c; (C) - d, (D) - a, b				
A/R	34	(a)	35	(a)	36	(c)
	37	(b)	38	(a)	39	(b)
	40	(d)	41	(c)		
INTEGER	42	454	43	3		

1. Ethers are capable of forming hydrogen bonds with water as well as alcohols. Alcohols too can form H-bonds with ethers and water. In higher alcohols alkyl group dominates, hence H-bond not possible.

2. (*a*) Phenol and HBr, both being acids, do not react with each other. Moreover, this reaction involves cleavage of the C—O bond which is difficult because C—O bond acquires double bond character due to resonance. Reaction (*b*) will lead to elimination reaction rather substitution. In reaction (*c*) vinylic chlorine will not be replaced, rather allylic chlorine will be replaced by —OCH_3.

9. (a, b, d)

(a) $Me-OCH_2-CH_3 \xrightarrow[(S_N2)]{\text{Anhydrous HI}} Me-I+Et-OH$

(b) Order of basicity in aqueous medium
$Me_2NH < Me-NH_2 < Me_3N$

(c) With $SOCl_2$ complete retention is obtained

(d) Isocyanide is major product not nitrile

10. (a, b) $CH_2 = CH-O-CH_3$

11. (a, b, c)

Second epoxidation is faster because of activation by the epoxy oxygen.

12. (b) The mechanism of this reaction is represented as follows.

Benzylic carbocation (stable)

13. (a, d) The aromatic ethers are cleaved to give phenol as one of the products.

14. (b, d) The combination $C_6H_5Br + CH_3CH_2OH$ has non-reactive C_6H_5Br, while in the combination $C_6H_5OH + Me_3CBr$, Me_3CBr being *tert*-halide will undergo elimination reaction rather substitution. Hence, only combinations (*a*) and (*c*) can be used for preparing ether.

$C_6H_5OH + (CH_3)_2SO_4 \xrightarrow{S_N} C_6H_5OCH_3$;

$p\text{-}NO_2C_6H_4Br + CH_3CH_2OH \xrightarrow{Ar\,S_N} p\text{-}NO_2C_6H_4OCH_2CH_3$

Sol. (Q-25-27) :

(R)

Sol. (Q-28-30) :

28. (c) **29.** (d) **30.** (a)

42. 0454

(a)   156   I = 127 $C_2H_5 = 29$

(b)   156   I = 127   Me = 15

(c) Me – I   142

156 + 156 + 142 = 454

43. 3

CH_3OCH_3, $CH_3OCH_2CH_3$, $C_2H_5OC_2H_5$.

EXERCISE 12.3

1. (*a*)   1-Chloro-2-methoxyethane   (*b*)   4-Ethoxynitrobenzene   (*c*)   *n*-Propoxycyclohexane
(*d*)   Benzyloxyethene   (*e*)   5-Methoxy-2-pentanol.

2. Ethyl alcohol and *n*-propyl alcohol, both are 1° alcohols ; hence they undergo S_N2 mechanism leading to the formation of three different ethers ; diethyl ether, di-*n*-propyl ether and ethyl *n*-propyl ether. On the other hand, *tert*-butyl alcohol may form quite stable *tert*-butyl carbocation which will react with the nucleophile (ethyl alcohol) easily to form *tert*-butyl ethyl ether.

3. (*a*)

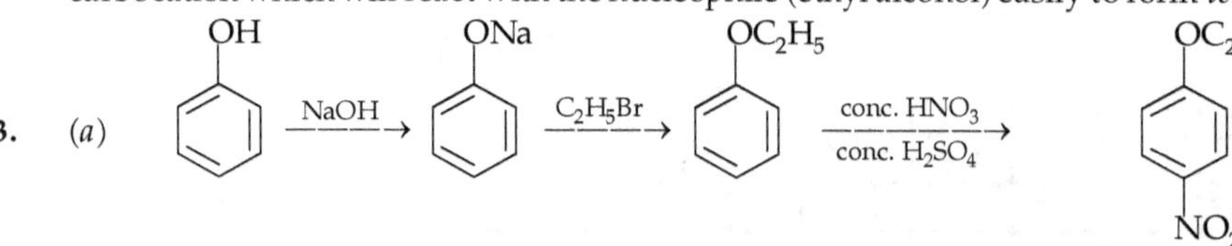

p-Nitrophenyl ethyl ether

In the preparation of aryl alkyl ether, halide component should be taken in the form of alkyl halide, because aryl halides do not readily undergo S_N^2 reactions. Further note that since ArOH is much more acidic than ROH, it is converted to ArO^- by OH^- instead of by Na as in ROH.

(b)

$$C_6H_6 \xrightarrow{Br_2,\ Fe} C_6H_5Br \xrightarrow[\text{Cu, > 200°C, no solvent}]{C_6H_5ONa} C_6H_5OC_6H_5$$

Diphenyl ether

Phenols do not undergo intermolecular dehydration. Although aryl halides can't be used as substrate in typical Williamson synthesis, they do undergo a modified Williamson-type synthesis at higher temperatures in presence of copper.

(c)

$$C_6H_5OH + CH_2N_2 \xrightarrow{H^+} C_6H_5OCH_3 \quad \text{or} \quad C_6H_5OH \xrightarrow[(ii)\ CH_3I]{(i)\ Na} C_6H_5OCH_3$$

(d) $\quad C_6H_5CH_3 \xrightarrow[\text{light}]{Cl_2} C_6H_5CH_2Cl \xrightarrow[H_2O]{OH^-} C_6H_5CH_2OH \xrightarrow[(-H_2O)]{H_2SO_4} C_6H_5CH_2OCH_2C_6H_5$

(e) $\quad CH_2 = CH_2 \xrightarrow{HOCl} ClCH_2CH_2OH \xrightarrow[\text{heat}]{H_2SO_4} ClCH_2CH_2{-}O{-}CH_2CH_2Cl \xrightarrow{\text{alc. KOH}} CH_2 = CH{-}O{-}CH = CH_2$

Divinyl ether

Remember that vinyl alcohol, $H_2C = CHOH$, can't be used as a starting material because it is not stable and rearranges to CH_3CHO. Hence, in the above preparation double bond must be introduced after the ether bond is formed.

Formation of hydroperoxide is a free-radical reaction, involving following steps.

Initiation step. $RCH_2OCH_2R + \cdot \ddot{O}{-}\ddot{O}\cdot \longrightarrow R\overset{\cdot}{C}HOCH_2R + H{-}\ddot{O}{-}\ddot{O}\cdot$

Propagation step. $R\overset{\cdot}{C}HOCH_2R + \cdot \ddot{O}{-}\ddot{O}\cdot \longrightarrow$ R—CHOCH$_2$R with $\dot{O}$—$\dot{O}$

$$\underset{\overset{|}{O}-O\cdot}{RCHOCH_2R} + RCH_2OCH_2R \longrightarrow \underset{\overset{|}{O}-OH}{RCHOCH_2R} + R\overset{\cdot}{C}HOCH_2R$$

Hydroperoxide

$$\underset{CH_3}{\underset{|}{CH_3}}\overset{C_2H_5}{\underset{|}{CH}}{-}O{-}CH_3 \xrightarrow{H^+} CH_3\overset{C_2H_5}{\underset{|}{CH}}{-}\overset{+}{\underset{H}{O}}{-}CH_3$$

The above protonated ether may react with Br^- either through S_N^2 or S_N^1. In case of S_N^2, the attack of the Br^- will be at the least hindered methyl group to form CH_3Br and *sec*-butyl alcohol which is in accordance with the given product. Since bond to chiral carbon is not cleaved, configuration and optical purity of the product will be identical to that of the starting material. In case the mechanism were S_N^1, carbocation would have been formed leading to racemic *sec*-butyl alcohol.

(a) $\quad CH_2 = CH\,CH{-}O{-}C_3H_7\text{-}n$ with OOH

(b) $\quad n\text{-}C_3H_7{-}O{-}CHC_6H_5$ with OOH

Attack by oxygen on the given carbon will form more stable allylic radical in (a), and benzylic radical in (b).

(a) Like water and alcohols, ethers are basic, hence they dissolve in conc. H_2SO_4 with evolution of much heat.

$$\underset{\text{Base}_1}{ROR} + \underset{\text{Acid}_2}{H_2SO_4} \longrightarrow \underset{\text{Acid}_1}{[R_2OH]^+} + \underset{\text{Base}_2}{HSO_4^-}$$

(b) 1° and 2° alcohols are oxidizable and hence give positive tests with acidic potassium dichromate (orange colour turns green). 3° Alcohols give turbidity immediately on adding Lucas reagent. Ethers give negative results to these tests.

(a) Water is stronger base than ether and removes proton from protonated ether, R_2OH^+

$$\underset{\text{Acid}_1}{[R_2OH]^+} + \underset{\text{Base}_2}{H_2O} \longrightarrow \underset{\text{Base}_1}{R_2O} + \underset{\text{Acid}_2}{H_3O^+}$$

(b) Due to unshared electron pairs, ethers act as Lewis bases and hence easily react with Lewis acids like BF_3 and RMgBr to form coordinated compounds.

$$(C_2H_5)_2\ddot{O}: + BF_3 \longrightarrow (C_2H_5)_2\ddot{O} \longrightarrow \overset{+}{B}F_3$$

$$2(C_2H_5)_2\ddot{O}: + RMgBr \longrightarrow (C_2H_5)_2O \to \underset{Br}{\overset{R}{Mg}} \leftarrow O(C_2H_5)_2$$

Note that two molecules of ether coordinate tetrahedrally with one Mg^{2+}.

9. (*a*)

H_3C—⟨benzene ring⟩—OCH_3 (Strong activator) $\xrightarrow{\text{mononitration}}$ H_3C—⟨benzene ring⟩—OCH_3 with NO_2

p-Methylanisole   2-Nitro-4-methylanisole

(*b*)

HO—⟨benzene ring⟩—OC_2H_5 (Stronger activator) $\xrightarrow{\text{monobromination}}$ HO—⟨benzene ring⟩—OC_2H_5 with Br

p-Ethoxyphenol   2-Bromo-4-ethoxyphenol

10. All are S_N^2 reactions, except (*c*) which has S_N^1 mechanism because of the stability of the intermediate benzyl carbocation, $C_6H_5\overset{+}{C}HCH_2O$

(*a*) $C_6H_5CH(OH)CH_2CN$ (*b*) $C_6H_5CH(OH)CH_2N_3$

(*c*) $C_6H_5CH\!\!-\!\!CH_2$ (epoxide) $\xrightarrow{H^+} C_6H_5\overset{+}{C}H\!\!-\!\!CH_2OH \xrightarrow{Cl^+} C_6H_5CHCH_2OH$ with Cl

(*d*) $C_6H_5CH(OH)CH_2NH_2$ (*e*) $C_6H_5CH(OH)CH_2D$

(*f*) $C_6H_5CH(OH)CH_2SCH_2CH_3$.

11. (*a*) $CH_3\cdot CH\!\!-\!\!CH_2$ (epoxide) $\xrightarrow[\text{CH}_3\text{OH}]{\text{HCl}} CH_3CHCH_2OH$ with OCH_3 **(Acid-catalyzed cleavage)**

(*b*)   In the absence of acid, methanol (an *extremely weak base*) would have to displace the strongly basic alkoxy oxygen on ring-opening which cannot occur. However, in presence of acid, oxygen atom of the epoxide is displaced as weakly basic —OH group which possible.

(*c*) $CH_3CH\!\!-\!\!CH_2$ (epoxide) $\xrightarrow[\text{CH}_3\text{OH}]{\text{CH}_3\text{ONa}} CH_3CHCH_2OCH_3$ with OH **(Base-catalyzed cleavage)**

12.

⟨cyclohexene with CH_2Br⟩ $\xrightarrow[\text{heat}]{C_2H_5OH}$ ⟨cyclohexene with $\overset{+}{C}H_2$⟩ ⟷ ⟨cyclohexane ⊕ with CH_2⟩ $\xrightarrow{C_2H_5OH}$ ⟨cyclohexane with CH_2 and OC_2H_5⟩   **III**

↓ C_2H_5OH ↓ $-H^+$

⟨cyclohexene with $CH_2OC_2H_5$⟩   ⟨cyclohexadiene with CH_2⟩

I   **II**

13. (*a*)   Cold *aq.* $KMnO_4$ or OsO_4 containing H_2O_2 (*b*)   Performic acid

14. (*a*)   CHO.CHO   (*b*)   No reaction   (*c*) $O = CH(CH_2)_3CH = O.$

15. There are four adjacencies, $CH_2\!=\!O$ and CH_3CHO are formed by oxidation of the terminal C—OH groups, while 3HCOOH indicates the presence of three —CH—OH groups in the middle of the molecule.

$$\begin{array}{c} H \quad H \quad H \quad H \quad H \\ | \quad\ | \quad\ | \quad\ | \quad\ | \\ H\!-\!C\!-\!C\!-\!C\!-\!C\!-\!C\!-\!CH_3 \\ | \quad\ | \quad\ | \quad\ | \quad\ | \\ OH\ OH\ OH\ OH\ OH \end{array}$$

16. (*a*) $(CH_3)_2CO + O = CH_2 \longleftarrow (CH_3)_2\underset{OH}{C}\!-\!\underset{OH}{CH_2}$ (*b*) $OHC(CH_2)_4CHO \longleftarrow$ ⟨cyclohexane with two OH⟩

17.   ⟨bicyclohexylidene structure⟩

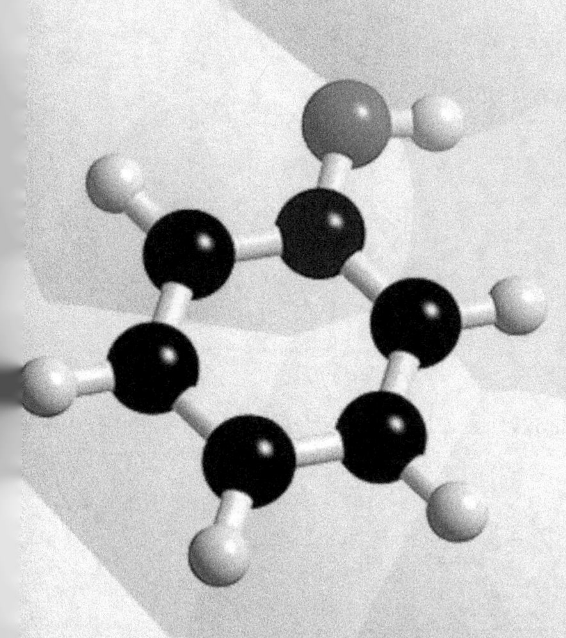

13

Phenols

13.1   Nomenclature

Compounds in which hydroxyl group is directly attached to a benzene ring are called *phenols*. The parent compound of this group of compounds is simply called phenol, C_6H_5OH. Remember that phenols differ from alcohols in the respect that in the former the —OH group is directly attached to the carbon atom of an aromatic ring, *i.e.* to an sp^2 hybridised carbon, while in alcohols the —OH is attached to an sp^3 hybridised carbon ; however they resemble enols where —OH group is attached to an sp^2 hybridised carbon.

OH   OH   OH

Cyclohexanol   Phenol   Cyclohexenol

Although the systematic name for phenol is *benzenol*, phenol and hydroxybenzene are also acceptable IUPAC names. The three methylphenols and the three dihydroxybenzenes are generally named by their common names (given in bracket)

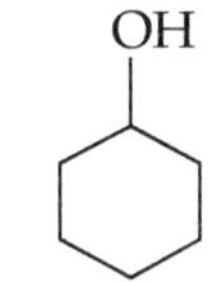
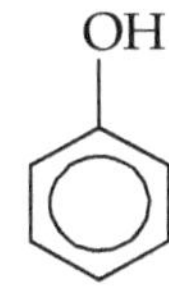
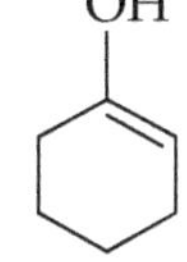
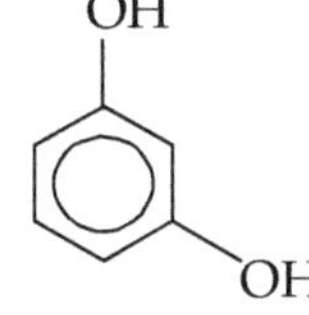
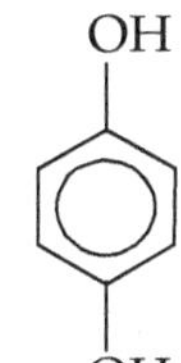

Phenol	3-Methylphenol	o-Dihydroxybenzene	m-Dihydroxybenzene	p-Dihydroxybenzene
(Carbolic acid)	(*m*–Cresol)	1, 2-Benzendiol (Catechol)	(Resorcinol)	(Hydroquinone) or Quinol

Like the dihydroxybenzenes, the isomeric trihydroxybenzenes have unique names.

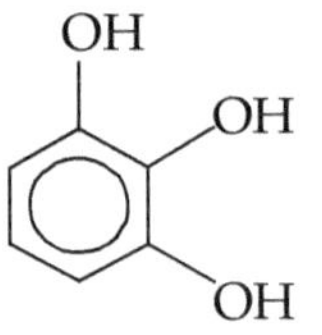

1, 2, 3-Trihydroxybenzene   1, 2, 4-Trihydroxybenzene 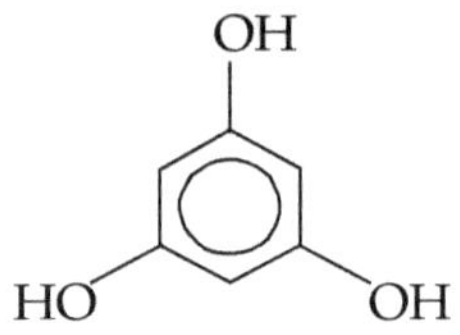   1, 3, 5-Trihydroxybenzene
(Pyrogallol)   (Phloroglucinol)

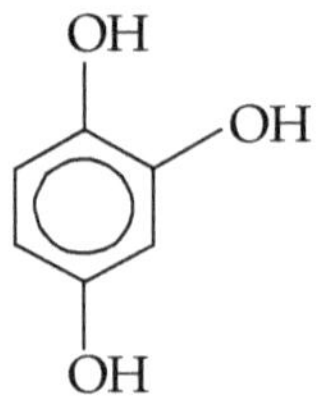

Carboxyl and acyl groups take precedence over the phenolic hydroxyl, and hence it is treated as a substituent in these cases.

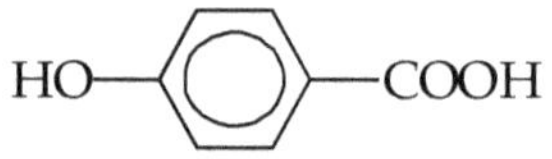

p-Hydroxybenzoic acid 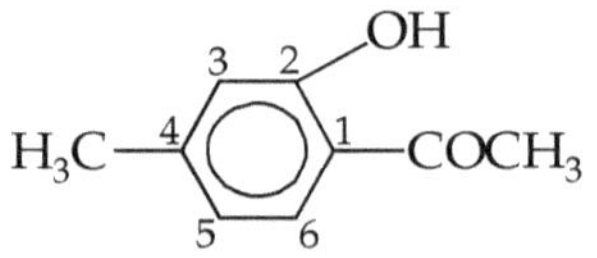   2-Hydroxy-4-methylacetophenone

TEST YOUR UNDERSTANDING - 13.1

1. Write IUPAC names for the following :

(a)   (b) 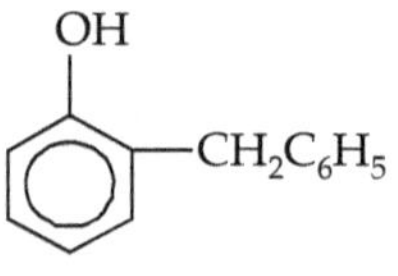   (c)

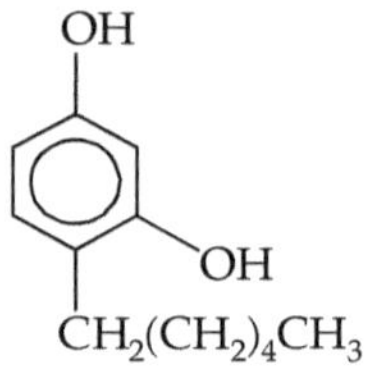

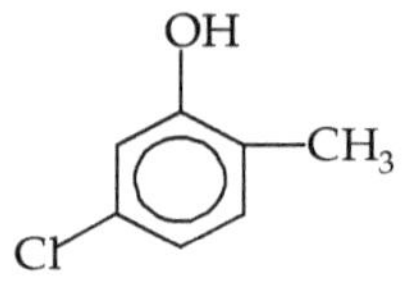

2. Write the structure for the following compounds.

   (a)   Phenoxyacetic acid   (b)   Phenyl acetate

   (c)   2-Hydroxy-3-phenylbenzonic acid   (d)   *p*-Hydroxyanisole.

13.2   Preparation of Phenols

Phenol was first of all isolated from middle oil fraction of coal-tar distillation.

1. **By hydrolysis of arenediazonium salts.** This is a highly versatile method of making phenols because the conditions required for the preparation of diazonium salt (diazotization step) and its hydrolysis are mild. (Details are given in the chapter on diazonium salts).

$$ArNH_2 \xrightarrow[0-5°C]{HONO} ArN_2^+ \xrightarrow[heat]{H_2O} ArOH + N_2$$

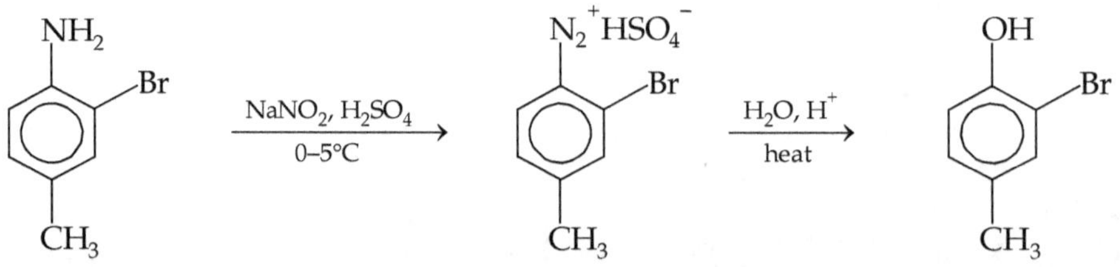

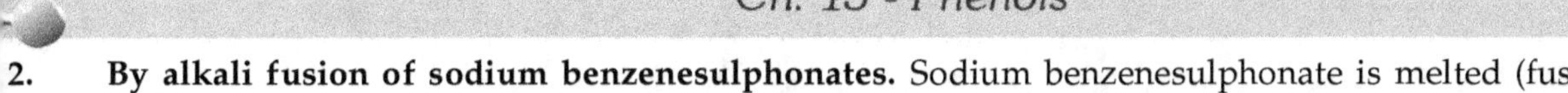

2. **By alkali fusion of sodium benzenesulphonates.** Sodium benzenesulphonate is melted (fused) with sodium hydroxide at 350°C to produce sodium phenoxide which is converted into phenol on acidification.

Sod. phenoxide

However, the condition required to bring about the reaction are so vigorous that this method cannot be used for the preparation of many phenols.

3. **By hydrolysis of chlorobenzene (Dow process).** Although chlorobenzene is inert to aq. NaOH under ordinary conditions, it can be converted quantitatively into phenol by heating at high temperature and under high pressure. Remember that conversion of chlorobenzene to phenol under these vigorous conditions takes place *via* benzyne mechanism (*elimination-addition mechanism*).

However, aryl halides containing strongly electron-withdrawing groups in *ortho* and *para* positions to the halogen easily undergo usual **(nucleophilic substitution)** reaction with aq. NaOH.

2, 4-Dinitrochlorobenzene   2, 4-Dinitrophenol   2, 4, 6-Trinitrophenol

2, 4-Dinitrophenol can be easily converted into 2, 4, 6-trinitrophenol **(picric acid)** by nitration.

4. **From cumene hydroperoxide (Commercial method).** Commercially, nearly all phenol is made today from isopropylbenzene, commonly known as *cumene*. Cumene is converted by air oxidation into cumene hydroperoxide, which is converted by aqueous acid into phenol and acetone. Cumene, in turn, can be easily obtained by the Friedel-Crafts alkylation of benzene with propene.

Benzene   Cumene   Cumene hydroperoxide

Phenol   Acetone

Note that this method involves the conversion of two relatively inexpensive organic compounds (benzene and propene) into two valuable industrial chemicals, phenol and acetone.

This step involves migration of phenyl group to electron-deficient oxygen.

TEST YOUR UNDERSTANDING - 13.2

1.   (*a*)   Give mechanism involved in the conversion of *p*-toluenesulphonic acid to *p*-cresol.

      (*b*)   Write a stepwise mechanism for the hydrolysis of chlorobenzene with aq. NaOH under high pressure and at high temperature (370°C).

2.   Try to prepare (*a*) catechol (1, 2-dihydroxybenzene), and (*b*) resorcinol (1, 3-dihydroxybenezene) from benzene.

13.3   Physical Properties

Physical properties of phenols are strongly influenced by hydroxyl group, which permits phenols to form hydrogen bonds with other phenol molecules causing high melting and boiling points, and also with water, causing some (*partial*) solubility in water. This accounts why phenols have higher melting and boiling points and are more soluble in water than arenes and aryl halides of comparable molecular weight. Phenols, themselves, are colourless and the colour, if any, associated with phenols is either due to the presence of some other colour producing group, *viz.* —NO_2, or due to the presence of some oxidised product of phenol as impurity.

An interesting example of comparative solubility and boiling point is observed in the three isomeric (*o*-, *m*-, and *p*-) nitrophenols. *p*- Nitrophenol is capable of forming intermolecular H–bond between themselves and with water too, hence it has high higher m.p. and more solubility in water. *m*-Nitrophenol also behaves in the same way.

p-Nitrophenol (intermolecular H-bond between two *p*-nitrophenol molecules)   (intermolecular H-bond with water)   *o*-Nitrophenol (intramolecular H-bond restricts intermolecular H-bonds)

However, *o*-nitrophenol is capable of forming intramolecular H-bond because the newly formed ring will be 6 membered. Due to intramolecular H-bonding, it does not form intermolecular H-bond neither with its second molecule nor with water. Hence *o*-nitrophenol has low m.p. and low solubility in water than the corresponding *m*- and *p*-isomers.

TEST YOUR UNDERSTANDING - 13.3

1.   Which of the following compounds is expected to have intramolecular hydrogen bonding ?

      (*a*)   *o*-Hydroxybenzaldehyde   (*b*)   *o*-Nitroaniline

      (*c*)   *o*-Hydroxybenzonitrile   (*d*)   Salicylic acid (*o*-Hydroxybenzoic acid)

      (*e*)   *o*-Fluorophenol   (*f*)   *o*-Cresol.

13.4   Acidity of Phenols

The most characteristic property of phenols is their acidity. Phenols are more acidic than alcohols which are even more weakly acidic than water, but phenols are less acidic than carboxylic acids.

$$R—COOH > Ar—OH > H—OH > R—OH \qquad \textbf{(Acidic character)}$$

Acidity of phenols has been discussed at large in the chapter on "Carboxylic Acids". However, a summary of acidic character of phenols is given here.

(i) Greater acidity of a phenol than an alcohol is due to possibility of resonance in phenol which leads to electron-deficient oxygen atom. Presence of electron-deficient oxygen atom (see structures II, III and IV) in turn weakens

the $-\overset{+}{O}\longleftarrow H$ bond, and thus facilitates release of proton.

$$I \longleftrightarrow II \longleftrightarrow III \longleftrightarrow IV$$

Such structures are not possible in alcohols.

(ii) Once hydrogen atom is removed from phenol, the ion (phenoxide) is very much stabilized due to delocalization of its negative charge.

$$V \longleftrightarrow VI \longleftrightarrow VII \longleftrightarrow VIII$$

Resonance in phenoxide ion (note that structures VI to VIII are equivalent)

Remember that phenoxide ion is very much more stable than the parent compound phenol because phenoxide ion does not involve charge separation, while in phenol three equivalent resonanting structures (II to IV) involve charge separation.

(iii) Electron-withdrawing substituents increase the acidity of phenols ; while electron-releasing substituents decrease acidity. Thus substituents affect acidity of phenols in the same way as they affect acidity of carboxylic acids ; it is of course, opposite to the way these groups affect basicity of amines.

G withdraws electrons, thus disperses the –ve charge of the ion, stabilises it and hence increases ionization of the parent phenol.

(where G = $-NO_2$, $-CN$, $-CHO$, $-COOH$, $-\overset{+}{N}R_3$, $-X$)

G releases electrons, thus intensifies the -ve charge of the ion, destabilises it and hence decreases ionization of the parent phenol.

(where G = $-R$, $-OR$, $-NR_2$)

13.4.1 Relative Acidic Characters of *o*-, *p*- and *m*- Isomers

For assessing the comparative acidic character of an organic compound, always remember that the presence of an electron withdrawing group increases the acidity while that of an electron-releasing group decreases acidity mainly due to resonance effect and inductive effect ; although sometimes hyperconjugation and H–bonding also plays important role.

(i)   Since resonance operates from *ortho-* and *para*-positions (**not from meta**-), such group will affect acidity, nearly to equal extent, only when present in *o-* or *p*-position.

(ii)   Since inductive effect operates from all the three positions (*o-*, *m-*, and *p*-), it will affect acidity of the compound from all positions. However, since the effect diminishes with the increase in distance between two groups, the effect will be maximum in *ortho*, then in *meta-* and least in *para-*.

(iii)   When the resonance and inductive effects operate in opposite directions, generally resonance effect predominates over inductive effect, except in some cases where the group is highly electronegative as in *o*-chlorophenol.

$$-\text{OH} \qquad \text{Here} \quad -\text{I}_{\text{of Cl}} \;>\; +\; \text{R}_{\text{of Cl}}$$

(iv)   Whenever the acidic group is capable of forming H–bond with the *ortho-* substituent as in *o*-nitrophenol, *o*-fluorophenol, and *o*–nitrobenzoic acid, it becomes relatively difficult to remove acidic hydrogen as proton. Hence such compound will be less acidic than the corresponding *p*-isomer, although the —I effect (acid-strengthening effect) in the *o*-isomer is more than in the corresponding *p*-isomer.

(v)   In somes cases hyperconjugation also plays important role, *viz.* in cresols (*o-*, *m-* and *p-*) where acidic character is influenced by + I effect of the —CH₃ group. Since the + I (acid-weakening) effect is maximum in *ortho*-position, followed by *meta-* and least in *para*, the acidic character of the three cresols should follow the following order.

Least + I effect		Maximum + I effect

Theoretical relative acidic character, on the basis of + I effect.

However, in practice the order is found to be somewhat different.

Mid-way + I effect	Min. + I effect	Max. + I effect
No hyperconjugative effect	+ve Hyperconjugative effect	+ve Hyperconjugative effect

Hyperconjugation (no-bond resonance), which here is acid-weakening, is also possible in case of *o-* and *p*-isomers, but not in *m-*. Since in *m*-isomer, hyperconjugation does not operate, it will be stronger acid than the other two isomers where this effect operates and thus decreases their acidity.

TEST YOUR UNDERSTANDING - 13.4

1.   In each of the following pairs, which is the stronger acid ?

    (a)   Phenol or *p*-hydroxybenzaldehyde   (b)   *m*-Nitrophenol or *p*-nitrophenol

    (c)   *o*-Fluorophenol or *p*-fluorophenol   (d)   *m*-Chlorophenol or *p*-chlorophenol

    (e)   *o*-Aminophenol or *m*-aminophenol.   (f)

2.   Arrange the following in increasing acidic character.

    (a)   Phenol, benzyl alcohol, benzenesulphonic acid and benzoic acid.

    (b)   Phenol, benzoic acid, *p*-nitrophenol and carbonic acid.

    (c)   Phenol, *p*-chlorophenol, *p*-nitrophenol and *p*-cresol.

    (d)   Phenol, *m*-chlorophenol, *m*-nitrophenol, and *m*-cresol.

3. Arrange the following compounds in decreasing order of acidity.

    (*a*)   Phenol (*A*), *o*-nitrophenol (*B*), *m*-nitrophenol (*C*), *p*-nitrophenol (*D*).

    (*b*)   Phenol (*A*), *o*-chlorophenol (*B*), *m*-chlorophenol (*C*), *p*-chlorophenol (*D*).

    (*c*)   Phenol (*A*), *o*-cresol (*B*), *m*-cresol (*C*), *p*-cresol (*D*).

13.4.2 Separation of Phenols from Alcohols and Carboxylic Acids

Since phenols are more acidic than water, phenol dissolves in sodium hydroxide according to the following reaction.

$$C_6H_5OH + NaOH \underset{\longleftarrow}{\overset{H_2O}{\longrightarrow}} C_6H_5O^- Na^+ + H_2O$$

Stronger acid (slighly soluble in water), Stronger base, Weaker base (completely soluble in water), Weaker acid

The corresponding reaction of 1-hexanol with aqueous sodium hydroxide does not occur to a significant extent because 1-hexanol is a weaker acid than water.

$$CH_3(CH_2)_4 CH_2OH + NaOH \underset{H_2O}{\overset{\longrightarrow}{\longleftarrow}} CH_3(CH_2)_4 CH_2O^- Na^+ + H_2O$$

Weaker acid (very slightly soluble), Stronger base, Stronger acid

The fact that phenols dissolve in aqueous sodium hydroxide, whereas most alcohols with six or more carbon atoms do not, gives us a convenient means for distinguishing and separating phenols from most alcohols. (Note that alcohols with five or less carbon atoms are quite soluble in water, and hence they also dissolve in aqueous sodium hydroxide even though they are converted to sodium alkoxides in appreciable amounts, the solubility is actually due to H-bond with water molecules).

Opposite solubility properties of phenols and their salts (the salts being soluble in water and insoluble in organic solvents, while phenols are very less soluble in water and soluble in organic solvents) is applied in the isolation and separation of phenols. Aq. NaOH converts phenols into their salts which are converted back to phenols, on adding mineral acids.

$$ArOH \underset{H^+}{\overset{OH^-}{\rightleftharpoons}} ArO^-$$

A phenol (acid) (Insoluble in water), A phenoxide ion (salt) (soluble in water)

Most phenols are weaker acids than carbonic acid, hence, unlike carboxylic acids, which are stronger than carbonic acid, they (phenols) do not dissolve in aqueous bicarbonate solution. Indeed, phenols are conveniently liberated from their salts by the action of carbonic acid.

$$CO_2 + H_2O \rightleftharpoons H_2CO_3$$

$$H_2CO_3 + ArO^- Na^+ \longrightarrow ArOH + HCO_3^-$$

Stronger acid, (Soluble in water), Weaker acid (Insoluble in water)

Thus phenols can be separated (*i*) from non-acidic compounds by means of its solubility in base; and (*ii*) from carboxylic acids by means of its insolubility in bicarbonate.

TEST YOUR UNDERSTANDING - 13.5

1. Account for the fact that

    (*a*)   unlike most phenols, 2, 4-dinitrophenol is soluble in aqueous sodium bicarbonate.

    (*b*)   Carboxylic acids are soluble in $NaHCO_3$ solution, while phenol not. Explain

2. Draw a flow sheet for the separation of a mixture of C_6H_5OH, $C_6H_5CH_2OH$ and C_6H_5COOH.

13.5   Chemical Properties of Phenols

1.   **Ester formation.** Phenols react with acylating agents, such as acid chlorides and carboxylic acid anhydrides, *the absence* of $AlCl_3$*, to form esters (O-acylation). These reactions are quite similar to those of alcohols.

$$\text{C}_6\text{H}_5\text{—OH} + \text{CH}_3\text{COCl} \xrightarrow{\text{base}} \text{C}_6\text{H}_5\text{—OCCH}_3$$

Phenyl acetate

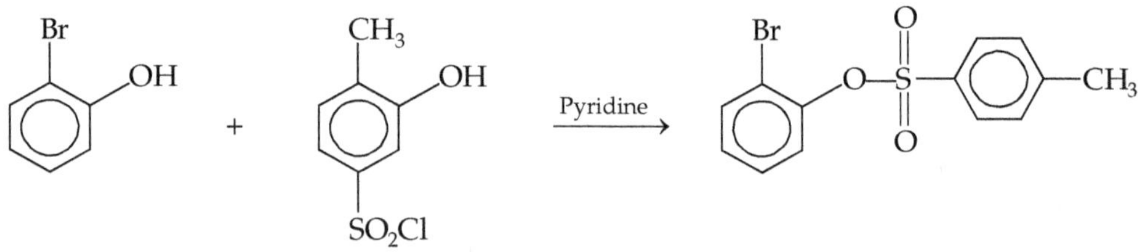

o-Bromophenol   p-Toluenesulphonyl chloride   o-Bromophenyl p-toluenesulphonate

The O-acylation of phenols with carboxylic acid anhydrides can be conveniently catalyzed in either of two ways.

(a)   In one method, the acid anhydride is converted to more powerful acyl transfer agent, due to protonation of one of its carbonyl oxygens, by adding a few drops of sulphuric acid.

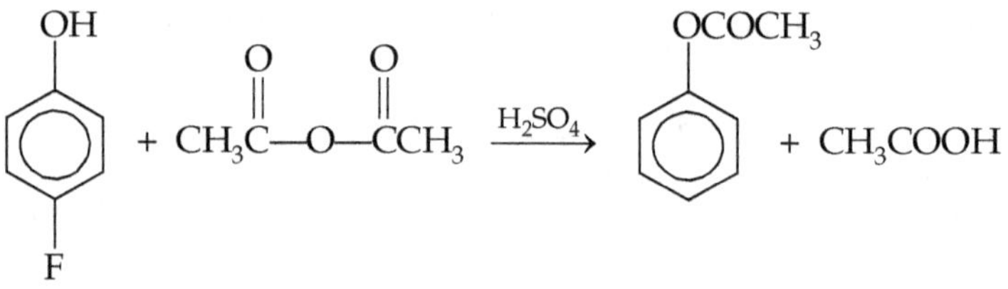

$$p\text{-F-C}_6\text{H}_4\text{OH} + \text{CH}_3\text{C—O—CCH}_3 \xrightarrow{\text{H}_2\text{SO}_4} p\text{-F-C}_6\text{H}_4\text{OCOCH}_3 + \text{CH}_3\text{COOH}$$

(b)   In another method, the nucleophilicity of the phenol is increased by converting it to its phenoxide anion by adding base like aq. NaOH.

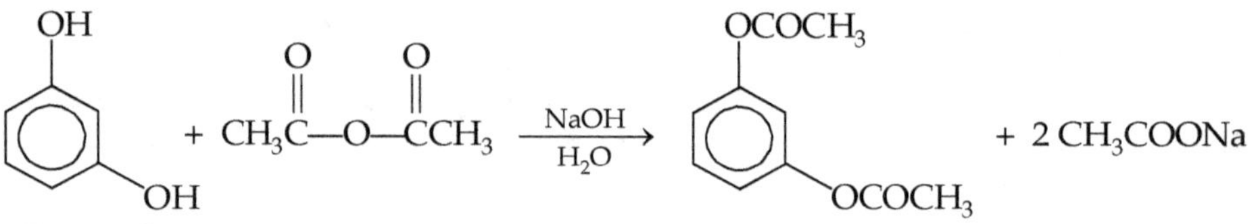

$$\text{Resorcinol} + \text{CH}_3\text{C—O—CCH}_3 \xrightarrow[\text{H}_2\text{O}]{\text{NaOH}} \text{1,3-Diacetoxybenzene} + 2\,\text{CH}_3\text{COONa}$$

Resorcinol   1, 3-Diacetoxybenzene

When esters of phenols are heated with aluminium chloride, the acyl group migrates from the phenolic oxygen to an *ortho* or *para* position of the ring, thus forming a ketone. This reaction, called the **Fries rearrangement**, is often used instead of direct C–acylation leading to the synthesis of phenolic ketones.

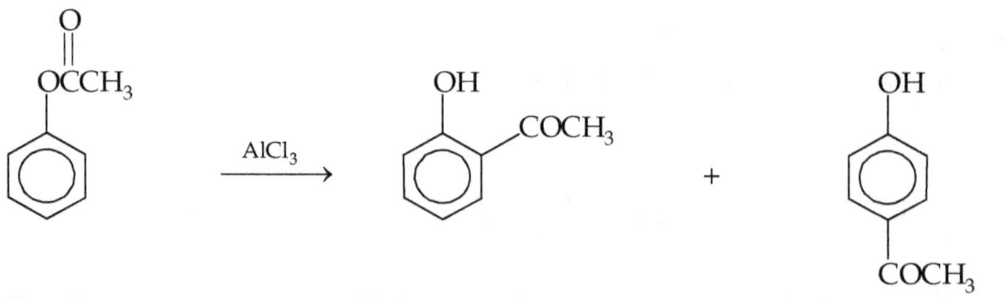

Phenyl acetate   o-Hydroxyacetophenone   p-Hydroxyacetophenone
                      (Volatile in steam)   (Non-volatile in steam)

---

*   In presence of $AlCl_3$, phenols react with acid chlorides and carboxylic acid anhydrides to form *o*- and *p*-acyl phenols (Friedel-Crafts reaction, C–acylation).

Role of AlCl₃ in Fries rearrangement

$AlCl_3$ forms complex with the phenolic oxygen leading to the formation of acylium ion, RC^+O (an electrophile) which then attacks the ring as in Friedel Craft acylation.

[Reaction scheme showing phenyl acetate + AlCl₃ forming a complex, then rearranging to o-hydroxyacetophenone and p-hydroxyacetophenone]

TEST YOUR UNDERSTANDING - 13.6

1. (*a*) Predict the product in the following reaction.

$$\text{Phenol} + C_6H_5COCl \xrightarrow{OH^-} [A] \xrightarrow{1\ \text{mole}\ Br_2\,/\,Fe} \text{Product}$$

(*b*) *m*-Nitrophenyl acetate does not respond Fries rearrangement. Explain

2. Ether formation (Williamson synthesis). Phenols are converted into alkyl aryl ethers by treating its alkaline solution with 1° alkyl halides*. For preparing, aryl methyl ethers, methyl sulphate is frequently used because it is cheaper than methyl halides.

$$ArOH \xrightarrow{NaOH} ArONa \xrightarrow{R-X} ArOR + NaX \quad (\text{where, } X = Cl, Br, I\ \text{or}\ OSO_2OCH_3)$$

(*a*) [Phenol] + $CH_3OSO_2OCH_3$ $\xrightarrow{\text{aq. NaOH}}$ [Anisole] + $CH_3OSO_3^-\ Na^+$

Phenol   Dimethyl sulphate (Methyl sulphate)   Anisole

(*b*) [Phenol] + $CH_3CH_2CH_2Br$ $\xrightarrow{\text{aq. NaOH}}$ [phenyl propyl ether, $OCH_2CH_2CH_3$]

Remember that due to low reactivity of aryl halides toward nucleophilic substitution, they can't be used as one of the components of Williamson synthesis; *i.e.* the following pair can't be used for preparing ether.

$$CH_3CH_2CH_2ONa + \underset{\text{(low reactivity)}}{BrC_6H_5} \longrightarrow \text{No Reaction}$$

However, when the aryl halide has an electron-withdrawing substituent it can be applied for preparing ether with alcohols, *e.g.*

[p-fluoronitrobenzene] + CH_3OH $\xrightarrow[25°C]{CH_3OK}$ [*p*-Nitroanisole] ; [2-chloro-4-nitro... + nitro] + $NaOC_2H_5$ $\longrightarrow$ [OC_2H_5 dinitro product]

p-Nitroanisole

Recall that such aryl halides undergo nucleophilic aromatic substitution by the addition-elimination mechanism rather than S_N2 mechanism.

---

*   2° or 3° Alkyl halides may lead to elimination reactions.

(c) 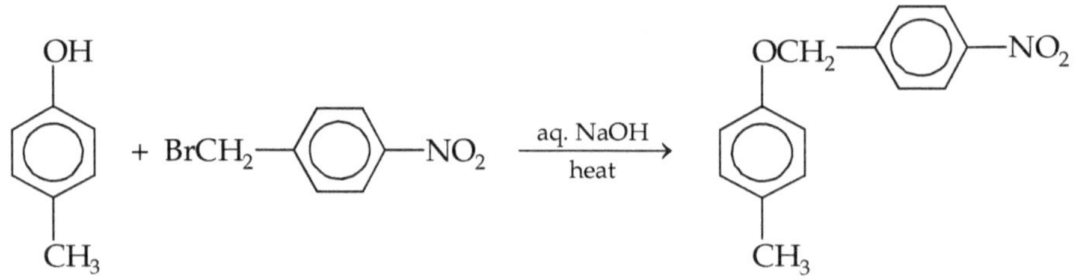 [structure: p-cresol] $+$ $BrCH_2$—[benzene ring]—NO_2 $\xrightarrow[\text{heat}]{\text{aq. NaOH}}$ [structure: OCH_2—[ring]—NO_2 on tolyl]

p-Nitrobenzyl *p*-tolyl ether

(d) $C_6H_5OH + ClCH_2COOH \xrightarrow[\text{heat}]{OH^-} C_6H_5OCH_2COONa \xrightarrow{HCl} C_6H_5OCH_2COOH$

Phenoxyacetic acid

(e) 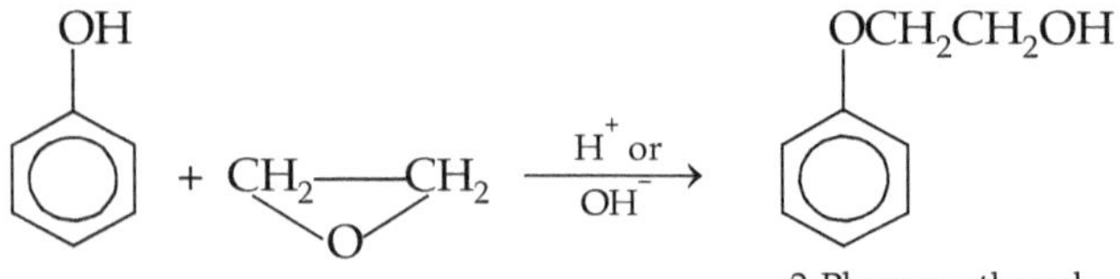 [structure: phenol] $+$ $CH_2\!\!-\!\!CH_2$ (epoxide, O) $\xrightarrow[OH^-]{H^+ \text{ or}}$ [structure: OCH_2CH_2OH on benzene]

2-Phenoxyethanol

The last reaction is considered as a modification of the Williamson synthesis.

(f) 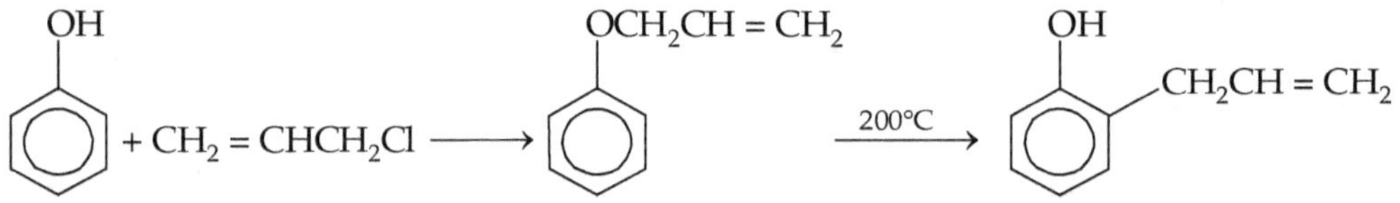 [structure: Phenol] $+$ $CH_2 = CHCH_2Cl$ $\longrightarrow$ [structure: $OCH_2CH = CH_2$ on benzene] $\xrightarrow{200°C}$ [structure: OH and $CH_2CH = CH_2$ on benzene]

Phenol   Allyl chloride   Allyl phenyl ether   *o*-Allylphenol

Allyl aryl ethers, when heated, undergo rearrangement to form *o*-allylphenol. This reaction, known as *Claisen rearrangement,* involves migration of the allyl group from O to the ortho position of the ring. Remember that it is the C 3 (indicated by C^{14}) that becomes bonded to the benzene ring.

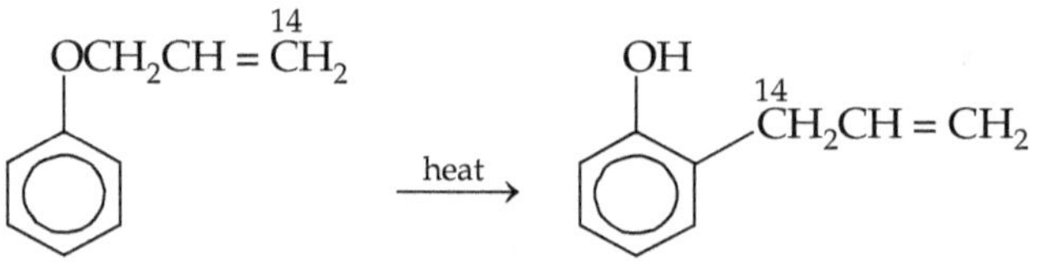

[structure: $OCH_2CH = \overset{14}{CH_2}$ on benzene] $\xrightarrow{\text{heat}}$ [structure: OH and $\overset{14}{CH_2}CH = CH_2$ on benzene]

Like other ethers, alkyl aryl ethers are cleaved by hot conc. HBr or HI. Because of low reactivity at the bond between oxygen and an aromatic ring, alkyl aryl ethers undergo cleavage at the alkyl-oxygen bond and yields phenols and alkyl halides.

$$Ar\!-\!O\!-\!R + HI \xrightarrow{120-130°C} Ar\!-\!OH + RI$$

Remember that the phenol does not react further with hydrogen halide to form aryl halide again due to strong nature of the bond between oxygen and the aromatic carbon.

TEST YOUR UNDERSTANDING - 13.7

1. Why methyl sulphate is considered to be a good methylating agent ? Suggest another class of compounds that can be used in place of alkyl halides in the Williamson synthesis.

2. ' Predict the product of the following reaction.

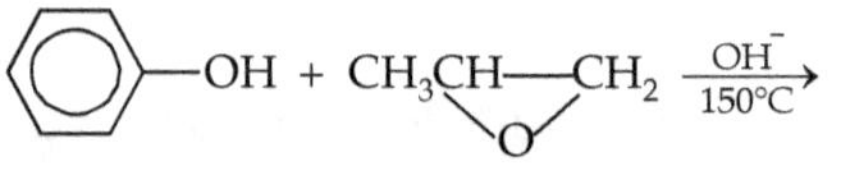

[structure: [benzene ring]—OH $+$ $CH_3CH\!\!-\!\!CH_2$ (epoxide, O) $\xrightarrow[150°C]{OH^-}$]

3. Alkylation of phenoxide ion with allyl chloride gives phenyl allyl ether along with some amount of *o*-allylphenol. Explain.

Other salient features of aryl alkyl ethers. Aryl alkyl ethers undergo electrophilic substitution in the *o-* and *p-*positions, because —OR groups are *o-*, *p-* directing with moderately activating effect. The alkoxy group is a much stronger activator than —R because the former involves the following especially stable intermediate oxonium ions where every atom (except hydrogen) has a complete set of electrons.

However, alkoxy group is much weaker electron-releasing than the —OH group, hence aryl ethers do not generally undergo those electrophilic substitution reactions which require the especially high reactivity of phenols, like coupling, Kolbe reaction, Reimer-Tiemann reaction, etc. This difference in reactivity is due to the fact that, unlike a phenol, an ether can't dissociate to form the extremely reactive phenoxide ion.

Due to lower reactivity of the ring, aromatic ethers are less sensitive to oxidation than a phenol, hence alkyl groups present on the ring of an ether can be easily oxidised to —COOH group.

$$CH_3O \longrightarrow \langle \rangle \longrightarrow CH_3 \quad \xrightarrow[\text{(ii) } H^+]{\text{(i) } KMnO_4 \,/\, OH^-, \text{ heat}} \quad CH_3O \longrightarrow \langle \rangle \longrightarrow COOH$$

p-Methylanisol   Anisic acid

$$HO \longrightarrow \langle \rangle \longrightarrow CH_3 \quad \xrightarrow[\text{(ii) } H^+]{\text{(i) } KMnO_4 \,/\, OH^-, \text{ heat}} \quad HO \longrightarrow \langle \rangle \longrightarrow COOH$$

p-Cresol   **(Not formed)**

3. **Displacement of phenolic —OH group.** Like aryl halides, it is difficult to replace the —OH group of phenols. Thus, unlike ROH, phenols do not react with HX, $SOCl_2$ or phosphorus halides. However, phenols can be converted to hydrocarbons by distillation with zinc dust (replacement of —OH by H).

$$\text{Phenol} \quad \xrightarrow[\text{heat}]{\text{Zn dust}} \quad \text{Benzene} \; + \; ZnO$$

Displacement of phenolic —OH by —Cl. The —OH group attached to benzene ring is very less reactive, however when treated with PCl_5 it gives chlorobenzene, although in low yield because of formation of triphenyl phosphate.

$$C_6H_5OH + PCl_5 \longrightarrow C_6H_5Cl + POCl_3 + HCl$$
$$3C_6H_5OH + PCl_5 \longrightarrow (C_6H_5)_3\,PO_3 + 3HCl$$

4. **Electrophilic aromatic substitution.** The —OH and even more so the —O⁻ (phenoxide) ion are strongly activating and *op*-directing. High reactivity of phenol can be attributed to exceptionally high stability of intermediates, which are oxocations, in which every atom (except hydrogen) has a complete octet of electrons. Hence they are formed tremendously faster than the carbocations derived from benzene itself.

Oxonium cations

Phenoxide ion forms even more stable, and hence more rapidly formed, intermediates—the unsaturated ketones.

Fairly stable unsaturated ketones

Hence, like amines, special mild conditions are needed to achieve electrophilic monosubstitution in phenol because their high reactivity favours both polysubstitution and oxidation.

(a) **Halogenation.** Treatment of phenols with aqueous solution of bromine and even in absence of a catalyst results in replacement of every hydrogen *ortho-* or *para* to the —OH group, and may even cause displacement of certain groups, like —SO_3H (*bromodesulphonation*, see example *iv*).

(i) Phenol → (Br_2/H_2O) → 2, 4, 6- Tribromophenol

(ii) *o*-Crersol → (Br_2/aq.) → 4, 6-Dibromo-2-methylphenol

(iii) → (Br_2, H_2O) →

(iv) → (Br_2/H_2O) →

Monobromination can be achieved with non-polar solvents (like CS_2, $CHCl_3$, CCl_4 or CH_2ClCH_2Cl) to decrease the electrophilicity of Br_2 and also to minimize phenol ionization.

+ Br_2 → (CS_2/0°C) → *o*-Bromophenol   +   *p*-Bromophenol **(Major)**

(b) **Nitration**

Conc. HNO_3 → 2, 4, 6-Trinitrophenol **(Picric acid)**   + Oxidation product

However, picric acid can quantitatively be prepared by treating phenol -2, 4-disulphonic acid with nitric acid.

Phenol -2, 4-disulphonic acid → (HNO_3) → 2, 4, 6-Trinitrophenol

Two nitro groups (at position 2 and 4) are introduced by *nitrodesulphonation* (displacement of —SO_3H by electrophile, NO_2^+) while the third —NO_2 group at position 6 is introduced by direct nitration, note that this position (6) is favoured by all the three substituents already present in the molecule. Since, there is less destructive oxidation by the nitrating agent, this method gives a good yield.

Mononitro products, of course in poor yield, can be obtained by using dil nitric acid at a low temperature.

o-Nitrophenol   p-Nitrophenol

Recall that the two isomeric nitrophenols can be easily separated because the o-isomer is steam volatile. Since direct nitration of phenol even under mild conditions gives low yield, these are better obtained *via* nitrosation or by hydrolysis of chloronitrobenzenes.

Phenol   p-Nitrosophenol   p-Nitrophenol   p-Chloronitrobenzene

(c) **Sulphonation.** Phenol reacts with concentrated sulphuric acid to give mainly the o-sulphonated product at 20°C and mainly the p-sulphonated product at 100°C. This is another* example of thermodynamic (or equilibrium) versus kinetic (or rate) control of a reaction.

o-Phenolsulphonic acid
(rate-controlled)

p-Phenolsulphonic acid
(equilibrium-controlled)

The reason for the formation of two different products at different temperatures is due to *reversible nature of sulphonation. The ortho isomer is formed more rapidly* and thus it will be the major product at low temperature, *while the para isomer is more stable* and thus it will be the major product at high temperature.

(d) **Friedel-Craft's alkylation and acylation.** Since RX and $AlCl_3$ give poor yields because $AlCl_3$ coordinates with oxygen of phenol, the latter is alkylated with the help of alkene or alcohol in presence of acid like H_2SO_4 or HF.

$+ p$-Isomer

$+ p$-Isomer

---

* Addition of HBr on 1, 3-butadiene is also such example.

$$CH_2 = CHCH = CH_2 \xrightarrow{\text{HBr}} CH_3CH(Br)CH = CH_2 \ + \ CH_3CH = CHCH_2Br$$

1, 2-Product
(rate or kinetic controlled)

1, 4-Product
(thermodynamic or equilibrium controlled)

However, phenolic ketones are best prepared in two steps by means of Fries rearrangement (discussed earlier).

m-Cresol $\xrightarrow{(CH_3CO)_2O}$ *m*-Cresol acetate $\xrightarrow{AlCl_3}$ Main product at 26°C + Main product at 160°C

(e) Gattermann reaction

$$C_6H_5OH + HCN + HCl \xrightarrow{ZnCl_2} p\text{-}CHO.C_6H_4.OH$$

(benzene-1,3-diol) $+ HCN + HCl \xrightarrow[(ii)\ H_2O]{(i)\ ZnCl_2,\ ether}$

(f) Nitrosation. Since phenols are highly reactive, they also undergo electrophilic substitution by the weak electrophiles, like nitrosonium ion $(N\overset{+}{O})$ and diazonium ions $(ArN_2{}^+)$.

Phenol $\xrightarrow[7\text{--}8°C]{HONO}$ *p*-Nitrosophenol $\rightleftharpoons$ Quinone monoxime

Since —NO group is readily oxidized to the —NO_2 group by nitric acid, nitrosation route is considered to be better way to synthesize *p*-nitrophenol than the direct nitration which may lead to oxidation of phenol.

(g) Coupling with diazonium salts with phenols gives azophenols.

p-Hydroxyazobenzene

(h) Mercuration. Mercuriacetate cation, $\overset{+}{Hg}OAc$ is another weak electrophile which substitutes in *ortho* and *para* positions of phenols. This reaction is used to introduce an –I on the ring.

Phenol $\xrightarrow[C_2H_5OH]{Hg(OAc)_2}$ HgOAc (*o*-, and *p*-) $\xrightarrow{NaCl}$ HgCl (*o*- and *p*-) $\xrightarrow{KI}$ I (*o*- and *p*-)

(i) Kolbe reaction *or* **Kolbe-Schmidt reaction.** Treatment of sodium phenoxide phenol (activated toward electrophilic substitution) with carbon dioxide (a weak electrophile) at 125°C under pressure yields sodium salt of *o*-hydroxybenzoic acid. This reaction, known as *Kolbe reaction*, brings about substitution of the —COOH group for hydrogen of the ring.

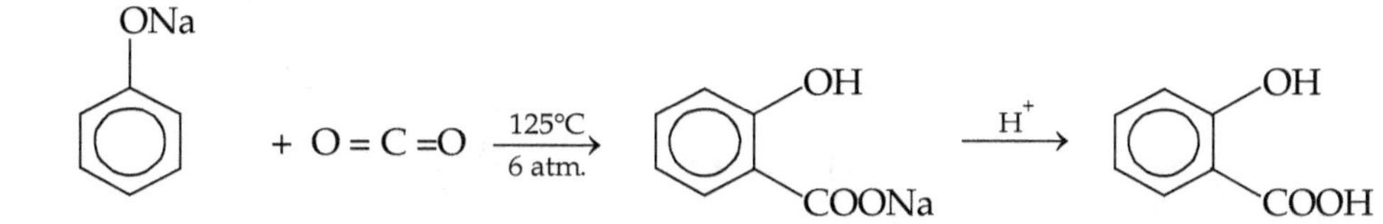

Sodium phenoxide   Carbon dioxide   Sod. salicylate   Salicylic acid
(Weak electrophile)

Mechanism.

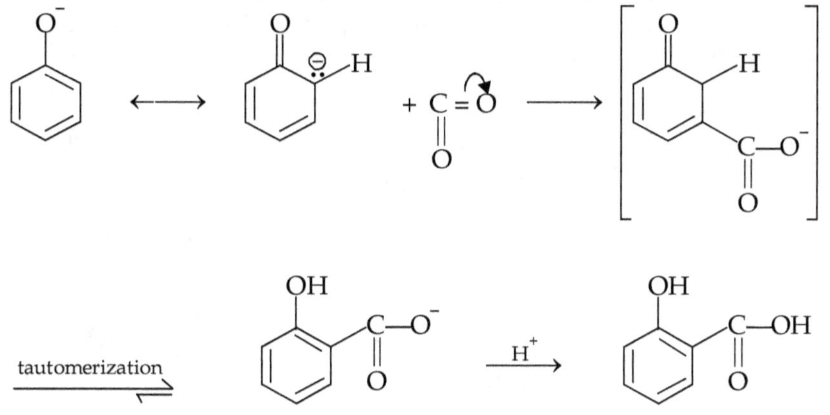

tautomerization   Salicylate anion   Salicylic acid

The Kolbe reaction is an equilibrium process governed by thermodynamic control. The position of equilibrium favours formation of the weaker base (salicylate ion) at the expense of the stronger one (phenoxide ion). Thermodynamic control is also responsible for the pronounced bias toward *ortho* over para substitution. Salicylate anion is a weaker base than *p*-hydroxybenzoate and so is the predominant species at equilibrium.

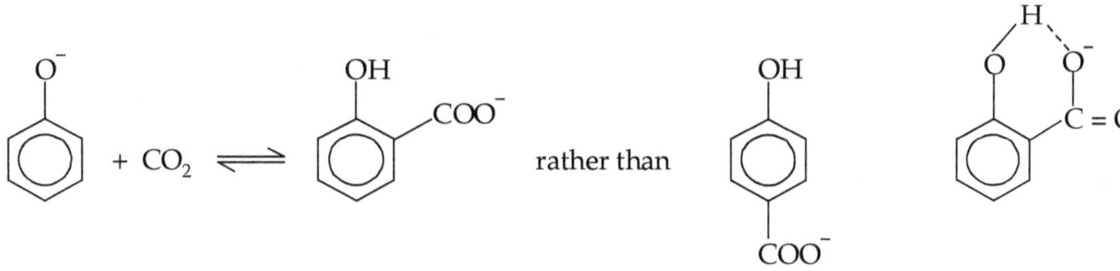

Phenoxide ion   Salicylate anion   *p*-Hydroxybenzoate anion
(strongest base)   (weakest base)   (weaker base)

rather than

Weaker basic character of the salicylate anion than *p*-hydroxybenzoate anion is because of its stability due to intramolecular hydrogen bonding.

Salicylic acid is very important compound as it is used for preparing *o*-acetylsalicylic acid, also known as *Aspirin*, by acetylation with acetic anhydride.

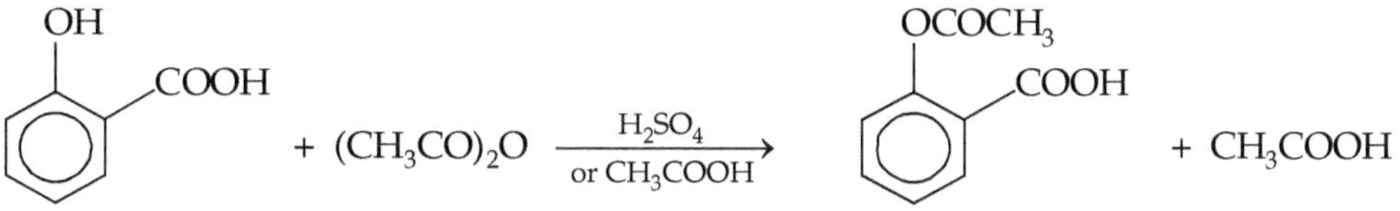

o-Acetylsalicylic acid
(Aspirin)

Aspirin has several medicinal properties, hence it is used as an *analgesic* (for relieving pain), *antipyretic* (for reducing fever) and *anti-inflammatory agent* (for relieving swelling associated with arthritis and minor injuries).

Phenols bearing alkyl groups behave very much like phenol, while phenols bearing strongly electron-withdrawing groups give low yields because their corresponding phenoxide anions are less basic.

p-Cresol $\xrightarrow{\text{(i) NaOH; (ii) CO}_2\text{, 125°C, 7 atm.; (iii) H}^+}$ 2-Hydroxy-5-methylbenzoic acid

(*j*) **Reimer-Tiemann reaction.** Treatement of a phenol with chloroform (or cabon tetrachloride) and aqueous hydroxide introduces an aldehyde (or —COOH) group in the o-position to the —OH group ; this reaction known as *Reimer-Tiemann reaction*.

Phenol + HCCl$_3$ + NaOH $\xrightarrow{70°C}$ Salicylaldehyde

Phenol + CCl$_4$ + NaOH $\longrightarrow$ Salicylic acid

Mechanism. The reaction involves electrophilic substitution on the highly reactive phenoxide ring. Here the electrophile is dichlorocarbene, $: CCl_2$, generated from $CHCl_3$ (or CCl_4) by the action of a base

$$HCCl_3 + OH^- \longrightarrow H_2O + {}^-:CCl_3 \longrightarrow Cl^- + \quad :CCl_2$$

Note that C has only a sextet of electrons

A benzal chloride

Salicylaldehyde can also be prepared by heating phenol with hexamethylenetetramine, glycerol and boric acid (**Duff reaction**).

Phenol $\xrightarrow{\text{(i) (CH}_2)_6\text{N}_4\text{; (ii) H}^+}$ Salicylaldehyde $\xrightarrow[\text{NaOH}]{\text{H}_2\text{O}_2}$ Catechol

Salicylaldehyde, on oxidation with alkaline hydrogen peroxide is converted into 1, 2-dihydroxybenzene (**Dakin reaction**).

Three important derivatives of salicylic acid are **aspirin** (acetylsalicylic acid), **salol** (phenyl salicylate) and **methyl salicylate** (oil of wintergreen).

Methyl salicylate (flavouring agent) $\xleftarrow[\text{Conc. H}_2\text{SO}_4]{\text{CH}_3\text{OH}}$ **Salicylic acid** $\xrightarrow{\text{(CH}_3\text{CO})_2\text{O}}$ Aspirin (an antipyretic)

Phenyl salicylate (an antiseptic) $\xleftarrow[\text{POCl}_3]{\text{C}_6\text{H}_5\text{OH}}$ **Salicylic acid** $\xrightarrow{\text{heat}}$ $\xrightarrow[\substack{\text{molecule of} \\ \text{salicylic acid}}]{\text{2nd}}$ Phenyl salicylate

(k) **Condensation with formaldehyde.** When phenol is heated with formaldehyde (an electrophile) in presence of alkali or acid, a high-molecular-substanace (polymer), known as bakelite, is obtained in which many phenol rings are held together by —CH_2— groups.

o-Hydroxymethylphenol

Bakelite

Base-catalysed mechanism. Base catalyzes reaction by converting phenol into the more reactive (more nucleophilic) phenoxide ion

Nucleophile   Electrophile

Acid-catalysed mechanism. Acid catalyzes reaction by protonating formaldehyde and thus increasing the electron deficiency of the carbonyl carbon

Nucleophile
(weaker than $C_6H_5O^-$)

Electrophile
(stronger than CH_2O)

(l) **Condensation of phenol with phthalic anhydride** in presence of conc. H_2SO_4 forms phenolphthalein (an acid-base indicator) which gives pink colour with NaOH

Phthalic acid

Phthalic anhydride

Phenolphthalein

This reaction is used for detecting the presence of *o*-dibasic acid, *viz.* phthalic acid under the name of **phthalein test.** Condensation of resorcinol with phthalic anhydride in presence of conc. H_2SO_4 gives **fluorescein.**

TEST YOUR UNDERSTANDING - 13.8

1. Which of the compound reacts faster, with the given reaction, in each of the following pairs ?

(a) 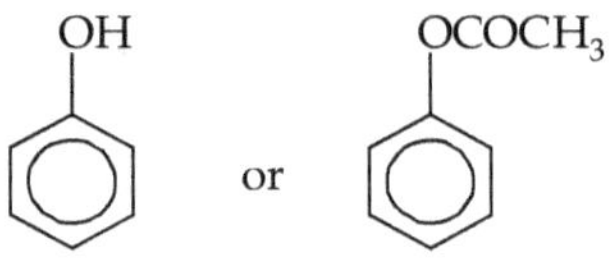 [phenol (OH)] or [phenyl acetate (OCOCH₃)]   (for nitration)

(b) 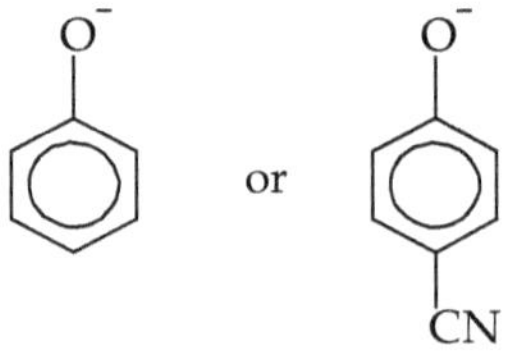 [phenoxide (O⁻)] or [4-cyanophenoxide (O⁻ with CN para)]   (for reaction with $C_6H_5CH_2Cl$)

(c) 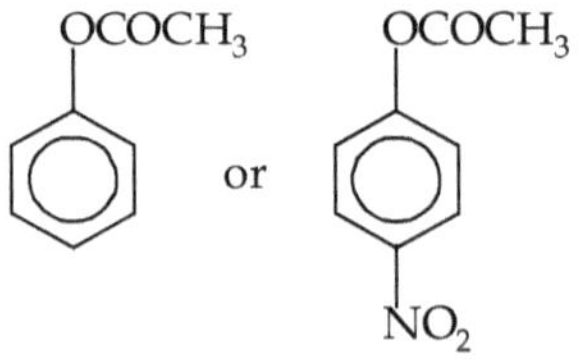 [phenyl acetate (OCOCH₃)] or [4-nitrophenyl acetate (OCOCH₃ with NO₂)]   (for base-catalysed hydrolysis)

(d) 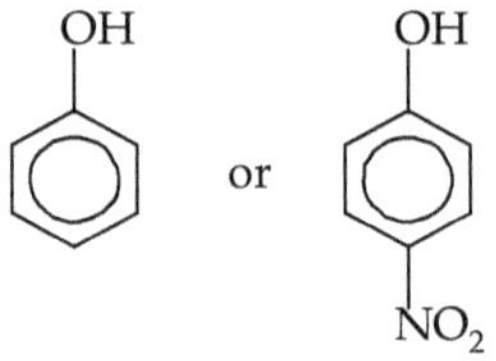 [phenol (OH)] or [4-nitrophenol (OH with NO₂)]   (for acid-catalysed esterification)

2. Give major product in each of the following reactions.

(a) 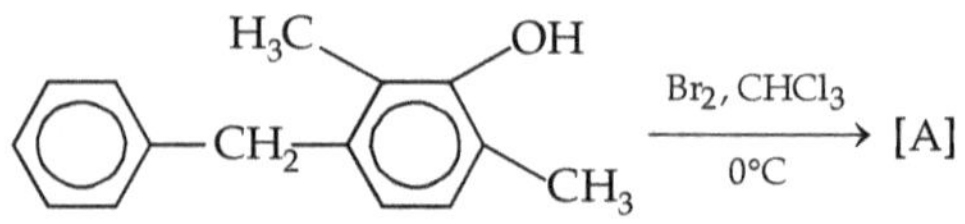 [aromatic compound with H_3C, OH, CH₃ and CH₂ linked to benzene ring] $\xrightarrow[0°C]{Br_2,\ CHCl_3}$ [A]

(b) 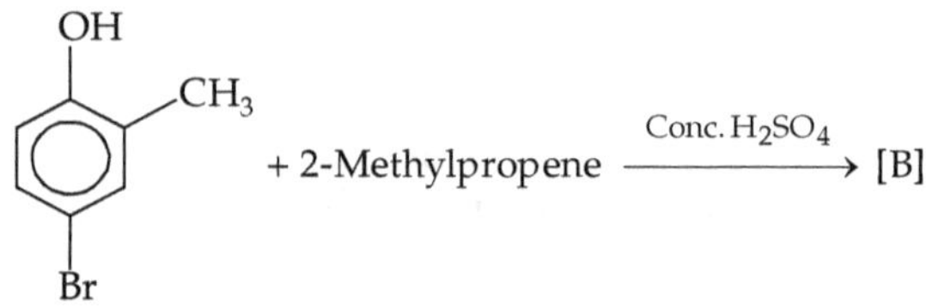 [phenol with OH, CH₃, Br substituents] + 2-Methylpropene $\xrightarrow{Conc.\ H_2SO_4}$ [B]

(c) [compound with H_3C, OH, $CHMe_2$ substituents] $\xrightarrow[\text{(ii) dil.HNO}_3]{\text{(i) NaNO}_2,\ HCl}$ [C]

(d) [o-cresol with OH, CH₃] + $CHCl_3$ + NaOH $\xrightarrow{70°C}$ 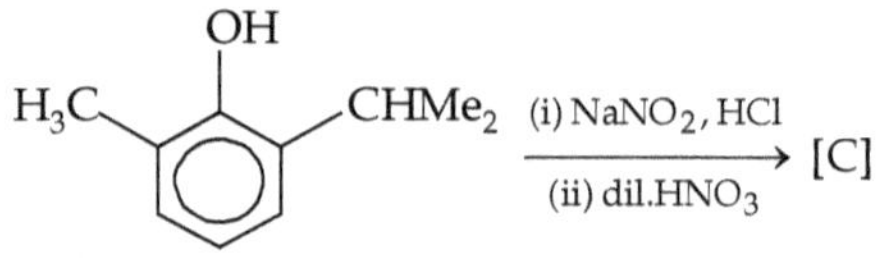 [D]

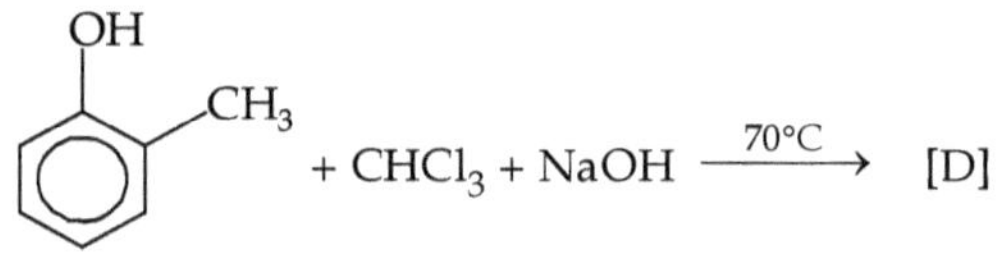

(e) 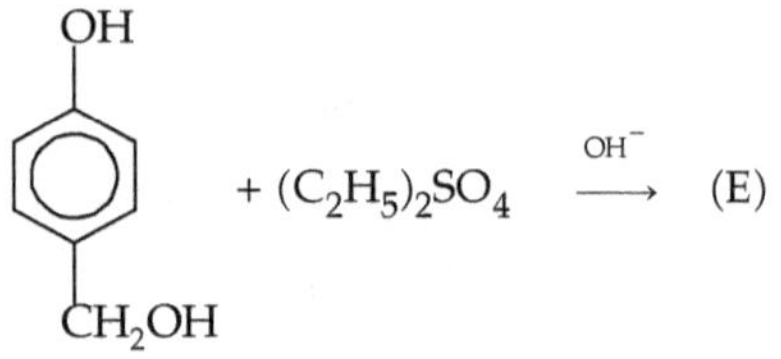 [phenol with OH and CH₂OH] + $(C_2H_5)_2SO_4$ $\xrightarrow{OH^-}$ (E)

(f) [compound with $OCH_2CH=\overset{14}{CH_2}$, H_3C, CH₃] $\xrightarrow{heat}$ (F)

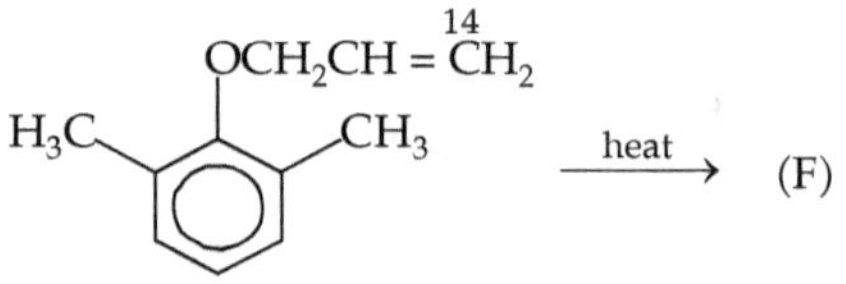

(g) 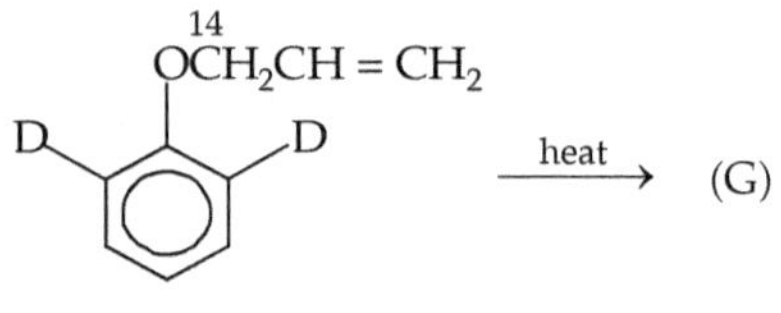 [compound with $O\overset{14}{CH_2}CH=CH_2$ and two D substituents] $\xrightarrow{heat}$ (G)

(h) [compound with OH, isopropyl and methyl substituents] $\xrightarrow[HCl]{NaNO_2}$ (H)

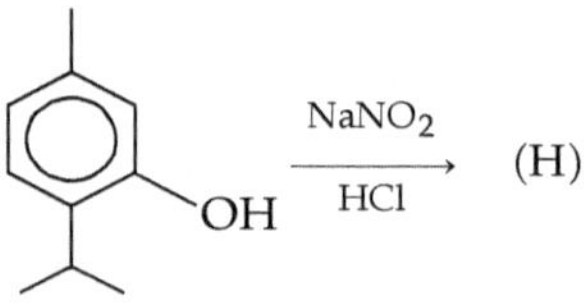

(i) 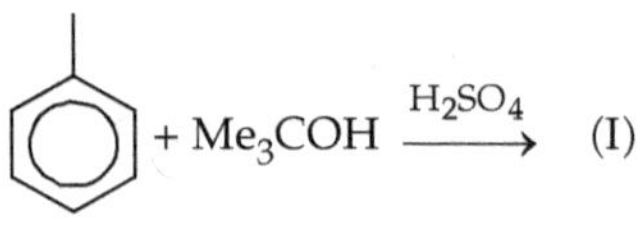 [toluene with CH₃] + Me_3COH $\xrightarrow{H_2SO_4}$ (I)

(j) [compound with OCH_3, NO₂, NO₂ substituents] $\xrightarrow[heat]{KOH,\ C_2H_5OH}$ (J)

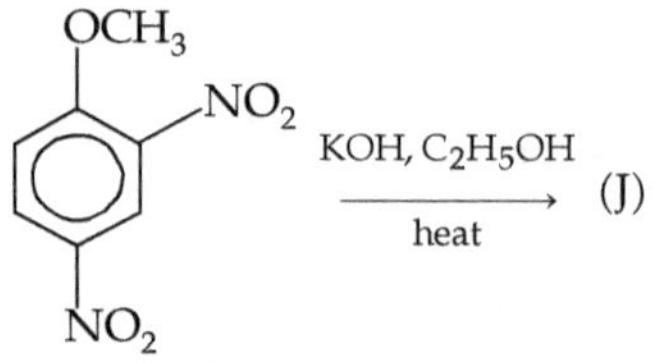

(k) 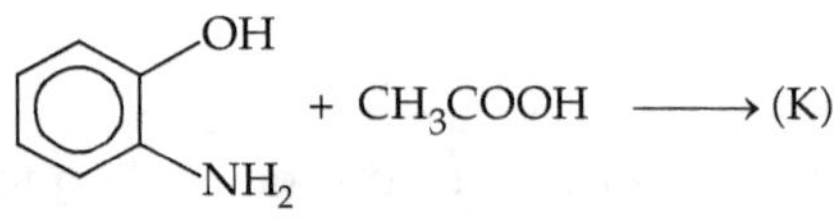 [aminophenol with OH and NH₂] + CH_3COOH $\longrightarrow$ (K)

(l) 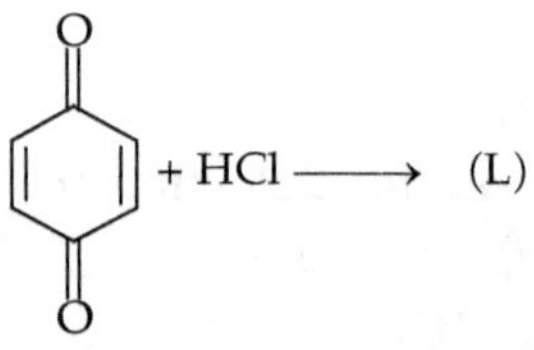 [1,4-benzoquinone] + HCl $\longrightarrow$ (L)

(m) [p-benzoquinone] + H_2SO_3 + H_2O $\longrightarrow$ (M)

(n) [4-nitrophenol] + $CH_2(OC_2H_5)_2$ $\xrightarrow[H_2SO_4]{Conc.\ HCl}$ (N)

(o) [phloroglucinol / 1,3,5-trihydroxybenzene] $\xrightarrow{NH_2OH}$ (O)

---

5. **Oxidation of phenols.** Phenols are more easily oxidized than alcohols. The oxidation can be brought by chromic acid to form conjugated dicarbonyl compounds, called **quinones.**

$$\text{Phenol} \xrightarrow[H_2SO_4]{Na_2Cr_2O_7} \text{p-Benzoquinone}$$

Hydroquinone is easily oxidised because it already has two oxygen atoms to the ring. Even very weak oxidants like silver bromide can oxidize hydroquinone.

[Hydroquinone] + 2Ag$\overset{*}{\text{Br}}$ (Activated AgBr) $\longrightarrow$ [p-benzoquinone] + 2Ag $\downarrow$ + 2HBr

This reaction has been used in black-and-white photography. A film containing small grains of AgBr is exposed by a focussed image. When light strikes the film, AgBr grains are activated. The film is then treated with a hydroquinone solution (the developer) to reduce the activated AgBr to metallic black silver. This is the negative image, the dark (black) areas indicate the area exposed to light.

$$\text{4-Methylpyrocatechol} \xrightarrow{Ag_2O} \text{4-Methyl-1, 2-benzoquinone}$$

6. **Hydrogenation of phenols.**

$$\text{Phenol} + 3H_2 \xrightarrow[15\ atm]{Ni,\ 175°C} \text{Cyclohexanol}$$

13.6 Analysis of Phenols

(i) Phenols have peculiar type of acidity. Most of them are stronger acids than water but weaker than carbonic acid. Hence, most of phenols dissolve in aqueous NaOH but not in aqueous $NaHCO_3$.

(ii) Many (*but not all*) phenols form coloured complexes, ranging from green through blue and violet to red, with ferric chloride. This test is also given by enols.

TEST YOUR UNDERSTANDING - 13.9

1. (*a*) Benzene ring of phenol is more easily oxdised than benzene itself. Explain.
   (*b*) Give the method for the preparation of *p*-benzoquinone, other than direct oxidation.
2. Use simple chemical tests to differentiate between each member of the following pairs of compounds.
   (*a*) Anisole and cresol
   (*b*) Anisole and benzyl alcohol
   (*c*) Salicylic acid and acetylsalicylic acid
   (*d*) Ethyl salicylate and ethyl acetylsalicylate
   (*e*) 2, 4, 6-Trimethylphenol and 2, 4, 6-trinitrophenol.

13.7 Illustrative Examples

Example 1 :

In industries phenol is prepared from cumene (isopropylbenzene) according to following steps.

$$C_6H_6 \xrightarrow[H_2SO_4]{CH_3CH=CH_2} \underset{\text{Cumene}}{C_6H_5CH(CH_3)_2} \xrightarrow{O_2} \underset{\text{Cumene hydroperoxide}}{C_6H_5-\overset{CH_3}{\overset{|}{C}}\underset{CH_3}{\underset{|}{}}-OOH} \xrightarrow{H_3O^+} \underset{\text{Phenol}}{C_6H_5OH} + (CH_3)_2C=O$$

Suggest a mechanism for the acid-catalyzed decomposition of cumene hydroperoxide to phenol.

Solution :

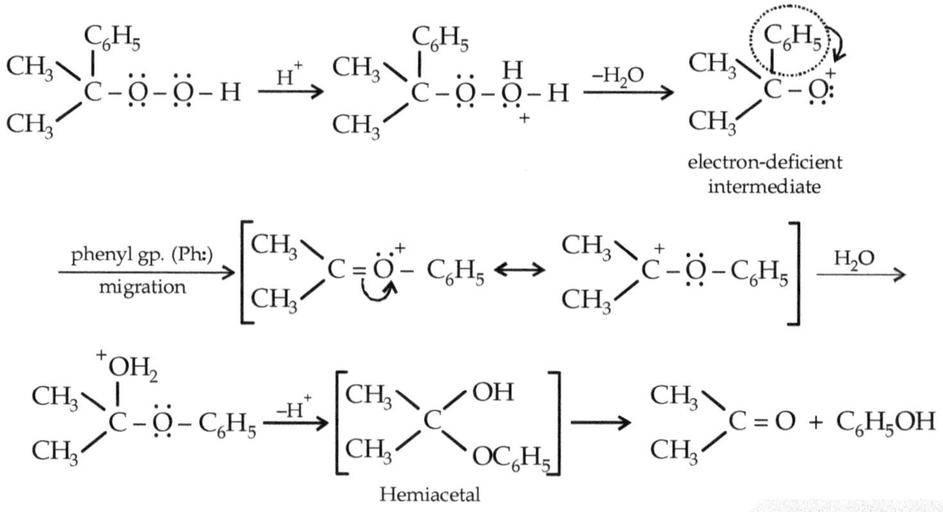

H⁺
–H₂O
electron-deficient intermediate
phenyl gp. (Ph:) migration
H₂O
–H⁺
Hemiacetal

Example 2 :

Give the structure of the products formed, when *m*-cresol is treated separately with each of the following reagent.

(a) Bromine in CCl_4 in the dark

(b) Excess of bormine in CCl_4 in the dark

(c) Excess of bromine in CCl_4 in the light

Solution :

(a)
OH
Br
CH₃
+
(b)
(c)
CBr₃

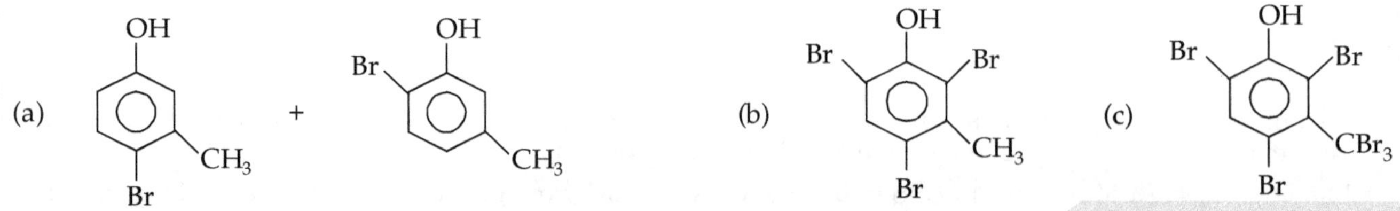

Example 3 :

Arrange the following three compounds in decreasing order of stability.

(a)   I   II   III   (b)   I   II   III

Solution :

(a)   The keto group (C = O) has large resonance energy and therefore its presence imparts stability in the molecule. Since each of the three compounds has three keto groups, these should be quite stable. However, the compounds II and III have two or more C = O's on the adjacent carbon atoms, these are destabilized. Hence the order of stability will be

$$\text{III} \; > \; \text{I} \; > \; \text{II}$$

(b)   The compound I has two adjacent C = O's which destabilize the *ortho* isomer relative to the para (II). Hence compound I is least stable. Relative stability between compounds II and III can be ascertained by the stability of their reduced products. Reduction of II will give a compound with a single benzene ring, while that of III gives a compound with two benzene rings, hence III will be more stable than II. Thus the stability order will be

$$\text{III} \; > \; \text{II} \; > \; \text{I}$$

Example 4 :

Give steps involved in the following conversion.

The intermediate undergoes hydrolysis through its triimino tautomer which gives corresponding triketo carboxylic acid. The latter, being a β-keto acid, readily decarboxylates to form triketo compound which readily tautomerizes to the more stable trihydric phenol. Higher stability of the phenol is due to presence of a very stable benzene ring.

Example 5 :

Give structures of the bracketed products in each of the following reactions.

(a) H_3C—⬡—NH_2 $\xrightarrow{CH_3COCl}$ [A] $\xrightarrow{HNO_3}$ [B] $\xrightarrow{OH^-}$ [C] $\xrightarrow[\text{(ii) } HPH_2O_2]{\text{(i) } HNO_2, 0°C}$ [D]

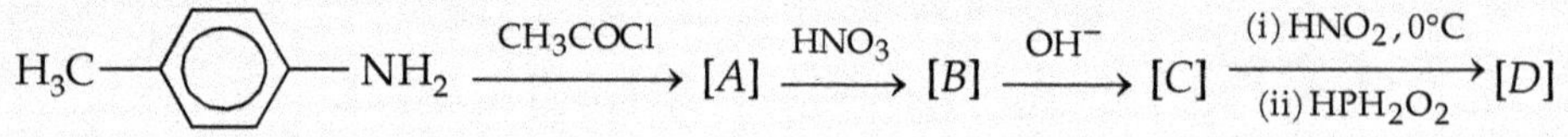

(b) $C_6H_5CH_3$ $\xrightarrow{HNO_3}$ [E] $\xrightarrow[\text{heat}]{KMnO_4, H^+}$ [F] $\xrightarrow[\text{(ii) } OH^-]{\text{(i) } Sn, HCl}$ [G] $\xrightarrow[\text{(ii) heat}]{\text{(i) } HNO_2, 0°C}$ [H] $\xrightarrow{SOCl_2}$ [I] $\xrightarrow{LiAlH(OCMe_3)_3}$ [J].

(c) (3,5-dimethyl benzene with CH₃ groups) $\xrightarrow[\text{H}_2SO_4]{HNO_3}$ [K] $\xrightarrow[\text{Fe}]{Br_2}$ [L] $\xrightarrow[\text{(ii) } HONO]{\text{(i) } Sn, HCl}$ [M] $\xrightarrow[\text{heat}]{H_2O}$ [N]

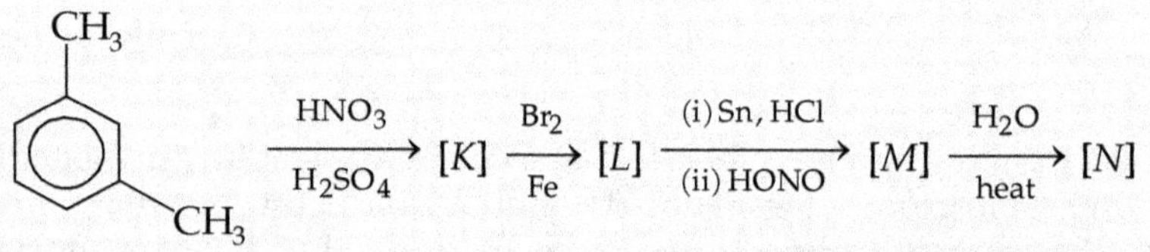

(d) (benzene) $\xrightarrow[\text{Fe}]{3Cl_2}$ [O] $\xrightarrow[\text{(ii) } HCl]{\text{(i) } [P]}$

(structure with OCH_2COOH, two Cl substituents)

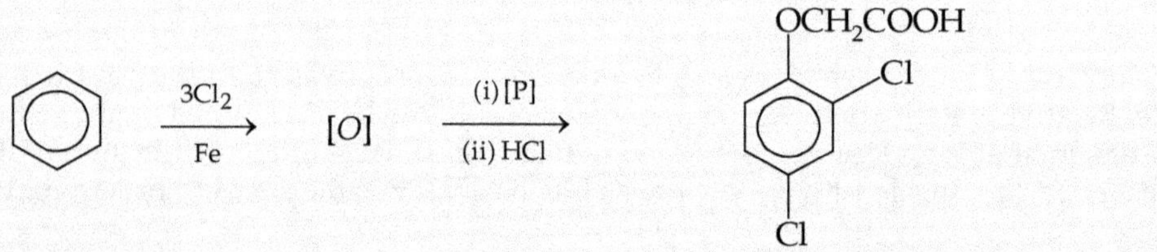

2, 4-Dichlorophenoxyacetic acid (a sea weed)

(e) (phenol with CH₃, i.e. 3-methylphenol) $\xrightarrow[\text{OH}^-]{(CH_3)_2SO_4}$ [Q] $\xrightarrow[\text{AlCl}_3]{Me_3CCl}$ [R] $\xrightarrow[\text{H}_2SO_4]{2HNO_3}$ [S]

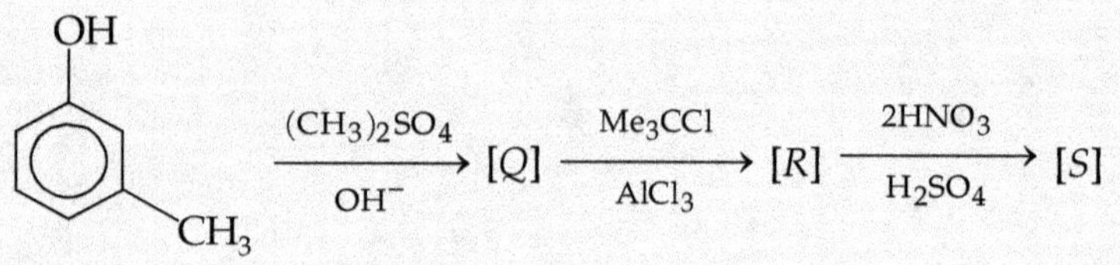

(f) (phenoxide ion) $+ T \longrightarrow$ [U] $\xrightarrow{\text{alc. KOH}}$ $C_6H_5OCH=CH_2$ $\xrightarrow{H_3O^+}$ [V] + [W]

(g) (2,4-dinitrophenol) $+ C_6H_5SO_2Cl \longrightarrow$ [X] $\xrightarrow[\text{DMSO}]{\text{NaF}}$ [Y]

(h) (catechol, benzene with OH and OH) $+ ClCH_2COCl$ $\xrightarrow{POCl_3}$ [Z] $\xrightarrow[\text{(ii) } H^+]{\text{(i) } NaOCl}$ $CHCl_3$

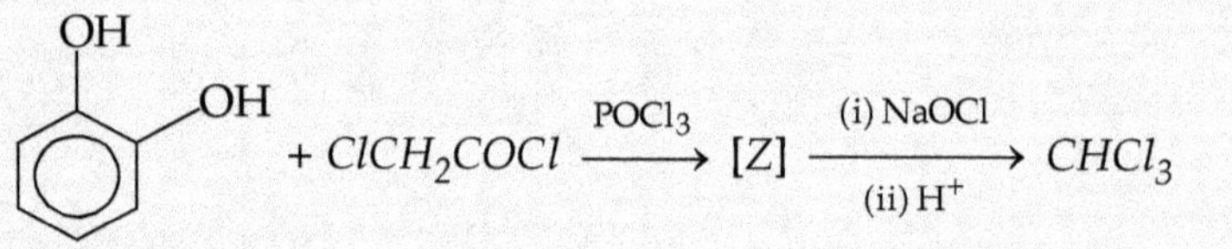

Solution :

(a)

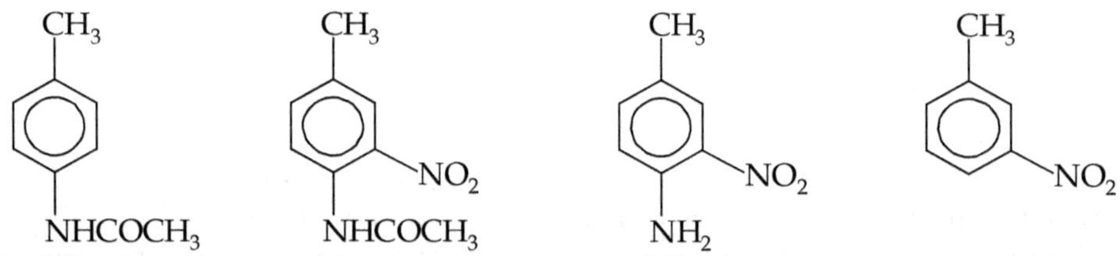

[A] : 4-methyl-N-acetyl aniline (CH₃ top, NHCOCH₃ bottom)

[B] : (CH₃ top, NO₂ ortho, NHCOCH₃ bottom)

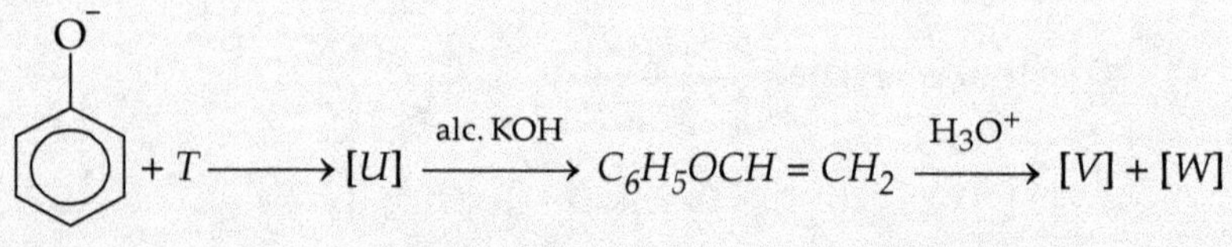

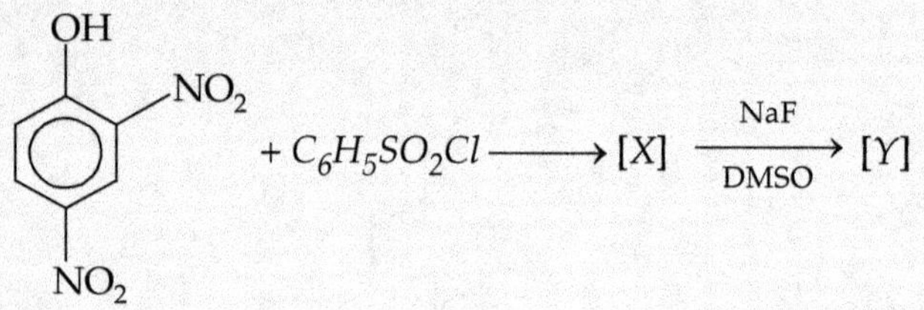

[C] : (CH₃ top, NO₂ ortho, NH₂ bottom)

[D] : (CH₃ top, NO₂ meta)

(b) [Structures E–J: para-substituted benzene rings]
- [E]: CH₃ (top), NO₂ (bottom) — p-nitrotoluene
- [F]: COOH (top), NO₂ (bottom)
- [G]: COOH (top), NH₂ (bottom)
- [H]: COOH (top), OH (bottom)
- [I]: COCl (top), OH (bottom)
- [J]: CHO (top), OH (bottom)

(c) [Structures K–N]
- [K]: CH₃ (top), CH₃ (right), NO₂ (bottom)
- [L]: Br (left), CH₃ (top), CH₃ (right), NO₂ (bottom)
- [M]: Br (left), CH₃ (top), CH₃ (right), $N_2^+Cl^-$ (bottom)
- [N]: Br (left), CH₃ (top), CH₃ (right), OH (bottom)

(d)
- [O]: Cl, Cl, Cl (trichlorobenzene)
- [P]: $^-OCH_2COO^-$

(e)
- [Q]: OCH₃ (top), CH₃
- [R]: OCH₃ (top), CH₃, C(CH₃)₃
- [S] A synthetic musk: OCH₃ (top), O_2N, NO_2, CH₃, C(CH₃)₃

(f)
$$BrH_2CCH_2Br \quad [T] \qquad\qquad C_6H_5OCH_2CH_2Br \quad [U]$$

$$C_6H_5OCH=CH_2 \xrightarrow{H_3O^+} [C_6H_5OCH(OH)CH_3] \longrightarrow C_6H_5OH + CH_3CHO$$
$$\text{hemiacetal} \qquad\qquad [V] \qquad [W]$$

(g)
[X]: OSO₂C₆H₅ (top), NO₂, NO₂ (bottom) $\xrightarrow[\text{DMSO}]{\text{NaF}}$ [Y]: F (top), NO₂, NO₂ (bottom)

Note that in the conversion of [X] to [Y], the very reactive unsolvated F⁻ displaces the good leaving group ($C_6H_5SO_3^-$) from the activated benzene ring.

(h)   Since Z undergoes haloform reaction, it must have —COCH₂Cl grouping. Hence Z is acylated product of catechol.

[Z]: OH (top), OH, COCH₂Cl (bottom) $\xrightarrow[\text{(ii) H}^+]{\text{(i) NaOCl}}$ [product]: OH (top), OH, COOH (bottom) $+ CHCl_3$

Example 6 :

Give structures of the bracketed compounds, A to H.

(a) [phenoxide with D, ortho] $\xrightarrow[\text{(ii) H}^+]{\text{(i) CO}_2}$ [A]

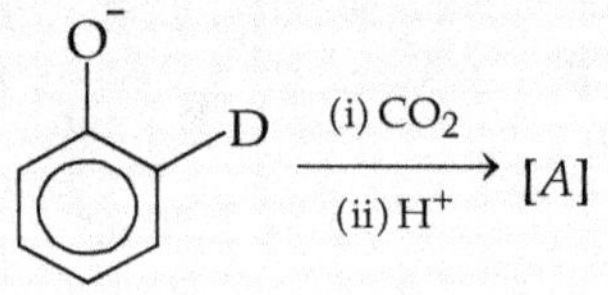

(b) [phenoxide with D, ortho] $\xrightarrow[\text{(ii) D}^+]{\text{(i) CO}_2}$ [B]

(c) [phenoxide with D at both ortho] $\xrightarrow[\text{(ii) H}^+]{\text{(i) CO}_2}$ [C]

(d) [phenoxide with D at both ortho] $\xrightarrow[\text{(ii) D}^+]{\text{(i) CO}_2}$ [D]

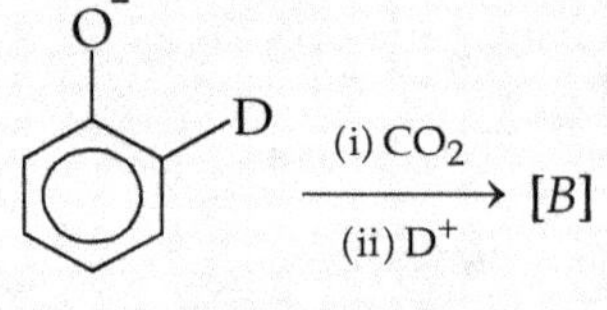

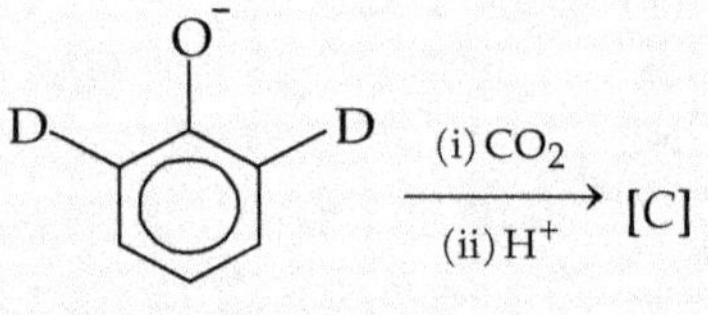

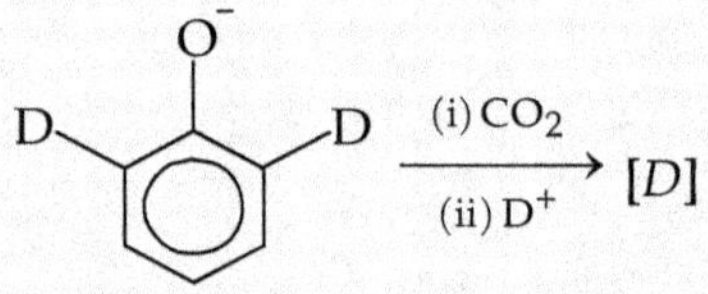

(e) [phenol] $\xrightarrow[\text{(ii) H}^+]{\text{(i) CCl}_4,\ \text{OH}^-}$ [E] $\xrightarrow{\text{heat}}$ [F]

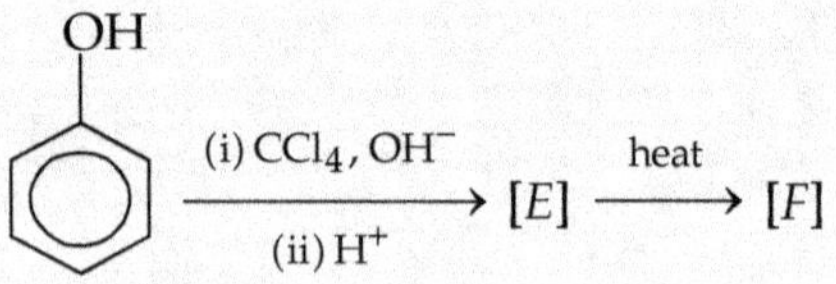

(f) [H] $\xleftarrow{\text{HNO}_3}$ [E] $\xrightarrow{\text{Br}_2 \text{ water}}$ [G]

Solution :

Note that reactions (a) to (d) are examples to Kolbe's reaction. For knowing the structure, students should know the mechanism of Kolbe reaction.

(a) [structure of [A]: salicylic acid with HOOC, OH and D]
[A]
(C—D bond is stronger than C—H)

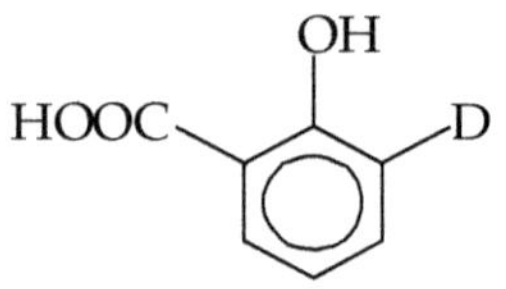

(b) [structure of [B]: with DOOC, OH and D]
[B]

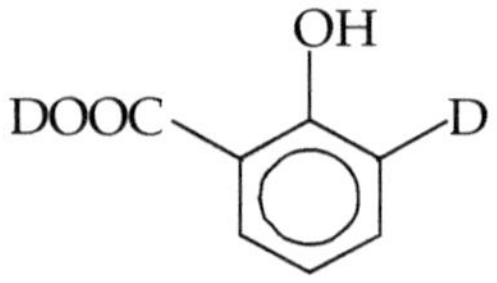

(c) [structure of [C]: with OD, D and COOH]
[C]

(d) [structure of [D]: with D, D and COOH]
[D]

(e) [structure of salicylic acid with OH, COOH]
Salicylic acid
[E]
$\xrightarrow[(-\text{CO}_2)]{\text{heat}}$
[structure of Phenol]
Phenol
$\xrightarrow[\text{of salicylic acid}]{\text{2nd molecule}}$
[structure of Phenyl salicylate]
Phenyl salicylate
[F]

(f) [structure of [H]: with OH, O$_2$N, NO$_2$, NO$_2$]
[H]
$\xleftarrow{\text{HNO}_3}$
[structure of [E]: salicylic acid with OH, COOH]
[E]
$\xrightarrow[\text{water}]{\text{Br}_2}$
[structure of [G]: with OH, Br, Br, Br]
[G]

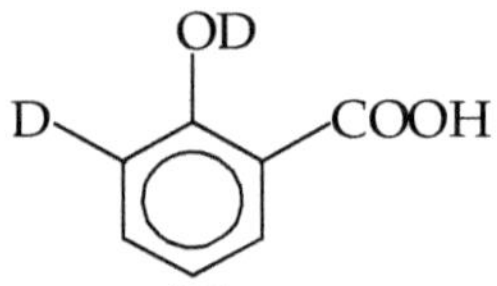

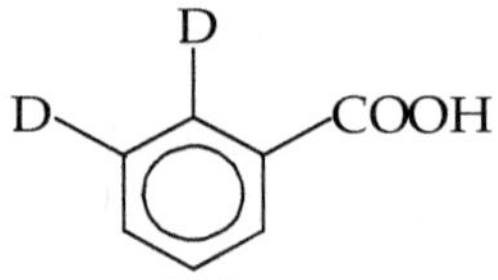

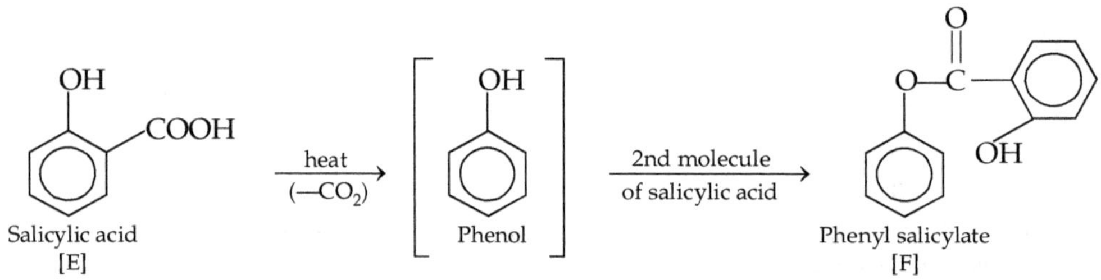

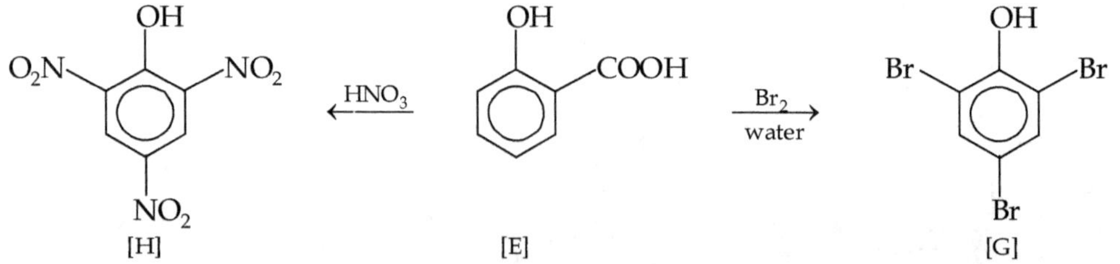

Example 7 :

Give steps involved in following conversions.

(a)

$$Ph\text{-}O\text{-}C(Ph)(Ph)\text{-}Ph \xrightarrow{H^+} HO\text{-}C_6H_4\text{-}C(Ph)(Ph)\text{-}Ph$$

(b)

$$CH_2 = CH\text{-}O\text{-}Ph \xrightarrow{H^+} CH_3CHO + C_6H_5OH$$

Solution :

(a)

$$Ph\text{-}\ddot{O}\text{-}CPh_3 \xrightarrow{H^+} Ph\text{-}\overset{+}{\underset{H}{O}}\text{-}CPh_3 \longrightarrow$$

$$\left[C_6H_5\text{-}OH + \overset{+}{C}Ph_3 \right] \xrightarrow[\text{substitution}]{\text{electrophilic}} HO\text{-}C_6H_4\text{-}CPh_3$$

(acts as electrophile)

(b)

$$CH_2 = CH\text{-}\ddot{O}\text{-}Ph \xrightarrow{H^+} CH_3\text{-}CH = \overset{+}{\ddot{O}}\text{-}C_6H_5 \xrightarrow[(-H^+)]{H_2O} \left[CH_3\text{-}\underset{OH}{CH}\text{-}O\text{-}C_6H_5 \right] \longrightarrow CH_3CHO + C_6H_5OH$$

A hemiacetal

Example 8 :

Outline method for converting o-cresol to salicylic acid in quantitative yield.

Solution :

At first step, it seems that CH_3 group can directly be oxidised to —COOH group by $KMnO_4$, but this can cause damage to the benzene ring due to the presence of —OH (an activating) group. So, in order to get quantiative yield of the acid, —OH group must first be protected

$$\underset{\text{}}{\text{o-cresol (OH, CH}_3) } \xrightarrow{CH_2N_2} \underset{(\text{—OH gp. protected})}{(OCH_3, CH_3)} \xrightarrow{KMnO_4} \underset{}{(OCH_3, COOH)} \xrightarrow{HI} \underset{(\text{—OH regenerated})}{(OH, COOH)}$$

Example 9 :

Prepare (a) 2, 4-dichlorophenol, and (b) 2, 4, 6-trinitrophenol from benzene.

Solution :

(a)

$$\text{benzene} \longrightarrow \text{2,4-dichlorophenol (OH, Cl, Cl)}$$

At first sight, it seems that the conversion can be affected by first converting benzene to phenol and then chlorinating the phenol.

Benzene $\xrightarrow[\text{(ii) Sn, HCl}]{\text{(i) HNO}_3}$ Aniline (NH$_2$) $\xrightarrow[\text{(ii) H}_2\text{O}]{\text{(i) HONO, 5°C}}$ Phenol (OH) $\xrightarrow{\text{Cl}_2}$ 2,4-Dichlorophenol (OH, Cl, Cl)

However, this method is not feasible because phenol is susceptible to oxidation by Cl_2. Hence the following scheme should be adopted.

Benzene $\xrightarrow[\text{Fe}]{3Cl_2}$ 1, 2, 4-Trichlorobenzene $\xrightarrow{\text{OH}^-}$ 2, 4-Dichlorophenol

Remember that ordinarily chlorine present on benzene nucleus is difficult to be replaced. However, when it has electron-withdrawing group in the *o*- and *p*-position it is easily replaced. Here chlorine present on C_1 is *ortho* to one chlorine (electronegative group) and para to other, hence it is replaced. Other two chlorines (at C_2 and C_4) are present at *meta* position to at least one chlorine, hence these are not replaced.

(b)   Benzene $\longrightarrow$ 2,4,6-Trinitrophenol (OH, O$_2$N, NO$_2$, NO$_2$)

Here again following route is not feasible because of high susceptibility of phenol to oxidation by HNO_3.

$$C_6H_6 \longrightarrow C_6H_5OH \xrightarrow[\text{H}_2\text{SO}_4]{\text{HNO}_3} \text{Oxidised products}$$

Thus following scheme is adopted.

Benzene $\xrightarrow[\text{Fe}]{\text{Cl}_2}$ (Cl) $\xrightarrow[\text{H}_2\text{SO}_4]{\text{HNO}_3}$ 2,4-Dinitrochlorobenzene (Cl, NO$_2$, NO$_2$) $\xrightarrow[\text{(ii) H}_3\text{O}^+]{\text{(i) NaOH}}$ 2,4-Dinitrophenol (OH, NO$_2$, NO$_2$) $\xrightarrow[\text{H}_2\text{SO}_4]{\text{HNO}_3}$ 2, 4, 6-Trinitrophenol (OH, O$_2$N, NO$_2$, NO$_2$)

Note that :

(i)   2, 4-Dinitrochlorobenzene can't be nitrated further because the Cl and two NO_2's deactivate the ring toward further electrophilic substitution.

(ii)   2, 4-Dinitrophenol can be nitrated because the two deactivating NO_2's prevent ring oxidation. Moreover, the third NO_2 group is directed at the desired site by all the existing three groups.

Example 10 :

Devise laboratory synthesis for the following compounds from the given organic compound.

(a)   *m*-Iodophenol from benzene

(b)   3-Bromo-4-methylphenol from toluene

(c)   2-Bromo-4-methylphenol from toluene

(d)   *m*-Aminophenol from benzene

(e)   2-Hydroxy-5-methylbenzaldehyde from *p*-toluidine

(f)   *m*-Methoxyaniline from benzenesulphonic acid

(g)   2, 4-Dinitrophenyl phenyl ether from chlorobenzene

(h)   4-Amino-2-hydroxybenzoic acid from nitrobenzene

(i)   2, 4-Diaminophenol from chlorobenzene

(j)   5-Methylresorcinol from toluene.

Solution :

(a)

Either of the group can't be introduced directly at the required site, hence these are introduced indirectly through diazotisation.

m-Iodophenol

(b)

Here OH group in *para* position to CH_3 group can be easily introduced through nitration, reduction, diazotisation and heating the product. But note that Br is present in *m*-position to the —OH group, so it can not be introduced at the final stage. Hence it should be introduced at some intermediate step which is after nitration of $C_6H_5CH_3$ because in such case —Br at the required site will be directed by both of the existing groups (—CH_3 as well as —NO_2)

Toluene

(Position of —Br is favoured by CH_3 as well as NO_2)

(c)

Note that here Br is present *ortho* to OH and *meta* to CH_3, so it must be introduced prior to OH and, of course, aft[er] the introduction of NH_2 which will give OH at the desired site because NH_2 is stronger activating group than CH_3.

$$CH_3\text{-benzene} \xrightarrow[\text{Sn, HCl}]{\text{HNO}_3,\ \text{H}_2\text{SO}_4} \xrightarrow[\text{(ii) Br}_2]{\text{(i) Ac}_2\text{O}} \xrightarrow[\text{(iii) H}_2\text{O, heat}]{\text{(i) H}_3\text{O}^+,\ \text{(ii) HNO}_2}$$

(NH_2 gp. is protected since Br_2 is oxidising agent)

(d) benzene $\longrightarrow$ 3-aminophenol (OH, NH_2)

$$\text{benzene} \xrightarrow[\text{H}_2\text{SO}_4]{2\text{HNO}_3} \text{1,3-dinitrobenzene} \xrightarrow{\text{NH}_4\text{HS}} \text{3-nitroaniline} \xrightarrow[\text{(ii) H}_2\text{O, heat}]{\text{(i) NaNO}_2,\ \text{HCl}} \text{3-nitrophenol} \xrightarrow[\text{(ii) OH}^-]{\text{(i) Sn, HCl}} \text{3-aminophenol}$$

(e) 4-methylaniline (NH_2, CH_3) $\xrightarrow[\text{(ii) H}_2\text{O, heat}]{\text{(i) HONO, 5°C}}$ 4-methylphenol (OH, CH_3) $\xrightarrow[\text{(ii) H}_3\text{O}^+]{\text{(i) CHCl}_3,\ \text{NaOH}}$ 2-hydroxy-5-methylbenzaldehyde (OH, CHO, CH_3)

(f) benzenesulfonic acid (SO_3H) $\xrightarrow[\text{H}_2\text{SO}_4]{\text{HNO}_3}$ 3-nitrobenzenesulfonic acid (SO_3H, NO_2) $\xrightarrow[\text{(ii) H}^+]{\text{(i) NaOH, heat}}$ 3-nitrophenol (OH, NO_2) $\xrightarrow[\text{(ii) Zn, HCl}]{\text{(i) (CH}_3)_2\text{SO}_4}$ 3-anisidine (OCH_3, NH_2)

(g) chlorobenzene (Cl) $\xrightarrow[\text{H}_2\text{SO}_4]{\text{HNO}_3}$ 1-chloro-2,4-dinitrobenzene (Cl, NO_2, NO_2) $\xrightarrow{\text{C}_6\text{H}_5\text{O}^-}$ 1-phenoxy-2,4-dinitrobenzene (OC_6H_5, NO_2, NO_2)

(–Cl activated by two —NO_2 gps.)

(h) nitrobenzene (NO_2) $\longrightarrow$ 4-amino-2-hydroxybenzoic acid (COOH, OH, NH_2)

4-Amino-2-hydroxybenzoic acid

(i) ... 2,4-Diaminophenol (**Amidol,** a photographic developer)

(j) ... 5-Methylresorcinol (**Orcinol,** a constituent of litmus dye)

Example 11 :

A phenol ($C_8H_{10}O$) having two methyl groups as substituent, when treated with dilute nitric acid, gives two isomeric products. Give the structure of the isomers and the possible way for separating them.

Solution :

The phenol should have two CH_3 groups in 3 and 5 positions because only this can give two isomeric products.

3, 5-Dimethylphenol

Intramolecular H-bonding possible, hence it can be steam-distilled

+

(It is non-volatile)

Example 12 :

(a)   An organic compound (A) of the molecular formula C_7H_8O gives following reactions :

      (i)   It dissolves in NaOH but not in $NaHCO_3$ (ii)   It reacts with Br_2 rapidly forming B, $C_7H_5O\ Br_3$.

      Give structures of A and B.

(b)   What would be A, if it did not dissolve in NaOH ?

Solution :

(a)   (i)   Molecular formula of A (C_7H_8O) indicates 4° of unsaturation (molecular formula of saturated parent hydrocarbon with C_7 is $C_{17}H_{16}$). Since the compound A has very less hydrogen atoms, it must have a benzene ring which accounts for its 4° of unsaturation (three for 3 double bonds, and one for ring).

     (ii)   Solubility of A in NaOH and insolubility in $NaHCO_3$ indicates that A contains a phenolic group.

     (iii)   The seventh carbon atom of A can be present as CH_3 group ; hence A can be $CH_3C_6H_4OH$ (C_7H_8O).

     (iv)   Since A reacts with bromine to form tribromo product, the two substituents (CH_3 and OH) must be present in the *m*-position to each other.

$$\text{A } (C_7H_8O) \qquad + 3Br_2 \longrightarrow \qquad \text{B } (C_7H_5OBr_3)$$

A (C_7H_8O)
(—OH can direct Br to
two *ortho* and one *para* positions)

(b)   The isomer of phenol that is insoluble in NaOH is ether, hence B should be anisole, $C_6H_5OCH_3$.

Example 13 :

Two isomeric compounds A and B with the molecular formula $C_{10}H_{12}O$ are insoluble in aqueous NaOH and decolorize Br_2 in CCl_4. Each is vigorously oxidized to p-methoxybenzoic acid (p-anisic acid), and give the same products, on ozonolysis. Identify compounds A and B. Is any other isomer possible for the compounds A and B that too gives p-anisic acid on oxidation, if so give a chemical reaction to distinguish it from A and B ?

Solution :

(i)   Molecular formula ($C_{10}H_{12}O$) of *A* and *B* indicates 5° of unsaturation, four of which can be accounted to benzene ring as indicated by relatively fewer H atoms, and the fifth to $C = C$ bond as evidenced by positive test with Br_2.

(ii)   Insolubility in aq. NaOH indicates that *A* and *B* are not having phenolic —OH group. Moreover, oxidation of *A* and *B* to form *p*-methoxybenzoic acid indicates that they are having —OCH_3 group and an alkenyl group in *para* position to each other.

Since seven C's are accounted for by the ring and the C of OCH_3, the remaining three C's must be present in the form of alkenyl group (R).

$$[A] \text{ and } [B] \xrightarrow{\text{Oxidation}} \text{p-Methoxybenzoic acid}$$

(iii)   Since each gives the same ozonolysis products, they must have identical position of double bond. The isomerism, thus, may be *cis-trans* type; to exhibit this the side chain (R) should be   —CH = CHCH_3.

cis
[A]   and   *trans*
[B]   [C]   [D]

(iv) The structure of isomer of *A* and *B* should be *C* or *D* which explains all the given reactions.

Distinction between A/B and C

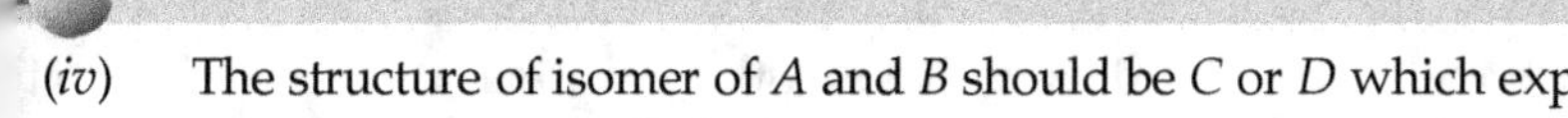

$$[A]/[B] \xrightarrow{\text{ozonolysis}} \text{(CHO, OCH}_3\text{ aromatic)} + CH_3CHO \quad \textbf{(Responds haloform test)}$$

$$[C] \xrightarrow{\text{ozonolysis}} \text{(CH}_2\text{CHO, OCH}_3\text{ aromatic)} + CH_2O \quad \textbf{(Does not respond haloform test)}$$

The isomer [D] can't be distinguished from A/B by ozonolysis followed by haloform test.

$$[D] \xrightarrow{\text{ozonolysis}} \text{(COCH}_3\text{, OCH}_3\text{ aromatic)} + CH_2O \quad \text{(Responds haloform test)}$$

Example 14 :

A sweet-smelling organic liquid A, $C_{10}H_{10}O_2$ gives the following reactions.

(a) It is insoluble in NaOH and does not give a colour with ferric chloride.

(b) On catalytic hydrogenation, it adds one equivalent of hydrogen.

(c) On ozonolysis it gives methanal and a compound B ($C_9H_8O_3$) which responds Tollen's reagent.

(d) On oxidation with $KMnO_4$, it gives a monocarboxylic acid C (N.E. = 166) which does not give colour with $FeCl_3$. However, acid C gives 3, 4-dihydroxybenzoic acid and methanal, when refluxed with conc. HI.

Identify compounds A, B, and C and explain the concerned reactions.

Solution :

(i) Molecular formula of A ($C_{10}H_{10}O_2$) indicates 6° of unsaturation, four of which must be due to benezene ring.

(ii) Since A does not dissolve in NaOH or give a colour with $FeCl_3$, it is not a phenol.

(iii) Ozonolysis product, methanal ($CH_2 = O$), of A indicates that A has a chain with a terminal $= CH_2$ grouping. Since the second ozonolysis product (B) responds Tollen's reagent, it has an —CHO group and hence A has —CH = CH_2 grouping.

$$\underset{\text{(A)}}{-CH = CH_2} \xrightarrow{O_3} \underset{\text{(B)}}{-CHO} + \underset{\text{Methanal}}{O = CH_2}$$

Note that the double bond accounts for the fifth degree of unsaturation.

(iv)   Since the oxidation product (C) is a monocarboxylic acid, it indicates that no other carbon is directly linked to the ring, had it been so a dicarboxylic acid should have been the oxidation product. This leads to the thought that the two oxygen's must be prsent as ether linkages probably present as a ring to explain the sixth degree of unsaturation. This is confirmed by isolating $CH_2 = O$ and 3, 4-dihydroxybenzoic acid on cleavage with HI. Formation of $CH_2 = O$ indicates that the two oxygen's are linked together through CH_2, hence acid C has following structure.

COOH $\xrightarrow{HI}$ COOH $+ \; O = CH_2$

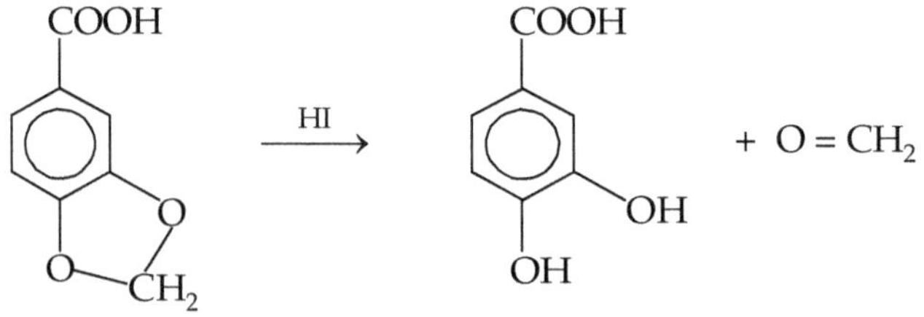

[C]   3, 4-Dihydroxybenzoic acid

Thus compounds (A) and (B) should have following respective structures.

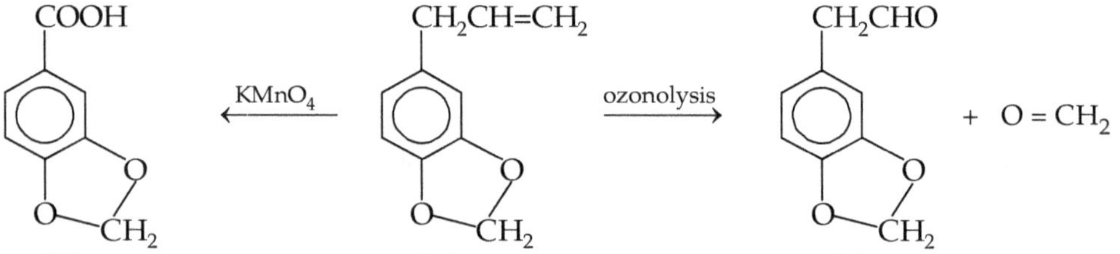

COOH $\xleftarrow{KMnO_4}$ $CH_2CH=CH_2$ $\xrightarrow{ozonolysis}$ CH_2CHO $+ \; O = CH_2$

[C]   [A]   [B]

Example 15 :

Give structural formula for the dicarboxylic acids with the molecular formula $C_6H_{10}O_4$ which satisfies following conditions.

(a)   **They are chiral, form anhydride easily but not decarboxylated easily.**

(b)   **They are achiral, do not form anhydride easily, but decarboxylated easily.**

Solution :

The dicarboxylic acids, $C_6H_{10}O_4$, should have structure as $HOOC(C_4H_8)COOH$. Now we know that 1,4- and 1,5-dicarboxylic acids on heating form anhydride, while 1,2- and 1,3-dicarboxylic acids form monocarboxylate and CO_2 on heating. Thus

(a)   the acid capable of forming anhydride should have following part structure.

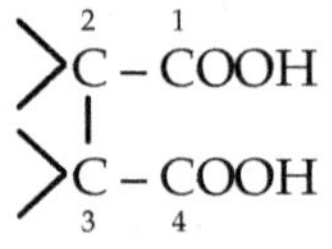

$$\begin{array}{c} \overset{2}{>}C - \overset{1}{COOH} \\ | \\ >C - \underset{4}{COOH} \\ {\scriptstyle 3} \end{array} \qquad or \qquad \begin{array}{c} \overset{2}{>}C - \overset{1}{COOH} \\ >C \\ \underset{3}{} \diagdown C - \underset{5}{COOH} \\ {\scriptstyle 4} \end{array}$$

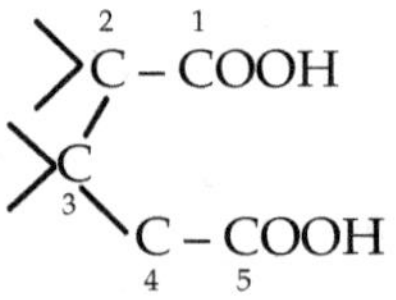

It needs two carbon and for being chiral it   It needs only one C,
can have a C_2H_5 on C_2 (or C_3) and H on C_3 and for being chiral it can
(or C_2); or it can have a CH_3 each on C_2 and C_3 have $-CH_3$ group at C_2 or C_4

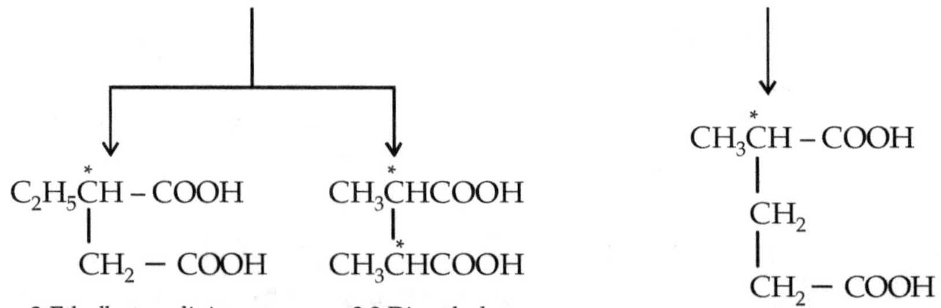

$C_2H_5\overset{*}{C}H - COOH$ $CH_3\overset{*}{C}HCOOH$ $CH_3\overset{*}{C}H - COOH$

$CH_2 - COOH$ $CH_3\overset{*}{C}HCOOH$ CH_2

                                                      $CH_2 - COOH$

2-Ethylbutanedioic   2,3-Dimethyl-   2-Methylpentanedioic acid
acid   butanedioic acid

(b) Since the dicarboxylic acids, HOOC (C_4H_8)COOH evolve CO_2 on heating, two acidic groups must be on same carbon atom, i.e. these are 1,3-dicarboxylic acids

$$\begin{array}{c} \diagup COOH \\ \diagdown C \\ \diagdown COOH \end{array} \xrightarrow{\text{heat}} \begin{array}{c} \diagup \\ \diagdown \end{array} C-COOH \ + \ CO_2\uparrow$$

The three carbon fraction can be present as C_2H_5 and CH_3, or n-C_3H_7 and H, or iso-C_3H_7 and H. Thus here also three isomeric dicarboxylic acids are possible.

Ethylmethylpropane-
dioic acid

Propylpropanedioic
acid

Isopropylpropanedioic
acid

Example 16 :

Give steps involved in the conversion of (R)-(+)-glyceraldehyde to

(i) **(R)-(+)-malic acid,**   **(ii) (S)-(–)-malic acid**

Solution :

(i)

(R)-(+)-Glyceraldehyde

(R)-(+)-Malic acid

(ii)

(R)-(+)-Glyceraldehyde

I

II

Both are same stereoisomer

(S)-(–)-Malic acid

Example 17 :

Carry out the following conversions in not more than four steps.

(a) [structure: methylenecyclohexane → cyclohexyl-CH$_2$COOH]

(b) [structure: 5-bromo-1-tetralone → 1-oxo-tetralin-COOH]

(c) $(CH_3)_3CCOOH \longrightarrow (CH_3)_3CCN$

Solution :

(a) [structure: methylenecyclohexane] $\xrightarrow[\text{ROOR}]{\text{HBr}}$ [cyclohexyl-CH$_2$Br] $\xrightarrow[\text{ether}]{\text{Mg}}$ $\xrightarrow{CO_2}$ $\xrightarrow{H_3O^+}$ Product

(b) [structure: bromo ketone] $\xrightarrow[\text{H}^+, \text{heat}]{CH_2OHCH_2OH}$ $\xrightarrow[\text{ether}]{\text{Mg}}$ $\xrightarrow{CO_2}$ $\xrightarrow{H_3O^+}$ Product

(c) $(CH_3)_3CCOOH \xrightarrow{SOCl_2} \xrightarrow{NH_3} \xrightarrow{P_4O_{10}}$ Product

Example 18 :

[reaction: cyclic acetal with CH$_3$ and CH$_2$COOH side chain, carbons labelled 1, 2, 3]
$\xrightarrow[\substack{\text{(ii) H}^+ \\ \text{(iii) evaporate}}]{\text{(i) aq. base}}$
[product: lactone with CH$_3$ and OH]

Answer the following questions regarding above reaction :

(a)   **Name the functional groups in the reactant and product**

(b)   **What is the effect of aq. base and acid in the reaction?**

(c)   **Label the positions of C$_1$ and C$_2$ of reactant into product.**

Solution :

(a)   Reactant has acetal and –COOH groups, while the product has a lactone and alcoholic group.

(b)   and (c) Since acetals are resistant to base, hence the compound will not undergo any significant change except that –COOH will be converted to –COO⁻Na⁺. Acids decompose acetals to CH_3CHO and a diol; the latter on heating undergo esterification to form cyclic ester, commonly called lactone.

[reaction scheme: acetal $\xrightarrow{H^+}$ CH_3CHO + diol $\equiv$ labelled diol $\xrightarrow{\text{heat}}$ lactone]

Example 19 :

Benzene tetracarboxylic acids have three isomeric structures. Write their structures and show how these can be distinguished by anhydride formation?

Solution :

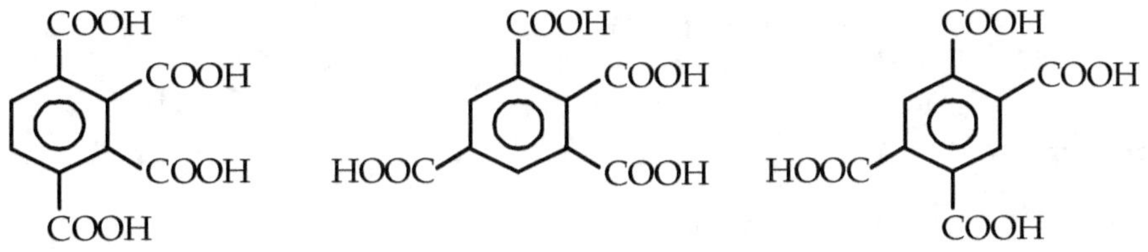

1,2,3,4– **(A)**　　　　1,2,3,5– **(B)**　　　　1,2,4,5– **(C)**

The three isomers can be distinguished by adding *an equivalent* amount of $SOCl_2$, when **(A)** gives two isomeric anhydrides, while **(B)** and **(C)** form one anhydride each; **(B)** and **(C)** can further be distinguished by adding second equivalent of $SOCl_2$ when only the monoanhydride from **(C)** will form a dianhydride.

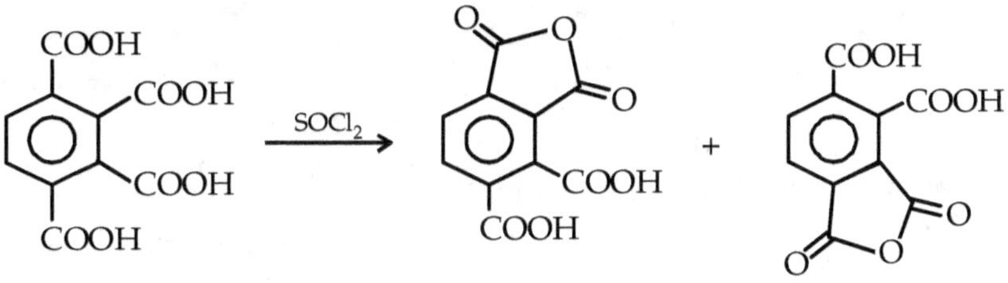

(A)

Two isomeric anhydrides

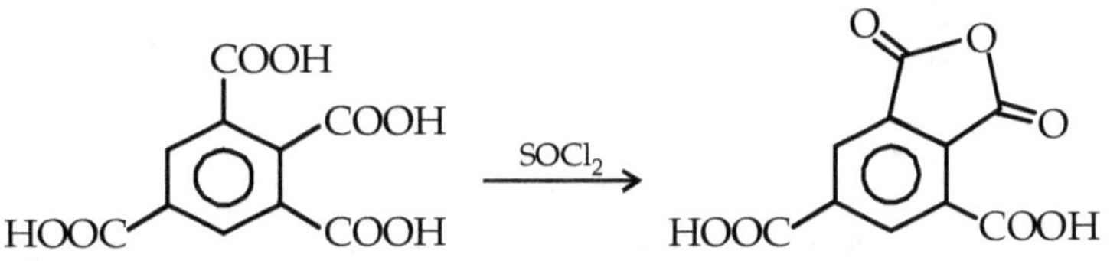

(B)

Only one mono-anhydride

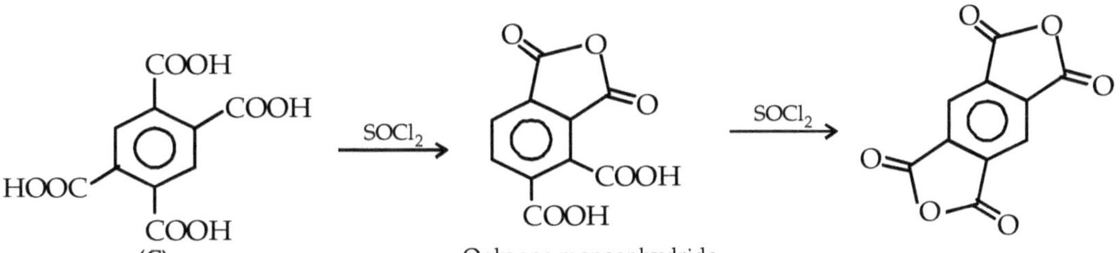

(C)

Only one monoanhydride

Dianhydride

EXERCISE 13.1 (MCQ - ONE option correct)

1. The compound, 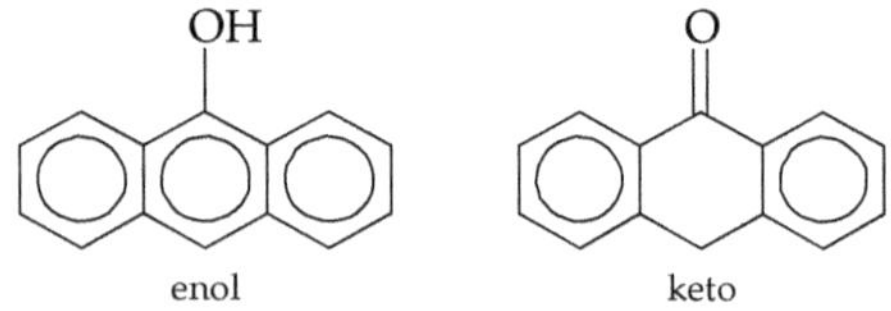 can be named as

   (*a*)   2-hydroxyanisole   (*b*)   catechol monomethyl ether

   (*c*)   Guaiacol   (*d*)   by all the three names.

2. The least accepted name for (structure) is

   (*a*)   2-mercaptophenol   (*b*)   2-hydroxythiophenol

   (*c*)   monothiocatechol   (*d*)   *o*-meraptophenol.

3. 9-Hydroxyanthracene (anthranol) shows keto-enol tautomerism, which of the tautomer is more stable ?

         enol   keto

   (*a*)   Keto   (*b*)   Enol

   (*c*)   Both are equally stable   (*d*)   It can't be predicted.

4. Which of the following isomer of nitrophenol is steam volatile?

   (*a*)   *ortho*   (*b*)   *meta*

   (*c*)   *para*   (*d*)   none.

5. Cumene (isopropylbenzene) is obtained by two cheap hydrocarbons, namely

   (*a*)   Benzene + *n*-Propane   (*b*)   Toluene + Ethylene

   (*c*)   Benzene + Propene   (*d*)   Benzene + Propyne.

6. Well-known antiseptic 4- *n*-hexylresorcinol is prepared most easily from which of the phenol ?

   (*a*)   Catechol   (*b*)   Resorcinol

   (*c*)   Quinol   (*d*)   From all the three.

7. Which of the following phenol will give lower yield during Kolbe-Schmidt reaction ?

   (*a*) (structure with CH₃)   (*b*) (structure with OCH₃)

   (*c*) (structure with NO₂)   (*d*)   All will give good yield.

8. Which of the following method gives better yield of *p*-nitrophenol?

   (*a*)   Phenol $\xrightarrow[20°C]{dil.HNO_3}$ *p*-Nitrophenol

   (*b*)   Phenol $\xrightarrow[\text{(ii) HNO}_3]{\text{(i) NaNO}_2 + H_2SO_4, 7-8°C}}$ *p*-Nitrophenol

   (*c*)   Phenol $\xrightarrow[\text{(ii) Conc. HNO}_3]{\text{(i) NaOH}}$

   (*d*)   None of the three.

9. Which of the following method is preferred for preparing 2, 4, trinitrophenol ?

   (*a*)   (benzene) + Conc. $HNO_3 \longrightarrow$ (2,4,6-trinitrophenol)

   (*b*)   (phenol-2,4-disulphonic acid) + Conc. $HNO_3 \longrightarrow$ (trinitrophenol)

   (*c*)   Both (*a*) and (*b*) give similar result

   (*d*)   None of the two.

10. What happens when, 2, 4, 6-trinitrochlorobenzene is just warmed with water ?

   (*a*)   No reaction takes place

   (*b*)   A hydrate is formed

   (*c*)   2, 4- Dinitrophenol is formed

   (*d*)   Picric acid is formed.

11. O_2N-(ring with NO_2 and Cl)$\xrightarrow{\text{dil. NaOH}} O_2N-$(ring with NO_2 and O^-)

   Which one is ture about the above representation ?

   (*a*)   It is an example of electrophilic substitution

   (*b*)   It is an example of substitution through benzyne intermediate

   (*c*)   It is an example of activated nucleophilic substitution

   (*d*)   Above reaction is not possible since C—Cl bond is very strong.

12. Which is true about the C—O bond lengths in the following compounds ?

        (cyclohexene a O—H)   (cyclohexane b O—H)

   (*a*) $a = b$ (*b*) $a > b$

   (*c*) $a < b$ (*d*)   all the three.

13. Which of the following has minimum pK_a value ?

   (*a*) (phenol)   (*b*) (o-cresol, OH with CH₃)

   (*c*) (naphthalenol)   (*d*) (naphthol with OH)

4. Which one of the following has highest dipole moment ?

(a) 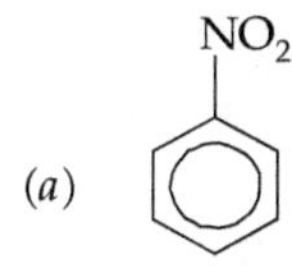

(b)  [NO₂-phenyl with OH para]

(c) 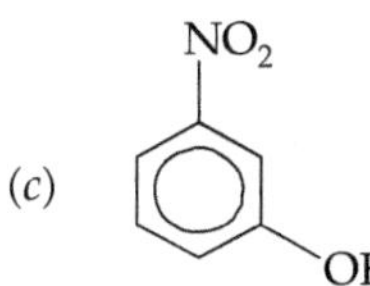 [NO₂-phenyl with OH meta]

(d) 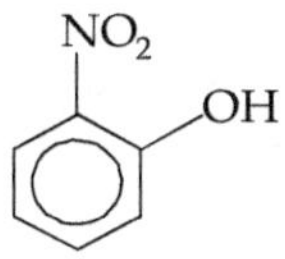 [NO₂-phenyl with OH ortho]

15. Choose the reagent to carry out following reaction :

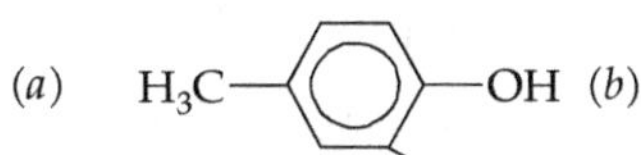

(a) Br_2 water
(b) Br_2 in CCl_4
(c) Either of the two
(d) Reaction not possible.

16. 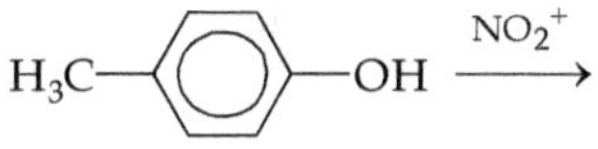 H_3C—⟨ ⟩—OH $\xrightarrow{NO_2^+}$ P. Here P is

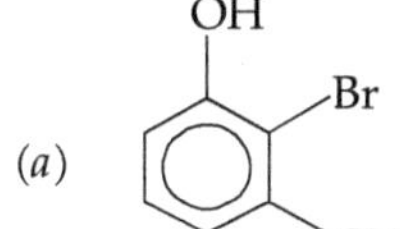

(a) H_3C—⟨ ⟩—OH (with NO_2)

(b) 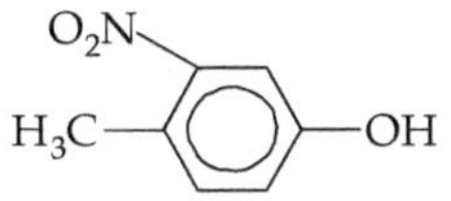 H_3C—⟨ ⟩—OH (with O_2N)

(c) Both (a) and (b)
(d) Reaction not possible.

17. What should be the product in the following reaction ?

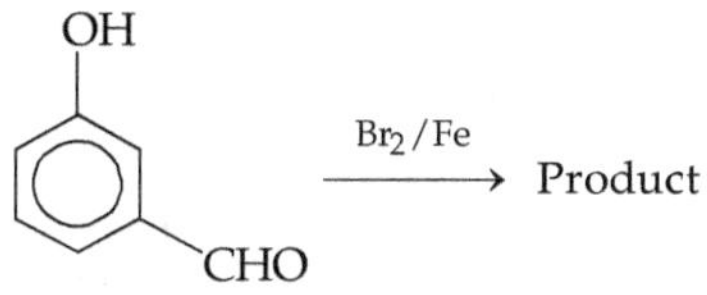

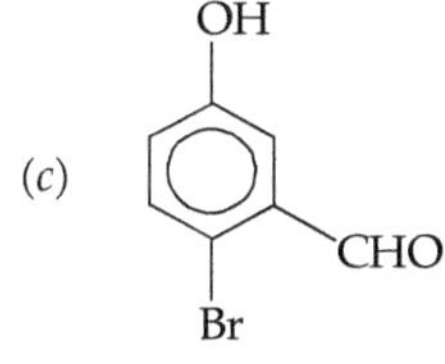

[meta-hydroxybenzaldehyde] $\xrightarrow{Br_2/Fe}$ Product

(a) [OH, Br ortho, CHO]
(b) 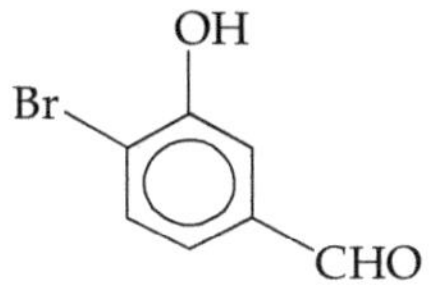 [OH, Br ortho, CHO]
(c) [OH, CHO, Br]
(d) 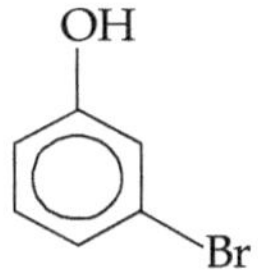 [OH, Br]

18. Predict the nature of P in the following reaction.

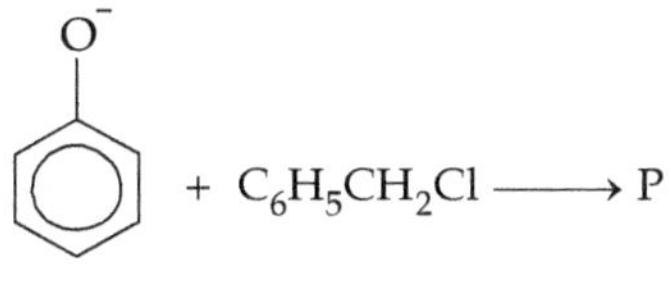

[phenoxide O⁻] $+ C_6H_5CH_2Cl \longrightarrow$ P

(a) 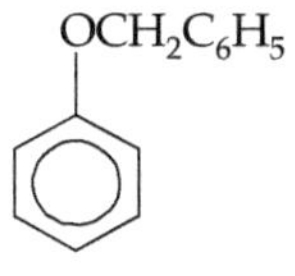 $OCH_2C_6H_5$ [on ring]
(b) 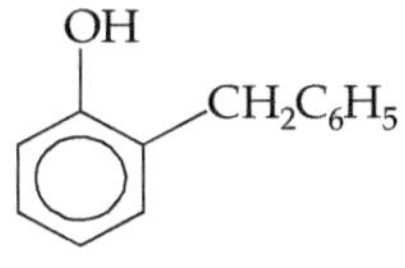 OH, $CH_2C_6H_5$ [on ring]
(c) Both (a) and (b)
(d) Reaction is not possible.

19. Direct the nature of the product in the following reaction :

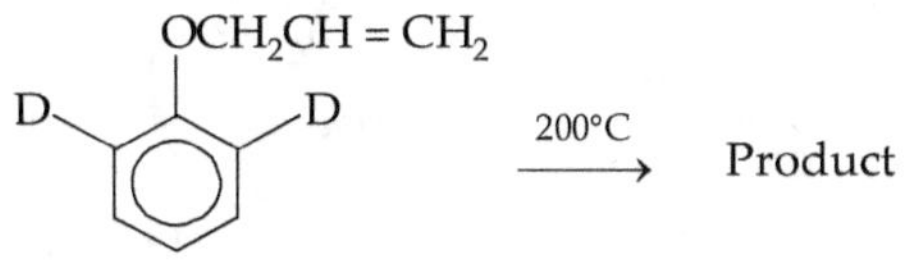

[$OCH_2CH = CH_2$ ring with D, D] $\xrightarrow{200°C}$ Product

(a) [OH ring, D, $CH_2CH = CH_2$]

(b) [OH ring, D, D, $CH_2CH = CH_2$]

(c) [OD ring, D, $CH_2CH = CH_2$]

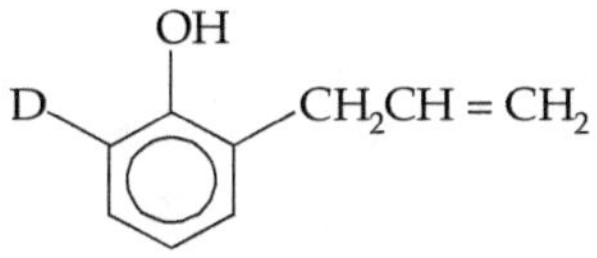

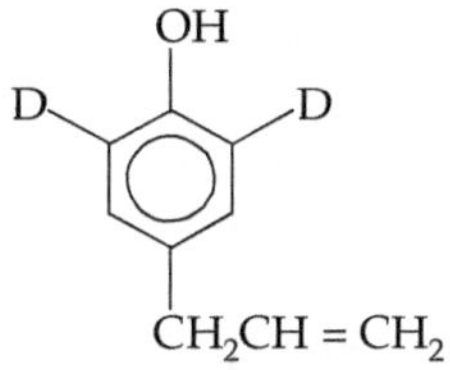

(d) [OD ring, $CH_2CH = CH_2$]

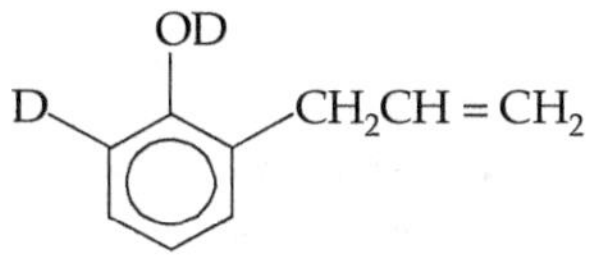

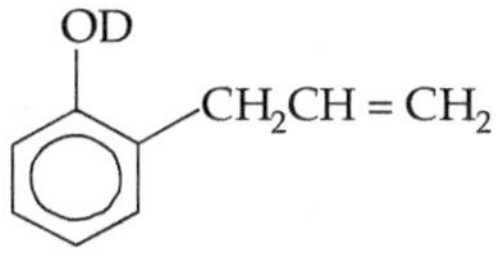

20. Predict the product Z in the following reaction :

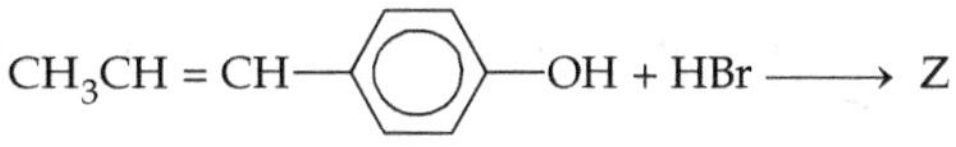

$CH_3CH = CH$—⟨ ⟩—OH $+ HBr \longrightarrow$ Z

(a) 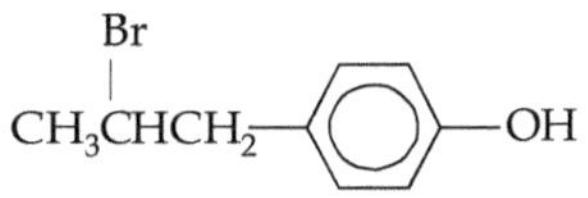 $CH_3\underset{\underset{Br}{|}}{CH}CH_2$—⟨ ⟩—OH

(b) 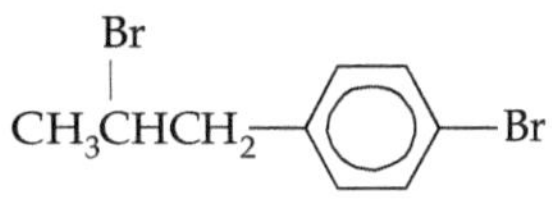 $CH_3\underset{\underset{Br}{|}}{CH}CH_2$—⟨ ⟩—Br

(c) 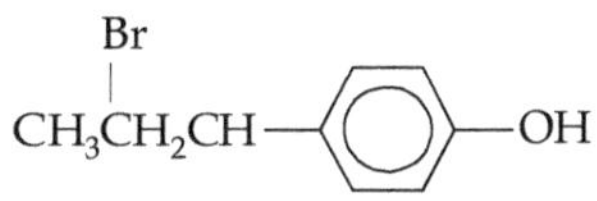 $CH_3CH_2\underset{\underset{Br}{|}}{CH}$—⟨ ⟩—OH

(d) 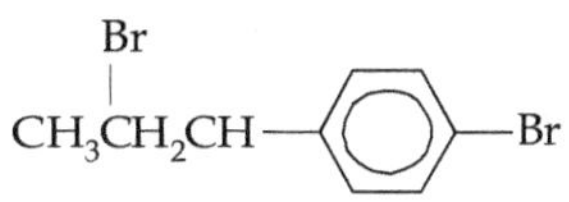 $CH_3CH_2\underset{\underset{Br}{|}}{CH}$—⟨ ⟩—Br

21. Identify the end product

$C_6H_6 \xrightarrow[\text{heat}]{2H_2SO_4} [A] \xrightarrow{NaOH, 270°C} [B]$

(a) 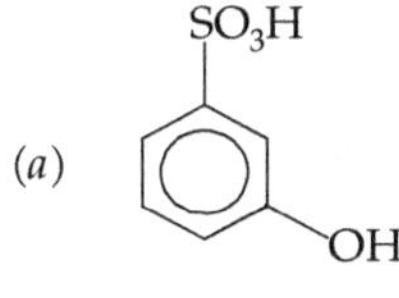

(b) 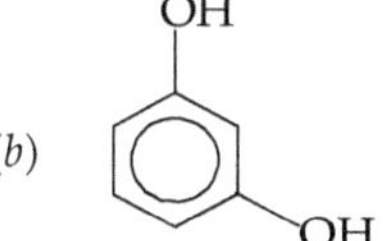

(c) 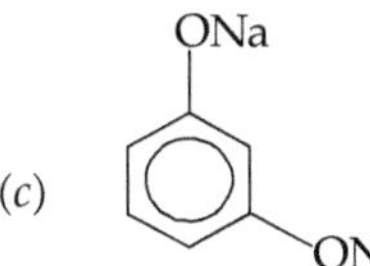

(d) 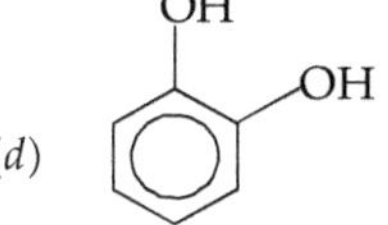

22. Identify the end product in the following series of reactions :

$$C_6H_5NO_2 \xrightarrow[\text{(ii) NaOH}]{\text{(i) Sn, HCl}} [A] \xrightarrow[\text{H}_2\text{SO}_4]{\text{Na}_2\text{Cr}_2\text{O}_7} [B] \xrightarrow[\text{H}_2\text{O}]{\text{SO}_2} [C]$$

(a) 2-hydroxybenzenesulfonic acid (SO₃H ortho to OH)

(b) 4-hydroxybenzenesulfonic acid (SO₃H para to OH)

(c) benzene-1,2-diol with extra OH

(d) benzene-1,4-diol with extra OH

23. Phenol is

  (a)   a base weaker than ammonia

  (b)   an acid stronger than carbonic acid

  (c)   an acid weaker than carbonic acid

  (d)   a neutral compound

24. —NO_2 group is acid-strengthening group ; when present in *para*-position of phenol and benzoic acid. Which statement is true about this ?

  (a)   It increases acidity of both to the same extent.

  (b)   It increases acidity of phenol more than that of benzoic acid.

  (c)   It increases acidity of benzoic acid more than that of the phenol.

  (d)   It does not increase acidity of any of the compound.

25.

$$\text{C}_6\text{H}_6 + \text{Cl}-\text{CH}_2\text{CH}_2-\text{CH}_3 \xrightarrow{\text{AlCl}_3} P \xrightarrow[\text{(ii) H}_3\text{O}^+]{\text{(i) O}_2/\Delta} Q + \text{Phenol}$$

The major products P and Q are

(a) isopropylbenzene and CH_3CH_2CHO (b) isopropylbenzene and CH_3COCH_3

(c) isopropylbenzene and CH_3COCH_3 (d) isopropylbenzene and CH_3CH_2CHO

26. When phenol is reacted with $CHCl_3$ and NaOH followed by acidification, salicyladehyde is obtained. Which of the following species are involved in the above mentioned reaction as intermediates?

(a) cyclohexadienone with CHO/CCl₂   (b) phenol with CHCl₂

(c) cyclohexanone with CHCl/OH   (d) phenolate with CHCl₂

27.

$$\text{C}_6\text{H}_5\text{OH} + \text{C}_2\text{H}_5\text{I} \xrightarrow[\text{Anhydrous (C}_2\text{H}_5\text{OH)}]{^-\text{OC}_2\text{H}_5} \ ?$$

(a) $C_6H_5OC_2H_5$ (b) $C_2H_5OC_2H_5$

(c) $C_6H_5OC_6H_5$ (d) C_6H_5I

28. (indanol) $\xrightarrow[\text{2. MeBr}]{\text{1. One eq. NaOH}}$ (A);

Product (A) is :

(a) OMe on ring, OH on side chain

(b) OH on ring, OMe on side chain

(c) indene with OH

(d) None of these

29. Phenol $\xrightarrow[\text{distillation}]{\text{Zinc}}$ (A) $\xrightarrow[\text{Conc.H}_2\text{SO}_4 \text{ at } 60°C]{\text{Conc. HNO}_3}$ (B) $\xrightarrow[\text{NaOH}]{\text{Zn}}$ (C)

In the above reaction compounds (A), (B) and (C) are :

  (a)   benzene, nitrobenzene and aniline

  (b)   benzene, dinitrobenzene and *m*-nitroaniline

  (c)   toluene, *m*-nitrobenzene and *m*-toluidine

  (d)   benzene, nitrobenzene and hydrazobenzene

30. Salol can be used as

  (a)   Antiseptic   (b)   Antipyretic

  (c)   Both (a) and (b)   (d)   None of these

31. Which of the following compounds have higher enol content as per conditions given in paranthesis:

  (a) $CH_3-CO-CH_3$ (at higher temperature)

  (b) $CH_3-CO-CH_2-COOC_2H_5$ (in polar solvent)

  (c)   cyclohexenone (non polar solvent)

  (d)   All of the above

32.

Benzene $\xrightarrow{\text{Ni/H}_2}$ (P) $\xrightarrow[250°C]{\text{Cu}}$ (Q) $\xrightarrow{\text{NH}_2\text{OH}}$ (R) $\xrightarrow{\text{H}^+}$ (S)

In the above sequence, the product (S) is :

(a) adipic acid (diacid)

(b) cyclohexanone oxime (N–OH)

(c) caprolactam (N-H lactam)

(d) aminohexanamide (NH₂ / C(=O)NH₂)

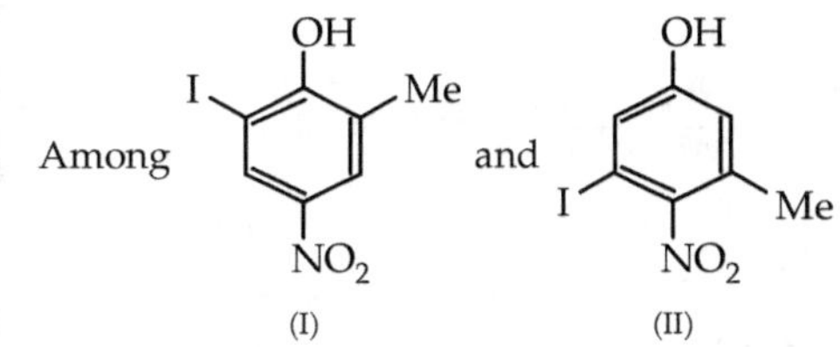

. Among 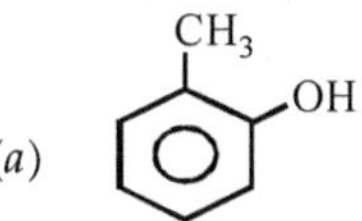 (I) and 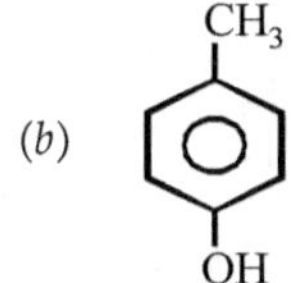 (II)

the acidic strength is
(a)　I > II
(b)　II > I
(c)　I = II
(d)　Cannot be predicted

. The structure of the compound that gives a tribromo derivative on treatment with bromine water is

(a)　CH_3, OH (ortho)
(b)　CH_3, OH (para)
(c)　CH_3, OH (meta)
(d)　CH_2OH

5. 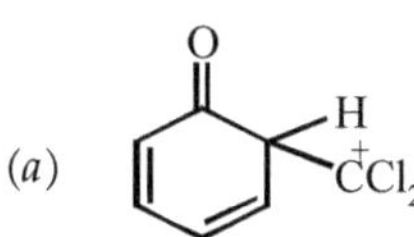 $+ CHCl_3 + NaOH \longrightarrow$ (o-$O^- Na^+$, CHO)

The electrophile involved in the above reaction is

(a)　trichloromethyl anion ($\overset{\ominus}{C}Cl_3$)

(b)　formyl cation ($\overset{\oplus}{C}HO$)

(c)　dichloromethyl cation ($\overset{\oplus}{C}HCl_2$)

(d)　dichlorocarbene ($:CCl_2$)

6. When phenol is reacted with $CHCl_3$ and $NaOH$ followed by acidification, salicylaldehyde is obtained. Which of the following species are involved in the above mentioned reaction as intermediate?

(a)　(cyclohexadienone with $\overset{+}{C}Cl_2$, H)
(b)　(OH, $CHCl_2$)
(c)　(cyclohexadienone with CHCl, OH, H)
(d)　(O^-, $CHCl_2$)

7. Arrange the following in the decreasing order of acidic strength

Phenol, p-nitrophenol, m-cresol, p-cresol
　I　　　　II　　　　　III　　　IV
(a)　II > III > IV > I
(b)　II > I > III > IV
(c)　II > I > IV > III
(d)　III > IV > II > I

8. Which of the following compound can react with hydroxylamine?

(a)　(OH, OH resorcinol type)
(b)　(OH, OH, OH)
(c)　(OH, HO, OH)
(d)　(OH, OH, OH)

39. Pyrrole is treated with alkaline chloroform to form two products A and B

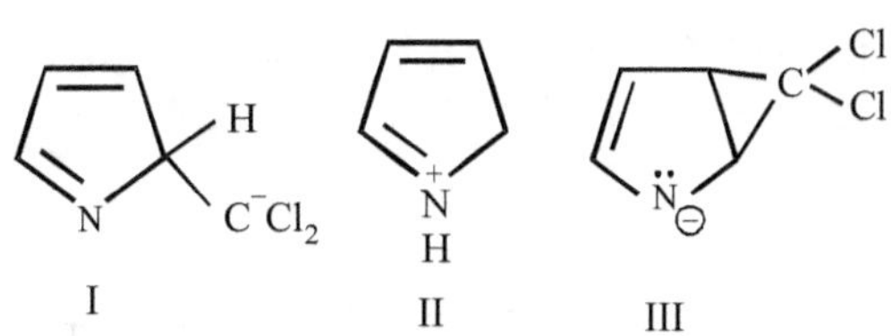

Which of the following intermediate is likely to be formed?

(structures I, II, III)
　I　　　II　　　III

(structure IV)
　IV

(a)　I and IV
(b)　I and III
(c)　III and IV
(d)　I, III and IV

40. 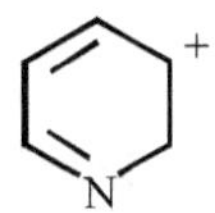 (OD, D) $\xrightarrow{NaOH}$ [Intermediate] $\xrightarrow[\text{(ii) } D^+]{\text{(i) } CO_2}$ P. Here P is

(a)　(HOOC, OD, D)
(b)　(DOOC, OD, D)
(c)　—
(d)　(DOOC, OH, D) Reaction not possible

41. (2,6-dimethylphenol H_3C, OH, CH_3) $\xrightarrow{CH_2=CHCH_2Cl}$ [ ] $\xrightarrow{200°C}$ P. Here P is

(a)　(H_3C, OH, CH_3, $CH_2\overset{14}{CH}=CH_2$)
(b)　(H_3C, OH, CH_3, $^{14}CH_2CH=CH_2$)
(c)　Both
(d)　(H_3C, $OCH_2CH=\overset{14}{CH_2}$, CH_3)

42. Phenol is converted into bakelite by heating it with formaldehyde in presence of alkali or acid. Which statement is true regarding this reaction ?
(a)　The electrophile in both cases is $CH_2=O$

(b)　The electrophile in both cases is $CH_2=\overset{+}{O}H$

(c)　The electrophile is $CH_2=O$ in presence of alkali and $CH_2=\overset{+}{O}H$ in presence of acid

(d)　It is a nucleophilic substitution reaction

43. Which of the following is not formed as an intermediate in the Reimer-Tiemann reaction between phenol and alkaline chloroform?

(a) [structure: cyclohexadienone with $\bar{C}Cl_2$ group]

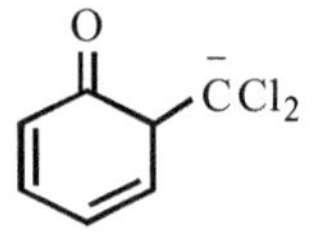

(b) [structure: cyclohexadienone anion]

(c) [structure: phenoxide with $CHCl_2$ group]

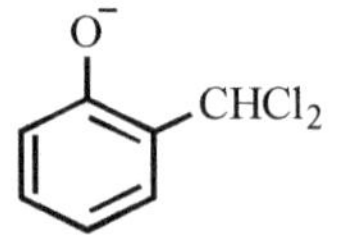

(d) $:CCl_2^{2-}$

44.

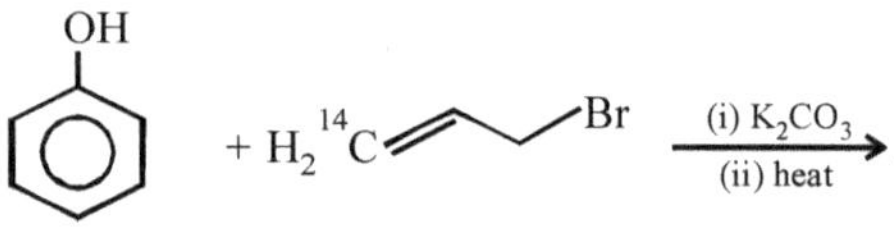

[structure: phenol] $+ H_2{}^{14}C\!\!=\!\!\!\diagup\!\!\!\diagdown\!\!Br$ $\xrightarrow[\text{(ii) heat}]{\text{(i) K}_2\text{CO}_3}$ Z. Here Z is

(a) [structure: phenol with $-CH_2CH\!=\!{}^{14}CH_2$ chain, ortho]

(b) [structure: phenol with $-CH_2CH\!=\!{}^{14}CH_2$ chain, ortho]

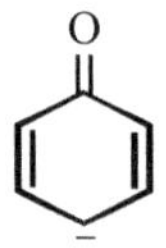

(c) [structure: phenol with $-CH\!=\!CH\,{}^{14}CH_3$ chain, ortho]

(d) [structure: $-OCH_2CH\!=\!{}^{14}CH_2$ ether]

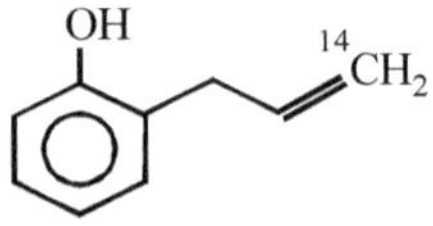

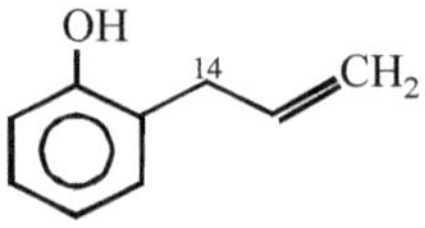

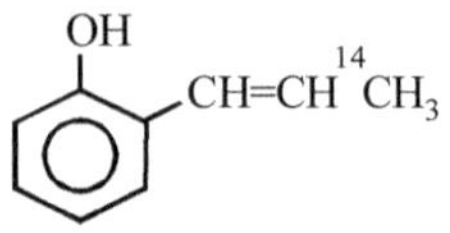

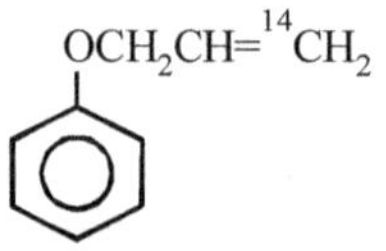

45.

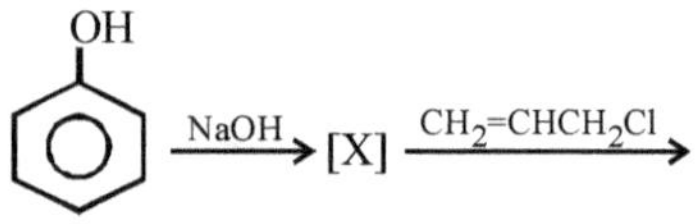

[structure: phenol] $\xrightarrow{\text{NaOH}}$ [X] $\xrightarrow{\text{CH}_2=\text{CHCH}_2\text{Cl}}$ [Y]. Here [Y] is a

  (a) single compound
  (b) mixture of two compounds
  (c) mixture of three compounds
  (d) no reaction is possible

46. Phenol undergoes electrophilic substitution more easily than benzene because
  (a) $-OH$ group exhibits $+M$ effect and hence increases the electron density on the o- and p-positions.
  (b) oxocation is more stable than the carbocation
  (c) both (a) and (b)
  (d) $-OH$ group exhibits acidic character

47. Identify the prodcut [B] in the following reaction

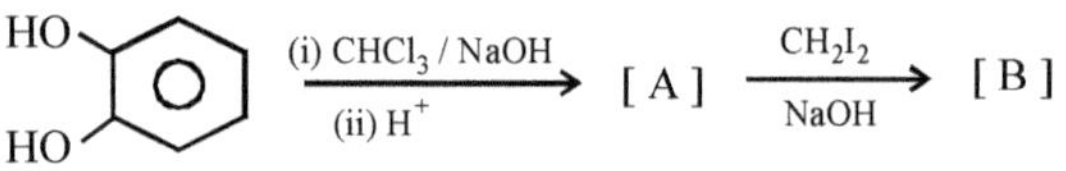

[structure: catechol (1,2-dihydroxybenzene)] $\xrightarrow[\text{(ii) H}^+]{\text{(i) CHCl}_3 \text{ / NaOH}}$ [A] $\xrightarrow[\text{NaOH}]{\text{CH}_2\text{I}_2}$ [B]

(a) [structure: dihydroxybenzene with $CH(OH)CHI_2$ group]

(b) [structure: dihydroxybenzene with $CHOHCHO$ group]

(c) [structure: dimethoxybenzene with CHO group]

(d) [structure: methylenedioxybenzene with CHO group]

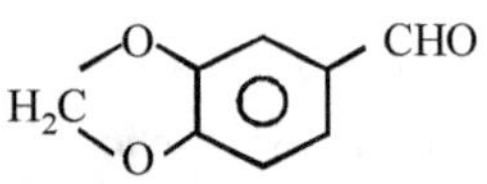

48.

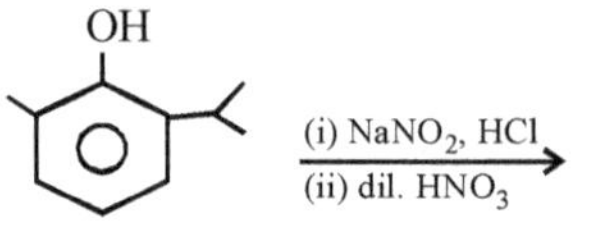

[structure: 2,6-dimethylphenol] $\xrightarrow[\text{(ii) dil. HNO}_3]{\text{(i) NaNO}_2, \text{ HCl}}$ Z. Here Z is

(a) [structure: 2,6-dimethylphenol with NO at para]

(b) [structure: 2,6-dimethylphenol with ON substituent]

(c) [structure: 2,6-dimethylphenol with NO_2 at para]

(d) [structure: 2,6-dimethylphenol with NO_2 at para]

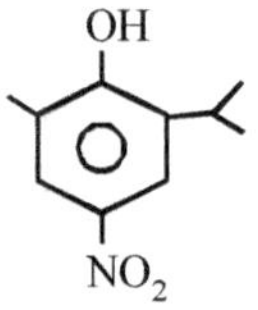

49. 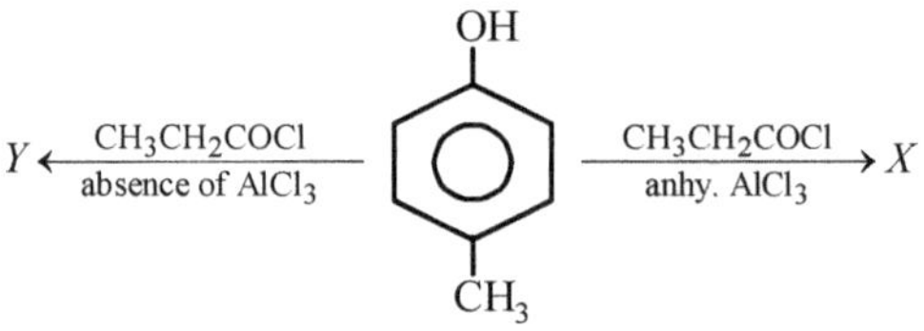 $Y \xleftarrow[\text{absence of AlCl}_3]{\text{CH}_3\text{CH}_2\text{COCl}}$ [structure: p-cresol] $\xrightarrow[\text{anhy. AlCl}_3]{\text{CH}_3\text{CH}_2\text{COCl}}$ X

X and Y respectively are

           X Y

(a) [structure: p-cresol with $-COCH_2CH_3$ ortho]   [structure: p-cresol with $-COCH_2CH_3$ ortho]

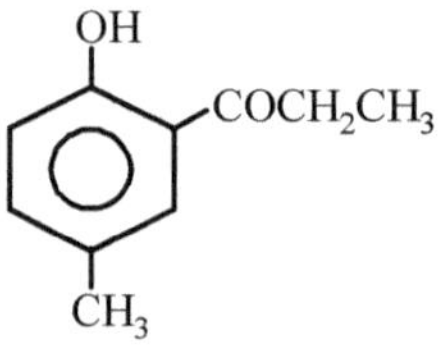

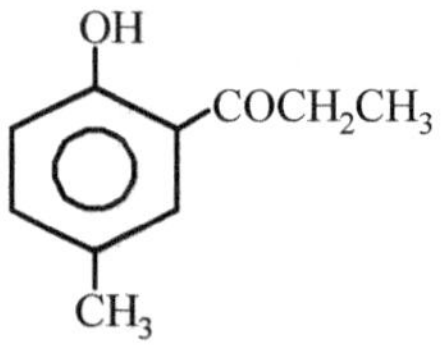

(b) [structure: p-cresol with $-COCH_2CH_3$ ortho]   [structure: p-cresol ester $OCOCH_2CH_3$]

(c) [structure: p-cresol with $-COCH_2CH_3$ ortho]   [structure: p-cresol with $-COCH_2CH_3$ meta]

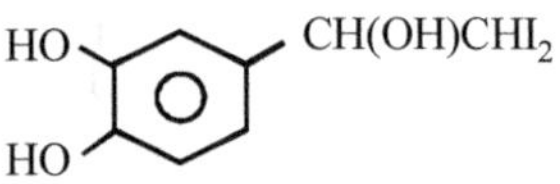

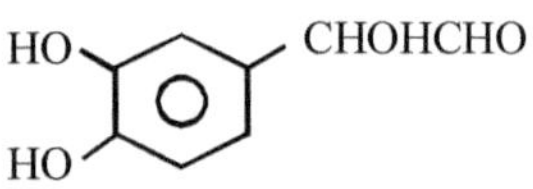

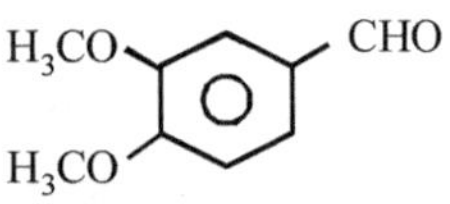

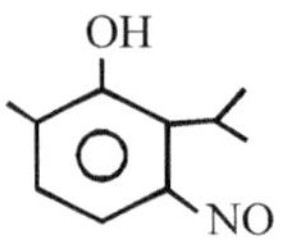

(d) [structure: p-cresol with $-COCH_2CH_3$ ortho]   No reaction

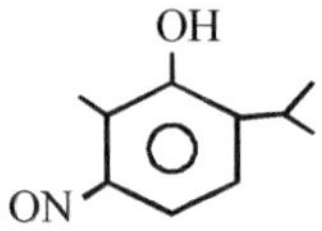

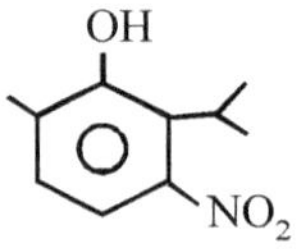

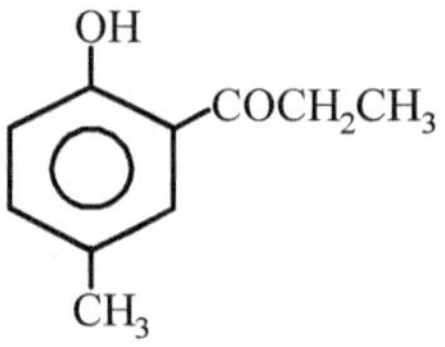

50. In the reaction [structure: anisole, $-OCH_3$] $\xrightarrow{\text{HBr}}$ the products are

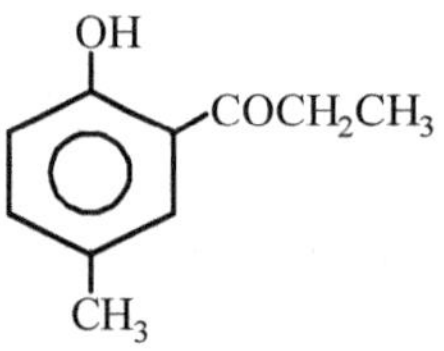

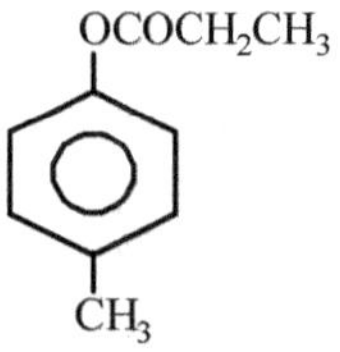

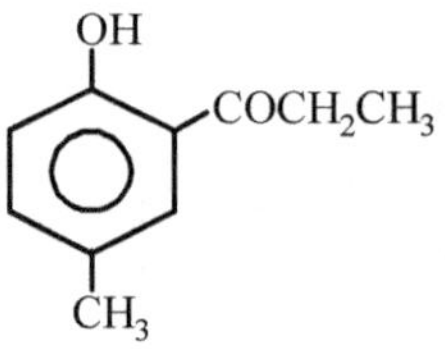

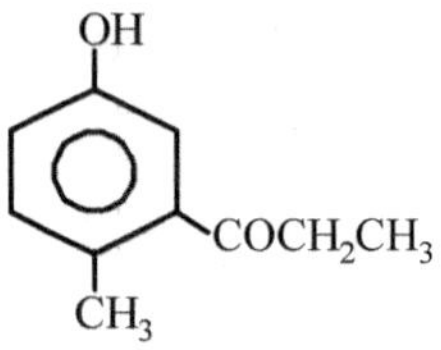

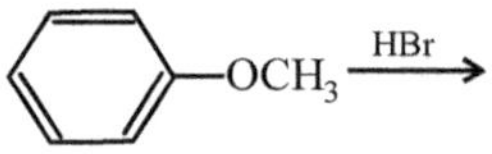

  (a) 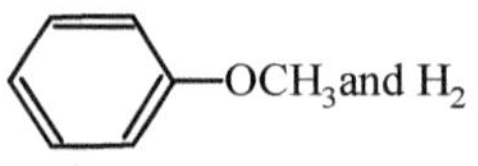 [structure: benzene ring] $-OCH_3$ and H_2

  (b) 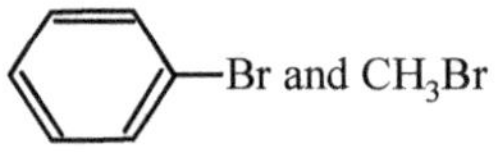 [structure: benzene ring] $-Br$ and CH_3Br

  (c) 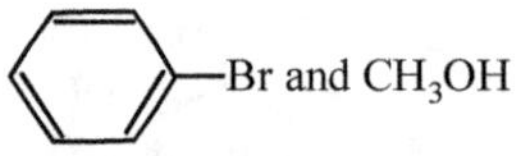 [structure: benzene ring] $-Br$ and CH_3OH

  (d) 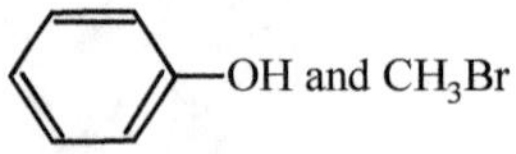 [structure: benzene ring] $-OH$ and CH_3Br

EXERCISE 13.2 (MCQ 1 or >1 option correct, Passage based, Matching, A/R)

DIRECTIONS for Q. 1 to Q. 14 : Multiple choice questions with one or more than one correct option(s).

1. Which of the following is correct name for OH⟨⟩OH

(a) Hydroquinone
(b) *p*-Benzenediol
(c) Quinol
(d) Resorcinol

2. Which of the following can't form intramolecular hydrogen bonding?

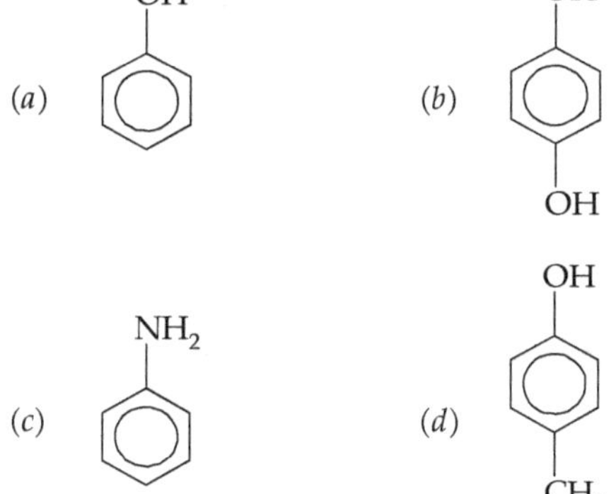

3. Which of the following combination can't be used for preparing an ether ?
(a) $C_6H_5OH + (CH_3)_2 SO_4$
(b) $C_6H_5Br + CH_3CH_2OH$
(c) $p\text{-}NO_2C_6H_4Br + CH_3CH_2OH$
(d) $C_6H_5OH + (CH_3)_3CBr$

4. Which of the following gives *p*-benzoquinone on oxidation ?

(a) [structure: phenol]
(b) [structure: hydroquinone]
(c) [structure: aniline]
(d) [structure: 4-methylphenol]

5. Phenol is less acidic than :
(a) acetic acid
(b) p-methoxyphenol
(c) p-nitrophenol
(d) ethanol

6. Which is/are less acidic than phenol?
(a) CH_3OH
(b) [structure: 2-methylphenol]
(c) [structure: 3-nitrophenol]
(d) H_2O

7. Resonating forms of phenoxide ion is/are :
(a) [structure]
(b) [structure]
(c) [structure]
(d) [structure]

8. When phenol is reacted with $CHCl_3$ and NaOH followed by acidification, salicyaldehyde is obtained. Which of the following species are involved in the above mentioned reaction as intermediates?

(a) [structure]
(b) [structure]
(c) $CHCl_3$
(d) [structure]

9. Which are the sources of phenol?
(a) Middle oil of coal-tar distillation
(b) Cumene
(c) Hydrolysis of benzene diazonium salts
(d) Reaction of diazonium salt with H_3PO_2

10. These reagents find application in photography :
(a) Hypo
(b) Quinol
(c) Hydrazine
(d) $AgNO_3$

11. Select the incorrect statement(s) from the following :
(a) Rate of sulphonation of C_6H_6 & C_6D_6 will be equal
(b) On treatment of [structure] with Br_2 / water (in excess) it results in a dibromo product.
(c) When HCOOEt is treated with MeMgBr in excess followed by hydrolysis it will results in the formation of tertiary alcohol.
(d) $MeCH_2 - \underset{\text{Optically pure}}{\overset{Me \quad Cl}{CH - CH}} - Me \xrightarrow[S_N 2]{aq. \, KOH}$ Product. Product is enantiomer of the reactant

12. In the Dow's process for the manufacture of phenol, chlorobenzene is fused with NaOH at high temperature under pressure.

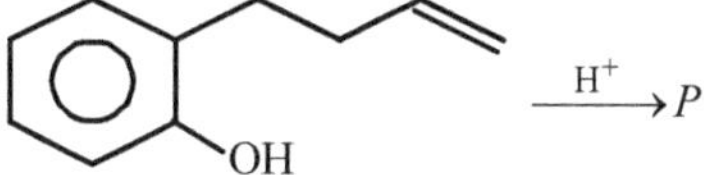

Which of the following statements is/are correct for the above set of transformations ?
(a) Phenol is formed via an intermediate that is aromatic
(b) Diphenyl ether is also formed as by-product
(c) *p*-Phenylphenol is also formed as by-product
(d) Biphenylene is also formed as by-product

13. Pick up the correct statements in the following reaction

[structure] $\xrightarrow{H^+} P$

(a) protonation occurs at −OH
(b) protonation occurs at C = C linkage
(c) *P* is [structure]
(d) *P* is [structure]

14. 2, 4, 6 -Tribromophenol can be prepared by the bromination of
   (*a*)   phenol
   (*b*)   salicylic acid
   (*c*)   *p*-hydroxybenzenesulphonic acid
   (*d*)   *p*-bromophenol

INSTRUCTION for Q. 15 to 31 : Read the passages given below and answer the questions that follow.

<u>PASSAGE 1</u>

Treatment of sodium peroxide with carbon dioxide at 125°C under pressure yields sodium salt of o-hydroxy benzoic acid, commonly known as salicylate ion. This reaction, known as Kolbe-Schmidt reaction, proceeds as below.

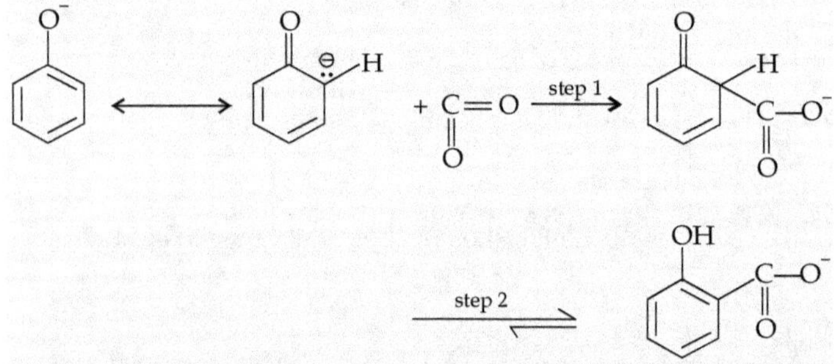

15. Which of the following statement is true ?
   (a)   Carbon dioxide is a strong nucleophile so requires a strong electrophile, the phenoxide ion.
   (b)   Carbon dioxide is a strong electrophile so requires strong nucleophile, the $C_6H_5O^-$
   (c)   Carbon dioxide is a weak electrophile, hence it requires a strong nucleophile like $C_6H_5O^-$
   (d)   Sodium phenoxide can be replaced by parent phenol.

16. Step 2 of the reaction involves
   (a)   addition of H^+ (b)   tautomerization
   (c)   resonance   (d)   None of these

17. Which of the following is correct explanation for the formation of *o*-hydroxybenzoate rather than the *p*-isomer.
   (a)   *o*-Hydroxybenzoate anion is a weaker base than phenoxide ion.
   (b)   *o*-Hydroxybenzoate anion is a weaker base than the *p*-hydroxybenzoate anion.
   (c)   Both of the two
   (d)   None of the two

<u>PASSAGE 2</u>

Two isomeric compounds A and B with the molecular formula $C_{10}H_{12}O$ are insoluble in aqueous NaOH and decolorize Br_2 in CCl_4. Each is vigorously oxidized to p-methoxybenzoic acid (p-anisic acid), and give the same products, on ozonolysis.

18. The degree of unsaturation and their nature in compound B are
   (a)   5-benzene, two C = C double bonds
   (b)   5-benzene, an aldehydic group
   (c)   4-benzene, a carboxylic group
   (d)   5-benzene, one carbon-carbon double bond

19. The isomers A and B show .... isomerism.
   (a)   Optical   (b)   Geometrical
   (c)   Conformational   (d)   Two of the three

20. The ozonolysis product of A undergoes haloform reaction, which is due to the formation of
   (a) CH_3COCH_3 (b) CH_3CHO
   (c) CH_3CH_2OH (d) $C_6H_5COCH_3$

<u>PASSAGE 3</u>

Riemer-Tiemann reaction introduces an aldehyde group, on to the aromatic ring of phenol, ortho to the hydroyl group. This reaction involves electrophilic aromatic substitution. This is a general method for the synthesis of substituted salicylaldehyde as depicted below.

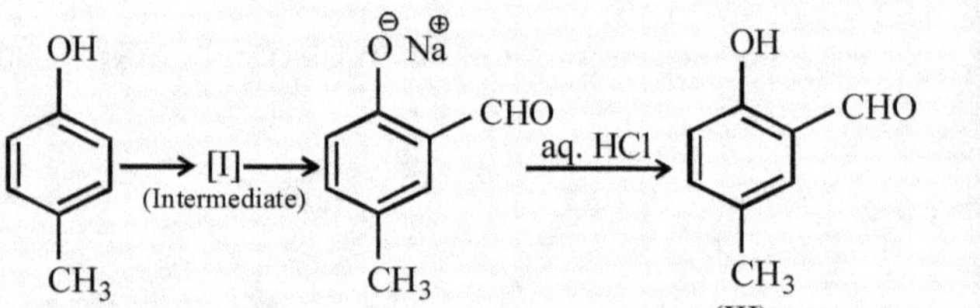

21. Which one of the following reagents is used in the above reaction?
   (a)   aq.NaOH + CH_3Cl (b)   aq.NaOH + CH_2Cl_2
   (c)   aq.NaOH + $CHCl_3$ (d)   aq.NaOH + CCl_4

22. The electrophile in the reaction is
   (a) $:CHCl$ (b) $^+CHCl_2$
   (c) $:CCl_2$ (d) CCl_3

23. The structure of the intermediate I is

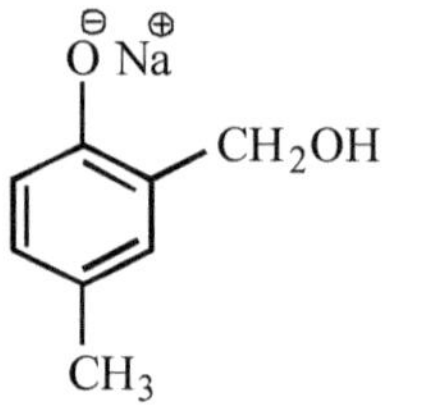

<u>PASSAGE 4</u>

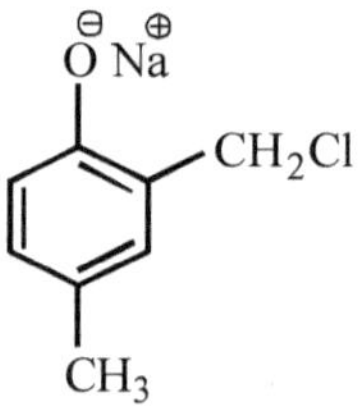

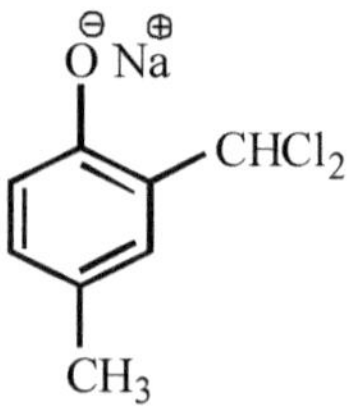

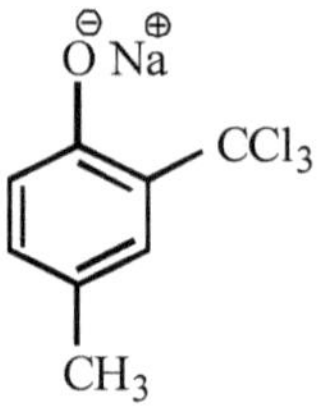

Although chlorobenene is inert to nucleophilic substitution, it gives quantitative yield of phenol when heated with aq. NaOH at high temperature and under high pressure. Phenol, so formed, is a weaker acid than the carboxylic acid; hence it dissolves only in strong bases like NaOH, but not weak like $NaHCO_3$. It reacts with acid chlorides and acid anhydrides in the absence of $AlCl_3$ to form esters. As far as electrophilic substitution in phenol is concerned, the –OH is an activating group, hence its presence enhances the electrophilic substitution in the *o*- and *p*-positions.

Condensation with formaldehyde is one of the important property of phenol. The condensation may take place in presence of acids or alkalis and leads to the formation of bakelite, an important industrial polymer.

24. Conversion of chlorobenzene into phenol involves
   (*a*)   modified S_N^1 mechanism
   (*b*)   modified S_N^2 mechanism
   (*c*)   both (*a*) and (*b*)
   (*d*)   elimination - addition mechanism

- The *o*-acylation of phenols with acid anhydrides can be catalyzed by
  - (*a*) sulphuric acid
  - (*b*) NaOH
  - (*c*) both
  - (*d*) none

- Phenol undergoes electrophilic substitution more readily than benzene because
  - (*a*) the intermediate carbocation is a resonance hybrid of more resonanting structures than that from benzene
  - (*b*) the intermediate is more stable as it has positive charge on oxygen, which can be better accommodated than on carbon
  - (*c*) in one of the canonical structures, every atom (except hydrogen) has complete octet
  - (*d*) the –OH group is *o*, *p*–directing which like all other *o*,*p*-directing groups is activating

7. Phenol undergoes electrophilic substitution more readily in presence of alkali than the phenol itself because
  - (*a*) of the formation of a more stable carbocation as an intermediate
  - (*b*) of the formation of a more stable carbanion as an intermediate
  - (*c*) of the formation of a more stable neutral intermediate
  - (*d*) in presence of alkali, a stronger electrophile is produced

8. Condensation of phenol with formaldehyde is an electrophilic substitution, in which
  - (*a*) $CH_2 = O$ as such is the electrophile in both acidic as well as basic medium
  - (*b*) $CH_2 = O$ is the real electrophile in acidic medium while in basic medium $\overset{+}{C}H_2 - O^-$ is the real electrophile
  - (*c*) $CH_2 = \overset{+}{O}H$ and $CH_2 = O$ are the electrophiles in acidic and basic medium respectively.
  - (*d*) $CH_2 = O$ and $\overset{+}{C}H_2 - O^-$ are the electrophiles in acidic and basic medium respectively

PASSAGE 5

Most of phenols are less acidic than carbonic and carboxylic acids and hence do not decompose $NaHCO_3$ evolving CO_2. Presence of electron-withdrawing group in the benzene ring increases acid strength, while electron donating group decreases the acid strength of phenols. The relative acid strength of *o*-, *m*- and *p*-substituted phenols, however, depends upon a combination of inductive and resonance effect of the substituent.

9. Increasing pK_a values of *o*, *m* and *p*-cresols is
  - (*a*) $o < p < m$
  - (*b*) $m < p < o$
  - (*c*) $m < o < p$
  - (*d*) $p < o < m$

10. Which of the following compounds decomposes $NaHCO_3$ solution?
  - (*a*) Phenol
  - (*b*) 2-Nitrophenol
  - (*c*) Methoxyphenol
  - (*d*) 2,4,6-Trinitrophenol

11. Choose the correct acidity order of the following phenols :
  - (*a*) *p*-nitrophenol > *p*-chlorophenol > *p*-cresol > phenol
  - (*b*) *p*-nitrophenol > *p*-cresol > *p*-chlorophenol > phenol
  - (*c*) *p*-nitrophenol > *p*-chlorophenol > phenol > *p*-cresol
  - (*d*) *p*-nitrophenol > phenol > *p*-chlorophenol > *p*-cresol

---

Instructions for Q. 32 & Q. 34 : Following questions are Multiple Matching type Questions :

32.

Column I	Column II
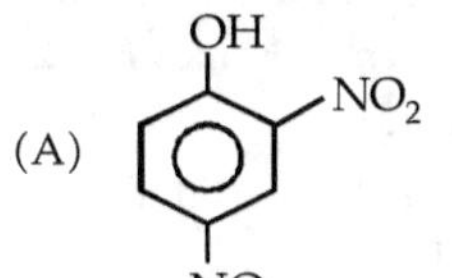 (A), (B), (C), (D)	(a) Oxidation of the ring by HNO_3
	(b) Nitration of the ring possible
	(c) Nitration of the ring not possible
	(d) Reaction with OH^- possible

33.

Column I	Column II
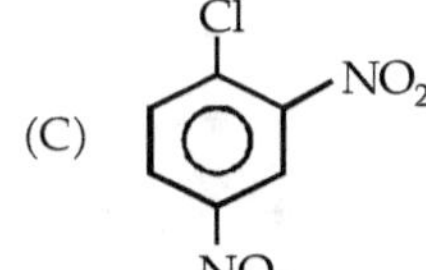 (A), (B), (C), (D)	(a) Coupling with $C_6H_5N_2Cl$ in presence of NaOH
	(b) Oxidation with AgBr
	(c) $KMnO_4$ oxidises $-CH_3$ to $-COOH$
	(d) $KMnO_4$ does not oxidise $-CH_3$ group to $-COOH$

34.

Column I	Column II
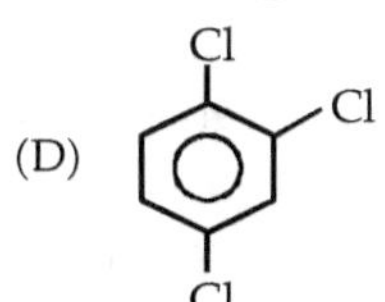 (A), (B), (C), (D)	(a) Reacts with sodium acetylide, $HC \equiv \overset{-}{C} Na^+$
	(b) Reacts with sodium hydroxide, NaOH
	(c) Reacts with sodamide, $NaNH_2$
	(d) Reacts with sodium bicarbonate, $NaHCO_3$

Instructions for Q. 35 to 43 : Following questions are Assertion and Reasoning Type Questions :

Note : Each question contains STATEMENT-1 (Assertion) and STATEMENT-2 (Reason). Each question has 5 choices (a), (b), (c), (d) and (e) out of which ONLY ONE is correct.

(a)   Statement-1 is True, Statement-2 is True; Statement-2 is a correct explanation for Statement-1.

(b)   Statement-1 is True, Statement-2 is True; Statement-2 is NOT a correct explanation for Statement-1.

(c)   Statement -1 is True, Statement-2 is False.

(d)   Statement -1 is False, Statement-2 is True.

(e)   Statement -1 is False, Statement-2 is False.

35.   **Statement 1 :** *p*-nitrophenol boil at high temperature than *o*-nitrophenol

    Statement 2 : In *p*-nitrophenol, the –OH group of one molecule forms hydrogen bonds with the –NO_2 group of the neighbouring p-nitrophenol molecule

36.   **Statement 1 :** *o*-nitrophenol has much lower solubility in water than *m*- or *p*-isomers.

    Statement 2 : In *o*-nitrophenol both the groups, –OH and –NO_2, are involved in intramolecular hydrogen bonding.

37.   **Statement 1 :** ortho-nitrophenol more acidic than orth[o]-methoxyphenol.

    Statement 2 : Nitro group (– NO_2) is an electron-withdrawi[ng] group while methoxy group (– OCH_3) is an electron releasi[ng] group.

38.   **Statement 1 :** The –OH group attached to a carbon of benze[ne] ring activates it towards electrophilic substitution

    Statement 2 : The –OH group is an electron-releasing grou[p]

39.   **Statement 1 :** Resorcinol turns $FeCl_2$ solution purple.

    Statement 2 : Resorcinol have phenolic group.

40.   **Statement 1 :** *p*-Nitrophenol is a weaker acid than *o*-nitrophen[ol]

    Statement 2 : Intramolecular H-bonding is present in orth[o] isomer. Intermolecular H-bonding is present in para isomer.

41.   **Statement 1 :** Phenol on chlorination in presence of $FeCl_3$ an[d] CS_2 gives *o*-chlorophenol as a major product.

    Statement 2 : *o*-Chlorophenol is thermodynamically mo[re] stable than *p*-chlorophenol due to intramolecular hydroge[n] bonding in the former.

42.   **Statement-1 :** Reimer-Tiemann reaction of phenol with CCl_4 [&] NaOH at 340 K gives salicyclic acid as the major product.

    Statement-2 : The reaction occurs through intermedia[te] formation of dichlorocarbene.

43.   **Statement-1 :** Phenol is more reactive than benzene toward[s] electrophilic substitution reaction.

    Statement-2 : In the case of phenol, the intermediate carbocatio[n] is more resonance stabilized.

EXERCISE 13.3 (Subjective Problems)

1.   (*a*)   Distinguish among alcohols, enols and phenols.

    (*b*)   Why phenols are more stable than enols ?

    (*c*)   Draw and name the two structures of phenol.

2.   Give the structural formula and (*i*) IUPAC, (*ii*) common, and (*iii*) CA names of the phenyl isomers of C_7H_8O.

3.   Explain the following :

    (*i*)   The C—O bond length in phenol is shorter than in alcohol.

    (*ii*)   The dipole moments of phenol (1.7 D) and methanol (1.6 D) are in opposite directions.

    (*iii*)   The dipole moment of *p*-nitrophenol (5.0 D) is greater than that of phenol or nitrobenzene (4.0 D).

    (*iv*)   Benzenol (C_6H_5OH) has a higher boiling point than benzenethiol.

    (*v*)   1, 4-Dihydroxybenzene (quinol) has a higher melting point than 1, 2-dihydroxybenzene (catechol).

4.   (*a*)   What do you mean by the term steam distillation ?

    (*b*)   What physical property most influences the ability of a compound to be steam distilled ?

    (*c*)   Why only *o*-nitrophenol is distilled, but *m*- and *p*- not ?

5.   Use chemical equations to compare the reactions of

    (*a*)   RCOOH and C_6H_5OH with aq. $NaHCO_3$.

    (*b*)   RCOOH and C_6H_5OH with aq. Na_2CO_3.

    (*c*)   RCOONa and C_6H_5ONa with CO_2.

    Predict which reaction is possible, and which not.

    Given pK_a for RCOOH, C_6H_5OH, H_2CO_3, and HCO_3^- are 5, 10, 6.4 and 10.3 respectively.

6.   Give the structural formula and name of the principal compound formed (if any) from the reaction of *p*-cresol with

    (*a*)   hot conc. HCl   (*b*) C_6H_5Cl, aq. NaOH

    (*c*) $C_6H_5CH_2Cl$, aq. NaOH

    (*d*) SO_2Cl (*e*) $C_6H_5SO_2Cl$

    (*f*)   phthalic anhydride   (*g*)   2, 4-dinitrochlorobenzene

    (*h*) $NaNO_2$ and dil . H_2SO_4, followed by HNO_3

    (*i*)   Cold dil . HNO_3 (*j*) H_2SO_4 at 15°C

    (*k*) H_2SO_4, 100°C   (*l*)   Bromine water

    (*m*) Br_2, CS_2

    (*n*)   *p*-Nitrobenzenediazonium chloride

    (*o*) CO_2, NaOH, 125°C, 5 atm.

7.   Arrange the compounds of each set in order of acidity.

    (*a*)   Carbonic acid, phenol, sulphuric acid, water

    (*b*)   *m*-Bromophenol, *m*-cresol, *m*-nitrophenol, phenol

    (*c*)   Benzenesulfonic acid, benzoic acid, benzyl alcohol, pheno[l]

    (*d*)   *p*-Chlorophenol, 2,4-dichlorophenol, 2, 4, 6-trichlorophenol

8.   Arrange the compounds of each set in order of reactivity toward[s] bromine.

    (*a*)   Anisole, benzene, chlorobenzene, nitrobenzene, phenol

    (*b*)   Anisole,   *m*-hydroxyanisole,   *o*-methylanisole, *m*-methylanisole.

    (*c*)

$$\underset{\underset{\text{OH}}{|}}{\overset{\overset{\text{OH}}{|}}{\bigcirc}} \ , \ \underset{\underset{\text{OCH}_3}{|}}{\overset{\overset{\text{OH}}{|}}{\bigcirc}} \ , \ \underset{\underset{\text{OCH}_3}{|}}{\overset{\overset{\text{OCH}_3}{|}}{\bigcirc}}$$

9. Outline steps involved in the following conversions :

(a) phenol (OH) to benzene-1,2-diol (OH, OH)

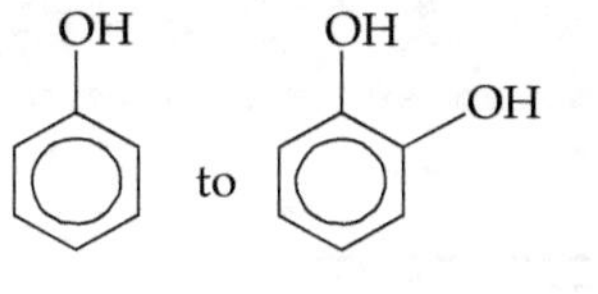

(b) benzene to benzene-1,3-diol (OH ... OH)

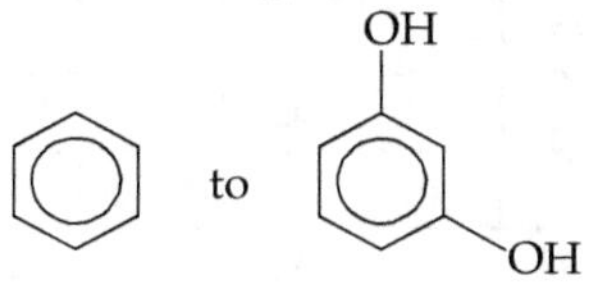

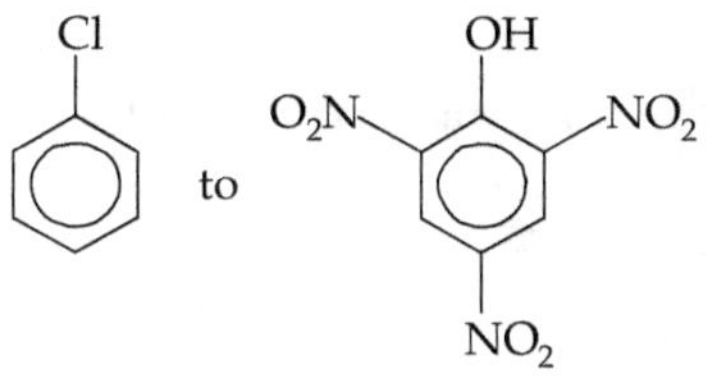

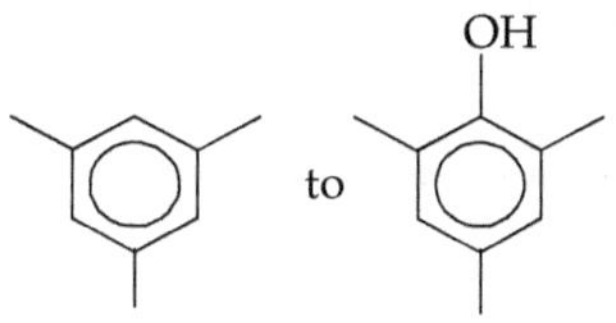

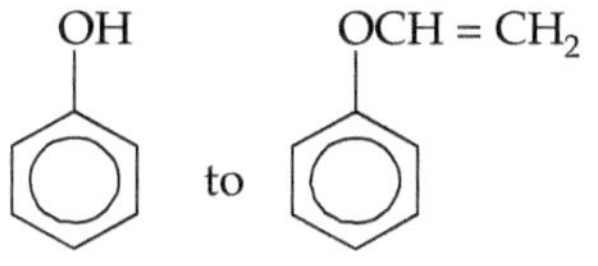

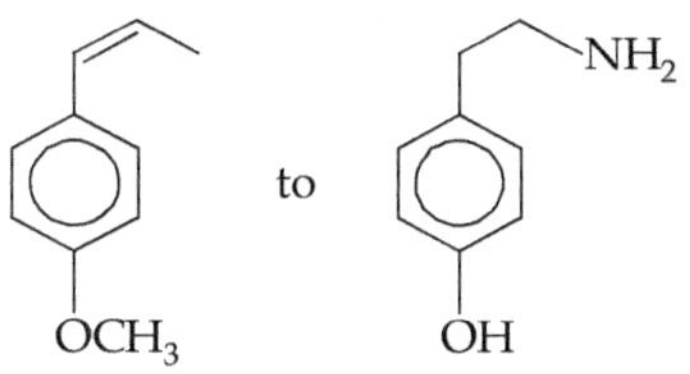

(c) chlorobenzene (Cl) to 2,4,6-trinitrophenol (OH, with O_2N, NO_2, NO_2)

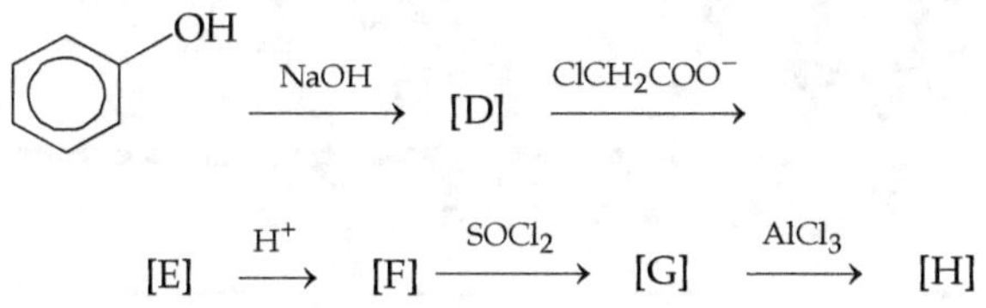

(d) 3,5-dimethylphenol to 2,6-dimethylphenol (OH)

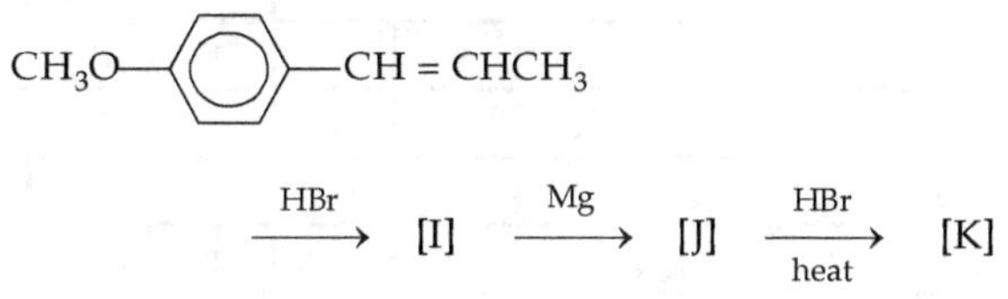

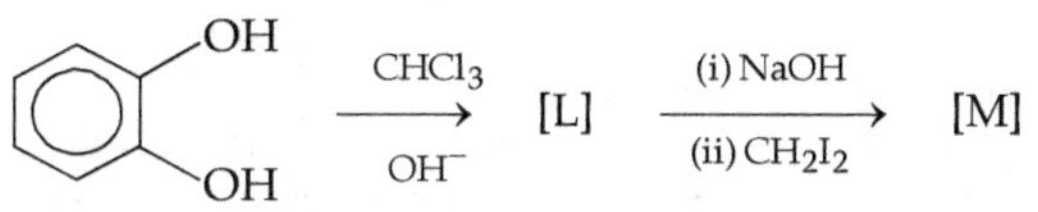

(e) phenol (OH) to phenyl vinyl ether ($OCH = CH_2$)

(f) anethole (1-propenyl-4-methoxybenzene, OCH_3) to 2-(4-hydroxyphenyl)ethylamine (NH_2, OH)

(g) 2-hydroxy-3-methoxybenzaldehyde (CHO, OCH_3, OH) to the aminoalcohol (HO, NH_2, OH, OH)

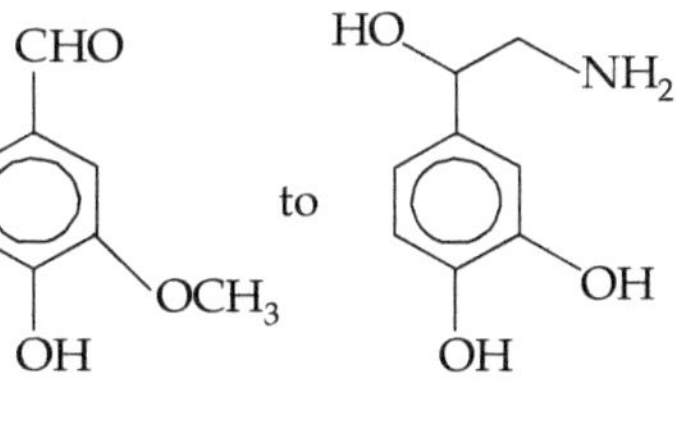

10. Complete the following :

(a)

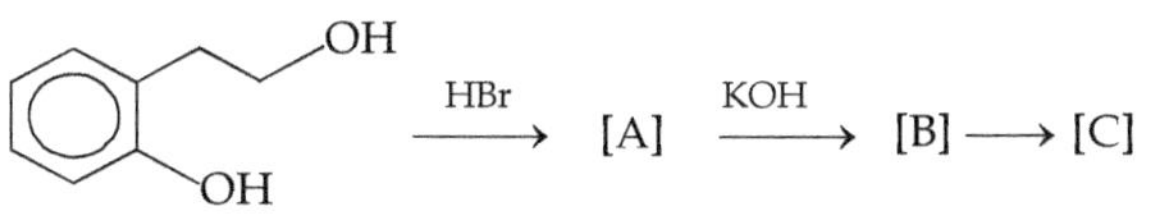

2-(2-hydroxyphenyl)ethanol (OH, OH) $\xrightarrow{\text{HBr}}$ [A] $\xrightarrow{\text{KOH}}$ [B] $\longrightarrow$ [C]

(b)

phenol (OH) $\xrightarrow{\text{NaOH}}$ [D] $\xrightarrow{ClCH_2COO^-}$

[E] $\xrightarrow{H^+}$ [F] $\xrightarrow{SOCl_2}$ [G] $\xrightarrow{AlCl_3}$ [H]

(c)

CH_3O—⟨ ⟩—$CH = CHCH_3$

$\xrightarrow{\text{HBr}}$ [I] $\xrightarrow{\text{Mg}}$ [J] $\xrightarrow[\text{heat}]{\text{HBr}}$ [K]

(d)

benzene-1,2-diol (OH, OH) $\xrightarrow[\text{OH}^-]{CHCl_3}$ [L] $\xrightarrow[\text{(ii) } CH_2I_2]{\text{(i) NaOH}}$ [M]

(e)

4-methylbenzoic acid (CH_3, COOH) $\xrightarrow[SO_3]{H_2SO_4}$ [N] $\xrightarrow[\text{(ii) } H^+]{\text{(i) KOH, fuse}}$ [O] $\xrightarrow[C_2H_5OH]{\text{Na}}$ [P]

$\xrightarrow{\text{HBr}}$ [Q] $\xrightarrow[\text{heat}]{\text{base}}$ [R] $\xrightarrow[H_2SO_4]{C_2H_5OH}$ [S] $\xrightarrow[\text{(ii) } H_3O^+]{\text{(i) } 2\,CH_3\,MgI}$ [T]

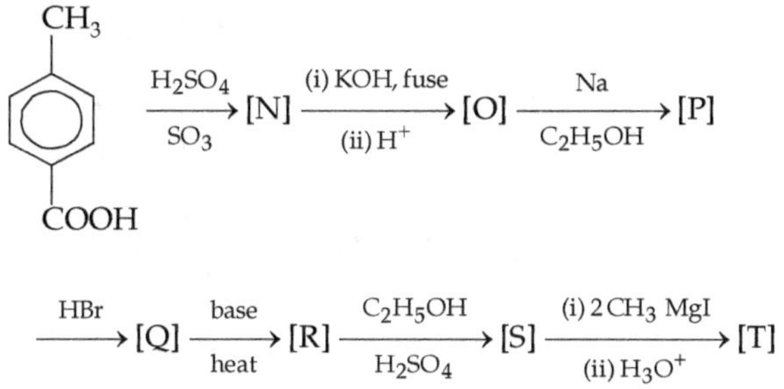

11. Deduce the structure of the compound Z from the following reactions.

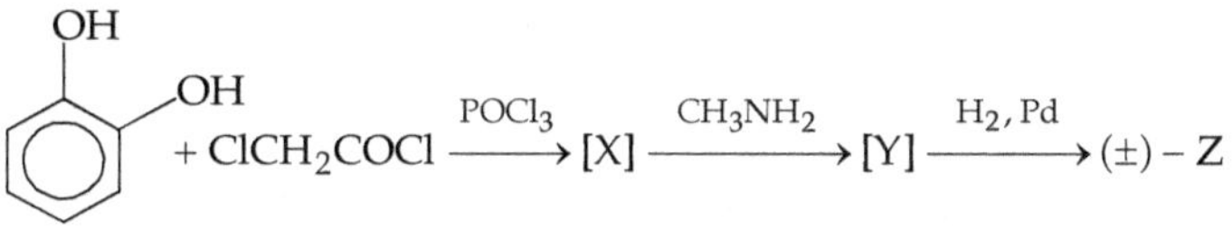

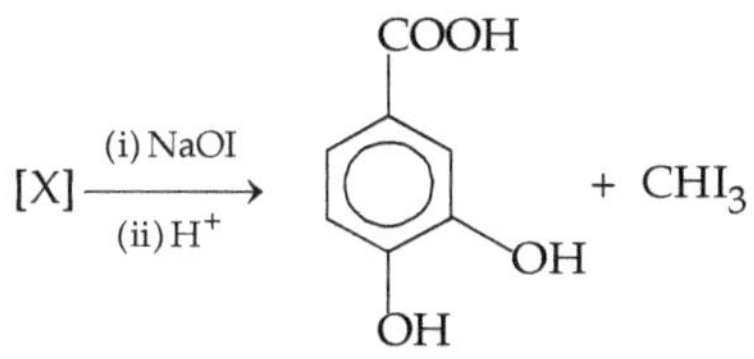

benzene-1,2-diol (OH, OH) $+ ClCH_2COCl \xrightarrow{POCl_3}$ [X] $\xrightarrow{CH_3NH_2}$ [Y] $\xrightarrow{H_2, Pd}$ $(\pm) - Z$

[X] $\xrightarrow[\text{(ii) } H^+]{\text{(i) NaOI}}$ 3,4-dihydroxybenzoic acid (COOH, OH, OH) $+ CHI_3$

12. An organic compound (A) of the formula $C_{10}H_{12}O_3$ is insoluble in water, dil. HCl, and dil. aqueous $NaHCO_3$ but soluble in dil. NaOH. Its solution in dil. NaOH is distilled and distillate is collected in an alkaline solution of iodine, when a yellow precipitate is formed. The alkaline residue in the distillation flask when acidified with dil. H_2SO_4 gives a solid residue (B) of the formula $C_7H_6O_3$. When this acidified mixture is boiled, the compound B is collected as steam distillate. The compound (B) is soluble in aqueous $NaHCO_3$ with the evolution of a gas. Give structures of (A) and (B) and explain the reactions involved.

SOLUTIONS

EXERCISE 13.1

1	(d)	6	(b)	11	(c)	16	(a)	21	(c)	26	(d)	31	(c)	36	(d)	41	(b)	46	(c)
2	(b)	7	(c)	12	(c)	17	(b)	22	(d)	27	(b)	32	(c)	37	(c)	42	(c)	47	(d)
3	(a)	8	(b)	13	(c)	18	(c)	23	(c)	28	(a)	33	(b)	38	(c)	43	(d)	48	(d)
4	(a)	9	(b)	14	(d)	19	(c)	24	(b)	29	(d)	34	(c)	39	(b)	44	(b)	49	(b)
5	(c)	10	(d)	15	(b)	20	(c)	25	(c)	30	(a)	35	(d)	40	(c)	45	(c)	50	(d)

1. All are correct name for the given structure.
2. —OH has priority over —SH.
3. The keto tautomer (anthrone) has two distinct intact aromatic rings in addition to the $C = O$, making it more stable than the enol tautomer (anthranol) which suffers a loss of aromaticity per ring because its three rings are fused.
4. *ortho*-Nitrophenol has low b.p. and low water solubility than the *m*- and *para*-isomers.

5.
$$\text{C}_6\text{H}_6 + CH_3CH = CH_2 \xrightarrow{AlCl_3} \text{CH(CH}_3)_2\text{-C}_6\text{H}_5 \quad \text{(Cumene)}$$

6. In resorcinol, the two —OH groups in the *meta*-positions reinforce each other in electrophilic substitution.

$$\text{resorcinol} + n\text{-C}_6\text{H}_{13}\text{Br} \xrightarrow{AlCl_3} \text{4-}n\text{-hexylresorcinol}$$

7. The corresponding phenoxide ion will be less basic, hence equilibrium will not lie favourably toward carboxylation.

$$\text{(4-nitrophenoxide)} + CO_2 \rightleftharpoons \text{(5-nitrosalicylic acid)}$$

Less basic due to —NO_2 group

8.
$$\text{Phenol} \xrightarrow[\text{7–8°C}]{NaNO_2,\ H_2SO_4} \text{p-Nitrosophenol} \xrightarrow{HNO_3} \text{p-Nitrophenol}$$

(Phenol → *p*-Nitrosophenol (NO) → *p*-Nitrophenol (NO_2))

Thus here, oxidation of phenol is minimised by forming *p*-nitrosophenol.

9. (a)
$$\text{Phenol} + \text{Conc. } HNO_3 \longrightarrow \text{Oxidised product formed}$$

(*b*) [structure: phenol with SO₃H groups] + Conc. HNO_3 ⟶ [structure: 2,4,6-trinitrophenol]

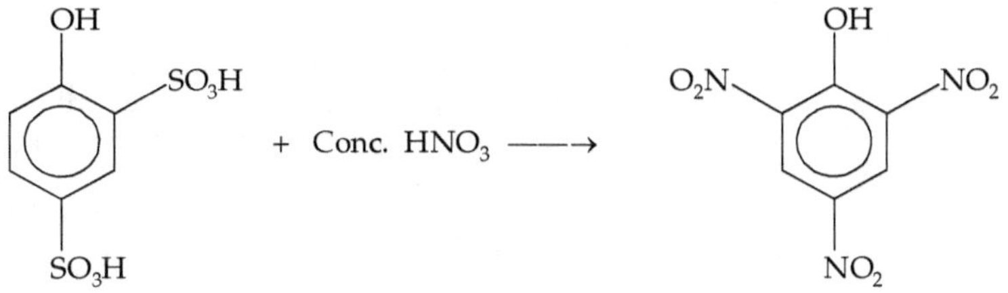

Two electron-withdrawing —SO_3H groups
deactivate phenol toward oxidation
(an example of electrophilic reaction)

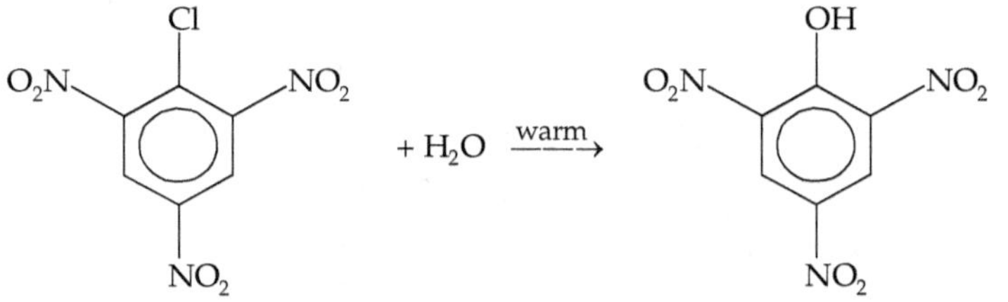

1. [structure: chloro-trinitrobenzene] + H_2O $\xrightarrow{\text{warm}}$ [structure: 2,4,6-trinitrophenol]

2, 4, 6 Trinitrophenol (Picric acid)

Three —NO_2 groups present in *ortho*- and *para*-positions strongly activate —Cl toward nucleophilic substitution.

1. Same as above.
2. In enols, carbon atom bonded to O is sp^2 hybridized, hence its bond length will be less than that in alcohols, where carbon atom bonded to O is sp^3 hybridized.
3. Phenoxide from α-naphthol has more resonating structures than that from β-naphthol and phenol.
4. Recall that dipole moment is an additive property.
5. Bromine water will cause polybromination, because phenol is a highly reactive molecule.
6. —OH group is more electron-releasing due to mesomeric effect than the —CH_3 group, hence electrophilic substitution is governed by —OH. Remember that nitric acid is not used, hence oxidation of phenol does not occur.

7. 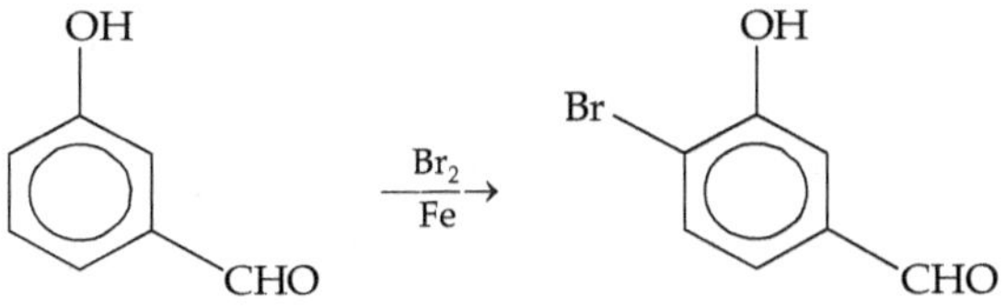 [structure: m-hydroxybenzaldehyde] $\xrightarrow[\text{Fe}]{\text{Br}_2}$ [structure: bromo-hydroxybenzaldehyde]

Position of Br is in accordance with the —OH group ; other two possible positions for Br are not observed due to steric factor.
8. $C_6H_5O^-$ is actually an ambident anion with a negative charge on O and on the *o, p*-ring positions. Hence attack by O^- gives the ether $C_6H_5OCH_2C_6H_5$ while attack by the *ortho* carbanion gives o-benzylphenol.
9. Consult mechanism of Claisen rearrangement.
0. It is an electrophilic addition reaction and involves the formation of carbocation, hence more stable is the cation more easily it will be formed. Recall that benzylic carbocation is very stable. Since phenols are very less reactive toward nucleophilic substitution, —OH will not be replaced by —Br.

1. 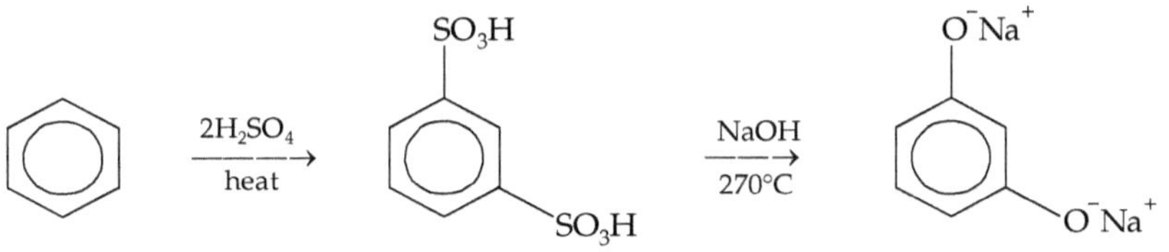 [structure: benzene] $\xrightarrow[\text{heat}]{2H_2SO_4}$ [structure: benzene-1,3-disulfonic acid] $\xrightarrow[\text{270°C}]{\text{NaOH}}$ [structure: disodium phenoxide]

2. 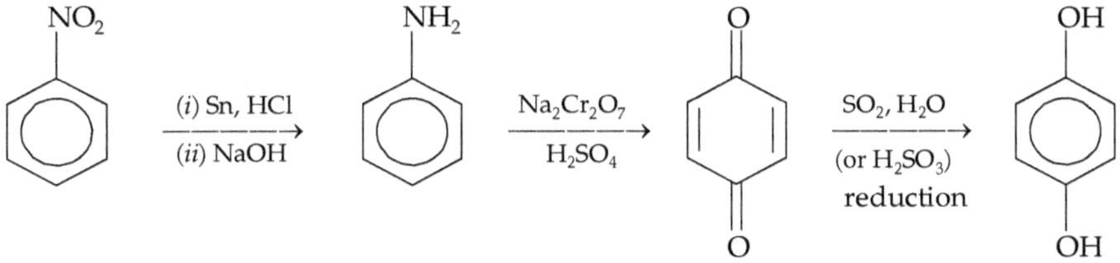 [structure: nitrobenzene] $\xrightarrow[\text{(ii) NaOH}]{\text{(i) Sn, HCl}}$ [structure: aniline] $\xrightarrow[\text{H}_2\text{SO}_4]{\text{Na}_2\text{Cr}_2\text{O}_7}$ [structure: benzoquinone] $\xrightarrow[\substack{\text{(or H}_2\text{SO}_3)\\ \text{reduction}}]{\text{SO}_2,\ \text{H}_2\text{O}}$ [structure: hydroquinone]

4. Charge delocalization in the *p*-nitrophenate ion is much more effective because of direct interaction between O^- and NO_2, which is not possible in the *p*-nitrobenzoate anion.

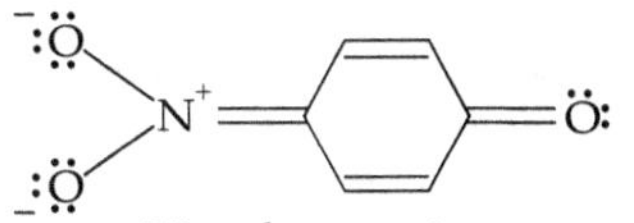

[structure: p-Nitrophenate anion]   [structure: p-Nitrobenzoate anion]

p-Nitrophenate anion   *p*-Nitrobenzoate anion
(direct extended π bonding)   (no direct extended π bonding)

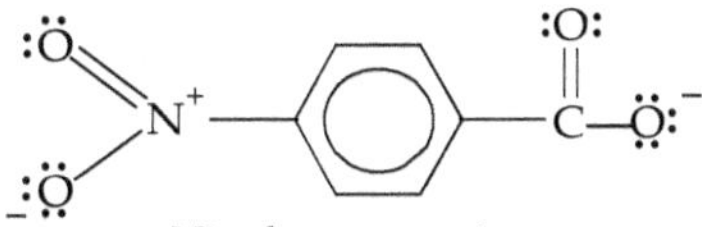

28. (*a*)

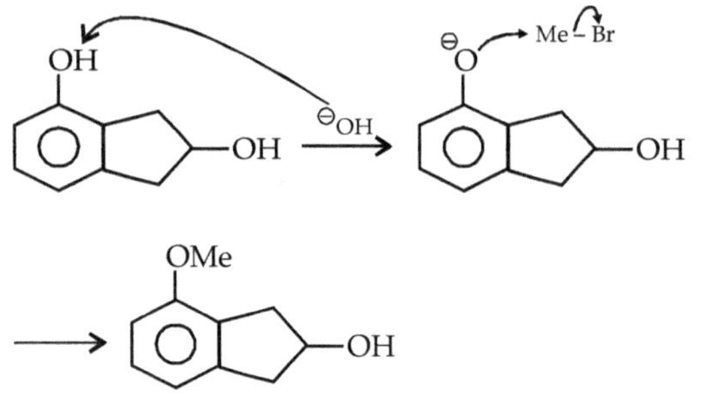

31. (*c*)   Enolic form is benzenoid.

32. (*c*)

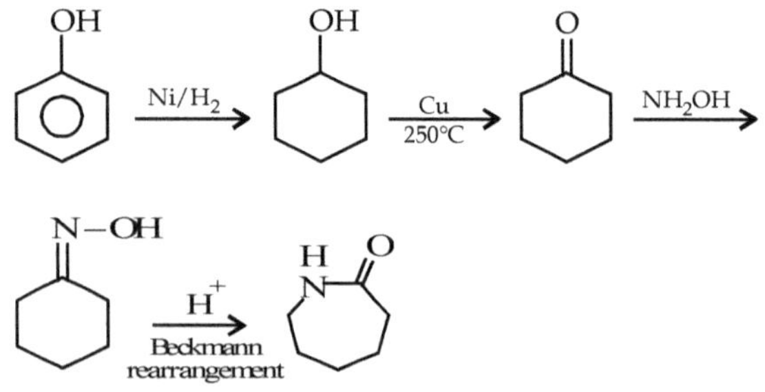

$$\text{(Beckmann rearrangement)} \quad \xrightarrow[\text{rearrangement}]{\overset{+}{H}}$$

33. (*b*)   In (I) steric inhibition is available.

34. (*c*)   *Note* : OH group activates the benzene nucleus.

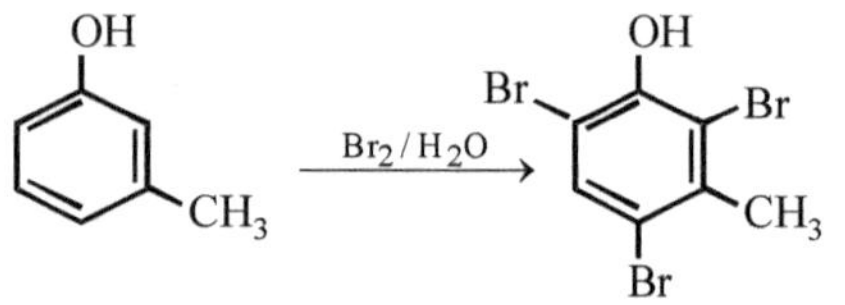

35. (*d*)   *Note* : This is Riemer-Tiemann reaction and the electrophile is dichlorocarbene.

$$H-\overset{Cl}{\underset{Cl}{\overset{|}{C}}}-Cl + NaOH \xrightarrow{\alpha\text{-elimination}} Cl-\overset{..}{C}-Cl + NaCl + H_2O$$
$$\text{dichlorocarbene}$$

36. (*d*)   Riemer-Tiemann reaction involves electrophilic substitution on the highly reactive phenoxide ring.

$$HCCl_3 + OH^- \longrightarrow H_2O + {}^-:CCl_3$$
$$:\overset{-}{C}Cl_3 \longrightarrow Cl^- + \quad :CCl_2$$
$$\text{Note the C has only a}$$
$$\text{sextet of electrons}$$

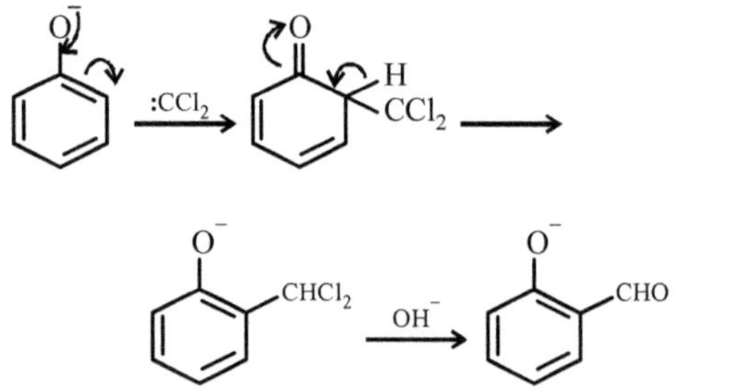

A benzal chloride

37. (*c*)   Recall that $-NO_2$ group increases, while $-CH_3$ decreases acidity of the phenol. Further, in case of $-CH_3$ group acid-weakening effect is due to +I effect, *m*-methyl will exert powerful +I effect than the *p*-methyl. Hence the acidic order will be

$$\underset{\text{II}}{p-\text{nitrophenol}} \; > \; \underset{\text{I}}{\text{phenol}} \; > \; \underset{\text{IV}}{p-\text{cresol}} \; > \; \underset{\text{III}}{m-\text{cresol}}$$

38. (*c*)   We know that phenols show keto-enol tautomerism and the stability of the keto form depends upon the number keto group (more the number of keto groups, higher will stability of the keto tautomer). Thus trihydric phenol should exist in keto form in considerable amount but only when the two keto groups are not on adjacent carbon atoms which decreases stability due to positive charge on adjacent carbon atoms.

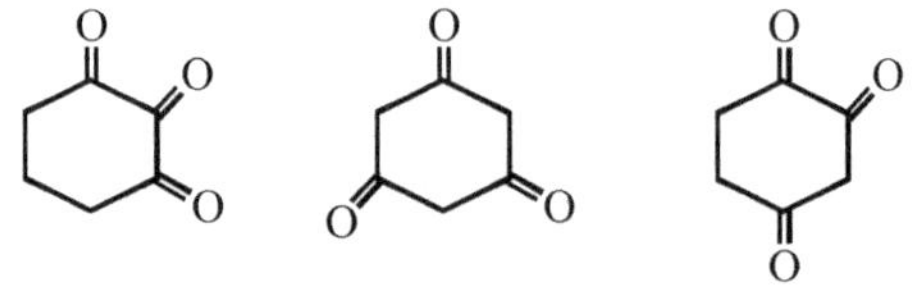

     Unstable   Stable   Unstable

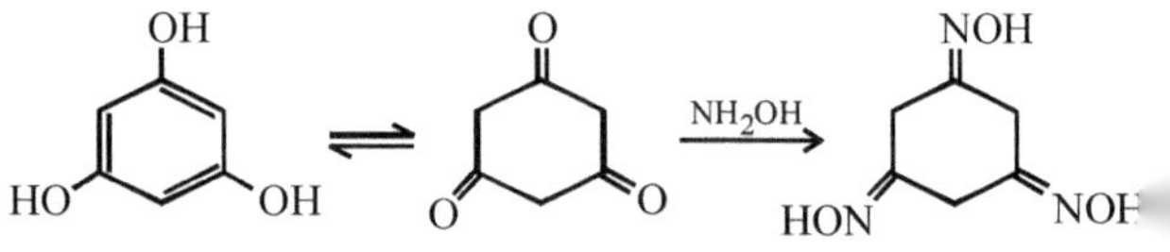

39. (*b*)   It is an example of Reimer-Tiemann reaction

$$CHCl_3 \xrightarrow{OH^-} :\overset{-}{C}Cl_3 \xrightarrow{-Cl^-} \quad :CCl_2$$
$$\text{Dichlorocarbene}$$

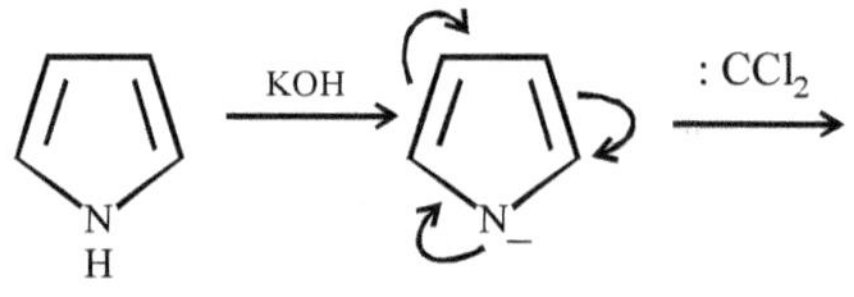

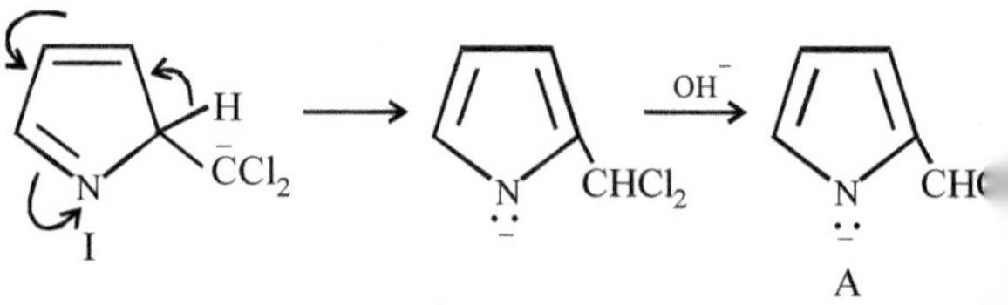

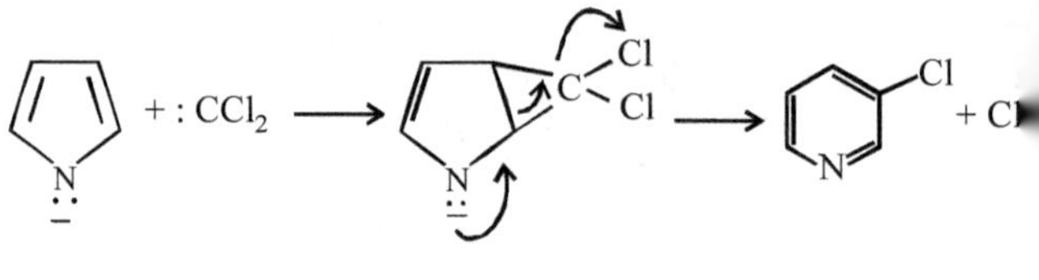

40. (*c*)

$$\text{(C-D is stronger than C} - \text{H)}$$

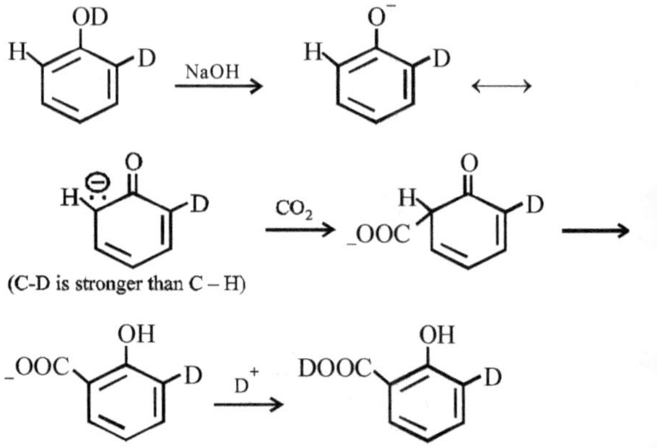

41. (*b*)   The reaction is an example of Claisen rearrangement in which allyl phenyl ethers, on heating, is forming *p*-allylphenol because *o*-positions are not free. Further, in the formation of *p*-product allyl group migrates twice, the labelled C^{14} comes to its original position.

42. (*c*) Condensation of phenol with formaldehyde is an electrophilic substitution reaction. Base converts phenol into phenoxide ion which, being more reactive, reacts easily with $CH_2 = O$ (a weak electrophile).

In presence of acid, $CH_2 = O$ (a weak electrophile) is protonated to $CH_2 = \overset{+}{O}H$ (a strong electrophile) which easily reacts with phenol (a weak nucleophile).

43. (*d*) Dichlorocarbene is a neutral species, not ionic.

44. (*b*)

45. (*c*)

46. (*c*)

+ M effect in phenol activates benzene ring   Oxonium ion (more stable)   Carbonium ion (less stable)

High stability of oxonium ion (oxocation) is because here every atom (except H) has a complete octet of electrons, while in carbocations, carbon bearing positive charge is having six electrons.

47. (*d*)

Reimer-Tiemann reaction

48. (*d*) Nitrosonium ion will go to *p*-position with respect to –OH group. Further dil. HNO_3 oxidises –NO group to –NO_2 group.

50. (*d*)

EXERCISE 13.2

MCQ > 1 CORRECT OPTION	1	(a,b,c)	2	(b,c)	3	(b,d)	4	(a,b,c)
	5	(a, c, d)	6	(a, b, d)	7	(a, b)	8	(a, d)
	9	(a, b, c)	10	(a, b)	11	(a, b, c, d)	12	(a, b, c)
	13	(b, d)	14	(a, b, c, d)				
PASSAGE 1	15	(c)	16	(b)	17	(b)		
PASSAGE 2	18	(d)	19	(b)	20	(b)		
PASSAGE 3	21	(c)	22	(c)	23	(b)		
PASSAGE 4	24	(d)	25	(c)	26	(c)		
	27	(c)	28	(c)				
PASSAGE 5	29	(b)	30	(d)	31	(c)		
Match the Following	32	(A) - b, (B) - a, c, (C) - c, d, (D) - c, d						
	33	(A) - a, d, (B) - a, c, (C) - a, (D) - a, b						
	34	(A) - a, b, c; (B) - a, b, c; (C) - a, b, c, d; (D) - a, b, c, d						
A/R	35	(a)	36	(a)	37	(a)	38	(a)
	39	(c)	40	(d)	41	(a)	42	(c)
	43	(a)						

1. All are correct name for the given structure, resorcinol is 1,3-isomer.

2. Compound II has —CH_3 group in the *ortho* position to —OH, hence it can't form H-bond ; although III has —$C \equiv N$ group which can form H–bond but due to its *sp* hybridized character, its carbon keeps N away from —OH group, hence here —$C \equiv N$ can't form intramolecular H-bond.

3. The combination $C_6H_5Br + CH_3CH_2OH$ has non-reactive C_6H_5Br, while in the combination $C_6H_5OH + Me_3CBr$, Me_3CBr being *tert* will undergo elimination reaction rather substitution. Hence, only combinations I and III can be used for preparing ether.

$$C_6H_5OH + (CH_3)_2SO_4 \xrightarrow{S_N} C_6H_5OCH_3$$

$$p\text{-}NO_2C_6H_4Br + CH_3CH_2OH \xrightarrow{Ar\,S_N} p\text{-}NO_2C_6H_4OCH_2CH_3$$

4. Aniline as well as phenol are highly activated compounds towards electrophilic reactions (oxidation), hence all the three will be easily oxidised to *p*-benzoquinone, but not (d).

11. (*a,b,c,d*)
    (a) Isotopic effect is observed in sulphonation.
    (b) Salicyclic acid gives 2,4,6-tribromophenol (i.e. decarboxy -bromination takes place)
    (c) Product is sec. alcohol.
    (d) Products are diastereomers.

12. (*a,b,c*)   The nucleophilic substitution of chlorobenzene by OH under drastic condition takes place via benzyne itermediate.

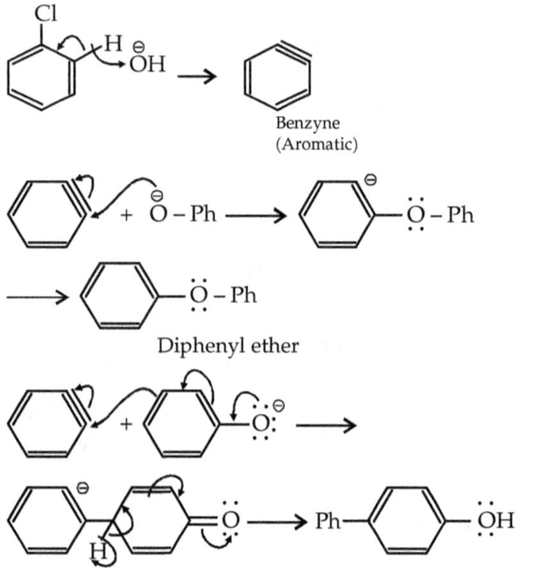

Benzyne
(Aromatic)

Diphenyl ether

p-Phenylphenol

13. (*b,d*) $\xrightarrow{H^+}$

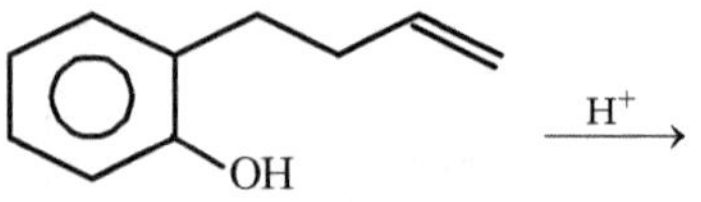

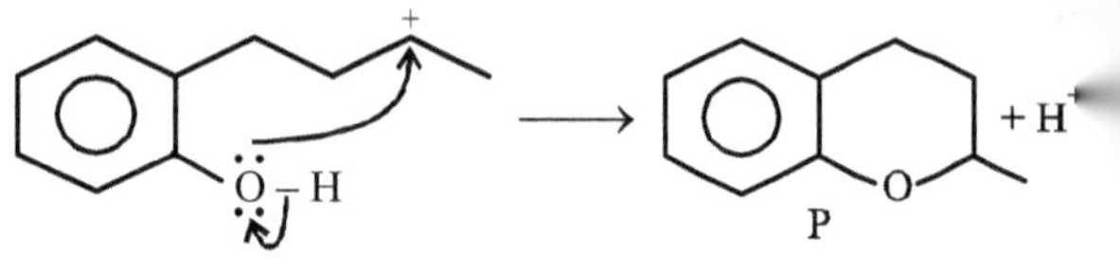

24. $\xrightarrow[\text{(elimination step)}]{\text{heat, pressure}}$ benzyne

$\xrightarrow[\text{(addition step)}]{OH^-}$

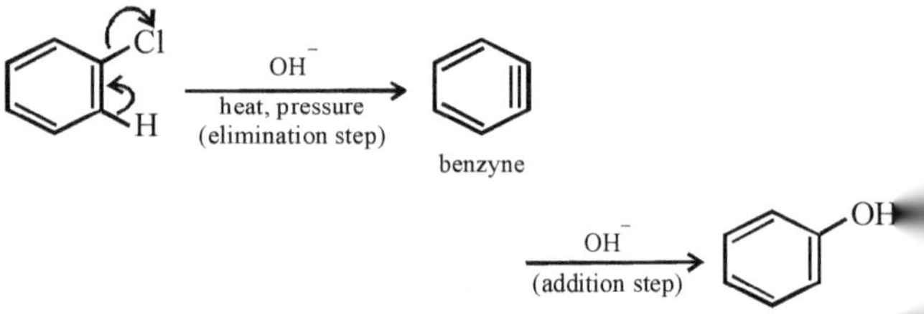

25. Acid (H_2SO_4) converts acid anhydride to the more powerful electrophile, $CH_3\overset{+}{C}=O$ group. On the other hand, base (NaOH) converts phenol to the more powerful nucleophile, phenoxide ion.

26. $\xrightarrow{E^+}$

Oxonium cation
(every atom has octet)

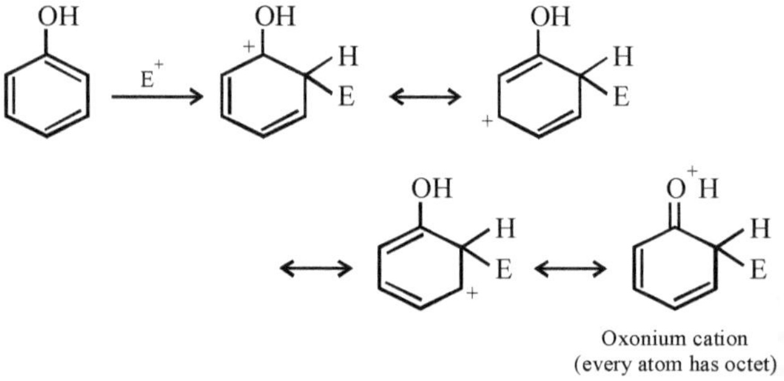

27. $\xrightarrow{E^+}$

Fairly stable neutral
conjugated ketone

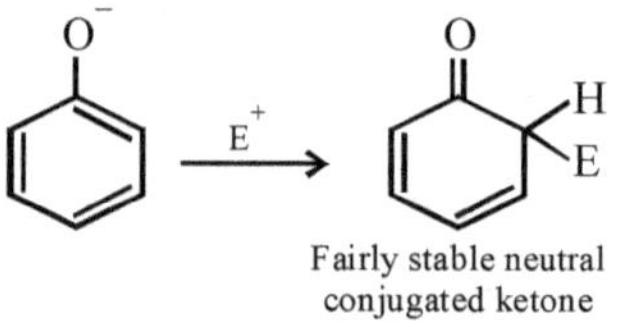

28. In presence of acids, $CH_2=O$ is protonated to form $CH_2=\overset{+}{O}H$ in which carbon is more electron deficient than that in $CH_2=O$. In presence of OH^-, phenol is converted into phenoxide, $C_6H_5O^-$ which being a stronger nucleophile is easily attacked by weaker nucleophile, the unprotonated $CH_2=O$.

34. (A)-a, b, c; (B)-a, b, c; (C)-a, b, c, d; (D)-a, b, c, d

40. Due to intra molecular H-bonding in ortho isomer H^+ ion may not release easily, so ortho isomer is weak acidic than para isomer. Here Statement 1 is wrong and Statement 2 is correct.

42. The correct reason is : Nucleophilic attack of phenolate ion through the *ortho*-carbon atom occurs on CCl_4 (a neutral electrophile) to form an intermediate which on hydrolysis gives salicylic acid (ArSE reaction).

43. Due to +M effect of $-\ddot{O}H$, its intermediate carbocation is more stable than the one in benzene.

EXERCISE 13.3

1. (*a*)   In alcohols, —OH group is attached to an sp^3 hybridized carbon, while enols have —OH group attached to sp^2 hybridized carbon. Further, when the —OH group is attached to a vinyl group, the compound is called enol, while when it is attached to a carbocylic aromatic ring it is called phenol.

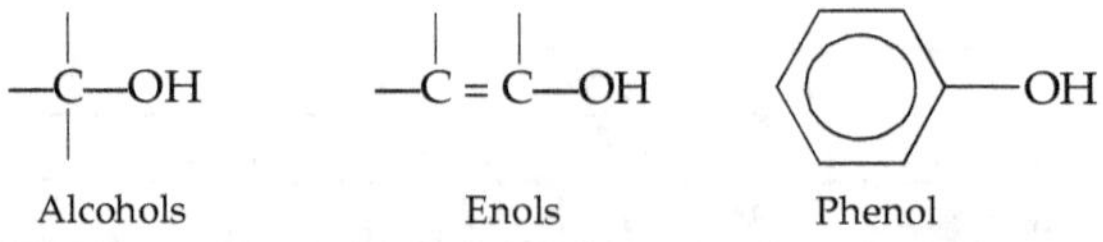

Alcohols   Enols   Phenol

    (*b*)   Both phenols and enols are considered as tautomers of a keto structure. The large resonance energy of C = O usually causes the keto tautomer to be much more stable than the enol.

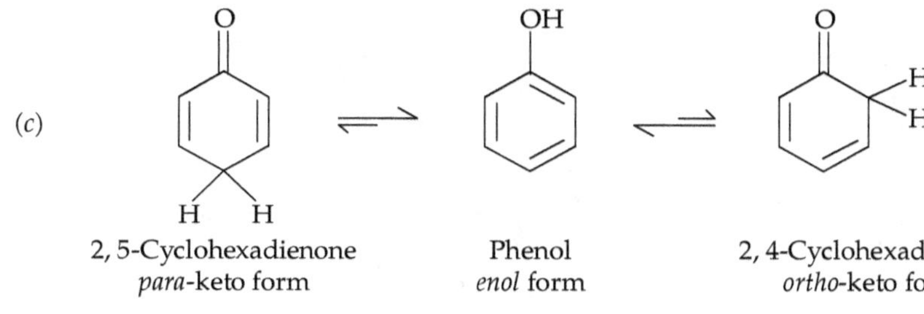

However, the keto form of phenol can be attained only with loss of the stable aromatic ring, hence it is very much stable than enol.

(c)

2, 5-Cyclohexadienone	Phenol	2, 4-Cyclohexadienone
para-keto form	*enol* form	*ortho*-keto form

1UPAC name	o-Methylphenol	m-	p-	Methoxybenzene
Common name	o-Cresol	m-Cresol	p-Cresol	Anisole
CA name	2-Methylbenzeneol	3-	4-	Methoxybenzene

Although the CA name for C_6H_5OH is phenol, substituted phenols are considered as derivatives of *benzeneol*.

(i) Remember that the bond lengths in C—X decreases with the increase in s character of the carbon.

$$\overset{sp^3}{C}\text{—OH} \qquad = \qquad \overset{sp^2}{C}\text{—OH}$$

	Alcohols		Enols (Phenols)
% of s character of C	25		33.3

Thus the C—O bond of ArOH's (having 33.3% s character) will be shorter than the C—O bond of ROH's (having 25% s character).

(ii) The delocalization of electron density from O to the ring causes the O of phenol to be positive end of the molecular dipole. In alcohols, delocalization of electrons is not possible and hence it is electronegativity of O atom that produces negative end of the dipole.

(iii) The electron-donation of —OH reinforces the electron-withdrawal of —NO_2.

(iv) Sulphur forms weak hydrogen bonding than O, hence intermolecular attraction (association) in C_6H_5SH is weaker than in C_6H_5OH.

(v) Molecules of *p*-isomer fit closer in the solid state causing it to have the higher melting point.

(a) When a compound is mixed (*but not soluble*) with boiling water and thus carried by steam, the compound is said to be steam distilled.

(b) The steam-distilled compound must have an appreciable vapour pressure at the boiling point of water.

(c) Attraction to water greatly lowers the vapour pressure, preventing steam distillation. Since the chelated *o*-isomer has a minimal attraction with water, it is steam distilled.

The equilibria of Bronsted acid-base reactions favour the side with the weaker acid and base. In each case, write the ionic equation as if it occurs and place the pK_a values under each acid. If the weaker acid is on the right-side, the reaction occurs but if the weaker acid is on the left-side, the reverse reaction occurs.

(a) $RCOOH + HCO_3^- \longrightarrow RCOO^- + H_2CO_3 (H_2O + CO_2)$
$pK_a = 5$ $pK_a = 6.4$ (weaker acid)

$C_6H_5OH + HCO_3^- \overset{\times}{\longrightarrow} C_6H_5O^- + H_2CO_3 (H_2O + CO_2)$
$pK_a = 10$ $pK_a = 6.4$ (stronger acid)

(b) $RCOOH + CO_3^{2-} \longrightarrow RCOO^- + HCO_3^-$
$pK_a = 5$ $pK_a = 10.3$ (weaker acid)

$C_6H_5OH + CO_3^{2-} \rightleftharpoons C_6H_5O^- + HCO_3^-$
$pK_a = 10$ $pK_a = 10.3$ (weaker acid)

The last reaction occurs, however the result is borderline and any substituted phenol that has $pK_a > 10.5$ may not react.

(c) $RCOO^- + \underset{pK_a = 6.4}{\underbrace{H_2O + CO_2}} \overset{\times}{\longrightarrow} \underset{\text{(stronger acid)}}{\underset{pK_a = 5}{RCOOH}} + HCO_3^-$

$C_6H_5O^- + \underset{pK_a = 6.4}{\underbrace{H_2O + CO_2}} \longrightarrow \underset{\underset{\text{(weaker acid)}}{pK_a = 10}}{C_6H_5OH} + HCO_3^-$

6. (*a*) No reaction

(*b*) No reaction. Aryl halides, unless activated, are inert toward S

(*c*) [structure: *p*-cresol benzyl ether, $OCH_2C_6H_5$ on ring with CH_3 para]

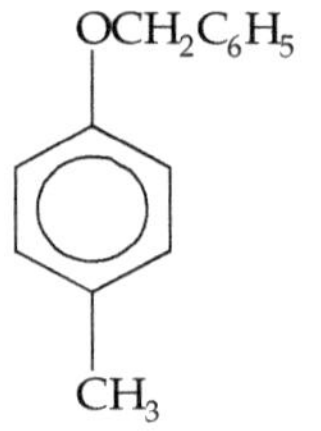

(*d*) No reaction

(*e*) [structure: $OSO_2C_6H_5$ on ring with CH_3 para]

(*f*) [structure: naphthalene-2,3-dicarboxylic, one COO esterified to *p*-tolyl (CH_3), other $COOH$]

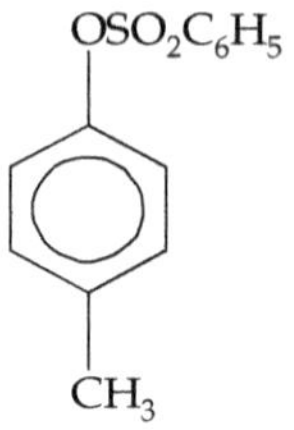

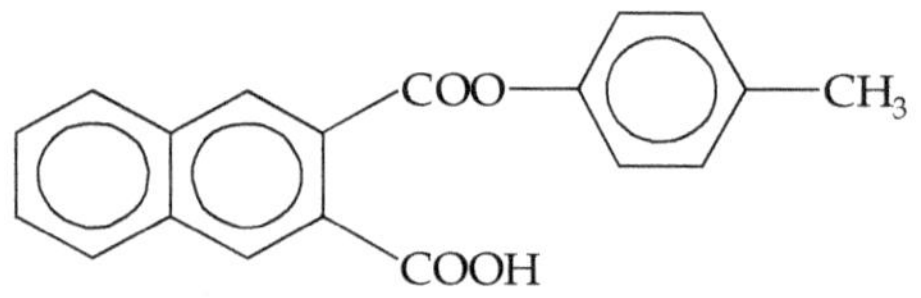

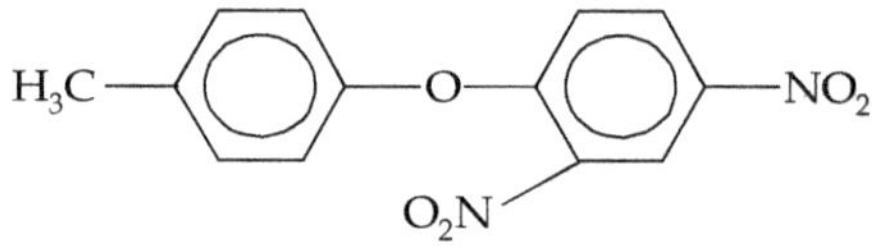

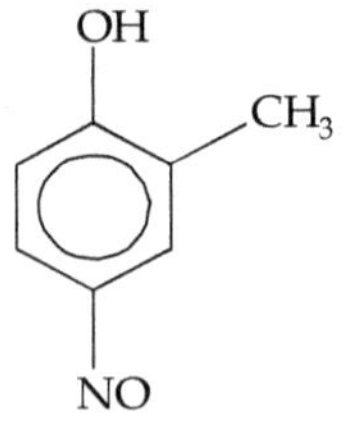

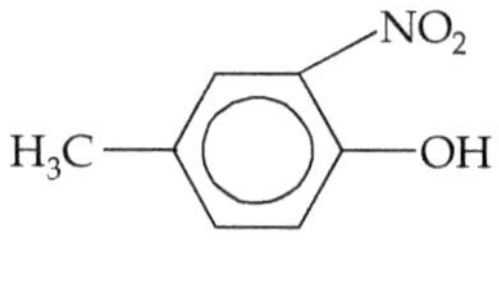

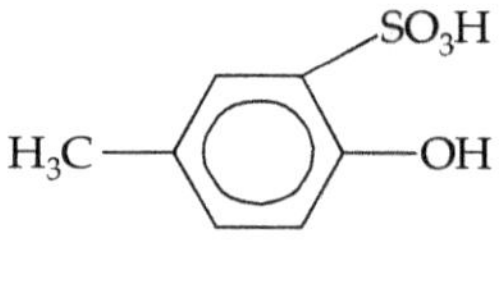

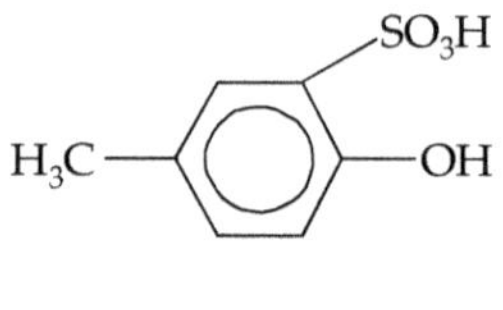

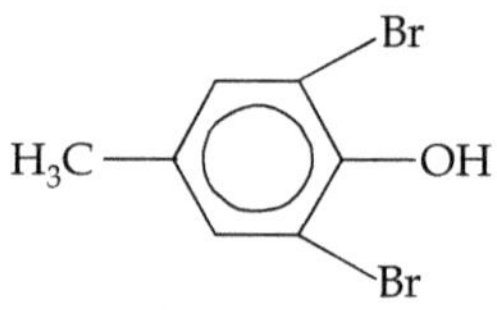

(*g*) H_3C—[ring]—O—[ring with NO_2 and O_2N]

(*h*) [structure: phenol with OH, CH_3 ortho, NO para]

(*i*) H_3C—[ring with NO_2 and OH]

(*j*) H_3C—[ring with SO_3H and OH]

(*k*) H_3C—[ring with SO_3H and OH]

(*l*) H_3C—[ring with Br, OH, Br]

(*m*) H_3C—[ring with Br and OH]

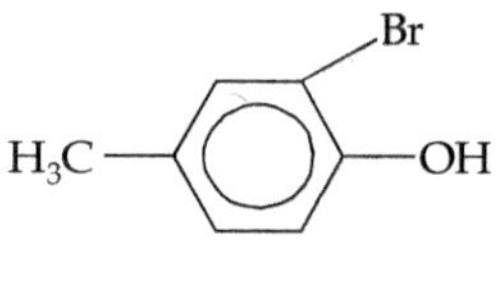

(Note *p*-position is not free)

(*n*) H_3C—[ring with OH, and $N=N$—[ring]—NO_2]

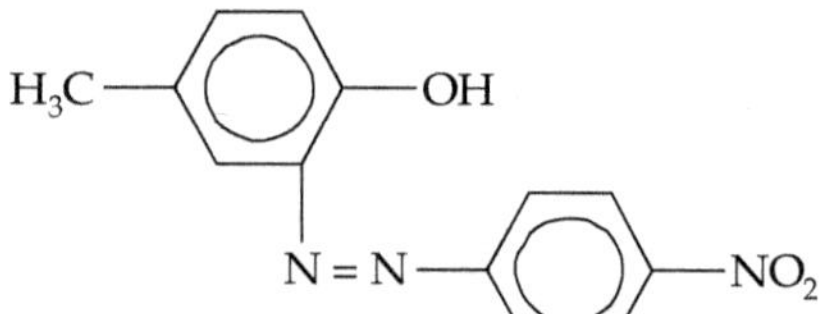

(*o*) H_3C—[ring with OH and COO^-]

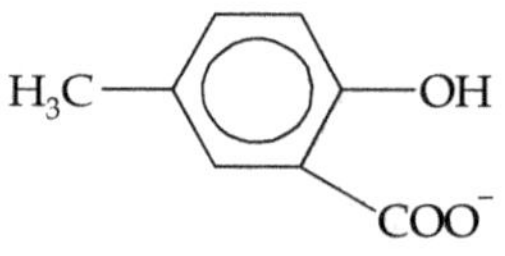

7. (*a*) $H_2SO_4 > H_2CO_3 > C_6H_5OH > H_2O$

(*b*) [phenol with OH, NO_2] $>$ [phenol with OH, Br] $>$ [phenol OH] $>$ [phenol with OH, CH_3]

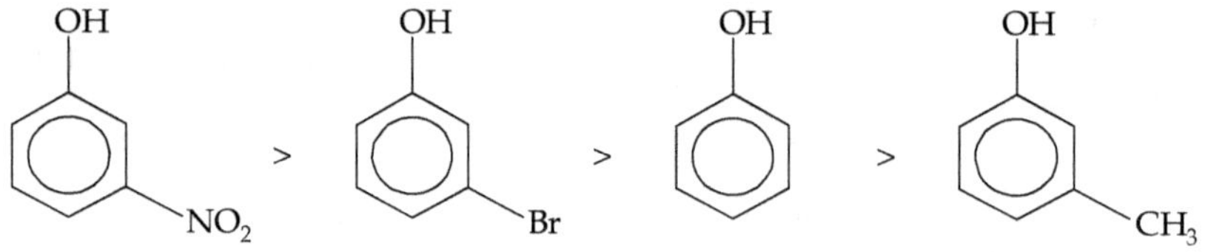

(*c*) $C_6H_5SO_3H > C_6H_5COOH > C_6H_5OH > C_6H_5CH_2OH$

(*d*) 2, 4, 6-Trichlorophenol $>$ 2, 4-Dichlorophenol $>$ *p*-Chlorophenol

8. Relative activating effect of the substituents toward electrophilic substitution :

$$—OH > —OCH_3 > —CH_3 > —H > —Cl > —NO_2$$

(*a*) $C_6H_5OH > C_6H_5OCH_3 > C_6H_6 > C_6H_5Cl > C_6H_5NO_2$

(*b*) [anisole with OCH_3, OH] $>$ [anisole with OCH_3, CH_3] $>$ [anisole with OCH_3, CH_3 ortho] $>$ [anisole OCH_3]

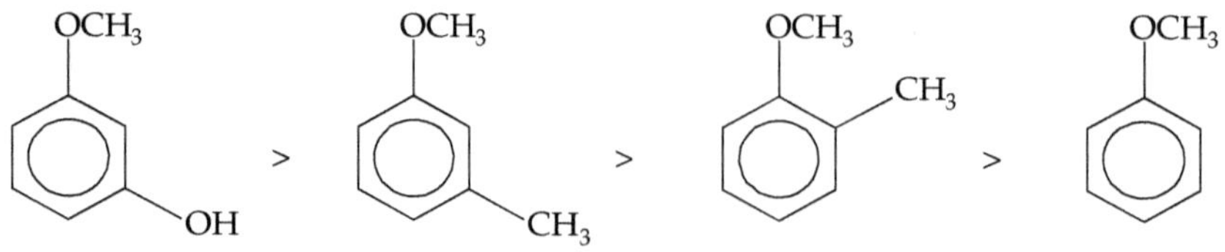

(*c*) [phenol with OH, OH para] $>$ [phenol with OH, OCH_3 para] $>$ [anisole with OCH_3, OCH_3 para]

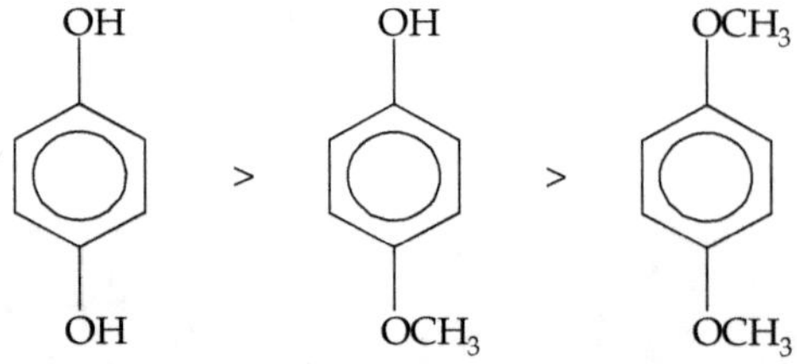

(a) C_6H_5OH $\xrightarrow[\text{low temp.}]{H_2SO_4}$ (o-phenol-SO$_3$H) $\xrightarrow{NaOH}$ (ONa, SO$_3$Na) $\xrightarrow[\text{Strong heating}]{NaOH}$ (ONa, ONa) $\xrightarrow{H^+}$ catechol (OH, OH)

(b) benzene $\xrightarrow[\text{heat}]{2SO_3,\ H_2SO_4}$ (benzene-1,3-di-SO$_3$H) $\xrightarrow[\text{(iii) }H^+]{\text{(i) NaOH};\ \text{(ii) NaOH, Strong heating}}$ resorcinol (OH, OH)

(c) chlorobenzene $\xrightarrow{HNO_3,\ H_2SO_4}$ (Cl, 2,4-dinitro) $\xrightarrow[\text{(ii) }H^+]{\text{(i) NaOH}}$ 2,4-dinitrophenol $\xrightarrow{HNO_3,\ H_2SO_4}$ 2,4,6-trinitrophenol (picric acid)

(d) 3,5-dimethylbenzene $\xrightarrow{HNO_3,\ H_2SO_4}$ (NO$_2$ derivative) $\xrightarrow[\text{(ii) HONO}]{\text{(i) Fe, }H^+}$ (N$_2^+$ diazonium) $\xrightarrow[\text{warm}]{H_2O,\ H^+}$ (OH, 2,4,6-trimethylphenol)

(e) $C_6H_5OH \xrightarrow{\text{NaOH aq.}} C_6H_5ONa \xrightarrow{BrCH_2CH_2Br} C_6H_5OCH_2CH_2Br \xrightarrow[\text{heat}]{KOH} C_6H_5OCH=CH_2$

(f) (p-OCH$_3$ styrene) $\xrightarrow[\text{H}_2SO_4]{K_2Cr_2O_7}$ (CHO, OCH$_3$) $\xrightarrow{CH_3NO_2,\ OH^-}$ (CH=CHNO$_2$, OCH$_3$) $\xrightarrow{H_2/Pt}$ (CH$_2$CH$_2$NH$_2$, OCH$_3$) $\xrightarrow{HI}$ (CH$_2$CH$_2$NH$_2$, OH)

(g) (CHO, OCH$_3$, OH) $\xrightarrow[\text{heat}]{HBr}$ (CHO, OH, OH) $\xrightarrow{CN^-,\ H^+}$ (CH(OH)CN, OH, OH) $\xrightarrow[\text{Ni}]{H_2}$ (CH(OH)CH$_2$NH$_2$, OH, OH)

10. (a) (o-bromoethyl phenol) [A]   [B]   (2,3-dihydrobenzofuran) [C]

(b) [D]   [E]   [F]   [G]   [H]

(c) CH_3O—C$_6$H$_4$—CHBr—CH$_2$CH$_3$ [I]

H_3CO—C$_6$H$_4$—CH(C$_2$H$_5$)—CH(C$_2$H$_5$)—C$_6$H$_4$—OCH_3 [J]

HO—C$_6$H$_4$—CH(C$_2$H$_5$)—CH(C$_2$H$_5$)—C$_6$H$_4$—OH [K]

(d)

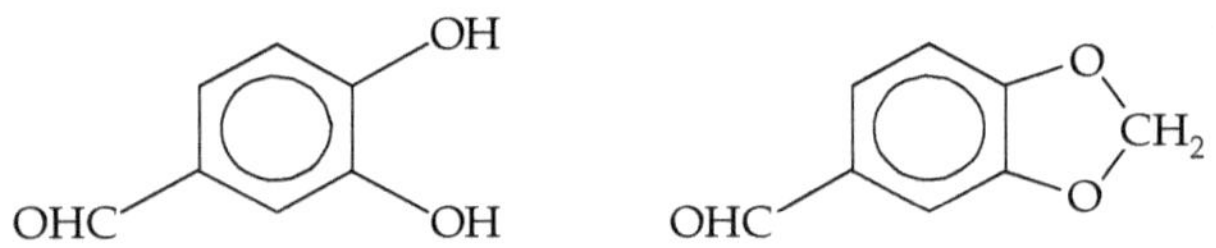

[L]   [M]

(e)

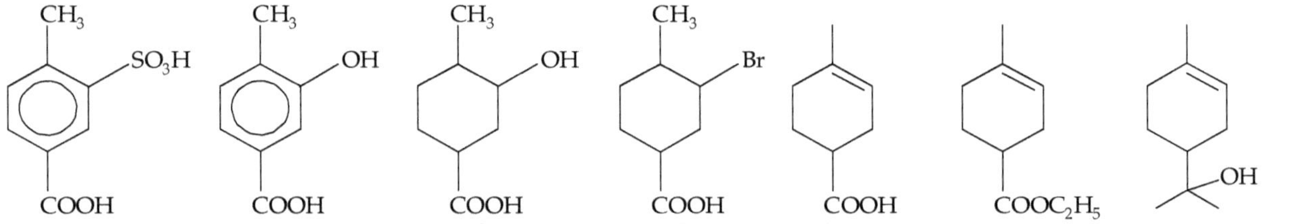

[N]   [O]   [P]   [Q]   [R]   [S]   [T]

11. There are three possible products for the reaction between catechol and chloroacetyl chloride.

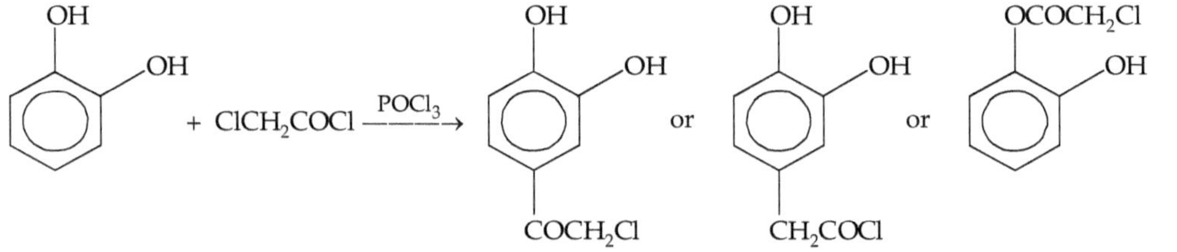

$$+ \ ClCH_2COCl \xrightarrow{\ POCl_3\ }$$

(X_1) or (X_2) or (X_3)

By ring acylation   By ring alkylation   By esterification

However, the compound [X] so obtained undergoes haloform reaction which is possible only in case of (X_1).

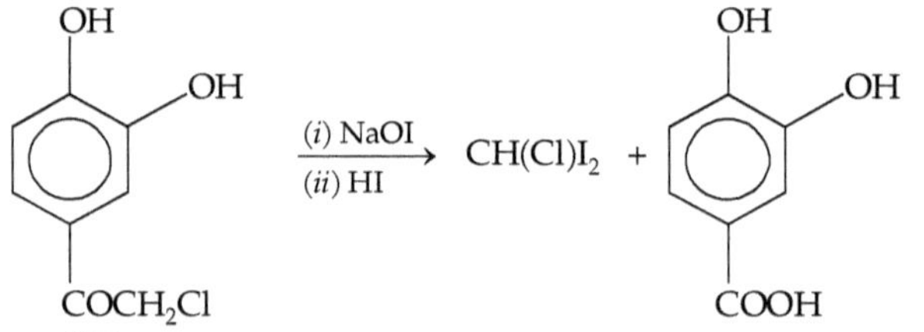

$$\xrightarrow[(ii)\ HI]{(i)\ NaOI} \ CH(Cl)I_2 \ +$$

(X_1) with $COCH_2Cl$ group $\longrightarrow$ product with $COOH$ group

Hence the compound [X] should be $[X_1]$ and thus the various reactions can be written as below.

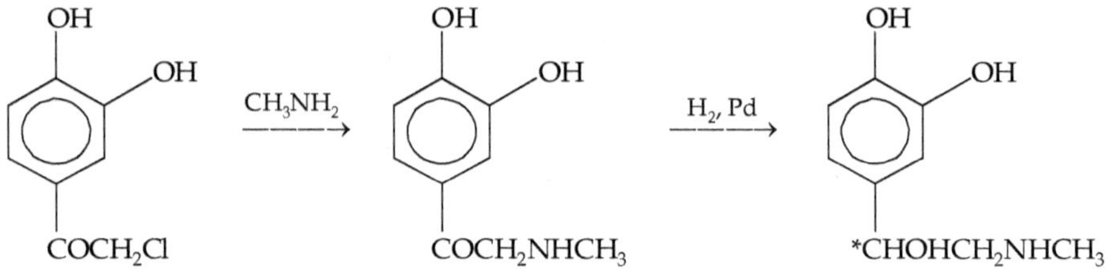

$$\xrightarrow{CH_3NH_2} \qquad \xrightarrow{H_2,\ Pd}$$

$COCH_2Cl$ $COCH_2NHCH_3$ $^*CHOHCH_2NHCH_3$

(X)   (Y)   ($\pm$)-Z

12. Solubility of the compound A indicates it to be a phenol. Alkaline hydrolysis of A also indicates presence of an ester group. Further since the distillate undergoes haloform test, alcoholic part of the ester should be $RCHOHCH_3$. Thus the structure of A can be written as below.

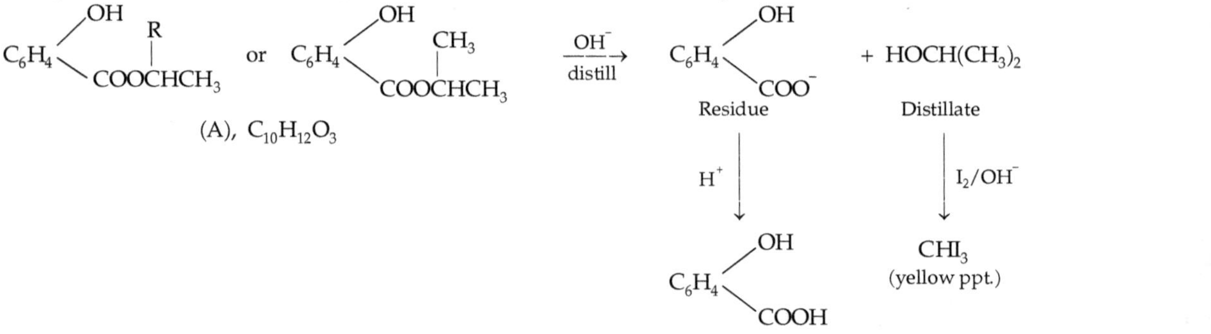

$$C_6H_4 \Big\langle {}^{OH}_{COOCHCH_3 (R)} \quad \text{or} \quad C_6H_4 \Big\langle {}^{OH}_{COOCHCH_3 (CH_3)} \xrightarrow[\text{distill}]{OH^-} \ C_6H_4 \Big\langle {}^{OH}_{COO^-} \ + \ HOCH(CH_3)_2$$

(A), $C_{10}H_{12}O_3$ Residue   Distillate

Residue $\xrightarrow{H^+}$ $C_6H_4 \Big\langle {}^{OH}_{COOH}$ (B)

Distillate $\xrightarrow{I_2/OH^-}$ CHI_3 (yellow ppt.)

Among the three hydroxybenzoic acids, only the *ortho* isomer (salicylic acid) is steam-volatile, hence B must be salicylic acid and A isopropyl salicylate.

ALCOHOLS, PHENOLS AND ETHERS

PAST YEAR QUESTIONS JEE ADVANCED/IIT-JEE (2013 - 2017)

MCQs with One Correct Answer

1. For the identification of β-naphthol using dye test, it is necessary to use **[JEE Adv. 2014]**
   (a) Dichloromethane solution of β-naphthol
   (b) Acidic solution of β-naphthol
   (c) Neutral solution of β-naphthol
   (d) Alkaline solution of β-naphthol

2. The acidic hydrolysis of ether (X) shown below is fastest when **[JEE Adv. 2014]**

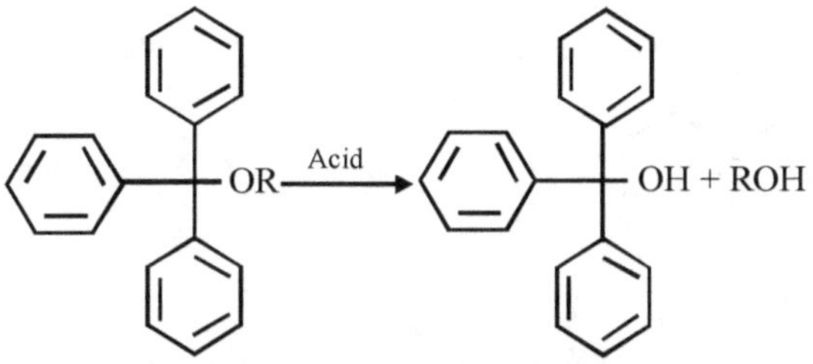

OR
Acid
OH + ROH

   (a) One phenyl group is replaced by a methyl group
   (b) One phenyl group is replaced by a *para*-methoxyphenyl group
   (c) Two phenyl groups are replaced by two *para*-methoxyphenyl groups
   (d) No structural change is made to *X*

MCQs with One or More Than One Correct

1. The major product(s) of the following reaction is(are) **[JEE Adv. 2013]**

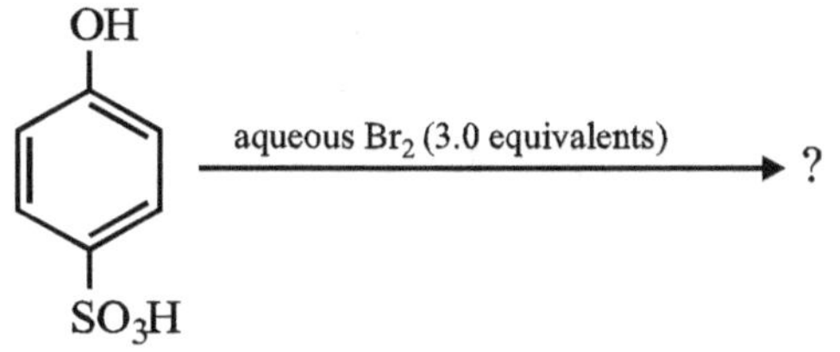

OH
aqueous Br_2 (3.0 equivalents)
?
SO_3H

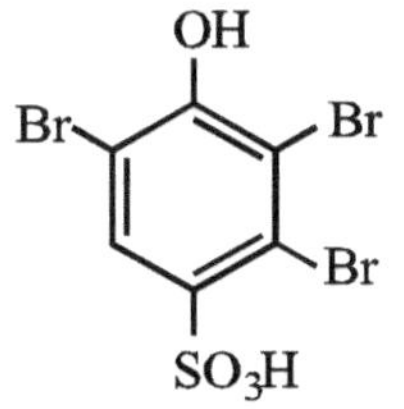

OH
Br
Br
Br
SO_3H

P

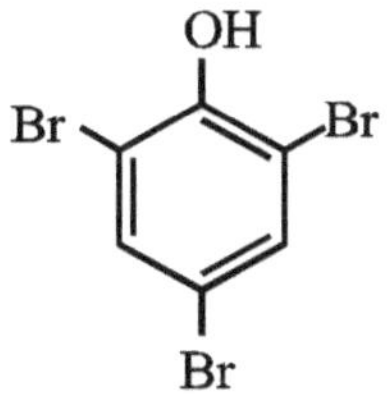

OH
Br
Br
Br

Q

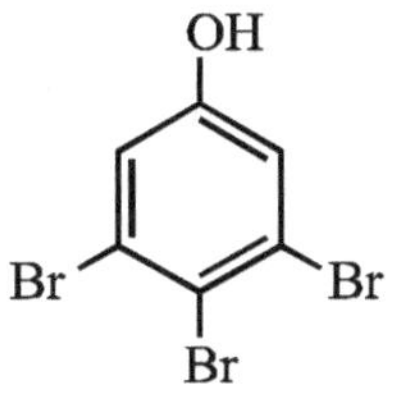

OH
Br
Br
Br

R

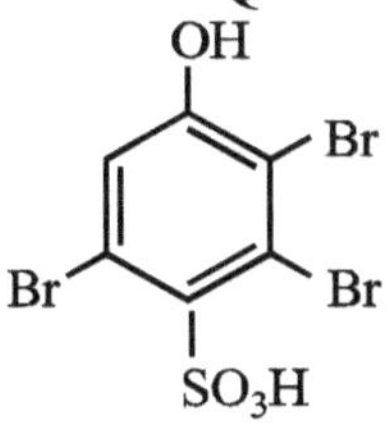

OH
Br
Br
Br
SO_3H

S

   (a) P (b) Q
   (c) R (d) S

2. The correct combination of names for isomeric alcohols with molecular formula $C_4H_{10}O$ is/are **[JEE Adv. 2014]**
   (a) Tert-butanol and 2-methylpropan-2-ol
   (b) Tert-butanol and 1, 1-dimethylethan-1-ol
   (c) n-butanol and butan-1-ol
   (d) Isobutyl alcohol and 2-methylpropan-1-ol

3. The reactivity of compound Z with different halogens under appropriate conditions is given below: **[JEE Adv. 2014]**

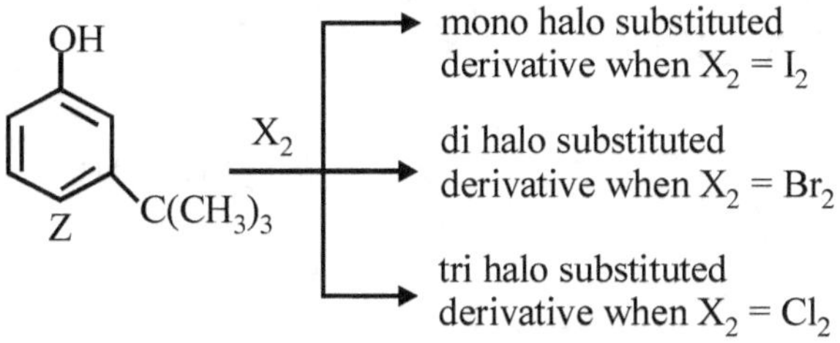

OH
Z
$C(CH_3)_3$
X_2
mono halo substituted derivative when $X_2 = I_2$
di halo substituted derivative when $X_2 = Br_2$
tri halo substituted derivative when $X_2 = Cl_2$

   The observed pattern of electrophilic substitution can be explained by
   (a) The steric effect of the halogen
   (b) The steric effect of the *tert*-butyl group
   (c) The electronic effect of the phenolic group
   (d) The electronic effect of the *tert*-butyl group

4. The major product U in the following reactions is

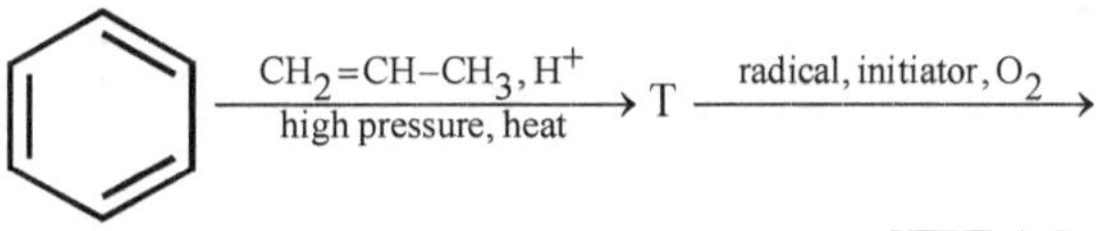

$CH_2=CH-CH_3, H^+$
high pressure, heat
T
radical, initiator, O_2

[JEE Adv. 2015]

   (a)

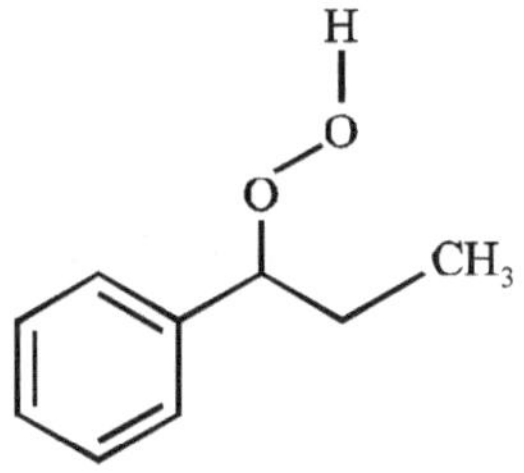

H
O
O
CH_3

   (b)

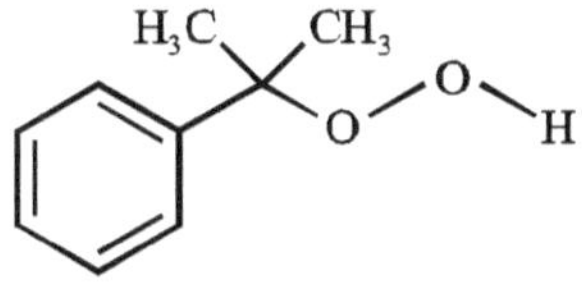

H_3C
CH_3
O
O
H

   (c)

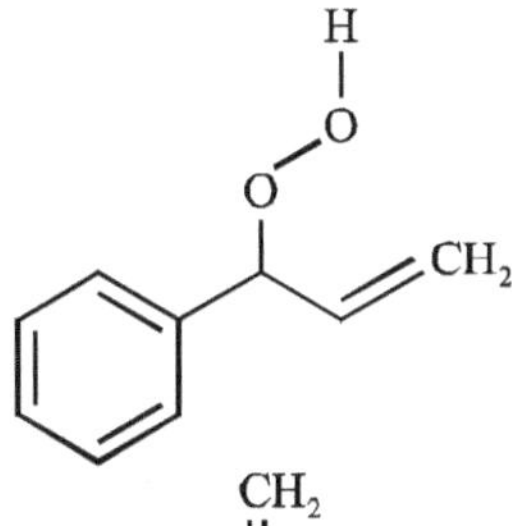

H
O
O
CH_2

   (d)

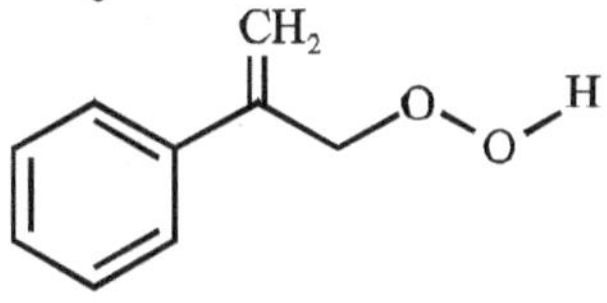

CH_2
O
O
H

Match the Following

1. Match the chemical conversions in List I with the appropriate reagents in List II and select the correct answer using the code given below the lists : *(JEE Adv. 2013)*

List I		List II

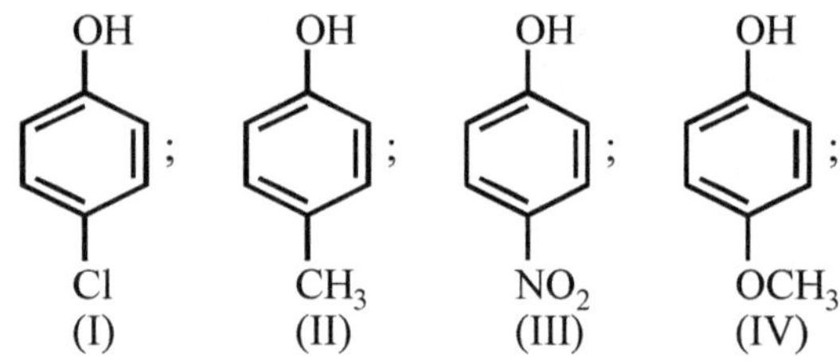

P. $\rangle$—Cl $\longrightarrow$ $\rangle=$ 1. (i) Hg(OAc)$_2$; (ii) NaBH$_4$

Q. $\rangle$—ONa $\longrightarrow$ $\rangle$—OEt   2. NaOEt

R. $\longrightarrow$ —OH   3. Et-Br

S. $\longrightarrow$ —OH   4. (i) BH$_3$; (ii) H$_2$O$_2$/NaOH

Codes :

	P	Q	R	S
(a)	2	3	1	4
(b)	3	2	1	4
(c)	2	3	4	1
(d)	3	2	4	1

Integer Value Correct Type

1. The number of resonance structures for N is *(JEE Adv. 201*

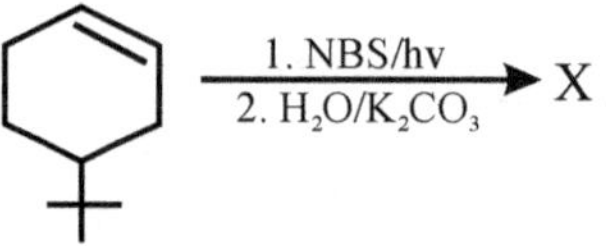

$$\xrightarrow{\text{NaOH}} N$$

2. The number of hydroxyl group(s) in Q is *(JEE Adv. 201*

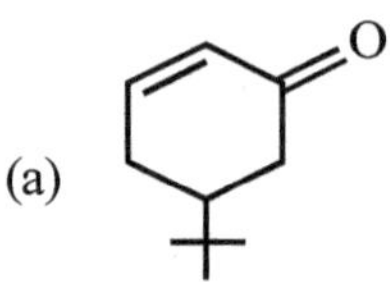

$$\xrightarrow[\text{heat}]{H^+} P \xrightarrow[0°C]{\text{aqueous dilute KMnO}_4 \text{ (excess)}}$$

PAST YEAR QUESTIONS JEE MAIN/AIEEE (2013 - 2017)

1. Arrange the following compounds in order of decreasing acidity : **[JEE M 2013]**

OH—C$_6$H$_4$—Cl (I) ; OH—C$_6$H$_4$—CH$_3$ (II) ; OH—C$_6$H$_4$—NO$_2$ (III) ; OH—C$_6$H$_4$—OCH$_3$ (IV)

(a) II > IV > I > III   (b) I > II > III > IV

(c) III > I > II > IV   (d) IV > III > I > II

2. An unknown alcohol is treated with the "Lucas reagent" to determine whether the alcohol is primary, secondary or tertiary. Which alcohol reacts fastest and by what mechanism : **[JEE M 2013]**

(a) secondary alcohol by S$_N$1

(b) tertiary alcohol by S$_N$1

(c) secondary alcohol by S$_N$2

(d) tertiary alcohol by S$_N$2

3. Sodium phenoxide when heated with CO$_2$ under pressure at 125°C yields a product which on acetylation produces C.

$$\text{C}_6\text{H}_5\text{—ONa} + \text{CO}_2 \xrightarrow[\text{5 Atm}]{125°C} B \xrightarrow[\text{Ac}_2\text{O}]{H^+} C$$

The major product C would be **[JEE M 2014]**

(a) 2-OCOCH$_3$-C$_6$H$_4$-COOH

(b) OH-C$_6$H$_3$(COCH$_3$)$_2$

(c) 2-OH-C$_6$H$_4$-COOCH$_3$

(d) 3-OCOCH$_3$-C$_6$H$_4$-COOH

4. Thiol group is present in : **[JEE M 201**

(a) Cysteine   (b) Methionine

(c) Cytosine   (d) Cystine

5. The product of the reaction given below is: **[JEE M 201**

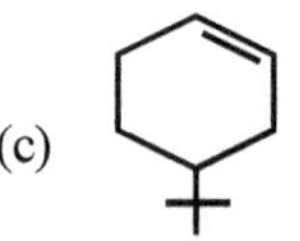

$$\xrightarrow[\text{2. H}_2\text{O/K}_2\text{CO}_3]{\text{1. NBS/hv}} X$$

(a)   (b)   (c)   (d)

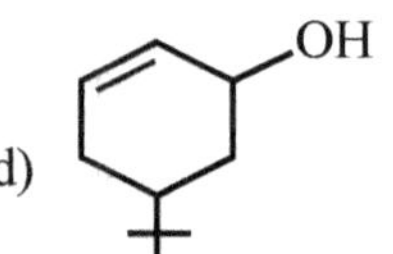

6. 2-chloro-2-methylpentane on reaction with sodium methoxide in methanol yields: **[JEE M 2016**

(1) $\text{C}_2\text{H}_5\text{CH}_2\text{C(CH}_3)_2\text{—OCH}_3$

(2) $\text{C}_2\text{H}_5\text{CH}_2\text{C}(\text{CH}_3)=\text{CH}_2$

(3) $\text{C}_2\text{H}_5\text{CH}=\text{C(CH}_3)\text{—CH}_3$

(a) (3) only   (b) (a) and (b)

(c) All of these   (d) (a) and (c)

SOLUTIONS

PAST YEAR QUESTIONS JEE ADVANCED/IIT-JEE (2013 - 2017)

MCQs with One Correct Answer

1. (d) In dye test, phenolic — OH group is converted to — O^- which activates the ring towards electrophilic aromatic substitution

2. (c) The given reaction proceeds through S_N^1 mechanism which involves carbocation as intermediate.

$$Ph_3C — O — R \rightleftharpoons Ph_3C — \overset{+}{\underset{H}{O}} — R \rightleftharpoons Ph_3C^+ + ROH$$

Thus, higher the stability of the carbocation, greater will be reactivity. Presence of electron releasing group (e.g., — OCH_3) in p-position of the phenyl group will disperse the positive charge of the carbocation by $+M$ effect, hence stabilizes the carbocation.

MCQs with One or More Than One Correct

1. (b)

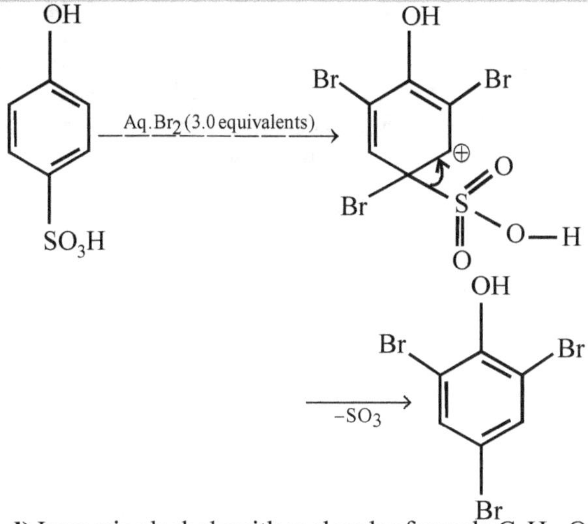

2. (a, c, d) Isomeric alcohols with molecular formula $C_4H_{10}O$ are

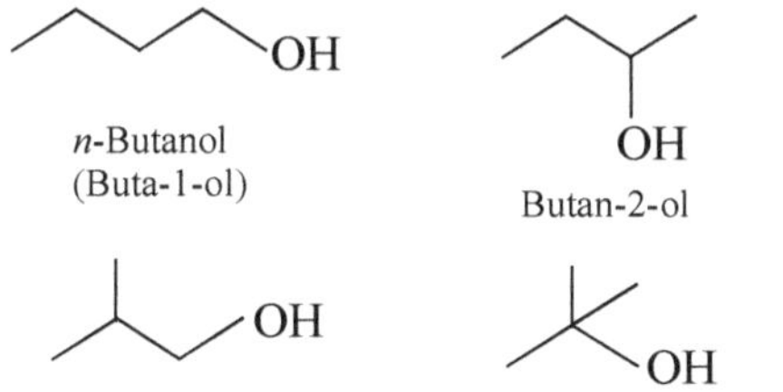

n-Butanol
(Buta-1-ol)

Butan-2-ol

Isobutyl alcohol
(2-methylpropan-1-ol)

tert-Butanol
(2-methylpropan-2-ol)

3. (a, b, c) —OH group is strongly activating and o, p-directing due to $+M$ effect. Thus positions a, b and c are the sites for attack by an electrophile. However, sites b and c are not preferred by bulky electrophile due to steric crowding. Thus more bulky electrophile (like I_2) can attack only site a, which is least sterically hindered, a bit smaller electrophile (Br_2) can attack at sites a and also b (relatively less sterically hindered site) and the smallest electrophile (Cl_2) can attack all the three sites, viz., a, b and c (most sterically hindered site).

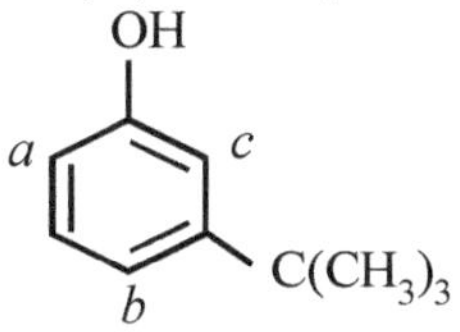

4. (b)

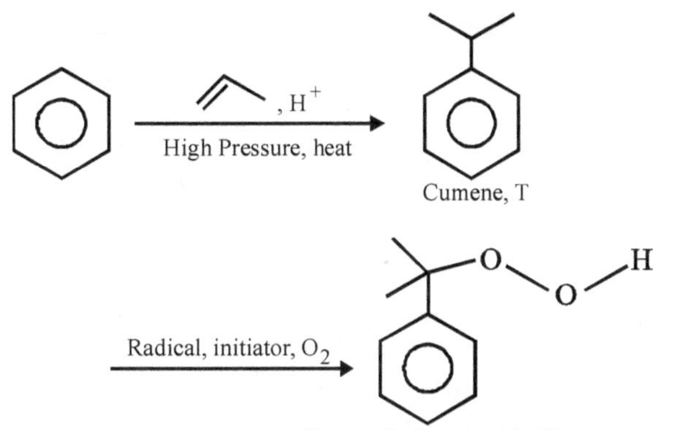

Cumene, T

Cumene hydroperoxide, U

Match the Following

1. (a)

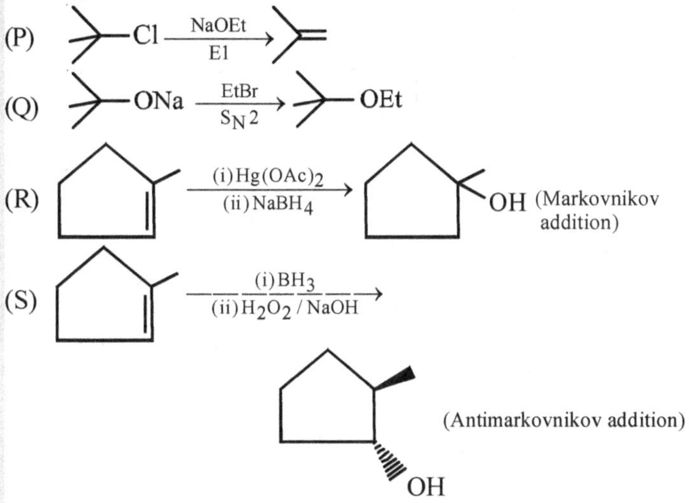

(P)

(Q)

(R) (Markovnikov addition)

(S)

(Antimarkovnikov addition)

Integer Value Correct Type

1. (9)

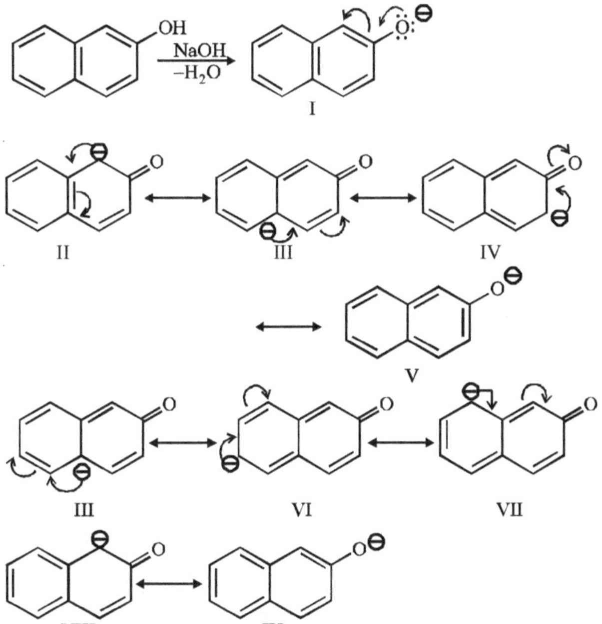

2. (4)

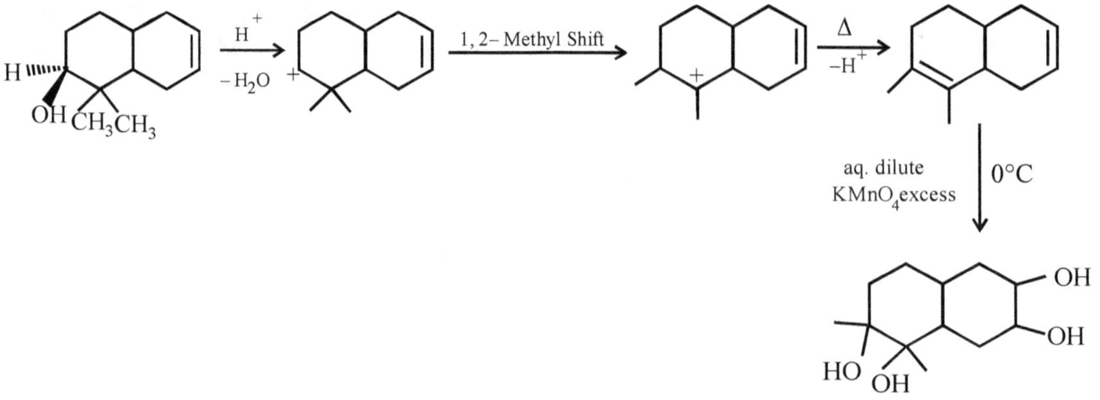

(Reaction scheme: starting decalin-type alcohol with H^+, $-H_2O$ → carbocation; 1,2-Methyl Shift → rearranged carbocation; Δ, $-H^+$ → diene)

aq. dilute $KMnO_4$ excess, $0°C$ → tetraol product

---

1. (c) Electron withdrawing substituents like $-NO_2$, Cl increase the acidity of phenol while electron releasing substituents like $-CH_3$, $-OCH_3$ decreases acidity. hence the correct order of acidity will be

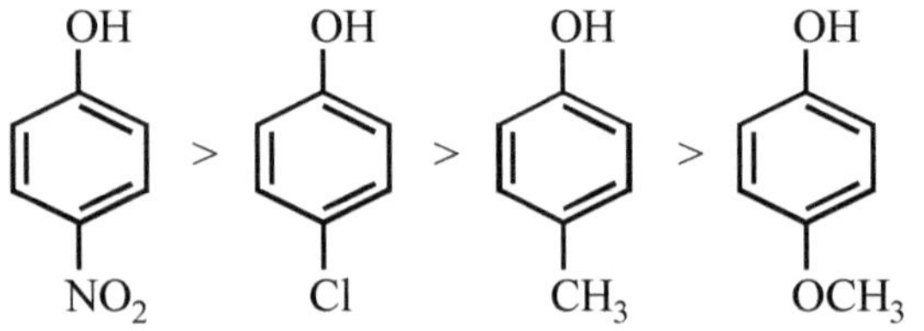

(Structures: phenol with NO_2 > phenol with Cl > phenol with CH_3 > phenol with OCH_3)

Further $(-I)\ NO_2 > (-I)\ Cl$ and $(+I)\ CH_3 > (+I)\ OCH_3$

2. (b) Tertiary alchols reacts fastest with lucas reagnet as the rate of reaction is directly proportional to the stability of carbocation formed in the reaction. Since most stable $3°$ carbocation is formed in the reaction hence it will react fastest further tetriary alcohols appears to react by $S_N 1$ mechanism.

Step 1. $(CH_3)_3 C - OH + H - Cl \rightleftharpoons (CH_3)_3 - \overset{+}{O}H_2 + Cl^-$

Step 2. $(CH_3)_3 C - \overset{+}{O}H_2 \rightleftharpoons (CH_3)_3 C^+ + H_2O$

Setp 3. $(CH_3)_3 C^+ + Cl^- \longrightarrow (CH_3)_3 C - Cl$
tert-Butyl chloride

3. (a)

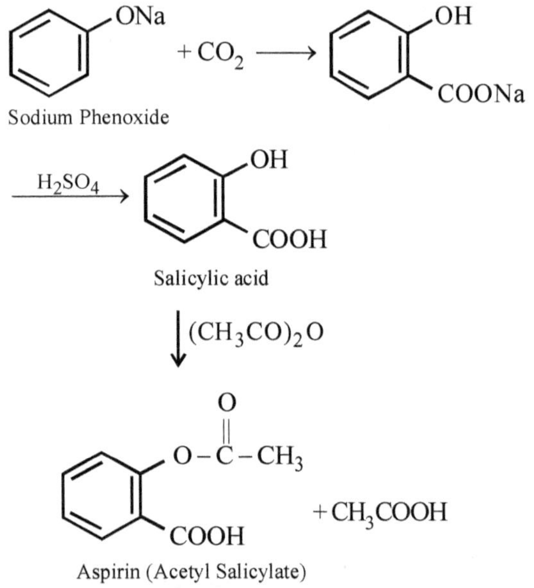

Sodium Phenoxide $+ CO_2 \longrightarrow$ (ortho-hydroxy sodium benzoate, OH and COONa)

$\xrightarrow{H_2SO_4}$ Salicylic acid (OH and COOH)

$\downarrow (CH_3CO)_2O$

Aspirin (Acetyl Salicylate) ($O-\overset{O}{\overset{\|}{C}}-CH_3$ and COOH) $+ CH_3COOH$

4. (a) Among 20 naturally occuring amino acids "Cysteine" has '– SH' or thiol functional group.

$\Rightarrow$ General formula of amino acid $\rightarrow$ R–CH–COOH (with NH_2)

$\Rightarrow$ Value of $R = -CH_2-SH$ in Cysteine.

5. (d) N – bromosuccinimide results into bromination at allylic and benzylic positions

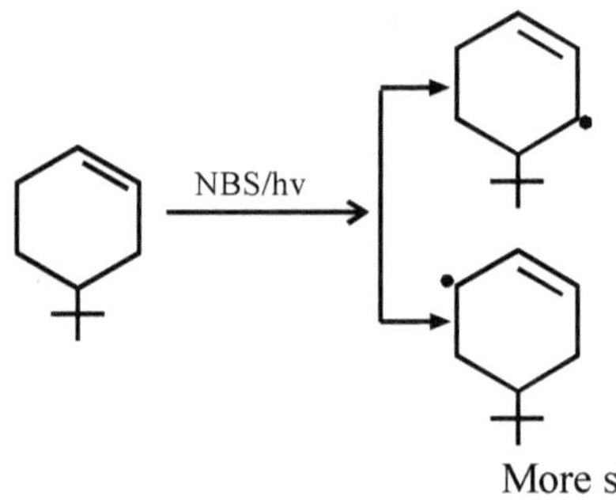

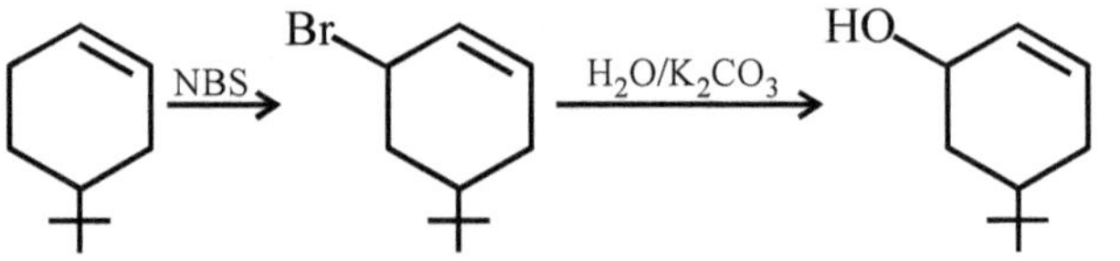

(Scheme: cyclohexene $\xrightarrow{NBS/hv}$ two allylic radicals, lower labelled **More stable**)

(Scheme: cyclohexene $\xrightarrow{NBS}$ allylic bromide (Br) $\xrightarrow{H_2O/K_2CO_3}$ allylic alcohol (HO))

6. (a) When tert -alkyl halides are used in Williamson synthesis elimination occurs rather than substitution resulting into formation of alkene. Here alkoxide ion abstract one of the β-hydrogen atom along with acting as a nucleophile.

$CH_3 - CH_2 - CH_2 - \underset{Cl}{\overset{CH_3}{\underset{|}{\overset{|}{C}}}} - CH_3 + Na^+\ {}^-OCH_3 \xrightarrow{CH_3OH}$

2-Chloro-2-methylpentane

$CH_3CH_2 - \underset{}{\overset{H}{\underset{}{\overset{|}{C}}}} = \underset{}{\overset{CH_3}{\underset{}{\overset{|}{C}}}} - CH_3 + CH_3OH + NaBr$

2-Methyl-pent-2-ene